COLETTE

Free and Fettered

To Chris —
My finest friend —
Jan — Easter 1980

COLETTE

Free and Fettered

by
Michèle Sarde

*Translated from the French
by Richard Miller*

WILLIAM MORROW & COMPANY, INC.
New York   1980

Library of Congress Cataloging in Publication Data

Sarde, Michèle.
    Colette.

    Translation of Colette, libre et entravée.
    Bibliography: p.
    Includes index.
    1. Colette, Sidonie Gabrielle, 1873-1954—Biography.
2. Authors, French—20th century—Biography. I. Title.
PQ2605.028Z8313   848'.9'1209 [B]   79-24978
ISBN 0-688-03601-5

Printed in the United States of America

First Edition

1   2   3   4   5   6   7   8   9   10

Book Design by Michael Mauceri

To my mother

Foreword

Who was Colette? There are many specious answers that those close to her might make to this specious question. For there is no "objective" Colette, just as there is no one entity that is "Colette."

My plan has been to create for you, who have read and loved Colette, and for those who do not already know her, the history of a particular subjectivity—her own—filtered through another subjectivity, mine. A process of selection. There are, of course, the facts, and yet for each fact, there are countless different interpretations. Interpretations . . . or deformations? Colette herself has already transformed for us those she loved, and even more those she did not love, or loved no longer. I have borrowed her opera glasses, forcing myself to see through them what she saw herself. Do not look for an impartial view in her own portraits of those around her; each person's truth is partial, minds cannot be studied as one studies the data of history. And when it becomes a matter of apprehending a character's surroundings, the field of vision becomes even more narrow, the world and others refracted in the distorting lens of "one sensibility," "one memory," "one imagination," "one single life." One might suggest I should have written other books; I did not choose to dwell on Willy, on Henry de Jouvenel, but on Colette. I have examined these men only through her eyes. In the wings of the theater where I have produced my drama for you, there is my encounter with a person I know only through the written footprints she has left behind. I do not try to conceal the backstage workings, the how and why of this book. In the light of Colette's life, I have questioned my own existence as a woman. Neither she nor I have all the answers.

I was first attracted to her because she was such an average woman, both in her ordinary social background and in her personality, which was basically normal and "well balanced." Nor was she different in her tastes, her aspirations, her intellectual interests. Millions of women can subscribe to what she said with her exceptional talent, even if they cannot say it with her genius.

Men have made the writer's work sacrosanct, and have thereby overestimated it. Colette always insisted on her own lack of vocation for writing; she saw no difference between a well-written page and a

7

well-carved pair of wooden shoes. Had it not been for Willy, she might well have written nothing but letters. It is because so many potential women writers throughout the centuries have not met their Willy that literature has remained a closed preserve for men.

And of course, other women did not have the same mother. The gift of mind with which Sido endowed her daughter demonstrates how a mother can be responsible for passing on to her daughter female insights as well as complexes. Sido was well ahead of her time. Because of her, the child Colette never really fulfilled the model of the well-behaved doll-child firmly convinced of her own inferiority. As an adult, she was therefore able to wage and to win a personal struggle during a time in history that was difficult for women. Yet neither Colette nor Sido regarded themselves as feminists. Sido was the very model of a "traditional wife," devoted to home, to domestic duties, and yet within this narrow frame, she was still a free woman. Colette played an important part in the feminine struggle, but after her own fashion, by writing of herself. The existentialists, rather out of fashion now, have noted the act of freedom that precedes the act of writing, her writing, and that "she alone has managed to account for a person in its totality." In his introduction to *Saint-Genet, comédien et martyr* (1952), Sartre announced his attempt "to reveal this freedom confronted by fate, first crushed by misfortunes, then turning against them and gradually controlling them. To prove that genius is not a gift, but rather the way out one invents in desperate situations, to rediscover the choices a writer makes of himself, his life and his sense of the universe in the actual formal matters of style and composition, in the structure of his images and the particularities of his taste; to retrace in detail the history of a liberation."

This is also the meaning I have attempted to give this book. Marx preferred Balzac to Zola, and yet Zola was the socialist, Balzac a monarchist and reactionary. In the latter, Marx found the materials that could fill out his own reflections on French society without dogmatic distortion. Colette's work, devoid of any ideological slant, comes across the footlights with far greater clarity than does the feminist writing of her day, and it is an invaluable aid in the consideration of woman and her history. Of course, in producing her books she had the benefit of a "unique style" and her own demanding, perfectionist sense of discipline. Almost eighty years after the publication of her first novel, Colette's books have aged not at all, not a wrinkle shows, and her dialogue can be transposed as is to the cinema or the stage.

It is for this reason that I have allowed her to speak as much as possible, to share with the reader the pleasure of this text, still brimming over with love of life. All of her writing—and particularly her novels—has served as a single document to assist in her rediscovery, "brought back alive" as she herself confessed, like the purloined letter, in the open, hidden by her very visibility.

In writing the life of a revolutionary figure, one cannot relegate her revolutionary activities to a footnote; the biography of a painter must take his paintings into account. Would I have written about Colette had she not been a writer? Literary critics are able to ignore biographical research à la Sainte-Beuve, but a text cannot be completely cut off from cause and effect; it is a long way from a life to the printed page. Neither can biographical research disregard that writer's work. In the heteroclite, eccentric process that is biography, including as it does historical, analytical, personal, sociological, detective elements—and poetry too—can there be any source superior to the text? For the text contains it all—in what it says and what it omits—Colette's share and the share we bring to it, the work of the imagination, of history, of truth. Facts and fantasies, her own and ours, intermingle and combine in a wished-for encounter. Sometimes, faced with certain repeated scenes and situations, we do not know whether they were imagined or lived. The "lying text," the "fictional text," overtly and unabashedly conceals truths; other documents—interviews, statistics, dates, critical works—are all merely related data to mislead us, my own book included.

—Michèle Sarde

Acknowledgments

I must at the outset express my gratitude to Mme Colette de Jouvenel for her invaluable suggestions and for her kind interest in this book.

For their warm hospitality and collaboration I should like to thank M. Bertrand de Jouvenel and Mme Jeanie Fromont.

I must also extend thanks to Mmes Danièle Delorme and Sanda Goudeket, and to M. Edouard Dermite.

I should like to pay a special tribute to the work done in researching and organizing the Colette Exhibition in 1973 at the Bibliothèque Nationale by Mmes Monique Cornand, Madeleine Barbin and Marie-Laure Chastaing.

Finally, for their devotion and the part they played in the creation of this book, my heartfelt thanks to Alain Mangin and Catherine Chevallier.

—MICHÈLE SARDE

Contents

Story of a Woman Without a Name

I was unable to conceal from him the jealous discouragement, the excessive hostility that overcome me when I find someone is seeking the living me in the pages of my novels.

Allow me the right to conceal myself in those pages, even if only after the fashion of the "purloined letter."

COLETTE

I
GABRIELLE
The Child's Way

One never recovers from one's childhood.

LÉON-PAUL FARGUE

A happy childhood is poor preparation for human contacts.

COLETTE

You cannot imagine what a queen of the earth I was when I was twelve years old. . . . Ah! how you would have loved me, and how I miss myself!

COLETTE

Gabrielle Sidonie Colette, the "baby," nicknamed Gabri by the family, Minet-Chéri by her mother, the golden trinket, the beauty, the masterpiece, Bel-Gazou as her father called her, meaning in Burgundian dialect a lovely warbler or fine speech—predestined to "beautiful language"—was born on January 28, 1873, at Saint-Sauveur-en-Puisaye in the region of Basse-Bourgogne.*

She had a painful time being born, half strangled and silent; her mother's labor was long, three days and two nights she labored, *struggled as women in labor know how to struggle;* with screams, with anguish she *drove her from her loins.*[1] The women assisting her lost their heads and forgot to tend the fire, but the child, overlooked in the crisis, showed a *personal will to live, and even to live for a long time.*[2] Through her daughter, Sido, the mother, recalled this birth of her fourth child: *I never regretted the pain. They say that children carried high as you were, and slow to descend to the light, are always the most precious because they have lived close to their mother's heart and leave it with reluctance.*[3]

One element of Colette's future destiny was fixed from the beginning: so slow to descend into the light, she would be one of the privileged who, having been content in the maternal waters, forever feel a vague and inexpressible nostalgia, a frustration they cannot afterward describe. To this first gift, these biological and genetic components, was to be added the all-important element of her childhood itself, throughout which her mother's presence, her love, were constant, protecting against any intrusion: a happy childhood. Here too she was to be content.

The room in which Sido sent her into the world was lacking in comfort, incongruously furnished with twin beds draped in flowered chintz, a shoebox with a curved lid that served as a seat, a mirrored

---

* Minet-Chéri, Bel-Gazou, "Dear Kitty," "Lovely warbler/speech," *Joyau-tout-en-or, Beauté,* etc., French terms of endearment are as fatuous in English translation as "Honeybun" and "Petsey" would be in French. Let us leave them in their original form.—Tr.

armoire in three unequal sections, made of rosewood and polished satinwood. In those days, when it was rare to give birth outside the home, the maternal bedroom was the matrix in the center of the house, the garden, forming a citadel that opened onto the village, the woods. The house was redolent of the mother's presence. The children were allowed to wander their chosen paths. Time went its own way. For fifteen years, at teatime, the short and slender spirit of the house would knead dough for the galette wearing white sleeves to protect her from the flour and the blue apron she had worn to wash the dog, thinking with urgency, with concern, "It's four o'clock, where are the children?" Six-thirty, will they be in time for dinner?

The children were always there. Love given, love received, love returned, a reciprocity of love. The mother remained, unchanging. Her daughter retained her always, in her garden, in her imagination, where she existed *at the center of an imaginary eight-pointed star, each point marked with the cardinal and collateral directions.*[4] Sido in her garden was to be the site where evil influences were abolished, the center of gravity of the universe and of Gabrielle's equilibrium.

She was to provide her daughter with the model of a woman proud to be a woman, a woman who loved others because she had begun by loving herself. No small gift. The gift of equilibrium, of solidity, of "normality" in the least conformist, least strict sense, a gift always suspect to those fascinated by the lower depths, by spiritual and mental imbalance. Because of her, Gabrielle would live in the harsh female world protected from its pitfalls, she would experience neither pathological depression nor any serious neuroses that would prevent her from living, from producing, she would tranquilly absorb the fearful contradictions she was to experience, as does everyone; she would surmount the everyday miseries that fell upon her.

If a protected childhood is also a protecting childhood, we have it with us always. The roof of the house in Saint-Sauveur, the arch created by Sido, covered an imagined space. It simultaneously covered all her future dislodgments, all the wanderings to come; it was to become flesh, the flesh with the cauterized scars that produce books. Not surprising that when M. Ducharne, the silk manufacturer who had bought her old home, offered to sell it to her, she refused. What need had she to live in a house she had never left! The only truth of the personality resides in the imagination. In Colette, the elemental image, the matrix of all images, is the house of her birth, an imaginary house.

We can still see it in Saint-Sauveur-en-Puisaye, the village Colette rebaptized Montigny-en-Fresnois in the Claudine novels: it was *large, with a high garret. The steep slope of the street made the stables, the carriage house, the poultry shed, the laundry, the dairy, huddle together on the lower level around a closed courtyard. . . . The upper garden overlooked a lower garden, an enclosed warm kitchen-garden devoted to eggplant and pimiento, where the odors of leaves and tomatoes mingled in July with the perfume of apricots ripening on the espaliers. In the upper garden there were twin fir trees, a walnut tree whose intolerant shadow killed the flowers around it, roses, untrimmed grass, a dilapidated arbor. . . . The main blackened façade had a double flight of stairs, large windows and no charm, a typical bourgeoise house in an old village, but the steep rise of the street somewhat upset its gravity, and its uneven steps, five on one side, ten on the other, were lopsided. A large, solemn house, harsh, an orphanage bell by the front door with its huge bolt like some ancient prison, a house that smiled only on its garden.*[5]

The house had belonged to Sido's first husband, Jules Robineau-Duclos, the son of gentlemen glassblowers, known as the "Savage" because of his ferocious character. There is a police report about him addressed to the Imperial prosecutor by the Justice of the Peace of Saint-Sauveur, dated November 15, 1865 [6]:

"M. Jules Robineau came into a considerable fortune at an early age as a result of his parents' demise. He had but one sister, Mme Givry, who is the mother-in-law of M. Cherest, the lawyer. M. Robineau was a man of perfect probity, frightfully ugly, almost an idiot. He took to drink at an early age to such a degree that in 1856 he was forbidden to bear firearms, and his worried brother-in-law sought a court judgment against him. In conformity with the morality of Saint-Sauveur, he took a concubine rather than marrying, and her association with him did not impoverish her. . . . M. Robineau's passion for drink, to which he increasingly became victim, brought about his total degradation. He no longer slept. From morning to night he kept by him a bottle of brandy which was refilled as he emptied it. His demise was imminent. It was only a question of one or two months."

Because of the property involved and probably to protect the interests of his sister that were threatened by the child of the resident concubine, certain members of the family, among them a Bourgoin de Mozilles, decided to take him in hand and marry him off. Their choice fell upon Sido.

⚜ SIDO, BENEFICENT GODDESS

Adèle Eugénie *Sidonie* Landoy, Colette's mother, who was born August 31, 1835, in Paris on the Boulevard Bonne-Nouvelle, was the daughter of Henri-Marie Landoy and Sophie Chatenay.

Henri-Marie Landoy, nicknamed *"Le Gorille,"* had been born on September 23, 1772, at Charleville in the Ardennes, where his father, Robert, owned a grocery and tobacconist's shop. In 1814, he had married Sophie Chatenay, from Versailles. The newlyweds set up housekeeping in Charleville and opened a grocer's shop.

Between 1815 and 1823, they were to have five children, of whom two boys, Eugène and Paul, survived. After 1823, there is no trace of the Landoy family in Charleville. Where were they living between 1823 and 1835, the year Sido was born in Paris? Some biographers believe that they went to Belgium, probably because later on both of the Gorilla's sons were to live there. It appears likely that Sophie Chatenay died in Paris a few weeks after the birth of her daughter Sido. Henri Landoy then moved to Lyons, where he remarried and died in 1854.

Regarding her maternal grandfather, Colette—who kept his daguerreotype portrait—noted that he looked like a *man of color, I believe a quadroon, with a high white cravat, pale and disdainful eyes, a long nose above the negroid lips that earned him his name.*[1] Might this genetic background—its truth is impossible to establish—be in part responsible for a certain rapport with the flesh, with sensations, with the paganism of Colette and her mother so often mentioned in later years? M. René Robinet, archivist at Mézières-Charleville,[2] "has traced [the family] back to 1640 and has established that on the Landoy side it was made up of skilled and unskilled laborers, several generations of whom lived at La Neuville(Ardennes) with no trace of black blood." If there is black blood, it must come from the family of Anne-Marie Mathis, the Gorilla's mother, since "the Mathis family, unlike the Landoys, were inclined to move about, being bargemen and merchants who traveled a good deal. The parish registers in Grandpré where Anne-Marie Mathis was born, however, were destroyed, and it has been impossible to pursue the investigations in this direction to discover if there had been a black ancestor." [3]

From her maternal grandmother Sophie Chatenay, Colette inherited a portrait on ivory dated 1830, stolen in Paris and found by her thirty years later as she was rummaging in a stall at the Saint-Ouen flea market with Charlotte Lysès, Sacha Guitry's first wife. *The miniature is of a young woman, her hair arranged in three loops with a huge loop at the top, and a bunch of curls like sausages on either side of her temples.*[4] The Parisienne of the Bonne-Nouvelle *died young, twenty times deceived by her husband.* Sido, her selective memory filtered through the no-less selective memory of her daughter, evoked her childhood in two ways: *The daughter of my father arrived when I was eight. The Gorilla told me "Pick her up, she's your sister." He used* vous *when he spoke to us. . . . I was holding her in my arms, and I noted that her fingers didn't seem to be tapered enough. My father was very fond of pretty hands. So then and there, with the cruelty children have, I began to work them, those soft little fingers that gave way beneath mine. . . . My father's daughter started out in the world with ten tiny blisters, five on each hand, around her pretty, shapely fingernails. . . . She cried. The doctor said, "I can't understand this digital inflammation." My "father's daughter" lived for several years in the house where my father manufactured chocolate, along with Sido, Eugène, Paul and Irma, and Jean, the big monkey. In those days, chocolate was made with cacao, sugar and vanilla. At the top of the house, the bricks of chocolate would be set to dry, laid out on the terrace while they were still soft. And every morning, the bars of chocolate would bear the imprints of the five-petalled flowers that betrayed the nocturnal passage of cats.*[5] A baby with blistered fingers and soft bricks of chocolate printed with flowers by the paws of a wandering cat, thus Colette in her fantasy recreates for us her mother's childhood: Sido, her mother dead, was put out to nurse with foster parents in Puisaye —in the biographies of the period foster parenthood plays a considerable role—farmers named Guillé who lived in the village of Mézilles some ten kilometers from Saint-Sauveur.

M. Amblard writes: "The reasons for this move are somewhat mysterious. I have been told that it may have been on orders from some secret society, Freemasons they still call them in the region." [6] And in this connection Crançon, the local justice of the peace, stated that Sido's parents "never paid for the months she spent with her

foster parents." We are in the days of Louis-Philippe, whose government was engaged in an open struggle against political clubs—1834
was the year in which Republican insurrections broke out in Lyons
and Paris. Fieschi's attentat took place in 1835. It is not inconceivable
that Sido's father and brothers may have been members of some
secret society; Puisaye with its thick surrounding forests had long
been a refuge for members of such groups when they were hiding
from the law. Truth, fiction? In any event, we do not know the
precise reasons for this move, nor the number of years the child
lived with the Guillé family.

We catch up with Sido after her father's death, living in Belgium
with her journalist brothers. "The elder brother, Henri-Eugène,
born in Charleville on October 17, 1816, was nineteen years older
than she, the second brother, Jules-Paulin, twelve years older. Another sister, Irma—there is no trace of her later on—lived with them
at the time. Eugène, the elder, had started out in Paris working for
a dealer in pearls, but he soon turned to journalism. He seems to have
emigrated to Belgium with his brother around 1840, perhaps for
political reasons. In 1840 he was a publisher in Brussels, where
he brought out books on the salons of 1842 and 1845. From 1850,
articles by him began to appear in *L'Illustration* and in Belgium he
was considered "one of the most distinguished members of the radical press." [7] Around 1863, he became the publisher of the *Journal de
Gand*, and until his death in 1890 he continued to be one of the important figures in Belgian journalism. The two Landoy brothers became Belgian citizens around 1850; Sido kept her French nationality.
In fact, Colette corroborates, *this French woman spent her childhood
in the Yonne and her adolescence among painters, journalists and
professional musicians in Belgium.*[8]

Happy years, "the best years of my life," for a girl who was relatively free, moving in enlightened and cultured circles. There was,
however, another side to it; Sido was, after all, nothing but an orphan
without a dowry. She usually went back to her foster parents in
Mézilles for her vacations. M. Bourgoin, who had been involved in
the plans to marry off the notorious Robineau-Duclos, latched on to
her and invited her to his home. There was some bargaining between
the families. On January 15, 1857, at half past twelve, she was
married to Robineau at the Sherberck city hall, near Brussels. Her
brothers had spent a week arguing over the marriage contract. Far-
sighted brothers; thanks to them Sido would inherit a tidy fortune

upon her husband's death. In the meanwhile, *terrified and silent, rolling her blond ringlets around her fingers, Sido listened to them. For a girl without fortune or profession, living at her brothers' expense, can do nothing but keep silent, accept her good fortune, and thank God.*[9] The words were written long afterward, from experience; Colette knew what she was talking about. And the same refrain echoes through the nineteenth century and beyond: What can a girl without a dowry do? Sido with all her love was to be powerless to lift this common curse from either of her two daughters. Widespread as it was, Sido continued to regard the curse of marriage as a real one. There was no salvation in it. Her entire philosophy of marriage can be summed up in that formula, and yet, paradoxically, she was later to be happy in her marriage with her second, chosen, husband.

But above all, she retained the kind of memories she invokes in a letter dated February 24, 1909, to her daughter, who had just divorced Willy: "I didn't tell you that I have taken poor Adélaïde back, and I'm going to keep her. She has an impressionable and delicate nature. No one but me would hire her. She tells me about her husband's brutality and she trembles before him. *If he were mine, I'd have killed him.* (emphasis added) One evening when he had been drinking, Jules Robineau tried to beat me—two months after my wedding. Ah! that was a great fight! I hurled everything on the mantle at his head, a little lamp with sharp edges among other things. It hit him in the face and he carried the scar to his grave. I was very pleased with myself. That taught him." [10] Such confessions are rare among women of the bourgeoisie. Colette was later to refer in passing to the fact that Willy had beaten her when she had been too recalcitrant. In Sido's case, the distrust that had so quickly turned into a rejection of all males was overtly passed on to her daughter. *I could not help but notice, at an early age, that Sido's gentle way with newborn babies, with all babies, with mothers who grew restless as their pregnancies drew to a close, did not extend to the male parent. She had a curt way of deflating the fatuity of young fathers gaping at the bedside of a bloodless female who had just given birth. Moffino, our hunting dog, was roughly removed from the benevolent watch he was keeping over a basket full of puppies . . .*

"But Maman," I whimpered, "they are his children."

"So you say," she replied.

"Poor Moffino," I sniffled, "where can he go?"

"Wherever his paternal calling takes him," my mother answered. "To the café, to play cards with Landre, to flirt with the woman who runs the draper's shop." [11]

For in the home there was a Power, a certain kind of Power, indivisible. Allied with the possession of a knowledge handed on from mother to daughter along with a way of life, it was embodied in an unwritten and innate Law in the family subconscious. The power of Sido was an inalienable power; women like Sido were not alienated. We might note in passing that this Law is biologically *encoded* throughout the animal kingdom, and that Sido made no more distinction between the dog Moffino and her husband the captain than Colette, with her percipience, would make between the living and the dead, man or beast. This is at the basis of her love of animals, a love that seems anthropomorphic only because it is excessively natural. Sido and Gabrielle speak about the dog as they would speak about a neighbor. And everyone knows that for a dog "flirting with the draper's assistant" takes other forms.

To return to Sido in her youth, however, she was *blonde, not unusually pretty, charming . . . a* liberated *young woman who was used to living on open terms with boys, with brothers and male friends, a girl without a dowry.*[12] (emphasis added) Forced by circumstances and the rules of society, she left the happy Belgian household full of youth and laughter, smelling of warm bread and coffee, and went to *the house with the stairways . . . in the harsh winter of the wooded countryside.*[13] Thus she embarked on the banal path of the unhappily married. Jules Robineau *rode alone, without a dog, without a companion,* flirted with the servants, and drank. Sido started out *filling the large house with flowers, cooked Flemish dishes herself, made raisin cakes, and began awaiting her first child.*[14] It took three years to arrive. To console her, the Savage went off one morning to the market town, Colette relates, to buy her a little mortar for crushing almonds and pastes, made of rare fire marble, and an Indian cashmere shawl. At last, surrounded by the "wily farmers" and hostile serving girls with whom she was forced to share her husband, Sido gave birth to her first daughter on August 19, 1860, Juliette "with the mongol eyes," perhaps a mark of her alcoholic heritage. After the birth, the mother was to become the village Bovary. At this moment, a young tax collector arrived in Saint-Sauveur, a proud-looking young man, even though he had lost a leg: Captain Colette.

The facts surpassed any fiction, and Colette never wrote the story. Of course, it had been written before, often, during the nineteenth century that was now drawing to its close. One can find it sketched out in many novels. Let us fill in the picture by referring to the report of Crançon, the justice of the peace, who may not have read Flaubert, but who gives a good reflection of village mentality. He wrote: "The conduct of Mme Robineau is probably known to you. First she was said to be the mistress of M. Adrien Jarry, who is purported to have only half denied it. Although there are doubts about this liaison, there is none with regard to her relationship with M. Colette, and everyone is convinced that Mme Robineau's second child is M. Colette's doing. . . . M. Jules Robineau died from a sudden apoplectic stroke one night in a separate room where his wife had left him alone, even though he was ill and foundering in his excessive drinking." [15] According to rumor, therefore, Sido was responsible for her husband's death. It was even whispered about that she had lent nature a hand. This was to be only the first in a long list of scandals. Jules Robineau died on January 30, 1865, and left his wife the usufruct of a fine fortune, estimated by R. Escholier as equivalent to some 50 million 1956 francs.[16] There were the house in Saint-Sauveur, well stocked with linens and silver, farms in La Forge and Lamberts, la Guillemette-sur-Mézilles, Massues, Champigneulles, Grivaux, and the woods in Villeneuve, the vineyard in Perreuse, and various other holdings, not to mention hard cash. The handsome young tax collector began looking after the widow's property, and as soon as the legal period of waiting was over, he married her, on December 20, 1865, at the city hall in Saint-Sauveur, at eight o'clock in the evening, in the presence of his parents from Toulon. After which there was a religious ceremony in Brussels attended by Sido's brothers.

Sido was impervious to scandal; like her daughter in later years, she was above petty conformity. Far ahead of her time, with her exceptionally open mind, her respect for none but her own self-imposed conventions—conventions dictated by her heart—she always shocked the narrow-minded. On two occasions, she hired unwed mothers to work for her; her only instructions were "Remove your corset, my girl!" She was condemned for keeping on a maid who was seven months pregnant, but *Sido preferred to run the risk of ostracism rather than put a mother and her child on the street.* Of course, such behavior was highly displeasing to the lawyers' wives in the district. *Immoral? My little neighborhood looked on it as non-existent, that morality that was over its head.*[17] But cursed be those who give rise to scandal. Bad enough when one is a man, but when

one is a woman! Long before her daughter, and completely naturally, Sido gave rise to scandal.

⚜ CAPTAIN JULES COLETTE, THE ONE-LEGGED ZOUAVE

And what of the "seducer," the dashing one-legged captain who
became a father, this time officially, of a second boy, Léo, in 1868,
and then of Gabrielle, our Gabrielle? Born in Toulon on September
26, 1829, he attended Saint-Cyr and graduated a second lieutenant;
he then served in Kabylia in the Zouave regiment under Bourbaki.
He sailed from Algiers on March 30, 1854, for the Crimea, where
he distinguished himself and where he was wounded in the battle of
Alma. Following Alma, he was promoted to lieutenant and became
a captain less than a year later, at twenty-six. The wars of the Second
Empire then took him to Italy, and he was wounded at Melegnano,
the famous battle of Marignan. Now an invalid, he was forced to
leave the army.

Colette has less to say about her father's family than her mother's.
Apparently Sido had little affection for her mother-in-law. As a
child, Gabrielle once received a Christmas tree from her grandmother and was disappointed—Christmas trees were unfamiliar
objects in Saint-Sauveur. "It looks like her," Sido murmured in
consternation. This woman, whom Sido accused of selfishness and
falsehood, apparently handed on to her son—and perhaps her granddaughter as well—an unhealthy, jealous nature. *My grandmother, the
bad one—so I distinguish her from the other, apparently good one—
followed my grandfather, when he was over sixty years of age, to
the very door of a public convenience and waited for him to emerge.
Haughtily, the jealous old lady told my shocked mother, "Ah, my
child, a man who is determined to cheat on you will get away
through even smaller holes than that!"* [1]

After the facts, legend. Colette set down her memories at the beginning of the Great War, when the wind of militarism was blowing
through the region. When her father, on his crutch and his cane, was
asked *"It was in hospital in Milan, wasn't it, that you were . . ."*

*"Yes," he would exclaim, in the complacent tones employed to
recount sexual escapades, "Ah! my friend, the Milanese women!
What memories! It was the most marvelous year of my life."* [2]

After his leg was amputated, he was visited by the Emperor while
still convalescent. Napoleon III passed from bed to bed, shaking
feverish hands, questioning the wounded. The Emperor asked:

"*And you my friend, you've been wounded?*"

"*A scratch, Sire.*"

"*A scratch! Show it to me.*"

The Zouave showed "it" to him, and one of the Emperor's aides-de-camp was never to forget the sight. After a pause, the Emperor said:

"*I'd like to do something for you.*"

"*But Sire, I've already got a cross and some medals.*"

"*Is there nothing more I can do?*"

"*Well, yes, Sire. A crutch.*"

Which he received, along with a post as tax collector in the Yonne.[3]

Colette, who shared her period's fondness for panache, retained what she deemed to be her share of the inheritance after her father's death: a ribbon from the Crimean campaign, a medal from Italy, the rosette of an officer in the Légion d'Honneur, and a photograph.

It seems strange to me now that I knew him so little. The attention and fervent devotion I felt for Sido were only fitfully distracted. And my father was the same, he contemplated Sido! Can it be stated more plainly—she herself expressed it, *in the cluster at Sido's side, in her arms, my father had equal weight with us, he scarcely sustained us*— and this reveals no guilt-ridden sense of loss, it is merely the statement that in the presence of the all-powerful and powerfully loved mother, father and children were equals, rivals.

All his life we disturbed the intimacy of which he dreamed, she wrote, evoking her father's "rival gaze." For example, Sido would unthinkingly begin singing under her breath a barrack's ballad whose off-color words had been handed down from the Republican army to the Imperial army. The Captain was somewhat straitlaced: "*Oh, don't mind us,*" *my father would say from behind* Le Temps. "*Oh!*" *my mother would gasp,* "*let's hope the child didn't understand!*" "*The child doesn't matter,*" *my father would reply* . . . "*The child doesn't matter!*" wrote that same child, who saw things clearly, *that was being frank, and how he struggled with his love, his only love!* [4]

Or Sido would return from shopping and attack her daughter with the question "*Where is your father?*" *I would follow her, vaguely disturbed . . . that she should be worrying about father. She had only left him a half hour ago, and he almost never went out! . . . She knew quite well where my father was.* Almost as urgent *was when she would say, for example,* "*Minet-Chéri, you're pale, Minet-Chéri, is something wrong?*" (emphasis added) Critics have often held that the men in Colette's books are unsubstantial

and weak. Yet this remark must be carefully qualified, for the relationship between the sexes is infinitely ambiguous. Here is how
the father and brothers are viewed: they are "sylphs," "fugitives,"
"exiles," "foreigners," always in flight. In a passage about the
"father," he *wanders far away*, he *floats*, he is *patchy, cloudy, seen
in fragments*, his white hand *escaped from mine*. To the earthbound
woman, the male is clearly a creature of the air. He escapes. Can one
more clearly express the subconscious desire that he be elsewhere?
Later on, of course, the young girl in love will make violent attempts
to hold onto her man. But he will escape nonetheless. At the time, for
both the daughter and the father, intimacy with Sido was constantly
being threatened by the other.

Thus the star that was Sido orbited within the home in Saint-
Sauveur, "Holy Savior," a fateful name. Thus fluttered around her
like butterflies the father, the four children, joined together by
jealousy mingled with tenderness, with mutual affection, drawn together by the special object of their love. It is hardly surprising that
seen alongside this woman he loved, the one-legged former soldier
should seem like some melancholy exile from some other world,
another realm, a foreigner. He seldom spoke, he preferred to sing,
to evoke the passionate Milanese women. The Captain would shut
himself away in his library to write . . . *on one of the topmost
shelves I can still see a series of volumes bound in cardboard backed
with black cloth . . . I cite from memory:* My Campaigns, The
Lessons of 1870, The Composition of Geodes, Elegant Algebra,
Marshal MacMahon as Seen by One of His Comrades in Arms, From
Village to Bedroom, Songs of the Zouaves, *and I forget. . . . When
my father died, the library was turned into a bedroom. The books
came down from the shelves.*
  One day my elder brother called to me, "Come look at this . . ."
  *The dozens of cardboard volumes yielded up their long-hidden
secret. Two-hundred, three-hundred pages per volume, fine, cream-
laid paper, lined and unlined, thick, carefully trimmed, hundreds
upon hundreds of blank pages . . . an imaginary work, the mirage
of a literary career.*[5] Jules Colette's verbal power had been amputated
along with his leg. And Colette is the daughter of this immense desire
to write, of this impotence before the blank sheet of paper. Later,
she would marry another verbal impotent and would perform his
duties as a writer for him. The same anxiety before the empty page,
the same inability to ink it in, would also be the tragedy of Willy,

that slave driver of letters, and of his wife. But Colette would write. Father and daughter would join in paying hommage to the same woman in their dedications, for *the only page that had lovingly been completed and signed of Jules Colette's unique and imaginary work was the first, "To my dear soul, From her faithful husband, Jules Colette."* [6]

He was to leave his exile on two occasions. The first was in 1870. The 1870s were happy years for the Colette family. They were living with the three children, Juliette, Achille, Léo, in the house left by Robineau-Duclos. The Second Empire fell apart with the Franco-Prussian War, the Commune. The family experienced it all through isolated historical side effects: the Prussians came to occupy Saint-Sauveur, whereupon Captain Colette, on his crutches, left the village to meet them with a small group of men, despite the snow. He was the only one who spoke German, who could make himself understood. *"Thanks to him, there was no pillaging, and not too much horror. They thought he was a brave man."*

"And where were you?"

"I looked after the house and the children. Your sister was twelve, your older brother seven, Léo was three. . . . Achille would scamper around in the street among the Prussian soldiers, he was already big for his age. But as he went by they would stop for a moment. You see, they'd never seen such wavy chestnut hair, such dark blue eyes, and especially not such a mouth . . .

"But you, Maman, did you see them?"

"Yes," Sido casually replied. "But I've also forgotten them a little. I only remember the first time."

"Was it frightening?"

"Why would it be frightening? God, how trite you are . . . it was growing dark, and in the middle of the road I saw a soldier with a pointed helmet . . . since it was late and foggy, you couldn't see the color of the uniform, or of his beard. For a moment I had the notion that the whole German army must be made up of men like that, gray clothes, gray face, gray hair, like printed pictures.

"What did you do?"

"I went back to the house and buried the good wine," Sido replied, with some pride. "The wine was from my first husband's day. Château-Larose, Château-Lafitte, Chambertin, Château-Yquem . . . wines ten, twelve, fifteen years old. The fine sand in the cellar made them even better." [7]

Thus the intimate album in which History is preserved. The current flows from generation to generation. Ripples of war, the wave of the Occupation, always more serious. A gray soldier against a background of fog. A tiny and fearless woman hurrying to bury her wine bottles in her cellar. Wars pass, the image remains valid. The only resistance possible was to preserve what one held dear, both for Sido and for Colette, when the Gestapo arrested her third husband, a Jew, in 1940.

1871. The smoke of Paris burning, shots fired by the Communards from behind their barricades, the last moans of the Federalists among the tombstones in Père Lachaise cemetery, all these are public images. None of this happened, none of it remained in Sido's memory to be passed on to her daughter. In the country, no one wanted to know, it was ignored; in Sido's house, on female ground, the laundry was done, seeds were planted, one suffered alongside a cat when she had kittens, another child was expected, Gabrielle, who would be born in 1873. What did that other Power, the Power tried by men in the scales of war and revolt, have to do with this? It is natural that a thorough spring cleaning have more weight with women than the October Revolution. The female psyche does not usually register events unless they directly threaten its balance. In this way, the mass of silent women stand together. Only in this way. Is Sido a marginal figure in History, or is it rather that our concept of History is marginal with regard to the female, to women?

In 1880, the year of his retirement, the tax collector left his retreat in Saint-Sauveur for the second time to stand for election to the district council in the Yonne. A longtime Republican, he had been attracted to politics from an early age. According to his speech to the electors, he had been "at the Hôtel de Ville in 1848, alongside Lamartine, Arago and Ledru-Rollin." His service records, on the other hand, show that he had been dismissed from the administration for a disciplinary infraction on December 26, 1848, and reinstated after a year, on December 23, 1849. Very probably the "disciplinary infraction" was related to his political views. In 1870, he had addressed a speech "To the Army, the People of France, and the Chambers, and had proposed measures for the defense of the homeland. Jules Colette was not the only candidate for the district council seat; there were three Republican candidates and one Bonapartist." [8]

Later, Colette recounted her own version of this electoral cam-

paign when, at eight or nine years of age, she had played a more
than minor role as her father's campaign manager.

*The worn Victoria and the old black mare were loaded up when
the time came with slide projectors, painted cards, test tubes, bent
pipes, the future candidate, his crutches, and myself. . . . After
the "instructive lecture" delivered by the Captain to the nearly empty
school hall . . . my lavish father could never abandon his somber
congregation without standing a round of drinks, at least to the
members of the municipal council. . . . A good southerner, my
father drank nothing but lemon soda, but his daughter . . .*

*"This little lady must warm herself up with a bit of hot wine."
A bit! Once the glass was in my hand, if the server were too quick
in withdrawing the pitcher, I knew how to say "Fill it up," to add
"Your health!" to touch glasses and to bend my elbow and tap on the
table with my emptied glass, to wipe my mustaches of mulled burgundy and say, pushing my glass toward the pitcher again, "That
felt good going down!" I knew how to behave!*

*My rustic manners loosened up the other drinkers, who sud-
denly saw that my father was a man like themselves—except for his
missing leg—a "good speaker, perhaps a bit cracked" . . . And the
boring meeting would end in laughter, with backslapping, with tall
stories. . . . Completely drunk, I would fall asleep with my head
on the table, lulled by the convivial tumult. . . . On the first occasion, upon our return, my beatific prostration surprised my mother,
who quickly put me to bed, reproaching my father for my tired
state. Then one evening, she discerned in my eyes a gaiety that was
somewhat too burgundian, and on my breath, alas, the proof of my
debauch.*

*The following day, the Victoria set off without me, returned in
the evening, and never left again.*

*"So you've given up your lectures?" my mother asked my father
a few days later. He threw me a melancholy and flattering glance
and shrugged, "I had to, you took away my top campaign manager!"* [9] So he was forced to give up, no more at ease in the end with
the men he was to administer than he was with his untamed family.
The idealistic Captain was a man of abstractions, cleaving to his hu-
manitarian dream in the face of the human realities that completely
escaped him. An honest man, he lost to a scoundrel, Dr. Merlou, a
Republican candidate from the Béarn, who—like the Captain—had
a penchant for public speaking. Merlou became a *conseiller général*

and a deputy, and his love affair with Mlle Terrain, the schoolmistress, was to create a scandal that mesmerized the religious faction
in the town that was against secular schooling. The affair inspired
the well-grounded attacks in *Claudine à l'école* aimed at the vile
Dr. Dutertre, a cantonal delegate and shady politician who was
deeply implicated in scandals about money and women, as like Merlou
as a brother. Here too, Colette was avenging the paternal honor,
marking up, perhaps subconsciously, one small victory over her
father's rival. Unjust or not, neither Sido nor Colette ever really
understood the ideological fantasies or the driving lust for power
that seemed to impel the men close to them into political careers.
Jules Colette was a failure, but Henry de Jouvenel, Colette's second
husband, was to be a senator and cabinet minister. Impervious as
these women were to History, they were clearly even more so when
it came to the motives that drove men to attempt to influence it.
"We who flourish at ease away from men" . . . They did not
understand that women can mix with men, can in addition try to influence them. To Sido, as to her daughter, the political stage was
an arena where "the human voice turns into human noise." They
recognized in the animal and in the human species only single individuals they could love, that they could understand or help. Where
the masses were concerned, they felt only distrust, at worst suspicion, at best indifference. Thus the trappings of male Power appeared, from the female point of view, very like female Power seen
from the male point of view: foolish and absurd.

Sido's curiosity and emotion before a timeless blackbird devouring
a cherry were metaphysical. The vision of the tomb belongs to another school, and there is usually less communication between the
two than one might think. Sido's words bear witness, nonviolent
witness. Nearer to us in time, Annie Leclerc has this to say of men:
"You are only able to amuse yourselves with conquest, power, the
morbid enjoyment of your fantasies. In this way, you subjugate,
stifle, kill, violate all living things." [10] Colette mentions the "per-
nicious clash of politics" that absorbed her father and her husband.
The attitude, it seems to me, is the same. A "feminist" Colette?
Everyone says no, everyone becomes indignant. And in her own
words, she clearly stated that she was not. But this is arguing over
terms. If being a feminist consists in joining the women's movement,
in becoming a militant lesbian, in taking an active part in the suffragist struggle and related struggles along with the bra-burners, the
women brandishing castrating scissors, no—Colette was not and

would never have been a feminist. But if it is a matter of making a "woman's voice" heard, if it is a question of attacking masculine Power when it becomes morbid or bogged down in sterile abstractions, if it is a question of waging an individual struggle for autonomy, then Colette is a feminist.

✤ CELEBRATING DEEDS AND DAYS

At a time when the Anglo-Saxon feminists were sacrificing to the feminist movement their lives or worse, their dignity—for they were destroyed by ridicule—the child Gabrielle Colette and her mother Sido were a long way from being feminists. The year of Gabrielle's birth was also the year of the first Marxist Internationale, the first Anarchist congress. In Saint-Sauveur, time was not in step with the pace of History, but moved with the changing seasons, the holidays.

First came spring, the *roasting spring that shortened the grass and the spears of wheat . . . the rose bush then loses its closed buds, the cherry tree its wrinkled cherries, the garlic is new, the shallots tender.*[1] A little girl sets out on a familiar path toward *the huge, twisted oak, to the humble farm where she is generously fed on cider and bread and butter. Here the yellow path divides, here the creamy white elders are surrounded by so many bees that from twenty paces one can hear the sound they make, like a wheat thresher.*[2] Then came the lovely summer, already being elbowed by autumn, that makes the wild game grow thin beneath its weight, *the hares lying flat, crouched low, with palpitating flanks. Where could she find some damp clay to make a dressing for the woodcock with its broken leg?*[3] The water in the springs fell to a trickle. A grass snake crosses the water, its tiny nostrils breaking the surface, and prevents the child from swimming. The swamp is full of creatures: swallows and warblers glide through the reeds, yellow rats and field mice, somnolent butterflies for older brothers to collect, huge frogs, bats, and sparrow owls whose mewing is like the mewing of cats. But August is a long month of patient waiting for a little girl out of school who plays mumblety-peg to pass the time, three-pebbles, jacks, counting the days that stretch between now and the eagerly awaited time when classes will begin. And then it is autumn, the favorite season. *The children are reborn in the rain, out of the cloudy west comes a blue light, feeble, brief. "But it's evening,"* my mother would cry, *"Already time to light the lamp!"* And I *would say to myself "finally the lamp!" . . . and then comes the fire, the wine, the red and windy skies, the flesh of the fruits, heady game, barrels and pulpy spheres.*[4] And Gabrielle would become drunk on the things autumn gave so freely, so prodigally, red sorb-apples, plums, mushrooms, triangular beechnuts, water chestnuts with their four horns called *cornuelles* in Puisaye, gathered with a skimming sieve and a flat-bottomed boat as one paddled in the chilly water wearing an old pair of trousers. Chilly, because winter had now come and the dawn was blue, with the red light of the lamp cast onto the snow fallen on the garden, the log fire dancing beneath the hood of the huge kitchen fireplace. Beyond the icy panes, Gabrielle hurried to school, to snowball fights, to the frozen skating pond, in the bite of the east wind. Against the background of the changing seasons, characters seemed to materialize out of children's books—Frisepoulet, *a majestic sylvan god whose white mane of hair and beard set off the dark luster of his sorcerer's gaze,*[5] who sold chestnuts and never spoke to the village folk or to the children, but cried out "Hot chestnuts, sizzling chestnuts, hot in the pocket, hot in the mouth." Frisepoulet, sometimes called "Bon Dieu," also re-paired umbrellas under a stairway. *He was known as the Man with the Rose, smelling of new shallots, green onions and bay, and he never spoke because his lips were perpetually closed around a rose held between his aged teeth.*[6]

Childhood can only be captured by evoking these early images that compose the primal imagination. Eternal and fantastic figures take form, figures that the adult can transform—one might say in-finitely, but in each life I believe they are finite, to scale. What strikes us in these images is their precision; when it comes to familiar objects, the domestic, intimate task, only women can know the reasons behind them, their purpose. Men can be moved by their fascination for the chance happening, for the meanderings of pure aesthetics. But their female counterparts have had long commerce with the interior life of the home, a life seen clearly, without *trompe l'oeil*, an inside view in which everything is real and has its function. The womb, the matrix, is not a pink marble basin around a precious spring in which men can lose themselves, or find themselves—it is a site where something produces itself, is reproduced. It is, in short, a factory, swollen with blood and with life. The matrix is not an *objet d'art*, not a thing to be venerated, something vacuous. It is an active place, the site of gestation and production. The same is true with the house: all the objects it contains are, for women, things to be handled. They must be cleaned, waxed, dusted, dyed, moved about, recovered, washed, varnished, aired, cooked, fried, reduced, grated, beaten, set to rise. Colette's imagination is filled with useful things. In her mind, the preserving pots are there, always ready to make jam. This is why she is accused of not "inventing" anything. How can one invent what one knows so well exists? Poverty of ideas perhaps exists in those writers who must invent because the real reality has eluded them. A lack of imagination, bound to appearances, such remarks have been aimed at Colette's work by the surrealists and existentialists contemptuous of her work (and of course dismissed with indifference, if not contempt). As if their own wings had not often been singed in their pursuit of the transcendent . . .

The figures of the imagination are hardened in the kiln of childhood. The figures in Colette's imagination stand out clearly against indelible backgrounds of *fir trees heavy with snow, the narcissus growing around the hidden spring, fiery geraniums, the family scene and little fields like decorative flower beds, an English teapot with a lid shaped like a convulvulus.*[7] A happy childhood is yielded up in words that satisfy us, that make us hungry, like the burning autumn cake flamed in rum and Frontignan wine served in stemmed glasses, like the hot summer-garden snack of meringues brimming with fresh cream and strawberries, passed around by maternal hands: *Sido's wide sleeves fluttered and cast on the table a gleam like that of a white nightlight. Her bare forearms were more graceful than the neck of the silver pitcher.*[8] Colette's conversation with her mother, her conversation with the world, is replete with feminine voluptuousness—she didn't need to seek the world, it was hers, given to her, it filled her stomach because of, for the sake of, her own overwhelming need, her own greediness.

"To live is happiness," the feminist Annie Leclerc has written, "seeing, hearing, touching, drinking, eating, urinating, defecating, diving into the water and looking at the sky, laughing, crying, speaking to someone one loves, seeing, hearing and touching and drinking someone one loves, mingling one's body with theirs, that is being happy." [9]

Colette's discourse is the discourse of this happiness, and we might add that—a bad omen for her future—it is a discourse previous to man. Reconstructed when she was old, it gives to the voices of childhood a retroactive lucidity. "The future," one of them once said, "is what does not happen."

Images of the seasons, images of the earth, images of celebrations. Gabrielle is *a child superstitiously attached to holidays, to dates marked by some gift, some flower, some traditional pastry . . . a child who instinctively ennobled the Christian holidays with pagan touches . . . a little girl attached to the five-sided cake that was sliced and eaten on Palm Sunday, to the crêpes of carnival time, to the overpowering aroma of the church during the month of Mary.*[10] The reverie of wintertime is bound up with the New Year, the December snows recall *the shiver of long ago when I would wait, the distant vibration mingled with the beating of my own heart, for the sound of the village drum to wake the sleeping town . . . it was the drum, and not the twelve strokes of midnight, that sounded for me the rousing beginning of the New Year.*[11] The drum, beaten in front of the houses of prominent citizens—Captain Colette among them—made the dawn break on a new morning, on new hopes, on some candies, some gilt-edged books, a dozen oranges, boxes of dates from the big city, for this child so fond of ritual and who had no knowledge of the objects—sophisticated toys and expensive clothes— of a consumer society. Christmas at the Colettes was not a religious holiday. Yet at ten years of age, Gabrielle was captivated by the curé and the devout little girls in the public school, she yearned for *the catechism, sung vespers, a white dress and a communion cap with a starched pleated ruffle . . .* [12] and for presents from the Christ child in her Christmas slipper. Sido was a skeptic, always ill at ease with exaltation, whether mystical or emotional, but on one single occasion she attempted to bend to her daughter's explicit demand for conformity. It was Christmas Eve, Gabrielle was in bed, the sheet and featherbed pulled up to her nose, her feet against the hot-water flask, in a frigid bedroom divided by the pink lamp into zones of light and darkness. In her voluminous dressing gown, Sido was standing by the fireplace, looking at the bed. "Are you asleep?" And in her sincerity, the child almost replied "Yes, Maman!" Sido held in her hand her daughter's wooden shoes and two packages she had decorated with a bouquet of hellebore, the Christmas rose. She was upset, however; she gazed distractedly out of the window onto the garden. Shaking herself, she turned back to the fireplace and with a quick gesture she picked up the presents Gabrielle would have found on New Year's morning next to her cup of steaming chocolate. Her only Christmas gifts were to be the ones Sido had shown her on that night, *her scruples, the hesitation of her pure and living heart, her self-doubt, the furtive homage her love had paid to the exaltation of a ten-year-old child.*[13] Instead of presents, there was the New Year ceremony of giving bread to the village poor. Vile paternalism? The child apparently saw it as another kind of ritual: *I would open the door to the baker bearing a hundredweight of bread, and until noon, serious and full of commercial importance, I would offer to all the poor people, the real and the fake, a slice of bread and the gold coin they would accept without humility or gratitude.*[14] "Happy New Year, Good Health, and Paradise to Come!" In the afternoon, the child would escape, her wooden shoes in her hand, *to join a group of children, tired of family holidays, who had been set free to play rough games.*[15]

⚜ THE PRIMAL SOURCE

On the threshold of old age, Colette did not so much describe Sido, her mother; she evoked her. It had taken more than fifty years for her to allow herself to call forth this beloved figure, this person who had made her so demanding when it came to other kinds of love. Sido's gifts to her had withstood the test of time. How many mothers offer their child Dawn as a special treat, how many awaken their daughter at three-thirty in the morning and send her off, an empty basket on each arm, to the marshy fields in the sharp bend of the river, where there were strawberries and bearded red-currants? Sido would watch her Beauté, her Joyau-en-or, and see her grow small in the distance; *the narrow-minded countryside was not a dangerous one.*[1] Yet she had misgivings at allowing her child, her fairy princess, to wander freely, and her anxiety increased as the child turned thirteen, fourteen, fifteen. Still, sacrificing her own peace of mind, she allowed her to run free. When her daughter, now an adolescent, would finally appear at the corner on her way home, Sido would hide, would pretend not to have been waiting for her. *Then, beneath the pale green globe of the hanging lamp, her ashen look, sharp and almost harsh, would examine me from head to toe, would read from my scratched cheek to my muddy shoes, adding up the damage: a trace of blood on the cheek, a tear at the shoulder, the hem of my skirt unsewn and damp, shoes and stockings sopping wet . . . that was all. That's all there was. Once again, thank God, that's all there was!*[2]

The child so indulgently given the dawn would turn back toward home at the sound of the bell for early Mass, but *not before I had tasted the water from the two hidden springs I so cherished. One of*

them gushed up out of the earth in a silver convulsion, with a kind
of sob, and traced out its own sandy bed. No sooner had it appeared
than it was gone again, under the ground. The other spring, nearly
invisible, brushed through the grass like a snake, flowing secretly
through a field where the narcissus blooming around it were the sole
witnesses to its presence. The first spring tasted of oak leaves, the
second of iron and of hyacinth stalk. . . . Just to mention them
makes me long for their taste to fill my mouth when the end comes,
so that I may carry away with me when I go this imaginary mouth-
ful.[3] A fantasy of hidden waters, tasting of oak leaf, of iron and
hyacinth stalk: the creation of the primal fantasy.

To reach Colette's imagined source, a field is crossed toward the
secret springs. The waters are not open to the sky, they stagnate
somewhere within the earth. The female waters are enclosed: thus,
they are fecund. Female imagery draws its power from these two
almost hidden sources, from the liquid element beneath the ground;
we can discover the hidden woman through the active magic of
mother, of spring. In later years, Colette was enchanted to find that
she had the gift of finding water beneath the ground. She had
simply "forgotten" that the spirit of the spring had been nourished
within her from childhood, from the hour of her birth.

The hidden woman is at once the prisoner of the spring and its
jailer; she possesses the keys to the female kingdom that are handed
down from mother to daughter. Sido's kingdom was all-embracing;
it included—beyond the nucleus of house, garden, neighborhood—the
narrow-minded village and, wider still, all of Puisaye with its springs
and woods—in short, all that the child's imagination could encom-
pass, to its furthest extent, for beyond and outside this kingdom
nothing existed. And we must understand Sido's own ambivalence
in offering this imaginative gift. She gave freedom freely, "Do whatever you want." The child would scamper off to her beloved springs
still bound by the invisible cord that linked her, unbreakably, to her
beloved mother. From mother to source, source to mother, an ambiguity was set up that was never to be resolved. Free and fettered,
Claudine could exclaim: *I feel bound by a cord, the other end of*
which unwinds and is tied to the old walnut tree in the garden in
Montigny.[4] As if in a fairy tale, Colette/Cinderella tastes in the two
springs the intoxicating brew of her first freedom, but at the sound
of the bell for early Mass, the coach turns back into a pumpkin, the
footmen into mice. Somewhere, the Good Fairy Sido is still waiting

for her daughter to come running breathless home. The wanderer must return. Restricted freedom; invisible chains. The fairy god-mother/mother with her magic wand enlarges the boundaries of her own limited kingdom: *beneath her sway and her solicitude, the walls grew higher, unknown lands lay beyond the barriers that I breached so easily, leaping from wall to wall and from branch to branch, and I witnessed familiar wonders!* [5] Before the eyes of the enchanted child, her mother's face would assume its glorious "garden" expression, so much lovelier than the careworn indoor visage. And yet nothing could prevent the springs from beckoning her on to the woods, from the woods to the village, the village to the garden, the garden back to the house. The wanderer could never resist the pull toward home, not even in later years when Sido's place in the house would be filled by a bearded man.

Every year, Gabrielle, who spent so much time at her springs, would catch a fever. She recovered quickly. *In our house, we fed a fever, and at intervals rice pudding with sugar, chicken breast, con-sommé, would be brought to me. . . . With a feverish hand, I would reject them all, and I would sigh "I want some Camembert."* Sido was so natural and imaginative that in those days of diet and purge when the sick often died from sheer weakness, she would allow her daughter to have her Camembert, or a fine-veined Roque-fort, or one of the flat cheeses rolled in charcoal, dry and transparent as old amber. *That*, Colette wrote proudly, *is what I call having had a proper upbringing.* [6] Throughout her childhood, she was a prey to fever; it allowed her both to escape from and hold onto her mother. Like the source, the wellspring, fever permitted her to escape into a light, dreamy delirium, still nurtured by Sido's actual presence.

When she was twenty-two, unhappily married, Colette fell ill from disappointment and despair; one way to bring Sido rushing to her side and to bring back the wonderful moments of childhood fever, was her rough small voice issuing from her languid face: "Maman, I want some Camembert!"

Throughout Colette's novels, all illnesses, particularly those caused by love, are symptomized by fever, real or imagined. Upset when Chéri leaves her, Léa takes to her bed, examines the thermometer and coldly notes that it isn't fever, but love. During her days as a music-hall performer, Colette Willy would wait until Missy had arrived in Belgium before catching a fever and being coddled. Sev-eral documents of the Missy era describe an attack of fever and the presence of her maternal friend. Like magic, illness enables the former child to return to the shelter of home, to the enchantments of the old house.

⚜ FEMALE LORE

The capital of an empire, a hive in which the primordial tasks of domestic life are performed, the house is also a place of apprenticeship. In former days, female lore was richly complex, full of mysteries whose meanings are now forgotten.

"Minet-Chéri, you've thrown the chestnut hulls into the fire again!"

"No, Maman."

"Yes, child."

My mother would brandish the guilty evidence under my nose at the end of the tongs.

"My ashes! Dirtying my precious ashes, apple wood, poplar, elm! And what about the laundry? I've told you twenty times . . . that the tannin in the hulls turns the wash yellow. . . . When will you learn the things a woman has to know, if you don't do it now?" [1] (emphasis added)

Gabrielle listened and tried to remember these practical hints, these household rules. Fifty years later, they reemerge in recipes, in bits of advice. Sometimes, however, inside the perfectly brought-up child, there is a rebel refusing to allow herself to be made into a housekeeper: *Although I knew how to turn a radish into a rose, although no one was better at making a grass flute, at turning an old coin into gold, at skimming off the pink foam that rose from the strawberries and currants in the preserve pan, on the other hand I let the butter burn, I sewed like a soldier, and while cleaning the mirror above my mantle I would stop to read standing up, the book open on the chimneypiece. . . . "And not only for the wash,"* Sido *would go on. "Ashes for the potato bed, you know that they have to be absolutely pure!"* [2]

It was a female universe in which Sido ruled over a domestic world consisting of dogs, cats, various other animals, day helpers, the occasional seamstress, a nurse-cook, a housemaid, Gabrielle, her sister with her long hair, two boys and a husband. When the house is what counts, only those in the house count. The father, once retired, pursued political and literary ambitions, both of which ended in failure. His military life was over. All that was left to him was his love for Sido. Like the others. And it was a love that Colette depicts as exclusive, passionate, wildly jealous, the love of a man of the south, almost Italian: "a man with a knife," an inquisitor, full of suspicions, timing his wife's trips to the butcher and making scenes like a young lover. As he grew older and to fear she might die before him, he would make scenes and rave with rage and anxiety when Sido was ill. *Sido recovered, she always recovered. But when they removed one of her breasts, and four years later the other breast, my father was overcome with an awful foreboding, even though each time she recovered.*[3] The father had a privileged position in the family constellation as one of her children, partly their rival. A stranger in the mysterious kingdom where mother and child communicated silently, openly, with each other, he was so "human" that he would hold out his hand to see whether it was raining, so human that he could not make any animal obey him, a citizen-poet who urbanely organized picnics for his wild children, for his children who cared only for unbeaten paths, for excursions into secret regions, who preferred to jump over the wall, to break the window, rather than come into the house through the open gate. For him, however, Sido kept her last gift: she gracefully allowed him to die before she did. *I mustn't die before him. Absolutely not! Can you see me, letting myself die, and then he'll try to kill himself and fail. . . . I have less to lose, you see, I'm only a woman!*[4] She kept her word, and he died in 1905, at seventy-four, holding the hand of the woman he loved. He was given a fine funeral in a country cemetery, *and my mother accompanied him without stumbling to the edge of the grave, tiny and resolute beneath her veils, murmuring under her breath words of love, for him alone.*[5]

Love lay at the base of everything. Colette received from Sido her love for the world, for springs, for animals, woods and plants, for the children of men, for females, for life in all its cruelty and misery, in all its absurdity. Sido was no victim of our contemporary "nausea"; in the face of the absurd she was merely surprised, she watched. Her curiosity was boundless. Murderous feelings, the contradictions and perversions of passion, the dialectics of power and violence, were not strangers to a world in which the words "The kitten has died," have more resonance than the mutiny on the Potemkin. Sido would fall silent: Look!

Look at the hairy caterpillar like a little gold bear! look at the first bean sprout, the cotyledon with a little cap of dried earth on its head. . . . Look at the wasp cutting a bit of raw meat with its

*jaws, like scissors. . . . Look at the color of the sunset sky fore-
boding wind and storm. What did tomorrow's tempest matter to us,
as long as we could admire today's fiery glow! Look quickly, the
black iris bud is about to burst! If you don't hurry, it will be quicker
than you!* [6]

So much mention has been made of Colette and her bestiaries,
Colette as a portrayer of animals, Colette as cat, Colette as a wild
animal, a fox, that this aspect of her has almost turned her into the
"mummy's ittle doggie" kind of person everyone detests. As if the
cliché could contain all her truths about animal life, all the relationships between animals and ourselves we would prefer to ignore. One
last remark: no, from a strictly scientific, from a biological or zoological point of view, Colette is not always right. Her analysis is always
literary, subjective. She describes a dog as she would describe a man,
employing her own perceptions. M. F. G. Lextrait has examined this
question; his doctoral veterinarian's thesis is entitled "The Animals in
Colette's World." He demonstrates that Colette's dialogues "with the
animal world are often nothing but monologues, in which she simultaneously poses questions and gives answers." She does the same thing
when she describes her teachers, her little niece. Lextrait makes a
fascinating analysis of *La Chatte*. The eponymous heroine, Saha, refuses to kiss her master the day after his wedding because the smell
of his hand has changed. Impossible, notes M. Lextrait, since cats are
animals with little sense of smell. Yet smell was one of Colette's most
highly developed senses; this can be amply demonstrated. Our conclusion: when Colette evokes or describes animals, she is not engaged
in a zoological study. She is writing poetry, fiction, life; she is involved too.

Let us also note that in Colette's work the animal kingdom is part
of a whole. There are no barriers, no kind of compartmentalization
exists between men and beasts. In her texts, passages about animals flow
into other passages. In real life, dogs, cats, even Ba-Tou the panther
Colette loved so much during her days on the Boulevard Suchet, live
in the same house with humans, alongside them, not set apart from
them. It is no accident that Saha the cat is one of the main characters
in *La Chatte*—which is not a book about animals—whose other protagonists are a man and a woman. Colette projects herself into Saha
just as she projects herself into Claudine, into Léa. No more, no less.
Her letters are full of the activities of the animals with which she
lived. And in the animal as in the human species, it is the females that
are described at greatest length, that are more readily brought to life:

cats in love, jealous bitch dogs, maternal rivalries, tender females changed into ferocious beasts by a male's desire, an offspring's need. Until her old age, Colette always had by her at least one animal, a dog or a cat, and from her observation and practice she took only what interested her most, revealing herself the more as she ceased feeling the need to dissimulate . . . for after all, they were only stories about animals.

In Sido's kingdom, the animal was a full citizen like any other, with duties and obligations and rights. The children and their mother did more than merely care for them; animals, their behavior, were a world full of marvels that constantly astonished, that lent magic to the home. The word "animal" had no meaning for Sido: there was Toutouque, there was Moffino, there was Moune or Noire from next door. Always seen specifically, in itself, the animal never seemed to be the representative of a species, but rather an individual capable of performing unique deeds: in Sido's house, a hound bitch would suckle a kitten, a cat would nap on top of the canary cage and its trusting inhabitants would peck from the sleeping animal some fur for their nest. Throughout one winter, two swallows, fed with great effort on dead flies, lived in the house, perched on head or shoulder, nested in the sewing basket, chirped beneath the cat's nose, went to school in the child's pocket and flew back home. The cat ate strawberries and, *poetic, absorbed, sniffed the blooming violets.*[7] There were spiders; one loved music, the other would swing down from the ceiling at three in the morning at the end of its filament to drink its fill from the bowl in which a creamy chocolate had been kept tepid overnight.

Sido tended the caterpillar of an Emperor butterfly that had been wounded in the stomach by a bird, making it a casing of dry sand, waiting for it to become a chrysalis.

The caterpillar ate all the leaves.

"Maman, she's eaten everything!"

"Eh! What can I do about it? For that matter, the box leaves she's eaten are what stifles the woodbine . . . I know, but what do you want me to do?"[8]

Far from being some idealistic withdrawal, some fake and naive pose, the love of beauty and living things, in Sido as in Colette, co-existed with destruction and decay, their love for the young and the healthy and for age and decline. Evil aroused nothing but interested curiosity, death aroused indifference. They were beyond evil and death. In the order of living things, however, one also had a right to

prejudices that were inexpressible, unjust: a repugnance for the old
and the sick, a marked preference for the young, the handsome—everyone agrees that up until her death Colette displayed a weakness for
anyone (man, woman, child) of a singular beauty. Life is made up
of hierarchies, a handsome child was worth the sacrifice of a rose:

*Sido hated to see flowers wantonly destroyed. I have seen her, she
who was so giving, refuse flowers to people who came to ask for
them to decorate a hearse or a grave . . . "No; no one has sentenced
my roses to die along with M. Enfert!" . . . Yet she would willingly
sacrifice a beautiful flower to a very small child, like the little boy of
our neighbor to the east who was brought proudly into our garden
one day. . . . She gave him a cuisse-de-nymphe-émue rose that he
seized joyfully, popped into his mouth and sucked, destroying the
flower with his strong little hands, tearing off the outer, blood-colored
petals, the image of his own lips. . . .*

"Stop, you naughty child," his young mother cried.

*But mine applauded with her eyes, her voice, the massacre of the
rose, and I, jealous, said nothing.*[9]

⚜ THE WILD BROTHERS

Few women have returned to their childhood with such poetic
rigor. It will be said that in entering Colette's I am following the text
of a mature woman, that *Sido, La Maison de Claudine, Journal à
rebours*, were all written at a time when, later in her life, experience
had colored her more distant memories of her earliest years. But
should it concern me whether, at the time they gathered chestnuts
together, Colette's childhood friend was called Yvonne or Claire, or
whether they were in fact gathering chestnuts and not something
else? I am following a trail of memories that lead to childhood.
Dates, exact days, months, years . . . these will come later. The
recurrence of the same details over intervals of many years, in different texts, is a guarantee of their authenticity. One example, out of
hundreds: in *Claudine à l'école*, written in 1900, Colette tells of the
forbidden possession of bottles for cool drinks that each student
would bring to school on very hot days: *At the first fifteen-minute
recess . . . everyone dashes to the pump to plunge the bottles under
water to cool them off. Three years before, one little girl fell on her
bottle and put out her eye; her eye is all white now.*[1] In June 1940,
forty years later, Colette was to note in her *Journal au rebours* the
following conversation, in which her brother corrects her memory:

You are mixing things up, Hélène Josset is the one who had the white eye, because when she was eight she fell on a bottle in the schoolyard.[2]

Apparently only her brother Léo surpassed her in detailed memories of their verdant youthful paradise. He was six years older than she, Achille ten, Juliette fifteen. She describes her wild brothers as creatures before the fall. They were also Sido's products and completely "pure," in the primitive sense of the word, that is, at peace with their own desires.

The unparalleled older brother, he of the light brown hair and gray green eyes, had at seventeen *a crimson mouth that smiled on us alone, and on a few pretty girls.*[3] The second brother was also handsome, with roughly cut black hair, slate blue eyes, sober, good, and so gentle that nothing bothered or upset him. At six, he was a model child, save for his habit of running off. One evening:

"I want two sous worth of prunes and two of hazelnuts!"

"All the shops are closed," my mother replied. "Go to sleep, you can have some tomorrow."

"I want two sous worth of prunes and two of hazelnuts," the gentle child again asked, the next evening.

"Why didn't you buy them during the day?" my mother asked, impatiently. "Go to bed."

Five evenings, ten evenings, the same teasing occurred. . . . One evening, as on the other evenings, he assumed his usual stubborn face and quiet voice:

"Maman!"

"Yes," mother said.

"Maman, I want . . ."

"Here they are," she said.

He was the first to lose his composure and burst into tears.

"But . . . but I don't like them," he sobbed.

"You don't like them? Why did you want them, then?"

And he let it out:

"I liked asking for them."[4]

This little boy whose place Gabrielle was to usurp as the youngest child, along with his seat in the maternal carriage, was evasive, agile; he managed to get lost everywhere, in the cathedral, in the municipal clock tower, in the attic above the spice store in town where he had climbed up the cast-iron pillar. He dismantled every clock, he could play the piano at birth, he collected epitaphs. Gabrielle participated in his "forbidden games" involving the fabrication of

cardboard tombs for the imaginary dead, for whom Léo would compose his inscriptions:

"'O, thou model of a Christian wife! Dead at eighteen, mother
of four. The sobbing of your weeping children could not stay your
departure. Your business bankrupt, your husband vainly begs pardon!'
That's as far as I've got."

"It's a good start. She had four children at eighteen?"

"That's what I said!"

"And what about her business bankrupt? What is a business
bankrupt?"

My brother shrugged:

"You wouldn't understand, you're only seven. Put the glue in
the double boiler. And make me two little wreaths of blue beads for
the tomb of those Azioume twins who were born and died on the
same day."

"Oh, were they nice?"

"Very nice," my brother replied.

At thirteen, Colette concludes, he didn't make much distinction
between the living and the dead.[5]

With Achille, Léo shared games from which the "baby" was
excluded, although they allowed her a certain complicity, treated
her with unaggressive condescension. She watched them as they played,
tolerated and uninvited. Smelling of mint and fresh hay, the young
savages would go off to chase butterflies—not just any butterflies,
but Mars, Moricos, Vanessas, that had to be captured intact, that were
uncompromisingly rejected if one were too pale or another too old.
Gabrielle would beg, "Give them to me."

"No, you'll keep them. That one isn't beautiful enough to be kept." [6]

Before the days of the motorcycle, the cinema, pop music and the
adolescent "hangout," before television, the telephone, organized sports,
before hitchhiking and charter flights, before pot and acid, adolescence was an untroubled time, if we are to believe Colette. Reading
and the pleasures of reading—day and night, everywhere, in trees,
in the hayloft—underlay everything. Games were invented. There was
the word "mignonne," detested, forbidden, which was counted up as
it occurred in every new book and credited with two sous in a kitty
each time it was found. A book in which the word did not appear
at all was worth ten sous. And of course, as adolescent children,
they misbehaved: They would select a victim, a school chum, who
they would persecute with a perversity equal to their affectionate

victim's pleasure. One day when they were gone, Mathieu came to see them. . . .

In the evening, Sido said, "He seemed surprised not to find you home."

"It doesn't take much to surprise him!"

To their little sister, trained not to betray them, they recounted their exciting afternoon spent in a woods overlooking the road, where the searching Mathieu had stopped to rest almost beneath their noses:

"It was a simple matter to kill him, wasn't it?"

The elder, stiff, his eyes closed, made no reply.

"You didn't really kill him, did you?" I asked in astonishment.

"No," said the elder, "we didn't kill him. I really don't quite know why."

The younger interrupted and gently promised me:

"We'll kill him next time." [7]

The elder son studied to be a doctor and moved to Châtillon-Coligny, where he had a love affair that resulted in a fine baby, to Sido's regret. In 1898, he married Andrée-Renée de la Fare, by whom he had two daughters, and he died prematurely in 1913, ten months after his mother. The younger brother became a notary's clerk in Levallois-Perret and was never to recover from his childhood. Sometimes, some sixty years later, he would come to visit his sister in the Palais-Royal in the damp twilight; he would tell her of a visit he had made to the Cour du Paté, the terrace of the ruined château in Saint-Sauveur. The slightest alteration or change would kindle his feeble indignation:

"Do you know what *they've* done?"

"No."

"*They've* oiled the gate," he would reply coldly.

⚜ MY LONG-HAIRED SISTER

The eldest child, the half-sister with the long hair, had an even more tragic fate. Colette dwells on her *black hair, with reddish strands, with soft waves* [1] that, when undone, covered her entire body. Today we have forgotten this symbol of slavery our grandmothers bore like a chain. The hair celebrated by Gabrielle was over five feet in length, nearly as long as she herself was tall. It was dressed in two long braids that could be used as *ropes to pass through the handles of the lunch basket, as brushes to dip into the inkwell or the paints, as whips to punish the dog, ribbons for the cat to play with.*[2] Because of her hair, the girl was forced to arise at dawn. On cold winter mornings, she would fall asleep again before the wood fire as her mother brushed and combed her nodding head for a full half hour. So long, strong and plentiful was her sister Juliette's hair that even for those days it was very like some congenital deformity. Yet there was no question of cutting it! The history of hair is an ambiguous one: in our society the way it is cut, clipped, or tonsured can be either a sign of liberation or a mark of slavery, or the stigma of infamy. Hairs from Juliette's head were to be found everywhere, despite her mother's continual brushing. Aside from their hair, however, the sisters were not much alike. Marked from birth, somewhat the victim of her mother's love for her second husband, her unparalleled brothers and the "child," Juliette was a stranger in the day-to-day life of the home. While her younger brothers and sister played their secret games, she would read, excessively as girls did at the time, in the days when the only available adventure was to be found in novels. She read everything she could lay her hands on, the younger Fromont and Risler the Elder, *La Chartreuse de Parme, Le Vicomte de Brage-lonne, Monsieur de Cahors, The Vicar of Wakefield* (in French, of course), *La Chronique de Charles VII, La Terre, Lorenzaccio, Les Monstres parisiens, La Grande Margot, Les Misérables,* serials cut out of *Le Temps* and sewn together, a collection of the *Revue des Deux Mondes,* the *Revue Bleue,* the *Journal des dames et des demoiselles,* Voltaire and Ponson du Terrail. What a trite and old-fashioned picture of provincial life in the 1880s! The girl was completely schizoid, and would encounter one of her brothers in the house with surprise; in the delirium of typhoid fever, she called her distracted mother Catulle Mendès or Octave Feuillet, popular writers of the period.

However, in 1885, Juliette's wedding was one of the great events of Colette's childhood. This "plain and pretty girl," who had not only a dowry but assurances of an inheritance from her father (her stepfather's disastrous financial affairs having not as yet become public), got engaged on the brink of becoming an old maid to a Dr. Roché, who is mentioned in guarded terms by Colette, as though there were something shamefully wrong with him. "*A man who smells of vermouth,*" Léo called him.[3] Was it the fiancé who upset the family, was it aversion to marriage, was it—more probably—the careful accounting Juliette's husband demanded from his unfortunate father-in-law? *In any case,* Colette was to write forty years later, *everyone spoke of it as a bad marriage, from the Rue de la Roche to the Rue Gerbaude, from Bel Air to Grand Jeu.*

"Juliette's getting married," people would say to my mother, "that's a real event."

"It's an accident," Sido would correct them.

"So Juliette's finally getting married! How unexpected! It was beginning to look hopeless!"

"No, desperate!" Sido would respond belligerently. "But who can stop a twenty-five-year-old girl?"

"And who is she going to marry?"

"Oh God, the first dog that came along." [4]

Was the family really so against the union? In any case, the ceremony took place: a photograph recalls it for us, with Juliette buried in silk faille and white tulle, *pale and lifting her strange Mongol's face, defiant and submissive, so that I was ashamed, up to an unknown man.*[5] Sido, unhappy, her face set, and Gabrielle, eleven years old, parading and pretty in her pink dress, beneath her long flowing hair.

At the first sound of the violins at the wedding ball, the elder of the two boys disappeared: *He jumped over the wall . . . into our garden, from the Rue des Vignes, wandered around the closed house, broke a window, and my mother found him in bed when she returned sad and weary from having handed her bewildered, trembling daughter over to a man. . . . "Just think," Sido said, "it was so that he could be alone, away from those sweating people . . . that he broke the windowpane. Was there ever such a wise child?"* [6]

Was there ever such an understanding mother—if her understanding is not actually a reflection of Colette's rose-colored hindsight? In any case, Sido must have exhibited the misanthropic behavior that can also be read as nonconformity, as distrust mixed with a savage shyness toward an intruder, a foreigner, and she passed this on to all her children. *Achille had attacks of misanthropy that would contort his face.*[7] When he was a doctor and the father of two daughters, he would dash into the garden whenever the bell rang unexpectedly. Léo was to live a solitary life. Even in the days of *Claudine*, Colette would shut herself away in a panic at the first visitor who arrived on the "day" Willy had set aside for her to be "at home." However, hers was a harsh schooling . . .

Juliette's wedding in 1885 marked the beginning of a dark period for the Colette family. We recall that Robineau-Duclos had left Sido a tidy fortune on his death. Unfortunately, Captain Colette was not a good manager. His salary as a tax collector had never been enough. "For either political or administrative" reasons, he was almost fired in 1862, almost transferred in 1863.

In 1864, the finance minister, from whom Jules Colette had requested fifteen days' leave to attend his sister's funeral, wrote to the prefect: "The last report on M. Colette indicates he is lacking in performance and commitment, that his collections of all kinds are greatly in arrears, and, finally, that many indications of negligence can be seen in his management of his own affairs." [8] From our vantage point, we are less surprised that this upright and dreamy Republican eager to "win people over by teaching them" was a poor tax collector lacking in the zeal his superiors demanded in collecting taxes from the poor than we might have been even forty years ago. Nor are we surprised that he was incompetent in managing his wife's property.

Jules Robineau had been feared as a landlord; he had understood the peasant mentality. Jules Colette rapidly allowed things to get out of hand; he borrowed money from his own farm tenants—who would then "forget" to pay him their rent—and he paid exorbitant interest. As early as April 1867, the year after his marriage to Sido, a building had to be sold, and in 1881 a house the Captain had inherited from relatives in Mourillon also went. By 1884, things had begun to pile up. Since Juliette was Robineau-Duclos's only daughter, her husband demanded an accounting. Captain Colette borrowed 120,000 francs from the Crédit Foncier on April 4, just before the signature of his stepdaughter's marriage contract on April 14. On September 4 of the same year there occurred the division of the estate left by Robineau-Duclos. Juliette's marriage brought to light the Captain's incompetence in handling her affairs, and after rancorous discussions between the Colettes and her husband, the families fell out. *The fearful machinery of notaries and lawyers was set in motion . . . there was talk of careless management, inexcusable extravagance. . . . My long-haired sister bowed to her husband's and her in-laws' demands and stopped seeing us.*[9]

Here was another scandal. The idle and mean-minded village found a new source of gossip to feed its hostility toward a family that was already regarded as being too "different." People showed no pity: *No one looked away out of charitable delicacy when they passed the woman who, overnight, had lost a child because of money troubles. Everyone was talking about us. People would congregate at Léonore's butcher shop in the morning in order to waylay my mother and get her to reveal the truth. . . . She would return home exhausted, panting like a hunted animal.*[10]

On the other side of the garden wall, the prodigal sister lived in a house and garden Sido could look down on from the upper story of her own house. A month passed, the girl *would walk stiffly by our door . . . but if she chanced to see my mother, she would flee.*[11] Sido suffered and, like all the Colettes, went into hiding. There were rumors that Juliette was going to become a mother. One evening, Colette chanced to see her mother hiding in the garden, listening, waiting: *A long drawn-out cry, high and thin in the distance, muffled by the wall, reached us both, and she brought her clasped hands violently to her breast. A second cry pitched on the same note . . . then a third. . . . And then I saw my mother grip her own loins with her hands and turn around, stamping on the ground, and she began helping, repeating with a low moan, with the convulsions of her tormented body and the clasping of her futile arms, with all her pain and maternal strength, the pain and strength of her ungrateful daughter so far from her who was in the process of giving birth.*[12]

When Colette gave birth to her own daughter, Sido was only recently dead, and we can imagine her drawing on this vision of motherhood shared, like an act of love, at a time when for most people birth was still the "most accursed festival, the one most persecuted and ravaged, in which man's fascist repression finds its victory in death."[13]

Juliette's child was a girl. In the end, she was reconciled to her mother, but when her marriage turned out badly, she made an unsuccessful attempt at suicide and succeeded in hanging herself in 1906, at forty-seven years of age, having first gone to Mass and taken Holy Communion. Colette never commented on these later tragic developments.

❧ "THE PURE AND THE IMPURE"

Colette preferred to respond to the sexual curiosity of her daughter Bel-Gazou with silence. *She is too close to truth, too natural, not to know as her birthright that all of nature recoils before that majestic and disturbing instinct, and that it is right to tremble, to keep silent, to lie when it is approached.*[1] Sido's position was probably similar. She does not seem to have given her daughter any very precise information about sex. There were plenty of analogies to be drawn by a country child surrounded by animals: *The mating of cattle, the tomcats covering the female like wild beasts falling on their prey, the almost austere peasant precision with which farm women talked about their virgin heifer or their daughter in labor.*[2]

And there were accidental discoveries: one April morning, Mélie, the nursemaid-cook, Marie-la-Rose the maid, and Milien, the handyman, went to gather apricot clippings with Gabrielle, who was ten or eleven years old.

"Mélie, spread out your apron so I can put the clippings in it."

I was on my knees collecting the flower-starred apricot twigs. Mélie crept playfully up behind me with a "Hou!", threw her apron over my head like a sack and tenderly rolled me over. I laughed in the pleasure of being small and giddy. But I needed air and emerged so suddenly that I caught Milien and Marie-la-Rose kissing, they had no time to break apart, and I caught the look of complicity on Mélie's face. . . . The clicking of the secateurs, a dry chatter of hard-beaked birds. They speak of budding, of early sunshine, sunburnt foreheads, cold shadows, incomprehensible repugnance, betrayed childish trust, suspicion, dreamy chagrin.[3]

"Repugnance," "dreamy chagrin," there is a mixture of attraction and repulsion, vague, unwilling to be named; before the discovery of adult infidelity, excitement turns into romantic melancholy.

With one's girl friends things were more basic. On Sundays there were white slippers, starched dresses, immature, mystical reveries; on Thursdays—the free day for French schoolchildren—in black smocks and hobnailed shoes, there were unsettling games with little friends. ʻThe whole of the mean-minded village with its greediness, its half-camouflaged yearnings, would be reflected in the faces, the games, issued through the mouths of these aware children. *Horrid stories of knavery and of illicit love affairs contorted their cherry-stained lips glistening with honey from their snacks . . . a deck of cards appears, the excitement mounts. Three out of the ten girls already know how to cheat, how to moisten the thumb when dealing, as they do in the bar, how to slap the trump down on the table. "That does it! You screwed it up, you've lost the point." . . . They shouted and imitated everything they had picked up in the village streets.*[4] It was a far cry from the whispered prayers of the convent. Straightforward little peasant girls did not identify with the veiled virgins and martyred saints they worshiped, but with the seamstress or the pharmacist's wife or the girl in the postoffice. All of them present or future wives of watchmakers, grocers, butchers, laundrymen.

"When I grow up, I'm going to be a harlot," Jeanne said.

"I'm going to be a sailor," Minet-Chéri *would interject, unable to come up with anything else,* a girl who didn't leave the borders of her canton over twice a year.[5] She would say "when I go round the world," as she might have said "I'm going to knock down some chestnuts," Colette adds fondly. And though she did not sail the seas, Gabrielle was the one who left in the end. Even though, she writes, the universe had been bounded *by the clear circle of light shed by the lamp, through which moved a beloved hand capped with a silver thimble, drawing a thread,*[6] one had still wanted to leave it.

The need, the urge to leave created the great anxiety of Sido and of Colette. When for so long one fears and desires the arrival of the wolf at the door, the wolf will one day knock, or break in. The man will come along . . . Sido rejected all thoughts of marriage, socially acceptable sex, for her daughter out of a complex of reasons, the main one being her desire to keep her at home, but she could also feel guilty about it. As for the child, she too turned away from sexuality, she did not want to leave her mother, to upset her; very naturally, she also craved it. Both mother and daughter had fantasies of abduction. From Sido:

"I can't go on like this," my mother said. *"I dreamed again last night that you were being carried off. I went to your room three times. And I didn't sleep at all."*

I looked at her with commiseration, for she seemed tired and worried. But I kept silent, since I didn't know of any remedy for her concern.

"And that's all it affects you, you little monster."

"But Maman, what do you want me to say? You seem to be blaming me that it was only a dream." [7] (emphasis added)

Juliette's marriage had freed the first-floor bedroom papered in cornflowers on a whitish gray background.[8] Gabrielle eagerly moved out of her old room, which was next to her mother's bedroom, but Sido continued to prowl around watchfully, fearful of gypsies and tramps.

"None of that is really serious," my father reassured her.

"Oh, you! As long as no one disturbs your midday cigarette or your dominoes. . . . You never consider that now the little one is sleeping upstairs, and that now she's separated from my room by the stairway, the dining room, the hallway, the salon. I'm tired of trembling for my daughters all the time. The older one has already gone off with some man." . . .

"What do you mean, gone off?"

"Well, got married. Married or not married, all the same she went off with some man she barely knew!"

She threw a glance of tender suspicion at my father.

"And you, after all, what are you to me? You're not even a relative." [9]

And from Gabrielle:

A little old-fashioned engraving hanging in the dim hallway suddenly caught my attention. It showed a carriage harnessed to two peculiar horses with long, extended necks. By the wide-opened carriage door stood a young man, bearing in one arm, with immense ease, a recumbent young woman whose tiny mouth opened in an O, whose rumpled skirts formed a corolla around her pretty legs, and who was making an attempt to express her horror. "The Abduction." In my innocent daydream, I cherished the word and the image.[10]

And now the mother and daughter share the same fantasy: *One windy night. . . . I was asleep, tired after a Thursday spent shaking down chestnuts in the fields and celebrating the new cider. Did I dream that my door creaked? . . . Two arms singularly expert at lifting a sleeping body went round my waist, my neck, at the same time wrapping the blanket and sheet around me. . . . Was I really awake? I doubt it. Only a dream, carrying a little girl out of her childhood, can fly her away and set her down without surprise or objection in the middle of hypocritical and adventurous adolescence. Only a dream can create in a tender child the ungrateful creature she will be tomorrow, the crafty accomplice of whoever comes along, the forgetful girl who will abandon the* maternal *home without a backward glance.* (emphasis added) *So I left for the land where the carriage, its bronze bells ringing, stops before a church, where a young man in taffeta and a girl like a blown rose in her disordered skirts . . . I did not cry out. The arms were so gentle, held me so close, watched out for my hanging arms at every doorway. . . . Some familiar rhythm seemed to be rocking me to sleep in those abducting arms.*

At dawn, I did not recognize my old garret, now filled with ladders and crooked furniture, where my worried mother had carried me during the night, like a mother cat who secretly moves her kitten's nest. Exhausted, she was sleeping and only woke when I cried out to the walls of my little room, "Maman . . . I've been abducted!" [11]

The dream of abduction, a version of the tale of the shepherd girl and Prince Charming, had such a hold on Colette that in 1904 it formed the basis for a short story entitled "Minne" (later revised, edited, and deformed by Willy, who turned it into *L'Ingénue libertine* in 1909), written when Colette was thirty-one years old. Minne, a high-strung adolescent, fourteen years and eight months old, who is the *only daughter* of a thirty-three-year-old mother who has been *widowed* for ten years, is torn between her everyday life in her bourgeoise home on the Boulevard Berthier and a fantasy world fed on reading low-life adventure stories in *Le Journal*. She devotes to one of these characters, Le Frisé, whom she imagines she meets every day near the fortifications, an attention that is at first passive and which gradually becomes charged with desires, with promise: one evening, thinking she has seen him go by, she runs off into the night after him, wanders aimlessly through the underworld district, and ends her hallucinatory and exhausting journey back home where her mother finds her in the morning in a dead faint.

In the meanwhile, the child has turned into a woman. This short story adds to the abduction fantasy the knowledge Colette had acquired from its enactment in real life (her abduction by Willy). The schema however is the same: the lure of abduction (rape, sexuality, marriage), an hallucinatory and actual return to the home (the womb, affection, the arms) of the mother.

Another episode illustrates the same progress: this is the episode of the maid Adrienne Septmance's wedding:

"We've been invited," my mother said. "Of course, I won't go. Adrienne asked me if the child could be a bridesmaid . . . it's very awkward!"

The child jumps up and rattles off her prepared speech:

"Maman, I can go with Julie David and the Follets. You know that with all the Follets you won't have to worry, it'll be as if I were with you, and Mme Follet's cart will take us and bring us back, and she said that the girls can't stay to dance after ten o'clock, and . . ."

I blush and fall silent, for my mother, instead of protesting, darts at me a look of contempt and extreme cunning:

"I've been thirteen and a half too," she says. "You don't have to keep it up. Why not just say 'I adore servants' weddings'?" [12] Here, her repugnance for the implicit sexual content of marriage is mingled with a social contempt for "servants' weddings" typical of the period.

There follows an evocation, filtered through a memory as accurate as clockwork, of the wedding, a poetic realization of a Renoir scene:

The arrival: Mme Follet drove the cart, *overflowing with us, with our laughter, her four daughters in blue, Julie David in shot alpaca, mauve and pink.*[13]

The four-hour meal: *What ancestor handed down to me, through my frugal parents, this almost religious feeling for sautéed rabbit, for lamb with garlic, for soft-boiled eggs in red wine. . . . Glass bowls of sugar lumps . . . are there so that between courses one can suck sugar dipped in wine, loosening the tongue, refreshing the appetite. . . . Five meat dishes, three sweets, and a nougat pièce-montée atop which trembles a plaster wedding scene.*[14]

Carousing, gluttony: *Labbé drinks white wine out of a milk pail, Bouilloux is handed a whole leg of lamb which he devours down to the bare bone, all by himself.*[15] Songs and ribaldry: *A tall bony peasant bellows patriotic songs, "Sauvons Paris! Sauvons Paris!" and is regarded with some awe . . . since he comes from so far away. "Just think, he's from Dampierre-sous-Bouhy! at least thirty kilometers from here!"*[16] And the full stomach at the end of the feast *which left me sitting there pleasurably stuffed with rabbit sauce, stewed chicken and sugared wine.* The mother of the bride inexplicably breaks down and cries (we are hardly surprised), Julie David gets a spot on her dress. The violins strike up a quadrille. Julie David and Gabrielle go for a walk in the kitchen garden, and Julie chatters: *"The Caillon boy kissed me. . . . I heard everything the groom was just saying to the bride. . . . He said 'One more schottische and we can be off.' . . . Armandine Follet threw up in front of everybody."*[17] And then, as if by chance, they arrive at the bridal chamber, with its *high, narrow bed, its featherbed plumped up with goose-down pillows, the bed where this evening reeking of incense, sweat, livestock and the fumes of the sauce would come to an end.*[18] Shocked out of the torpor of her overindulgence, the child began to run down the lettuce rows, across the ridges of the asparagus bed.

"Wait for me. What's got into you?" Julie caught up with me at the gate to the kitchen-garden . . . near the reassuring barn . . . where her impatience was finally given the most unexpected answer, bawled out by the confused child through her tears: "I want my mother!"[19]

An eloquent recollection of Juliette's wedding day, but here it is Gabrielle, not Achille, who is the adolescent both attracted and repelled, who wants to run to her mother. It will not be long now until this formless desire and anxiety will be aroused by another marriage,

so like the others, but this time it will be her own marriage, and there
will be no question of running to Maman. Freed and fettered! Like
a thread tied to the foot of a baby chick, immobilizing it, the invisible cord is ever more tightly tied to the pretty foot of the adolescent so eager to run off. From primal spring to wedding night, one
had come to believe oneself free, and suddenly one is a bride.

Marriage, however, is but one aspect of the great sexual mystery.
Another object of the child's curiosity is the immense ritual of the
flesh that so directly concerns her: motherhood. Here too she encounters a vacuum, a dearth of information, a dearth of example.
The "child is born, expelled from her own body. Instead of a body,
she has ringlets, bangs, polished shoes, pretty clothes." [20] Gabrielle
wonders. In a book of Zola sneaked out of Sido's library, which was
a broad-minded collection—"there are no wicked books"—she found
a terrifying response to her innocent questions. In the novel, the
feeble wife brings her child into the world *with a callous and crude*
abundance of detail, an anatomical precision, a wealth of color, smell,
posture, screams, in which I recognized nothing from my peaceful
country girl's experience. I felt deceived, terrified, threatened by my
young female fate.[21] She tried vainly to conjure up Sido's soothing
voice: *The words before my eyes described the lacerated flesh, the*
excrement, the unclean blood. . . . I fell down on the grass,
stretched out, soft as one of the baby hares that poachers would
bring fresh killed to the kitchen.[22] Fortunately, Sido was always
nearby, and her consoling words put both the beautiful things and
the lies in their proper place: *"Come, come, there's nothing terrible*
about the birth of a child. And the real thing is much more beautiful.
One's pain passes so quickly, it's always the men—what does he know
about it, this Zola?—who make things up about it." [23] Words repeated in our own day by Annie Leclerc who in the same spirit
writes of the discovery women make of their bodies' vital resources:
"When I discover that childbirth is a marvelous happiness, not some
pit of abject suffering, I am enchanted not only by the revelation of
some long-lost treasure, the splendid secret so pleasantly revealed
. . . what I then glimpse is the principle behind men's weapon; it is
aimed not only against women, their most threatening enemy because she is the more gifted for living, but against all living things,
since life is what can destroy them." [24]

Gifted for living, such was Gabrielle as her childhood drew to a
close. A female child warmed by her contact with another gifted
female. With this gift, what can the gift of writing be worth, that

worthless sideline? Deep down, Colette felt it to be worthless. She was sincere, she was right. But without that gift, the other would have benefited only herself.

How can we recapture adolescent female sexuality, with its great preoccupation with motherhood, its diffuse and disembodied love objects, its elements of homosexuality? We have the ambiguous relationship between Gabrielle and her mother's friend from Nerval, Adrienne de Saint-Aubin, which gives us an early example of the maternal component in Colette's own homosexuality.

When my mother and Adrienne were nursing, the former her daughter, the other her son, they had traded babies one day for fun. Sometimes Adrienne would say to me, laughing: "You, I nourished you with my milk." I would blush so hard that my mother would scan my face to discover the reason for my color. How was I to conceal from this lucid, steely and threatening gaze the image that tormented me, Adrienne's brownish breast, with its violet, hard nipple . . .

"So long at Adrienne's?" Not a word more, but her tone of voice! There was such clairvoyance, such jealousy in Sido, and such confusion in me, that as I grew older the friendship between the two women cooled. . . . It took a long time before I could make the association between that worrisome memory, a kind of warmth around the heart, the enchanting way I envisaged the woman and her home, and the notion of a kind of seduction.[25]

Of course, this prescient analysis must be set alongside other overtly homosexual texts by Colette. In her mind, homosexuality always had a maternal element, strongly sexual, tinged with guilt. The feeling of transgression included both the mother to whom she was unfaithful and a filial feeling that was supplanted by a repressed, forbidden eroticism. In this regard there are texts that more clearly set forth the relationship between an adolescent and a mature mistress. In these the lover's masculinity—with its feminine characteristics—allows for a wider latitude in erotic evocation. In Chéri's pressing his face into his Nounoune's bosom we sense a reference to this early fixation on a nursing female and Colette's awakening senses: Adrienne's swarthy breast with its violet nipple. Sido, a jealous mother wary of sexuality, had not been mistaken about the significance of this relationship.

The thirteen-year-old Gabrielle's romantic crush on a twenty-year-old law-student friend of her elder brother who loved music and always carried with him a photograph of his fiancée depicting her carefully coiffed and swimming in lace, is one of the common banalities of female adolescence; literature has dealt with it with a great deal of complacency. However, Colette's narration is different, and should be carefully examined. We have Gabrielle, pretty with her long hair, the buckled ribbon around her waist, wearing a huge straw hat. Maurice is spending the summer vacation with his friend, bringing with him all sorts of citified oddments, *candies, those monkeys made of silk chenille in old-gold and grenadine or peacock green that were so fashionable at the time, a purse made of turquoise velvet . . . but what were these gifts, compared to what I could steal? I stole from him and my brother everything I could get into my sentimental little magpie clutches: racy illustrated magazines, Oriental cigarettes, cough drops, a pencil with teeth marks on the end of it, and especially empty matchboxes . . . emblazoned with photographs of actresses . . . Théo, Sybil Sanderson, Van Zandt.*[26]

For a while, the love-struck girl daydreamed about these photographs of current celebrities, uniting them in a harem over which Maurice exerted an indolent, regal control. Then wisdom and good sense returned. One day, while they were alone together in the garden, Maurice handed her his fiancée's photograph:

"Oh," I said clumsily, "what a pretty dress."

He laughed with such lack of concern that I did not excuse myself.

"And what are you going to do when you get married?"

He broke off and looked at me.

"What do you mean, what am I going to do? I'm almost a lawyer already, you know."

"I know. But what will your fiancée do while you're being a lawyer?"

"How funny you are! She'll be my wife, naturally!"

"She'll wear other dresses with lots of little ruffles?"

"She'll look after the house and receive guests. . . . Why are you laughing? You know how married people live!"

"Not really. But I know how we've lived for the last month and a half."

"Who do you mean, 'we'?"

"You, my brother and me. . . . When you're married, you probably won't be able to come here for holidays. You'll never be able to walk with my brother holding the ends of my braids like reins."

He shrugged and answered, rather foolishly, "Well, of course not, that goes without saying."

He went off toward the house without another word, and for the

first time, mingled with my great sorrow at my imminent loss of
Maurice, I felt the faint victorious pang of a woman.[27]

The childish good sense is too natural not to have been derived
from her mother's natural anticonformity. Sido's hostility to the model
marriage had been proved right. However, even when the wisdom
and experience of a woman of the world is interposed between the
memory and the written page, there is a kind of candid clear-sighted-
ness in this encounter in which the female child is the adult, the young
man the ingénu, that contradicts the romantic, phallic picture of
ambiguous adolescence. This was not to be the last occasion on which
Colette would indulge in a liberating confusion of identities, in role
inversion.

What, other than these few fragments, can be retrieved from the
erotic universe of childhood? In isolating them, we have already distorted them. The text speaks with the diffuse sensuality of a young
animal overwhelmed with smells and sights, for whom duties and
play, the emotions of the mind and the heart, are inseparable. There
is no trace of the notorious Freudian penis envy, of sexual curiosity
about little boys. One turns to a passage of erotic byplay in *Claudine
à Paris*, bearing in mind that Willy's hand played its part in such
passages and that for successful sales he insisted on spice and gamy
description. Where spiciness is concerned, however, Colette's subconscious did the choosing and, after all, merely reconstructs the truth.

We sat in a hollow, in the clearing in the woods, in a circle, we big
girls, and opened our blouses.

Anaïs, the daring one, bared a patch of lemony flesh and announced
with aplomb: "They've grown quite a bit since last month." What do
you mean! The Sahara! Luce, all pink and white in her simple school-
girl shirt—long-sleeved without scallops, it was the rules—revealed a
"central valley" that was barely discernible and two little pink points
like Fanchette's nipples. Marie Belhomme . . . go on! And Claudine?
A little arched chest, about as much breasts as a somewhat plump
boy . . . at fourteen. . . . The exhibition over, we buttoned our
blouses with the intense conviction that each one of us had "more"
than the others.[28] A counterpart of those male competitions in which
members are compared for size, the competition between girls is
very like that between boys. There was apparently no desire to turn
their eyes toward the possessors of real or symbolic phalluses, and
they seem to have been content in their bodies, with their nascent,
childish female breasts.

In the sexual preoccupations of the young Gabrielle, the male appears but sporadically, as an abstraction, as the protagonist in the fight in which the adolescent girl dreams of playing a more or less passive role. He is the abductor, the one who goes off, a hero of evasion and the ambiguities of evasion. He whose role is to escape, to let go, will become at the proper social and biological moment a means of escape. In the real world, meanwhile, Sido's were the abducting arms.

⚜ SIDO, PRACTICING PAGAN

Sido's nonconformity is most clearly evidenced by her freethinking with regard to religious matters. In Catholic and bourgeoise France, religious concerns have always played a considerable role in literature. We need only list a few of Colette's great contemporaries, Péguy, Claudel, Gide, Mauriac, Bernanos. However, French society at the end of the nineteenth century, under the Third Republic, was marked almost as much by anticlericalism and freethinking as it was by Christianity. Women as a rule saw to the continuity of religious tradition in the family, and the man was a Republican, later a socialist. At the bottom of her heart, Colette was an unbeliever, impervious to all fanatical or transcendental mysticism, to all forms of intolerance, even to the secular Third Republic intolerance of priests. So was her mother.

1884 was the year of Leo XIII's encyclical *Humanum genus* condemning freemasonry and calling for the establishment of Catholic labor organizations. France during the Third Republic passed laws providing for secularized State education. Gabrielle was eleven at the time, the year of her first communion, of prepubescent yearnings toward mysticism. Sido had been baptized and married in the Church, but she had turned away from "childishness" and from Catholic ritual. *I should have inquired into the source of this withdrawal from any kind of organized religious practice,*[1] notes Colette, but she did not inquire, relating only that at eleven or twelve years of age, she wheedled from her skeptical mother permission to attend catechism classes and to learn the Canticles of Grace along with the other girls in the public school.

On the first of May, along with my catechism friends, I laid lilac, camomile and roses on the altar of the Virgin, and returned proudly home with my "blessed bouquet." My mother laughed irreverently, looking at my spray of flowers that was attracting the maybugs into the salon and into the lamp.

"Did you think it wasn't blessed before?"[2]

With her fundamental tolerance, Sido set no obstacle but her sarcasm in the path of her daughter's zeal. The catechism: *"Oh, how I hate that way of asking questions! What is God? What is this? What is that? All those question marks, all this mania for investigating, this inquisition, I think it's all most indiscreet!"* Confession: *"It's the last straw, it's too much! I turn red with indignation just talking about it! . . . Revealing, admitting, confessing and confessing, exhibiting all the bad things you've done! . . . Confession gets a child used to talking too much, this intimate disclosure soon gives him more vain pleasure than humility. . . . Mark my words! I'm very upset. And I'm going round to speak to the curé about it!"* [3]

And the tiny woman threw her black cashmere "visiting shawl" over her shoulders and dashed off, furious, to the curé, while her daughter, upset, imagined the dramatic meeting, the threats, the invective. But Sido returned all smiles:

"Well?" my father asked.

"That's it," my mother exclaimed, *"I've got it!"*

"The curé?"

"Of course not. The geranium cutting he was so stingy about."

"Did you read him out about the child?"

Standing in the doorway to the terrace, my mother threw him a look, blushing, taken aback.

"What an idea! Of course not. You haven't any tact. A man who's given me not only a cutting off his geranium, but who's promised me some of his Spanish honeysuckle . . ." [4]

Thus Sido, who was so suspicious of religion, but who managed to retain her sympathy for the curé and his flock. In her impertinent tolerance, her generous insolence, Sido got around every trap set by fanaticism and ideology: she kept to the rules: on Sundays, she rarely missed Mass. *In the wintertime, she would take her hand-warmer, in the summertime her parasol, in all seasons her thick black prayer book and her dog, Domino. . . .*

Old Millot, the curé . . . remonstrated with her one day that the Mass was not intended for dogs. She ruffled her feathers like an angry hen:

"My dog! Throw a dog out of church! Are you afraid of what he might learn there?"

"It's not a matter of . . ."

"A dog with irreproachable behavior! A dog that stands up and sits down along with the rest of the congregation!"

"That's very true, my dear Madam, but nevertheless he growled during the elevation last Sunday."

"Of course he growled during the elevation, I'd like to see him not growl during the elevation! I trained him myself to be a watchdog, he's supposed to bark whenever he hears a bell!" [5]

During Mass, the disbeliever would plunge into a book bound in black leather with gilt . . . the plays of Corneille. During the sermon, she would misbehave dreadfully; she would yawn nervously, her stomach would become upset, she would have palpitations and blush or grow pale, almost ill . . . until one day she found a remedy. *"I'll have to forbid Monsignor Millot to preach for more than ten minutes"* . . . *and she communicated this final ukase to him, but this time he sent her packing. The next Sunday, however, after the ten minutes had elapsed, she began to cough, to consult her watch ostentatiously, to drop her book. . . . The curé tried to struggle on, but he lost both his head and the thread of his sermon. Stuttering, he gave a sudden "Amen," with no rhyme or reason, and left the pulpit, blessing his flock with a distracted gesture—all his flock, not excepting the laughing face below him, gleaming with the insolence of a born reprobate.*[6]

From the daughter of such a mother, what can we expect? However, she took her first communion along with all of her friends, while beneath her veil and the feigned fervor of an untamed and graceful child there lurked the same suspicion, the same unimpeachable integrity, as her mother's. *The kind old curé who gave me my first communion fully believed that the silent child, her gaze fixed upon the altar, was awaiting a miracle, an imperceptible movement of the Virgin's blue veil. It's true! And I was so well behaved . . . and it is true that I was dreaming of miracles, but not the same as his. Glutted with the scent of the warm flowers, enchanted by their mortuary perfume, with the musky decay of roses, I, dear unsuspecting man, was in a paradise you could never imagine, peopled with my own gods, my animals that talked, my nymphs and lambs. . . . And as I heard you speaking about your hell, I was thinking of man's pride in inventing an eternal punishment for momentary crimes!* [7] Much has been said about Colette's paganism, her pantheism. Strong words to describe an attitude in which common sense and love of life, a feeling of fellowship, and her insatiable curiosity combined to create a certain reserve in the face of the great ideological and theological systems. This attitude remained unchanged until she died, and it would have been betrayed by formulation. An earthbound creature, she peopled her fantasies from an interior mythology that included all the creatures of the earth she loved, but deep down she had no interest in religion, in any religion, from either a dialectical or mystical point of view. And as for the evangelical spirit, she and Sido both saw it as separate from the practice of religion, just as she was to keep her concern for the exploited of the earth separate from any political or social dogma. Her morality was built on other foundations, and the quietism of her carnal attachment to living things was untroubled by any transcendental speculation. Metaphysical questions interested her no more than did political questions. Not even death. "Death does not interest me, not even my own," she remarked at fifty. Only the parapsychological aspect of the supernatural—clairvoyance, hypnotism, thought transference, kinesthesia—aroused her curiosity. She told many stories about seers. There was Mme B., for example, a plump and commonplace woman with white hair, who held forth in her modern, sun-filled apartment.

"*Then you can see the dead? What are they like?*"

"*Like the living," Mme B. replied frankly. "Behind you, for example . . . there is the spirit of an old man. He has an untrimmed beard, flowing, almost white. . . . He's watching over you a great deal right now.*"

"*Why now?*"

"*Because you represent for him what he would like to have been here on earth. You are what he wanted to be. He couldn't do it.*" [8]

This obvious reference to her father moved Colette deeply and gave her to think. Not, however, because of some credulous or superstitious belief, but because of the surprise we all feel in the face of some mysterious and enlightening coming together of hidden facts known to ourselves alone. The surrealists were also to be fascinated by this kind of poetic coming together, and they were militantly anticlerical. Colette was clear-sighted about the nature of her own interest: *Don't expect me to profess any kind of faith or develop a passion for consulting the privileged ones who have links with the invisible. It's just curiosity, very like the curiosity that compels me to consult, willy-nilly, Mme B., the "candle" woman, the dog who "counts," the rosebush that bears edible fruit, the doctor who adds some human blood to my own human blood, and so forth and so on. If I lose this kind of curiosity, they may as well bury me, for I will have ceased to exist.* [9] The curiosity that kept her alive cared nothing for ready-made truths or the revelations of bygone ages; it was interested solely in change, in particular discoveries.

⚜ THE PROVINCES

An English critic, Margaret Crosland, has noted that until 1900— and even after—the majority of French writers were members of the aristocracy. In France, Miss Crosland explains,[1] for the benefit of her English-speaking readers, women have always had importance not so much in and of themselves, but in relation to men. The Frenchwoman's main concern has always been concentrated in those areas for which men have considered her suited: the home, children, lovemaking. Her time and energies have been devoted to her life as housewife, as spouse, as mother and mistress. The only women with sufficient leisure time to devote themselves to more creative occupations were those who belonged to the nobility or the *haute bourgeoisie*. To this I would add that in a society that is still, in its most profoundly held values, aristocratic, the woman of noble family or the *haute bourgeoisie* is able to rise above her sex because of her elevated social status. For this reason, the *précieuses*, the mistresses of salons, the intellectual women and the feminists, have in general been products of this upper-class milieu. In France, there are no woman writers comparable to Jane Austen, the Brontë sisters, George Eliot, all those female British novelists of the Victorian age, all members of the middle class, often the daughters of the clergy. Probably the Protestant ethic, albeit more repressive where sex was concerned, encouraged women to educate themselves, to become individuals, without any particular sexual stigma. Catholicism, although in some ways more tolerant, set women apart, glorified them as women, by depriving them of tasks that were reserved for men. The only things—in the arts at any rate—that enabled them to overcome the blemish of being women were either nobility or social status, and this is why, in France, the gallery of female writers extends from Marie de France to Simone de Beauvoir, and includes Marguerite de Navarre, Mme de Lafayette, Mlle de Scudéry, Mme de Sévigné, Mme de Staël, George Sand, who was the Baronne Dudevant, and all of Colette's contemporaries, from Anna de Noailles to the Princesse Bibesco. Colette does not fall within this tradition. She is neither what a *mot* vaguely reminiscent of Restif de la Bretonne has called her, a "perverted peasant," nor was she noble: she is a pure product of the middle class. We will see that it took a great many circumstantial elements—her immense talent among them—and a good deal of luck to make her into what she became. As she herself wrote again and again, it was not "vocation." But then, what is a vocation?

I first thought that people would laugh if I told the story of a writer who didn't want to write. As I finish it, I find that the story is a melancholy one. For when love came into my life at seventeen, in spite of love and in spite of being seventeen, I had no desire to write about it or describe it, and I believed that love could get along without being written about, that it could meditate on itself in silence and be satisfied with the presence of the beloved, with no need to write a novel about itself. And yet I've spent my entire life writing. . . . The child of a family without money, I had learned no profession, I knew how to climb, to whistle, to run, but no one came along to offer me a career as a squirrel, a bird, a deer. The day when need forced a pen into my hand and I was given a bit of money for the pages I had written, I understood that from then on, slowly, tenderly, I would have to write, patiently joining sound with sense, I would have to get up early by preference, go to bed late out of duty.[2]

Without theses chance circumstances, she would have remained a provincial Sido—and Sido would have remained unknown to us. In France, the provinces are another country, different if not separate. Because of Sido, through Sido, Colette is by nationality a provincial. Margaret Crosland understood this when she entitled her first biography *Colette, a Provincial in Paris*. Provincial culture is more female-oriented than Parisian culture. It is in the provinces that the difficult art of making preserves, of doing huge laundries, of in-depth spring-cleaning, of seasonally embalming woolens and furs, reaches the peak of some mania for perfection. Colette is a part of this culture. Can one picture George Sand sewing nightshirts or Anna de Noailles hoeing her garden? These women, overendowed with class and intellect, reserved such menial tasks for their maids. Her possession of such knowledge makes Colette a unique figure in the French intellectual "establishment," mainly because of her interest in it, not that she always made use of it in her daily life. It is not surprising, then, that the literary effusions of many of her male or female contemporaries were foreign to her, and that she saw no difference between a page well written and a well-made pair of wooden shoes. This appreciation of work well done still exists in the provinces, although today we are more likely to confound this gradually disappearing provincial attitude with some vanished "prewar" mentality.

In addition to her sovereignty in domestic matters, the provincial woman reigns over a kingdom of romance, of tragic and adulterous love affairs, where there are parochial scandals and where vast networks of gossip are maintained. Colette and Sido were a part of this provincial society with its concealed hierarchies of awesome power, but were rejected by it because of scandal. They are citizens of the other provinces, the domestic provinces, the country of large, comfortable old houses filled with books, with old things: *Even had I not inherited it from her, I think she would have given me the love for the provinces, if by provinces we understand not only a place, a region far from the capital, but a feeling for caste, for morality, the pride of living in an ancient dwelling.*[3]

The provinces in all their pride have the particular quality, in a traditionally centralized France, of nonetheless referring everything back to Paris, of "keeping the eyes of the soul turned toward Paris." Sido's eyes were turned in this direction. On an average of once every other year, she would go to Paris, deriving a sustenance from her visit that would last her for the remainder of the time. *She would come home laden with chocolate bars, exotic foods, samples of material, but, above all, with theater programs and violet scent. . . . In a week she would have visited the mummy display, the new wing of the museum, the new department store, heard the latest tenor and a lecture on Burmese music. She would return with an inexpensive coat, everyday stockings, very expensive gloves.*[4]

Sido escaped being a typical provincial woman because she was without the mania for keeping track of napkins, lumps of sugar or full bottles. She also lacked—this woman who realized she was growing old when she began to polish her Chinese cups too slowly, with too much care—the denigrating spirit, which according to her daughter she replaced with a sharp critical sense that was clear-sighted rather than disparaging. *She would catch an unusual trait as it flew by, some shortcoming; in a flash, she could point out hidden beauties, she could shed a shining light into narrow minds.*[5]

The humor of a woman who was natural, at peace with herself, enlivens Sido's critical comments on Parisians: *"You've become very proud, Minet-Chéri, at living in Paris since your marriage. It makes me laugh when I see how proud the Parisians are that they live in Paris, the real Parisians because they think it makes them some kind of nobility, and the fake Parisians because they think they've come up in the world. You're like a dog on its hind legs because you've married a Parisian!"* [6]

Or: *"Ah, look at Mlle Thévenin strolling triumphantly down the street with her cousin from Paris. She doesn't need to tell us this Quériot woman comes from Paris—a lot of bosom, little feet, and ankles too fragile for the size of her body; two or three necklaces around her throat, hair very well done. . . . That's all you need to know that the Quériot woman must be a cashier in some big café! A Parisian cashier only has to dress up her head and her bosom, the rest of her is hidden all day. And she doesn't walk enough, her stomach gets fat. You'll be seeing a lot of top-heavy women like that in Paris."* [7]

Or: *"When will you give up trying to imitate Mimi Antonin and everything she does every time she comes to spend her holidays with her grandmother? Mimi Antonin is from Paris, you're from here. Children in Paris show their skinny legs without stockings in the summertime, and in the winter they show their little panties and their poor little red behinds. . . . And you don't need to start to wear stockings when you're eleven. Especially with the calves I've given you. You'll look like a tightrope walker, all you'll need is a tin cup."* [8]

How hard to be the mother in this play of mirrors reflecting Sido and Gabrielle, each with the same image. Sido always came back from Paris, returned to the things that *without her lost their warmth, their zest for living. She never knew that each time she returned the smell of her gray squirrel pelisse, impregnated with her scent, blonde, feminine, chaste, far from any base, bodily seductions, made me unable to speak or to show my feelings.*[9] One day, the daughter would not return.

In the meantime, Gabrielle too had her Parisian adventures: a short visit when she was six, which lived in her memory only as a series of loud noises, the train, the fiacre, the bus. Then when she was eleven, a whole week, of which she recalled only the dry heat, thirst, feverish fatigue, and the fleas in the hotel in the Rue Saint-Roch. She was overwhelmed by the tall buildings, but entranced by a photographer, who told her she was a "marvel." When she was sixteen, *after two weeks of theaters, museums, stores, I brought back with me among my memories of flirting and eating, mingled with regrets, hopes and contempts that were as ardent, as candid and as awkward as myself, an astonishment and a melancholy aversion for what I called "houses without animals."* [10]

Each time she returned home with the same eager anticipation, wanting to return to the nest, inseparable from her mother. At nineteen, however, she made another visit to Paris, staying with a Mme Cholleton. Here began the idyll that was to end in her married imprisonment. From then on, she returned to the provinces infrequently, and Sido would become the one to suffer the long periods of waiting in an empty house filled with the memory of the girl from Saint-Sauveur. Girls do not come back. In the journey from the provinces to Paris, the abduction fantasy takes its concrete form. The abduction must be to Paris. The provinces are conservative: regrets, homesickness, rancors, passions, brief encounters, all are slowly preserved in the act of waiting, in expectation, as in a brine, as it was with Nana Bouilloux. But little girls who are abducted are never brought back to their mothers by their abductors. The provinces stand for Sido, a paradigm that is lost by being abandoned.

⚜ PUBLIC SCHOOL AND SOCIAL DECLINE

> Democracy has a choice to make, a life and death choice, and, citizens, the choice must be made. Women must belong either to the realm of knowledge, or they belong to the Church.
>
> JULES FERRY,
> *Discours sur l'égalité d'éducation*
> Salle Molière, April 10, 1870

> Young girls used to grow up in poetic ignorance of the mystery of things. . . . We are going to eradicate such young girls.
>
> *Le Gaulois*, November 25, 1880

Gabrielle's schooling took place during the revolution in public education under the Third Republic. Born in 1873 and educated in the 1880s, Colette was to experience the problems of the three great and divergent educational choices of that period: free public education versus religious schooling, education for the upper classes versus universal education, and boys' schools versus girls' schools.

The legislation enacted can be summed up with a few dates: in 1833, the Guizot Law established lay primary education. This marked the end of the Church's monopoly on education. In 1836, this law was extended to cover girls' schools. On March 15, 1850, the Falloux decree departmentalized the universities and extended freedom of education to the secondary level. In 1881, the Ferry Law established free public primary schools, and in 1892 primary lay schooling was made compulsory. At the same time, a law of April 10, 1867, ordered communes with more than 500 inhabitants to provide girls' schools and made it obligatory for the *départements* to support teacher-training schools for women. In 1880, Camille Sée established a day school system for girls. For boys' schools, the battle for lay education had been won in the first half of the nineteenth century. The delay in providing facilities for the training of lay female teachers for girls' schools was largely responsible for giving members of religious communities a privileged position with regard to female primary education. Secular legislators believed that girls would benefit from the religious instruction from which boys were exempted. The female teachers who replaced the nuns were badly received in some of the villages where these women, most of them former students of religious schools, had to engage in the struggle for lay education without sufficient training. After the enactment of the 1879 law, the number of teacher-training schools for girls increased from forty-one in 1881 to eighty-one in 1886 and to eighty-five in 1891. At the time, the increase in boys' schools was at a lower rate. The girls' schools began to catch up with the boys' from the inception of the Third Republic. The organization of female secondary education was slower: after passage of the 1880 law, high schools and female colleges began to increase, from 23 in 1883 to 71 in 1901 and to 138 in 1913. Opinion was slower to change. Julie Daubie was allowed to sit for the baccalauréat examination in 1861 thanks only to the combined personal intervention of both the Empress Eugénie and Victor Duruy, the Minister for Education. In 1900, there were still a mere 21,200 girls attending secondary schools, as against 84,500 boys.*

To these two factors, freedom of education and sex discrimination, was added the third factor of class. In the nineteenth century, there were two kinds of schools in France, those for the upper classes and those for the masses. The bourgeoisie made an effective attempt to set itself apart from the lower class. From the primary grades on, there were several options open to upper-class children: education at home with the mother or a tutor had been prohibited by conservatives during the debate on compulsory schooling; special classes had therefore been set up in 1853, in Mulhouse, in which bourgeoise children were separated from working-class children. After elementary education, the split was even more evident: second-

* The figures are taken from Prost: *Histoire de l'enseignement en France*, Paris: Armand Colin, 1968.

ary schooling was restricted to the bourgeoisie, while higher primary education or professional schools were designed for the working class.

Against this three-tiered background, how was Gabrielle's own schooling carried out? We have noted Colette's own fairly free-thinking attitude. Her father was a Republican, her mother a skeptic. Her brothers had attended public schools. Socially, the family was considered upper class by the village: the Captain was a graduate of Saint-Cyr, a decorated soldier, his position as tax collector due to his distinguished service on the field of battle. His wife was the widow of a landowner and a gentleman. Their sons were therefore sent to secondary school in the Collège in Auxerre, their elder daughter had gone to boarding school. What was to happen to Gabrielle? When she reached school age, in around 1880, the Captain retired. At the same time, farms began to be sold off and the Colettes started down the road to bankruptcy. Financial difficulties had already begun to poison the family's life at the time Gabrielle turned twelve, and by the time she was completing her studies it had ended in ruin. Her family was probably unable to pay for expensive schooling. In any event, she was sent to the communal elementary school in Saint-Sauveur, where she was looked on as having come down in the world, where she was surrounded by the daughters of peasants. *I never had friends of my own sort*, Claudine was to say, *since the few bourgeoise families in Montigny habitually sent their children to boarding schools in town, and almost all the pupils in the school were the daughters of grocers, farmers, policemen, and laborers.*[1]

Colette was unable to attend either a convent school or go on to a secondary school. In her version, she is modestly silent about the economic reasons that dictated her education. *I remember two older brothers sent off to the Collège in Auxerre. Dirty and thin, flea-bitten in summer and swollen with chilblains in winter, they lived out their sentences in silent hatred. However, that was long ago, the time when I would also see my elder sister come home from her boarding school in town, altered, melancholy and nervous. The imprisonment of the three older children led to my own freedom. "Oh no, not this one!" my mother would murmur, gazing at me.*[2]

Although the child's own unwillingness to go away to school, and Sido's desire to keep her at home since there was a school in Saint-Sauveur may have played a part, the question of money must have been the predominant factor: Gabrielle would have to attend the rural school for poor girls; paradoxically, in later life she was to regard this as having been to her advantage. "Such female education was based on those concepts of feminine needs held by the upper classes. As proof, those needs were totally overlooked when it came time to establish primary education for working-class girls, which came later than it did for boys, but which was based on identical pedagogical standards. In fact, the peasant girl, submissive to and controlled by her husband, had little leisure to ponder her femininity." [3] The bourgeoise lawmakers' contempt for rural girls led to their being lumped in with the boys, which may explain why Colette's description of her schooling depicts a milieu that was amazingly homogeneous and tolerant, one in which traditional discrimination had not led to prejudice. Jean Larnac, one of Colette's earliest biographers, hints at this: "Confronted by the lack of discipline of her girls, the poor woman [Mlle Veillard, the teacher] could only weep. During recess periods, she would assist, powerless, at their boyish revels: they would crowd into the restricted schoolyard and play with marbles and climb trees without a thought to any immodest display of their underclothes." [4] Mlle Veillard's displeasure is aroused by the girls' unruly tomboy behavior, so contrary to the discipline and submissiveness expected of them. In a discriminatory society, coeducation will obviously reveal more insidious and insurmountable injustices. Elena Gianini Belotti's study, *Du côté des petites filles*,[5] gives a striking demonstration of this by describing the establishment of differences between girls and boys in the home and continued on in coeducational institutions before the age of five. At the girls' school in Saint-Sauveur, the same educational program and the same treatment was given as in the boys' school next door: there was no sexual privilege.

Gabrielle was allowed the opportunity to develop within an open school society, in which her status as a middle-class child gave her certain advantages over her rougher companions. She retained a vivid memory of her *poor school, dilapidated, unhealthy, but oh, so much fun! . . . On the ground floor were our two classrooms, one large and one small, incredibly ugly, dirty rooms, with tables the like of which I've never seen anywhere else, nearly worn away with use, at which we ought, by any normal standards, to have become hunchbacks after six months. The smell of those classrooms after they had been occupied for three hours in the morning and three in the afternoon was literally enough to knock you down.*[6]

In 1887, a series of advanced courses was added to the school. Mlle Veillard, who did not have her high-school teaching degree, was forced to relinquish her post as schoolmistress to Mlle Terrain, a young woman of twenty-four and the mistress-protégée of Dr. Merlou, Jules Colette's old political rival who was by now the deputy-mayor of Saint-Sauveur. The battle was joined. In Claudine's narrative, Dutertre is Merlou, and Mlle Sergent is Mlle Terrain; she gives a malicious but factual version of events that were discussed in every home in Saint-Sauveur at the time:

As for our teacher, poor Mme X., good, forty, ugly, uneducated, gentle and continually in terror of the primary school inspectors; Dr. Dutertre, our district superintendant of schools, wanted her post for his own protégée. In that part of the world, what Dutertre wants the Minister also wants. . . . When Mme X. was given her notice, she wept for an entire day, poor woman, and so did we; this gave me a fixed aversion to her replacement.[7]

The real-life Mlle Terrain finally won the rebel over, even though Colette would pretend to read the newspaper in class during the afternoon and would send her companions into shrieks of laughter at her pranks. In her old age, she recalled that thanks to this woman's prodding her handwriting improved, becoming clear and readable once again.

When interviewed by Jean Larnac, her teacher recalled that Colette had been a "very intelligent student with a perfect command of French, none or almost none of science, very musical, clever, witty."[8] (Teachers' evaluations will never change the world, or predict future vocations.) It is hardly surprising that Gabrielle had a "perfect command of French," especially when compared to the uncultured little peasants who surrounded her. The family library was lined with books and the child could pick them out in the dark; she had access to Musset, Voltaire, Littré, Larousse and Bequerel, d'Orbigny, Camille Flammarion, Elysée Reclus, Balzac and Shakespeare. At seven years of age she had read Labiche and Daudet, at eight Merimée, *Les Misérables*, and Dumas's *Le Collier de la Reine*. She had read Balzac and would continue to read him throughout her life; she knew him by heart. *I have been selling farms and buying houses all my life. But Balzac is one property from which I would never part.* The only forbidden writer—and then only some of his work—was Zola. What was banned, she read on the sly. The bookcase beside Sido's bed contained the twenty volumes of Saint-Simon's *Mémoires*; she was shocked that her daughter, at the age of eight, did not share her pleasure in that writer.

⚜ School Days

We could dwell upon this country school, so much more vivid than the school described in *Le Grand Meaulnes*, where at seven in the morning the students would arrive to sweep the classroom, *to break twigs in the shed and ruin our hands and carry in the logs and blow on the fire, receiving the acrid smoke in our eyes as we each in turn lit the rusty stove.*[1] The subjects set for compositions seem a bit bizarre: "Imagine the thoughts and sensations of a blind girl" or "Write a physical and moral description of a brother whom you haven't seen for ten years." As for sums, Colette in later years was still indignant and Claudine notes with amazement the impenetrable behavior of laborers *who contrive to complicate the possible amount of work they can accomplish when divided into two groups, one of which expends a third more energy than the other, while in revenge the second group works an additional two hours, or, the cost of needles a seamstress will use in twenty-five years if she uses needles costing 50 francs a packet for eleven years and needles at 75 francs a packet for the remaining time.*[2] These sadistic aberrations, however, did not stop Gabrielle from developing that sense of humor with its rich vein of impertinence that was to make her Claudine so successful.

"You've forgotten to bring down the zeros," the teacher says, and the saucy pupil replies: *"They should always be brought down, they deserve it."* [3] Rowdy behavior, giggling, slaps traded and gossip whispered around the stove, daily conspiracies, fistfights, music lessons (at which Gabrielle proved to be gifted), cleaning the classroom—hosed down up to and including the maps—tedious drawing lessons involving "the linear reproduction of an everyday object." The little girls in their wooden shoes, warmed by forbidden braziers in the wintertime, chattering in their Fresnois dialect, would play at marbles, jacks or one-legged hopscotch; they would fight like fishwives; they would eat—voluptuously comparing tastes—all kinds of school supplies: erasers, the lead out of Comté crayons, blotting paper, cloth samples from the Louvre department store or the Bon Marché, cigarette paper. They were merry, undisciplined, imaginative, creative and highly critical, refusing to extract square roots, yawning during classes in moral conduct, but very wide awake when they peered down from their windows into the boys' dormitory across the way—to which the girls were also detailed in shifts to carry up

water. The great symbol of repression was the school inspector, a fairly innocuous bugaboo, against whom both teachers and students were leagued in a shared repugnance.

For such young girls, who were being educated like boys almost inadvertently, any instruction in femininity occurred in fits and starts; there were sewing lessons, however, and there was instruction from that Bible of the rural public school, Louis-Eugène Bérillon's *Good Country Housewife: Simple Notions of Rural Domestic Economy for Use in Girls' Schools.*

The following passage from *Claudine à Paris* reveals the irreverence with which these clear-sighted and hard-to-deceive peasant girls regarded this pompous and virtuous manual so redolent of Third Republic France:

On rainy days, at one end of the playground that had recently been roofed over, we would huddle together, unable to play at tag or hopscotch, and quiz each other on the Good Country Housewife:

"Anaïs, tell us about the Good Country Housewife *and her ingenious way of dealing with cesspools."*

And Anaïs would pompously recite:

"The Good Housewife persuades her husband to construct for her, or she constructs for herself, on a sequestered spot in the north part of the garden . . . a kind of cabin that will serve as a convenience (that's exactly what it says—I'm not changing a thing). . . . This cabin, completely shrouded in greenery and creepers and flowering plants is less like a latrine than a pretty verdant bower."

"How charming! What a poetic concept, what style—and could I but direct my dreaming steps toward that flowery perfumed bower and rest there for a time! But get to the practical part of it, Anaïs, go on, I beg you!"

"Since over the course of a year the recrement of five or six individuals will be amply sufficient to manure a hectare of land, and that nothing in the nature of . . ."

"Ugh! That's enough."

Oh Bérillon, how you amused those wicked girls, of whom I was one! Marie Belhomme, a guileless soul, would lift her midwife's hands to heaven as, her voice throbbing with tender conviction, she mockingly apostrophized some peasant girl:

"Unhappy maid, how great your error! Ah, for your own sake and happiness, shun the hateful thought of leaving your parents and

the cot where you were born! If you but knew the price those whose luxuries you envy pay for the silk and jewels with which they bedeck themselves!"

"*Ten francs a night,*" Anaïs would interrupt. "*I think that's what they get in Paris!*" [4]

"Should I call my school a school?" Colette wondered years later. *No, rather a rough paradise in which disheveled angels split wood in the morning to light the stove and ate as their heavenly manna thick sandwiches, red beans in wine gravy spread thick over grayish bread kneaded in the farmhouse kitchens.* In the harsh winters of those bygone days, *beautified by the snow, fairy tales, pine trees and wolves* (for there were still wolves around Puisaye in 1880), each student carried with her a warmer, *a metal box containing live embers mixed with ashes, on which one put one's feet to keep them warm.*[5] Gabrielle's warmer, filled with poplar embers and fine ash, was the prettiest, the most solid; it was made of forged iron and weighed as much as a full suitcase. *Do you have any notion what my wrought-iron warmer could accomplish when employed as a weapon at recess time? I carry the ineradicable proof of one of these warmer battles: the cartilage of my ear was torn. Warmer, shield, projectile, stove . . . each girl in the first year—six to eight—in this poor denuded school had her own. Massive emanations of carbon monoxide issued from these braziers. The children, mildly asphyxiated, would nod off. . . . Sometimes, Mlle Fanny would rouse herself from her romantic dream and with a whinny announce the reading lesson . . . that year we were engaged in the New Testament. . . . Sometimes a very young pupil who had sat down on her warmer to relieve the chill would give a sharp cry as she seared her tiny bottom. Or a column of smoke would arise from one of them, spreading the odor of the chestnut, potato or winter pear that one of us was surreptitiously cooking in her warmer.*[6]

⚜ GIRL FRIENDS

At sixty-six, Colette looked back on her favorite girl friends, the Jollet sisters: *Four girls, only one boy . . . this was not what father and mother Jollet had counted on. So they worked their four daughters as if they had been boys; one never saw such avid and devoted workers. . . . Henriette, the eldest, worked alongside her mother in the house and kitchen, a smaller version of that slender countrywoman with her tiny hands. The second girl, Marie, looked after the*

*stable and found time to teach me to make grass whistles, rattles with
nutshell halves, to instruct me in the names of birds, the varieties of
edible mushrooms, how to stitch up huge gloves with which to up-
root nettles out of a rough, untearable material called ponyskin. . . .
Jeanne Jollet, the third girl, was always ready at any time to undertake the urgent odd job, and Yvonne, the youngest and my friend,
tended the sheep and the cows with me while waiting to grow up.*[1]
Yvonne (who is called Claire in *Claudine à l'école*) and Gabrielle
would herd sheep with traditional calls, "Prrrr, my pretty, prrr!"
and shout orders to the dog, Lisette, "Ta, ta Lisette, bring them
back!" "Ta, they're in the oats, Lisette!" or "They're in the beet
field, Lisette, in the beets!" And Lisette would guide her flock as
instructed, unerringly. *In the evening, Marie Jollet would stand in
the courtyard and call "Come, come, my cows!" And from a distant
field, six black and white cows would slowly rise and return, ambling
slowly, to the farm on their own.*[2] The Jollet girls were *always clean,
their slim feet in wooden shoes, with short bangs on their foreheads,*
and during the harvest, with Gabrielle's help, they would roll lunch
out to the harvesters: *Lunch consisted of putting the white part of
two twelve-pound loaves of dry bread on the clean white wooden
table, and with the palm of the hand—we call it uncrimping the bread
where I come from—you would roll it back and forth, the crust having been removed, until it turned to crumbs, and the crumbs, redolent of fresh rye, would be immersed in fifteen or twenty liters of
milk.*[3] This was served with thick slices of fat bacon with all the lean
removed, and eaten with white pickles cured for three days in vinegar, along with a demijohn of hard cider. In the evening, Gabrielle
would be sated and unable to touch her dinner, and Sido would gaze
at her in consternation. . . . Gabrielle also saw a great deal of the
Duchemin girl (the Luce in *Claudine à l'école*) and Odile Henrion
(tall Anaïs), who was sixteen months younger, the daughter of the
sergeant major of Saint-Sauveur; she later married M. Bouilly, a deputy and senator from the Yonne. She went on to teacher-training
school and headed the girls' school in Tonnerre, and later a school
on the Boulevard Alsace-Lorraine in Sens.

So Gabrielle turned thirteen, fourteen, fifteen, the year of her
"premature chignon, a leather belt drawn to the last hole, shoes that
pinched." At snack time, the teenage girls would crowd onto the two
stone benches that flanked the house of Mme Lachassagne, *bustling
like sparrows on the tiles of a hot chimney. Odile would feign a
giggling fit to attract the attention of a passing traveling salesman.*

Yvonne lay in wait for the new assistant teacher to show himself at the window of the upper school, and I plotted to knock my piano out of tune so that the tuner from town, the one with the gold pince-nez . . .[4] And there was Nana Bouilloux, the "Bouilloux girl," who was so pretty that everyone remarked on it, so pretty that when Sido met her in the street she would sigh, "Remarkable!"

The tale of the Bouilloux girl, as told by Colette, deserves closer attention. It is an old story celebrated in the popular songs of the nineteenth century, a trite story, except that its end was tragic rather than melodramatic.

As the years passed, the beautiful Bouilloux girl's "graces increased." On her first Communion day, she was taken to drink a half-pint of beer with her father, the sawyer, and in the evening to a dance at the public hall. All her days off, Sundays and Thursdays, she spent with her "unsuitable family," her eighteen-year-old cousins lolling on the doorstep, with her brothers who were apprenticed to the cartwright and who "wore neckties" at fourteen and smoked, and who would stroll with their sister on their arm from the fairground shooting gallery to the Widow Pimolle's tavern. *At thirteen, the Bouilloux girl left school and became an apprentice, trading her black school smock and her short child's dress for a long skirt and a blouse of pink satinette with pleats. General stupefaction!*

"Maman, I saw Nana Bouilloux. She went by the door. And Mama, she was wearing a long skirt! And a chignon, and high heels, and a pair of . . ."

"Eat, Minet-Chéri, eat; your cutlet will get cold."

"And an apron, Mama, such a pretty apron in alpaca, it was like silk! . . . Mayn't I . . ."

"No, Minet-Chéri, you may not."

"But since Nana Bouilloux can . . ."

"Yes, you want a whole outfit just like the Bouilloux girl? That consists of everything you've seen already, plus a letter tucked away in her apron pocket, a lover stinking of wine and cheap cigars, two lovers, three . . . and later on a lot of tears . . . a puny child who has to be kept hidden away and who was crushed in her belly by her corset stays for months. There, Minet-Chéri, that's the real outfit of girls like the Bouilloux girl. Is that what you want?"

"No, Mama, I only wanted to try the chignon."

My mother shook her head with mock seriousness:

"You can't have the chignon without the apron or the apron with-

out the letter or the letter without the high-heeled shoes, or the shoes
without . . . all the rest of it! It's up to you!" [5]

But Nana Bouilloux did not fulfill Sido's widely shared prediction;
she "behaved herself." One fine day two Parisians, the kind who come
to the country in the summer, friends of a neighboring landowner,
attended the village dance and their eyes fell on the Bouilloux girl,
that "swan among geese." One of them invited her to waltz, and
she danced with him, *silent and grave, her eyelashes, more beautiful*
than her glance, brushed now and then against her partner's mustache.
And then . . . and then . . . nothing else ever happened to the
Bouilloux girl. The Parisians never came back, neither they nor anyone
like them. Traveling salesmen, soldiers home on leave, notary's clerks,
all begged for her favors, and with honorable intentions, as she walked
up the steep street. In vain, she even refused to raise herself to the
rank of pharmacist's wife. *She awaited the coming of her kingdom,*
of the prince without a name,[6] and the prince never arrived.

⚜ SAINT-SAUVEUR: THE OTHER SIDE OF SCHOOL LIFE

In 1889 a great event occurred: Gabrielle simultaneously sat for
her upper school diploma and for the certificate of advanced primary studies. According to the novelistic version in *Claudine à l'école*
—and we know that Colette stuck close to the truth—the tests were
preceded by an immense amount of cramming . . . and then, off
to Auxerre, where the examinations were to be held. In the morning, the candidates and their teacher piled into the coach and then,
shrieking and excited, onto the train. After three hours, they arrived
at their hotel, climbed into their beds, and at five o'clock the following morning they got up and prepared for their written examination
in an old girls' boarding school. Is it true, as Colette describes, that
with their teacher's assistance the girls prepared themselves for this
ordeal, each in her own way? *Marie Belhomme had made up a min-*
uscule atlas that fit in the palm of her hand, Luce had written dates
on her white cuffs, details of reigns, a whole textbook. The Jaubert
sisters had noted down a mass of data on thin strips of paper that they
rolled up and inserted into the caps of their pens.[1] Gabrielle received
high marks on her written examination in spelling and dictation,
writing, French composition, arithmetic, metric system and logical
solution to a problem. In her orals she was given top marks for reading with commentary, arithmetic and metric system, French history,
civics and geography, *solfège* and sight-singing—the highest mark.

Her marks were lower for physical and natural science.² Her return to Saint-Sauveur must have been a triumph. The upper school in Saint-Sauveur had now given the girl all the education it was equipped to provide.

In 1889, however, she returned to her seat in the big building when September came. These were the days in which, under the Third Republic's policy of replacing the old makeshift buildings, the new red and white schoolhouses were being put up. The one in Saint-Sauveur was ready, and Gabrielle, the star pupil, was entrusted by the schoolmistress to recite the official speech of thanks to M. Denouvelle, the Minister for Agriculture and a great friend of Dr. Merlou. In *Claudine à l'école*, Colette recalls the political—and apolitical—circumstances of this great Republican school dedication ceremony in the bravura section that concludes that book. *The town crier gave out the news: endless revels were in store for us, the ministerial train was to arrive at nine A.M. . . . the town notables would meet the Minister at the station at the edge of town and escort him through the decorated streets to the bosom of the schools. There, on a dais, he was to address us! Then he would banquet with a large crowd in the great reception room in the town hall. After that, there would be a presentation of decorations to the notables (for M. Jean Dupuy was coming with some little green and violet ribbons for those to whom his friend Dutertre was obligated—a masterstroke on the latter's part). In the evening, there was to be a huge ball in the banqueting room.*³ The preparations were endless: dresses and wreaths, thousands of crepe-paper roses, rehearsals by the municipal chorus, an amassing of basketsful of donated or stolen flowers, the crucial deployment of curl-papers in a day when fashion dictated that all girls be frizzed like lambs. At the appointed time, Gabrielle recited her speech: *"Monsieur le Ministre, the schoolchildren of Saint-Sauveur, bearing the flowers of their native region, approach you with gratitude . . ."* ⁴ Then more speeches, a procession, a parade, and in the evening the dance, ending with a rousing scandal! Here is a version of the latter from the foreword to a pamphlet attacking Dr. Merlou that was published in 1906:

"For that matter, he was not totally successful in avoiding scandal. However, it was a ridiculous, amusing, farcical scandal giving rise to much laughter among the crowd of tipsy Burgundians that had gathered one evening at a dance in the main hall of the new school which the Minister of Public Education had opened that same morning. After dancing drunkenly for a time, he sneaked off to join his mistress, who was also the schoolmistress, in her room. Mme Sergent chanced upon them, and from the stairs this harridan shrieked with all her might, summoning boys, girls, and dancers—despite the supplications of the lovers, dismayed and horrified at the prospect of scandal—"Ah, you slut!" she screamed, "you didn't steal him, oh no! I've broken my broom over his backside . . . they didn't even lock the door! He's run off in his underwear in his bare feet, his filthy boots are still in her room!" [5]

This episode would long be remembered in pious households, and especially by the Church, which always relished any opportunity to criticize the public schools. Mlle Terrain, who had an illegitimate child well concealed from the families of her proper young pupils, today seems to us to have been merely another victim of the system. It was very difficult for an underpaid teacher at this period to refuse the protection of some highly placed official with total control over her career and her livelihood. The letters of rural schoolmistresses Ida Berger has brought to light bear witness to this. [6] As for the poor teacher, who seems to have been doomed to scandal, an even worse fate was to be meted out to her by her former pupil in the future. But who would have imagined that the daughter of an obscure and bankrupt country tax collector would one day become a popular writer?

✤ THE DAUGHTERS OF THE POOR IN THE NINETEENTH CENTURY

1889 was to witness the final chapter in the Captain's downfall. The house, the last possession, the final straw, was sold at public auction. Gabrielle watched as strangers took possession of everything that had made up the secret world of her youth, as it disappeared bit by bit: Sido's love seat, a commode with a *bombé* front, the Captain's armchair. She briefly referred to it in *Claudine à Paris*: *The physical horror of seeing the furniture being taken away, our everyday things packed up, made me shivery and bad-tempered as a wet cat. When I witnessed the departure of my little mahogany desk with its ink stains, my narrow walnut bed, the old Norman armoire I had used as a wardrobe, I nearly had an attack of hysterics.* [1] Dispossession, scandal—they seem to have punctuated Colette's life. This scandal marked her personality and her work, in which she was constantly to dwell on the need to renounce possessions. This conviction that all possessions are useless and should be renounced before one becomes overly attached to them was probably formed by the spectacle of Sido's household goods as they gradually disappeared under the gaze of the curious. The event also created a particular kind of nostalgia that is at the root of her nomadic life; as Colette somberly sums it up: "I belong to a country that I have left." The urge to write arises in part from the need to name this nostalgia. But writing is not enough to fill the void, "there are no words, pencils or colors enough to depict the sky of my country, above the violet tile roof with its red moss, that shone splendid over my childhood." Later, there would be other landscapes, but not seen with such clarity. Something unforgotten colors the later descriptions of first lover, of divorce, two divorces, of dozens of deceptions, of immense griefs that become homely, daily pain. Recalling Saint-Sauveur, she could count each minute speck of dust in the house that was sold, in the old demolished school. Away from Saint-Sauveur, things grew confused. The fact has to be faced, everything once abandoned in the past still continues to exist.

There was ambivalence in the paradise of school life. It meant society, friendships, a counterpoint to home, but it also had limits and restrictions. Within the school, life was full of emotion, of curiosity, there was solidarity, there were games, all under the aegis of benign powers. The evocation of school life in the Claudine books, albeit fictionalized, taken in conjunction with Colette's more autobiographical reminiscences, describes an atmosphere in which an intelligent, gifted adolescent girl, emotionally secure in her family milieu, managed to win autonomy. But beyond the world of school days was a no-man's-land, vaguely embodied in the advanced teacher-training school in the town; there was no precise notion of what went on there, about what one might become there, or any dreams of any kind of concrete future.[2]

In fact, there was no "future" in practice. For these pupils, the future was, literally, what was not to be. If the rural primary school did not bother to discriminate against girls, it was because it was a dead end. The famous manual by Lucille Sauvan, *A Training Course for Primary School Teachers*,[3] clearly and almost cynically notes that elementary and upper schooling was a way of "prolonging the childhood" of such girls, that the secular public school served as a transition between their deprived home life and some uncertain future.

Indeed, what were their prospects?

For the most gifted girls, the system offered the teaching profession. The material prospects for beginning teachers were precarious. In general, prospective teachers regarded the training school as a means of social advancement, as a way out of poverty. Meditating on girls who were going on for their teaching diplomas, Claudine provides us with a good description of them: *Five-sixths of these girls have their entire future at stake. To think that they're all going to become nothing but teachers, slaving from seven in the morning until five at night, trembling before the headmistress, who is usually harsh and unkind, just to earn seventy-five francs a month! . . . Out of the sixty girls, forty-five are the daughters of laborers or farmers; to escape working in the fields or at the loom they will turn their complexions sallow, become hollow chested and deform their right shoulders. They will bravely put in three years in some training college (getting up at five and going to bed at eight-thirty, with two hours free out of the twenty-four) and ruin their digestions, which rarely withstand three years of school fare. But they will wear hats, they will not sew other women's clothes, they will not tend animals or draw water out of wells, and they will learn to regard their parents with contempt.*[4] A laundress earned seventy-five francs a month. In 1886, "a servant earned from forty to seventy francs per month, a cook from fifty to seventy-five francs."[5]

Colette never attacked this question directly, but the heroine of *Claudine à l'école* rejected all urgings to go on to the training school "because it's like a prison," "because she had no vocation for teaching," and, above all, because that bourgeoise young lady had no intention of slaving away for a mere seventy-five francs a month, even if her parents were ruined. The majority of her companions remained in the village. Statistics indicate that 33 percent of the female population was employed in 1866, 36 percent in 1911. Female salaries were markedly lower than male salaries, and opportunities were extremely limited. In 1859, Julie Daubie, the first woman to sit for a baccalauréat degree, wrote a mémoire entitled *The Poor Woman in the Nineteenth Century*: "It may be said that for a female, education is an ornament rather than a meal ticket."[6] She laid stress on the lack of financial and moral support for poor girls desirous of entering the teaching profession and called for the extension of the rights and privileges granted wealthy girls who had received religious schooling to poor girls from secular public schools.

Poor country girls with primary certificates had limited choices within a narrow range of government jobs (in the post office or as railroad clerks, etc.), or in the private sector as salesgirls—and the insecure career of a kept woman (in *Claudine à l'école* we meet Luce, who later goes off to Paris and meets an older man who seduces her and keeps her); what then was available to a poor girl from the middle class, even so gifted a girl as Colette, with her ability to write, outside the sacrosanct institution of marriage? "All girls were forced to rely on marriage, and marriage was difficult for any girl without a dowry." [7] If she failed, she was faced with a life as a paid companion or governess—a status that cannot be considered a profession.

Gabrielle had never thought of literature as a way out. She says so many times. *No, I don't know how to write . . . in my youth I never never wanted to write. . . . No voice like a cold wind whispering in my ear ever urged me to write, to go on writing, to dull my avid or tranquil perception of the living universe by writing.*[8]

And even had it entered her mind, given her social status, it would have been in vain. Julie Daubie in her book raises the question of whether "a woman can have the same status as man in the career of literature," and reaches a negative conclusion.[9]

Fated by her petit-bourgeoise background to few socially acceptable professions, condemned by her rural public school education to limited and poorly paid careers, Colette was like thousands of others: if she didn't marry she was lost! And husbands didn't grow on trees for provincial young ladies without dowries.

Sido's anxiety increased as she faced the unknown future in store for her family during the auction of their possessions, their flight for refuge to Châtillon-Coligny, where Achille Robineau, the eldest son, having by now become a doctor, was to welcome his bankrupt clan. Colette was seventeen, a difficult age, an age for making emotional mistakes. The age for leaving one's mother. It is a time of life that can almost be pinned down to a few hours, to a minute period of time in which all must be decided, sometimes irrevocably. In those few hours, the choice of abductor is made, determining a woman's life. And what if a girl chooses the wrong abductor? It is easy to understand why mothers become anxious.

Sido at eighteen

The house at Saint-Sauveur-en-Puisaye

Colette at five

Reunion of family and friends in the garden at Saint-Sauveur; Colette is seated in the foreground.

Sido at forty-five

Colette at fifteen

Colette dressed up in a
Renaissance costume
(around 1895)

The Colette family at Châtillon-Coligny

Colette in 1897

Colette in a fur hat (around 1900)

Colette and Polaire

Polaire, Colette, and Willy at the races

Colette and La Marquise de Belbeuf, "Missy," around 1906

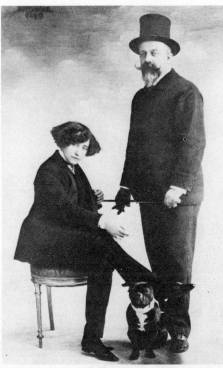

Colette and Willy

Colette with her bulldogs (around 1907)

The author of *La Vagabonde* (around 1910)

Colette as *Le faune* in a pantomime

Stage photographs

Colette in *La Chatte amoureuse* (1912)

Colette in an Egyptian costume (1912)

Renée Vivien

Nathalie Barney

Anna de Noailles

II
WILLY
Days of Contempt

The first man is the only one that kills you.
COLETTE, La Naissance du jour

*But no, that man is my husband. . . . I tremble at
the thought of him just as I tremble in his presence.
A creature restrained, unaware of its chain, this is
what he has made me. . . . Overwhelmed, I stub-
bornly search back to our past days as a young married couple, looking for some memory that will
bring back the husband I "believed" I had chosen.
Nothing, there's nothing . . . but my obedience,
like a whipped child, nothing but his smile, con-
descending, without kindness.*
COLETTE, Claudine s'en va

Sido's marriage to her Captain had occurred following a scandal; Gabrielle's marriage was also preceded by a scandal. Provincial scandals have their own special elements. They are based on tales of fortunes, on the vicissitudes of bourgeois married life. In Paris there are different elements. Gabrielle was to marry the most accomplished scandal-monger of the Belle Epoque, a man who made a good part of his living at it. But Colette had talents of her own. Even in the Paris of Pierre Louÿs and Alfred Jarry, people did not flout conventions with impunity. Such violations were outrages that had to be paid for, and they were easy for women to commit, since nearly everything was forbidden where they were concerned. Natalie Clifford Barney, the famous siren of Lesbos who publicly hymned her sapphic love affairs, wrote in her *Souvenirs indiscrets*: "In those days, people were still afraid to be involved in scandal. It took a certain courage to create one." [1] Or a certain ignorance. It must be said that during the "desert journey" of her first marriage, Colette had other things on her mind than a concern for other people's good opinion; she was in great danger of irrevocably losing her good opinion of herself.

But we anticipate. At the moment, Gabrielle and her family, totally ruined, the house in Saint-Sauveur gone, their furniture sold at auction in the public square, have sought refuge with Achille in Châtillon-sur-Loing (today Châtillon-Coligny). The house is smaller than the house in Saint-Sauveur; there is no counterpart to the lost garden: the Captain, eccentric and distracted, reads *Le Temps*; Sido— marked by events but still active and cheerful; Leo visits from time to time; and there is seventeen-year-old Gabrielle, thin and pretty with her long light chestnut hair, her triangular vixen's face, her lively speech with its Burgundian accent.

At nine, Gabrielle had had her seat in the paternal carriage during the municipal election campaign; at seventeen, she rode alongside her brother, the doctor. Through the long afternoons, a snack and a book on her knees, she would ride with him in the cabriolet, seated on his left in her old coat, holding the reins of the roan mare. Sharing the same passionate curiosity about nature and the sick, brother and sister would descend from time to time to gather bunches of wood hyacinth, to collect mushrooms, to dislodge the cocoons of butterflies to watch the "miracle." Their mutual interest in his profession led Achille to train her, to teach her to suture a wound, *to line up analgesic cachets, to use the delicate scales with its copper weights and platforms*.[2] And above all there was the companionship of their long trips, the hills climbed on foot to save the mare, inspections at the houses of wet nurses who allowed their unfortunate nurselings to smother pinned in their fetid cribs, scenes of sickness, of robust peasant births. Gabrielle, at an age when one seeks a vocation, dreamed of becoming a doctor, but—following contemporary dictates—she was to remain merely the doctor's assistant.

Aside from such activities, was life in Châtillon boring? Perhaps less so than during Colette's earliest years in Paris. Who could be bored in surroundings one loved and knew, in a place that contained all those one loved most? But we know that Gabrielle, like all girls her age, existed in a vaporous state of expectation created by sociological factors: idleness, a lack of any real occupation; by psychological factors: the identity crisis, her lack of emotional outlet or sexual and social future—virginity being the only natural, desirable state and no secondary satisfactions available now that school was over and life was lived within the confines of the family home. In such circumstances, the drives of youth come up against frustration. She was an avid reader. She devoured poetry and novels, and they had their usual effect: fretfulness, exaltation that was often suicidal. The dream of Prince Charming coexisted with the dream of some father-husband, with half-felt desires reflecting the female's social status within society: the desire to display herself, the desire to be *made* inferior. In the literature of the period, these elements can all be found, they have become clichés, these "romantic" girls with their unpredictable yearnings to become either nuns or whores. And in addition there are social strivings and ambitions, thirsts for power either frustrated or ineluctably diverted into the only accepted channel, marriage. Despite the brainwashing to which girls were subjected from an early age, these drives remained, and in the best of circumstances there was only one outlet available: marriage, power wielded over a male at second hand.

Colette herself has perfectly described this state in which inadmissible sexual feelings coexist with romantic daydreams stamped with the cultural code of the period. Two Gabrielles existed simultaneously. There was the one who leaned on her elbows in the eve-ing above some invisible provincial garden, her long hair descending from the balcony like a silken ladder: *The certainty of love flowed over me, and far from hanging back, my adolescent happiness reveled in it. . . . This triumphal, solitary night, crowned with wisteria and roses, was unspoiled by either my doubt or by my soft and gentle melancholy.*[3]

And there was the other Gabrielle, *a barely nubile girl dreaming of becoming the plaything, the entertainment, the licentious master-piece of an older man. . . . We have to say that when many a girl puts her hand into some hairy paw or offers her mouth to ravenous and impatient lips, gazing serenely at the huge male shadow cast on the wall by some unknown man, it is because her sexual curiosity has whispered powerful urgings into her ear. An unscrupulous man can in a few short hours turn an innocent girl into an accomplished liber-tine, disgusted by nothing. Disgust has never been an obstacle. That comes later, as does honesty. Once I wrote that dignity was a male flaw. I might rather have said that "disgust is not a female failing."* [4] And of course, disgust is not a weakness that all women can indulge. Although she is severe with herself, Colette is frequently unjust to other women. This is because she had eluded sociological fatality, had escaped the reality of oppression. By nature generous, she judges individuals by their existential choices, ignoring the fact that the choice made by an alienated person is an alienating choice.

⚜ HENRY GAUTHIER-VILLARS, FATHER/HUSBAND

So the father/husband appeared. More precisely, he had been there for some time. We do not know precisely at what age Gabrielle met him; he was an old friend of the family. In a letter to Rachilde dated 1900, Willy was to admit that he was indebted to his wife for much of the Claudine novels, to her school notebooks, to conversations they had had together: "We had chatted together ever since she was ten years old." [1] Biographers have placed this decisive meeting with Willy in 1889, during Gabrielle's visit to Paris at sixteen. Possibly she had known him earlier; the families were acquainted. Captain Colette and Henry Gauthier-Villars's father were both members of the Société de Géographie, and the former occasionally sent the lat-ter maps he had drawn and colored himself, or bought scientific books from him. Jean-Albert Gauthier-Villars had graduated from Saint-Cyr the year before Jules Colette, and both had served in the Crimean and Italian campaigns.

Henry Gauthier-Villars, Willy, was born on August 10, 1859, some thirteen years before Gabrielle, at Villiers-sur-Orge in the Seine-et-Oise; his mother had gone there to stay with his grandmother while his father was away in the Italian war. On his father's side, he was descended from old Dauphiné and Franche-Comté families; his mother's family were from the Ile-de-France and Normandy. In 1864, his father, a graduate of the Polytechnique and an engineer in the Postal and Telegraph Department, took over a printing establishment and publishing house on the Quai des Grands-Augustins in Paris. He would have liked Henry to have followed in his footsteps, as did his younger son, Albert. But Henry preferred to become Willy, the prodigal son of "tout Paris." One of Willy's friends, Sylvain Bonmariage, wrote that "The Gauthier-Villars family was of that class whose brilliance has so long honored France through the Ecole Polytechnique, and Gauthier-Villars père found it difficult to accept as his intimates or, in principle, as his sons-in-law, anyone who had not passed through that institution. . . . He himself looked after all the aspects of his business assisted by one or two selected Polytechnique graduates and protected by a kind of Catholic power bloc that existed up until 1919. I once had occasion to seek a printer for a handsome volume of Baudelaire that was being published by a house for which I was assistant manager. His reply was, 'We are extremely sorry. We are Catholic printers.' The Ecole Polytechnique and the Church were their pomp and circumstance, impossible to get around them." [2]

We can imagine the enthusiasm with which such a family must have welcomed an engagement to the daughter of a bankrupt village tax collector.

After completing his studies at the Lycée Fontanes and the prestigious Collège Stanislas, Henry started life as a well-brought-up young man with literary pretensions. In 1878, he published a collection of sonnets; in 1880 he did his military service in Le Mans, attached to the Third Artillery regiment, and was promoted to second lieutenant in the same company as the ill-fated Captain Dreyfus. He was stationed for a year in Besançon. Even before his time in the army, however, he had sent some articles, short stories and tales to a newspaper called *La Liberté du Jura*, and he was published in the *Nouvelle Rive Gauche*, later *La Lutèce*, in 1883, where he appeared under his first *nom de plume*, Maugis. He was to use several pseudonyms between 1885 and 1893, such as Jim Similey in *Art et Critique*;

he wrote for *La Batte, Le Bon Journal, Le Chat noir, Le Nouvel Echo* and *La Revue bleue*.

In 1887, he put his name to three "serious" articles on photography, of which he was later to admit that he had not written a single line (he was not always to be so frank). The time had come to win the good opinion of his father, who was beginning to find his son's literary activities somewhat frivolous. He became associated with the Gauthier-Villars publishing house and moved into a ground-floor office on the Quai des Grands-Augustins where he held open house for all sorts of fin-de-siècle celebrities: Catulle Mendès wrote a column about this locale, Mallarmé a quatrain; one might have met Marcel Schwob, Rémy de Gourmont, Henri de Régnier, Paul Verlaine, Claude Debussy, Jean de Tinan, Pierre Louÿs, the astronomer Camille Flammarion, and many others.[3]

Willy's favorite visitor was Charles Monselet, poet, columnist, gastronome. They would mysteriously shut themselves up in what Willy's brother referred to as the "intelligence sector." One day he investigated and discovered that for an hour and thirty-eight minutes, Willy and Charles Monselet had done nothing but bombard each other with puns.

Willy's great stroke of genius occurred in 1889. In October of that year, he began to write articles for *Art et Critique* on the Lamoureux concert performances which he signed "*Une ouvreuse du Cirque d'Eté*," "An usherette in the Cirque d'Eté," an alterego invented for the purpose. These light notes on music struck a novel tone and were hugely successful; they opened new doors for him, first at *Gil Blas*, and later at *L'Echo de Paris*, where he was employed from 1890 to 1907. The Usherette ended her long career in the pages of *Comœdia*.

Gabrielle, the gifted music student of Saint-Sauveur, had been reading the *Lettres de l'Ouvreuse* since 1889. The country girl was ripe to fall in love with the thirty-year-old Parisian cloaked in the prestige of his growing celebrity as journalist, writer, humorist and music critic—and probably one of the few bachelors to approach her.

At this period, however, Willy had much more on his mind than Gabrielle Colette and her sixteen years. He had embarked on an affair with a married woman whose divorce was not yet final and with whom he seems truly to have been in love. They lived together at 22 Rue de l'Odéon, and in 1889 their son Jacques was born there. Less than two years later, in December of 1891, the woman, not yet twenty-eight, died (the announcement appeared as Mme Germaine Villars, née Servan, wife of C). Marcel Schwob wrote many letters to Willy during this period in an attempt to console him, a bachelor father burdened with a child whose existence he dared not avow to his straitlaced parents. He turned to the Colette family for consolation; they were friends, and they lived in the country. At the beginning of 1892, therefore, the child was put out to nurse in Châtillon, where Sido looked after it for several months until Willy's mother, who had finally been told, agreed to see to his upbringing. In letters from Sido to her daughter Juliette (with whom she had just been reconciled) during this period, there are mentions of the Gauthier-Villars baby.

The brief months when the infant Jacques was kept in Châtillon were to be decisive. His father came to visit him, and he searched for ways to show his gratitude to the Colette family. His sorrow soon faded—Willy's emotions were superficial at the best of times, and he was an incorrigible ladies' man. The charms of the budding Gabrielle worked on this basically puritanical bachelor—puritanical as are so many libertines. The preface that Willy later wrote for *Claudine à l'école* is instructive in this regard (it appears in the first edition of 1900): "At present Claudine is seventeen years old. It would be amusing if she were one day to be chosen by some fine bachelor, the kind who is wary of linking up with some overexperienced Parisian girl and goes to the provinces to seek a virginal fiancée who will be completely innocent in every way." This classical scenario has become a cliché: the irresistible allure of a pure and music-loving shepherdess. The process was begun by Don Juan, the mechanism was well oiled, it didn't require much work. Gabrielle succumbed. Willy was enchanted. But should he seduce her or should he marry her? For alas, the dear child had no dowry. No dowry!—these fateful words had already caused centuries of female misfortune, centuries of sordid financial haggling over virgins. Gabrielle's story was to be slightly different. The fictionalized version contained in *Claudine à Paris* recounts the dénouement, the evening when Renaud, alias Willy, takes the provincial Claudine, alias Gabrielle, to the Brasserie Logre, alias Pousset, after the theater. Claudine gets a bit tight on a glass of Asti and babbles that she loves him, their tête-à-tête is interrupted by Maugis and some Parisian celebrities, and later in the cab Claudine abandons herself to her first long kiss from Renaud. When she later hears Marcel, Renaud's son, make a disobliging remark about the inequality of their respective fortunes, the poor girl decides to give the lie to his evil imputations and she offers to become the mistress of the man she loves. He, a chivalrous bachelor, declines her offer . . . and proposes marriage. All's well that ends well. Upon close examination, the text reveals Willy's and Gabrielle's own experience. All the elements are there, even Willy's son, whom the demands of fiction and the prejudices of the period have turned into Marcel, a seventeen-year-old pederast based on Marcel Boulestin. Colette had sublimated this entire structure so thoroughly that she would reproduce it in her last work of fiction, *Gigi*, written in 1944 when she was seventy-one.

And Willy collaborated on this version himself, removing the financial components that inspire the generous offer of the adolescent Gabrielle: "In sum, almost everything in *Claudine à Paris* is true. Even the day when Colette, to my great stupefaction, got tight on two glasses of Asti—after which she is supposed to have told me 'I'll die if I cannot be your mistress,' in the fiacre." Catulle Mendès saw her in the restaurant that same night, Eugénie Buffet saw her too, a charming girl with two long blond braids down to her ankles and so young-looking that both of them counseled me to 'Look out, Willy, you can't play fast and loose with the rules.'

"Alas, you can't play fast and loose with life either." [4]

✣ A CURIOUS ENGAGEMENT

And so they became engaged. Although Gabrielle pretended not to care for the advantages middle-class marriage could provide, she probably needed as little persuasion as Claudine. And in the end, it began to seem not so bad after all. A letter from Sido to Juliette sheds light on the approximate period when the engagement took place: on May 23, 1892, she writes "The Gauthier-Villars baby is also taking up a lot of my time. . . . Gabri spent two weeks in Paris with Mme Cholleton, and she had her fill of theater and concerts." [1]

Following letters mention events surrounding this curious engagement in veiled language. Marriage in French society almost never contains surprises, but this one was quite out of the ordinary. It was not on the books that the son of a good family, a son who dabbled in literature, should marry a poor girl without any particular artistic or intellectual leanings. Of course, there are many instances in literature of similar odd couplings, but facts and statistics all show that the Gauthier-Villars and Colette union was an exception rather than the rule. In the provinces, there was bound to be a lot of gossip about such an advantageous marriage for a girl who had come down in the world. And Willy was beginning to enjoy a somewhat questionable reputation in Paris. The effects of this were slow to be felt down in the country, but when they were, the scandal grew. It was the kind of scandal that was difficult to counter; the rumors and gossip reached such a pitch that anonymous letters began to be received, and there were remarks printed in gossip columns in the newspapers. In an attempt to put a stop to all this, the Colette family at one point let it be known that the engagement had been broken off.

On October 28, 1892, Sido wrote to Juliette: "No, we haven't had any more anonymous letters. I'm confident that the purported breaking-off of the engagement must have satisfied whoever was sending them. . . . Gauthier-Villars is still suffering with his arm, and it will soon be a month since he was wounded [in a duel]. So he will not be coming to see us, but Gabri is going to Paris with her father for a few days to meet the Gauthier-Villars family. . . . Gabri is terrified at the prospect of meeting them, and they are just as afraid of her. They would have much preferred marrying their son to a real heiress! They have a few lined up awaiting their chance. Keep everything I'm telling you to yourself, and go on pretending that Gabri's wedding has been postponed indefinitely." [2] A few days later, she writes again: "Gabri returns this evening. I'm sure she'll have a lot to tell me. Willy surprised her, he showed her their future apartment, completely furnished down to the row of shining pots and pans ready to be cooked in tomorrow. Keep this to yourself. Yes, both Willy and I have had anonymous letters, one of mine contained a newspaper clipping abusing Willy, still mailed from Roubaix."

In a letter of May 5, 1893, to Juliette's husband, Sido refers to an item that had appeared in *Gil Blas* on May 4 and had been forwarded to Achille along with some others. Obviously aimed at those with inside knowledge, the article mentioned no names, but stated: "There is a good deal of gossip in Châtillon about the frantic flirtation in which one of the wittiest of our Parisian club men is engaged with an exquisite blonde, famous in the region for her wonderful head of hair. There's no mention of the word 'marriage.' So we suggest that our beautiful owner of the incredible golden braids withhold her kisses, and obey the advice of Mephisto, 'until the ring is on her finger.' " Willy, an inveterate dueler, challenged the editor of *Gil Blas*, Lefebvre, and wounded him with a sword thrust to the midriff. "Lefebvre's wound," Sido wrote, with equanimity, "might just as easily have been Willy's, and at the thought Gabri is almost as upset as if it had been." [3] The burden of this letter, however, is mainly excuses for not inviting the Roches to the wedding —the Captain and his sons were not reconciled with Juliette—and to ask them to send "Gabri a small gift, mainly because of the Gauthier-Villars family." [4]

And so domestic, everyday concerns gradually dispelled the scandal, which faded into one of those incidents that seem to arise to create difficulties on the rough road toward marriage.

For her part, Colette never referred to the scandal. She recalled the time of her engagement as an uncertain, transitional period during which little seemed altered in her daily life. The principal element in her relationship with her fiancé was the correspondence they carried on. Willy came to see her infrequently, bringing her books, magazines and candy, and going off again. She would accompany him to the train station to catch the "slow local train" and afterward walk home with her dog, Patasson, to face her brothers' teasing about her suitor:

"*Did you notice how he's grown since the last time?*" *Achille would say to Léo.*

"*Grown? Are you sure?*"

"*What do you mean, am I sure? His forehead is outgrowing his hair.*"

"*Quiet!*" *Sido would say, "you're doing your best to upset the child.*"

"*Good enough for her,*" *the elder would reply. "She'll have plenty of that when she's married. I'm only trying to prepare her for it.*" [5]

Little did he know! And admittedly, Willy was no Adonis, if we refer to contemporary photographs, or to the portrait of him Colette paints in *Mes apprentissages: M. Willy was not large, so much as swollen. He had a powerful skull, protuberant eyes, a short rather formless nose between pendulous cheeks; all his features formed curves. A straight, delicate, rather nice mouth beneath very thick, grayish blond mustaches which he dyed for years, something English about his smile. He had a dimple in his chin, but since the chin was weak, small, even delicate, it was better to hide it. M. Willy therefore sported a kind of exaggerated Imperial, and later a short beard. He was said to resemble Edward the Seventh. To pay him a less flattering but more august compliment, I would say he looked like Queen Victoria.* Roundness, softness, baldness, all this is no help in explaining his success with women in general, or with Gabrielle in particular, unless we are willing to accept what today appears to be an historical, statistical fact: Don Juan is rarely an unusually handsome man. And he is also a man obsessed with impotence. Willy falls into this category too, but he had a flair for shocking people, a genius for lying, and a certain ability to denigrate with an acid tongue.

In addition, the true Don Juan does not marry, he only dangles the promise of marriage. Of course Willy too hesitated, and his letters do not evince any great enthusiasm.

On April 21, 1892, he wrote to his brother Albert, another graduate of the Polytechnique and from 1893 the director of the family publishing house, a man who had played by the rules and married Valentine-Claude Lafontaine, the rich daughter of a banking family in the Ardennes: "My dear Albert, just a word . . . I'm engaged to marry the daughter of a certain Captain Colette (from Châtillon), happy in this way to demonstrate my gratitude to a family that has been dreadfully good to Jacques. Of course she has no dowry, which doesn't please our parents. And by their lights they do have reason to wince. However, in all conscience I cannot do otherwise. Will you please inform Valentine, I suppose her family will also carry on. But a marriage like your own is so rare, so very rare, joining as it does the most exquisite tenderness and the . . . how shall I put it? . . . the more serious comforts. You have managed both a love match and a financially advantageous one, and that's an almost unheard-of stroke of luck. For my part, I'm not getting married for money, far from it. And if I were to ask myself if I have the right to think of marrying for love, I would perhaps have to answer that in the negative too. Love, great burning piercing love, is I think a romantic joke. And the possibility of achieving this great ideal is buried in Bagneux [where the mother of his son was interred], one cannot replace that." [6] A fine example of profound love! However, Willy could on occasion speak another language to Gabrielle, or to his friend Marcel Schwob, to whom he wrote at this same period to tell him how happy he was in Châtillon, "dreaming of marriage and completely captivated by the fluttering grace of my pretty little Colette. In a month we'll be married and I don't have a cent. All right!" [7] He never completely lost sight of certain stern realities. "I'll not have a cent" was a phrase to which Colette would become accustomed in her married life.

And in the end he outdid Don Juan and married her. Years later, in a "repeat" of the Claudine novels entitled *Imprudences de Peggy*, he had his second wife write: "My poor friend Taillandy [the name of a property belonging to his secretary Marcel Boulestin that Willy sometimes used as a pseudonym] married her all the same, this intelligent and clever provincial girl who was poor as a churchmouse and unable to find a husband in the district."[8] "All the same" clearly indicates Willy's state of mind, one that was not entirely devoid of second thoughts and regrets.

⚜ THE WEDDING

They were married on May 15, 1893, in Châtillon. Willy, for the first and the last time, was discreet and forwent publicity about his marriage. It is understandable. The scandal surrounding the engagement, his parents' coolness to the match (they did not attend the ceremony), perhaps some vestiges of feeling that lingered from the death of the woman who had been his companion so short a time before . . . It was a modest, almost melancholy wedding: there were few in attendance, the Colette family and the groom's witnesses, Adolphe Houdard and Pierre Veber. There was no nuptial Mass, only a simple benediction at four o'clock. The bride wore muslin embroidered with tiny flowers, a large blue ribbon in her hair and tied round her forehead like a Vigée-Lebrun portrait, her long tresses concealed in the folds of her white dress—no official photographs were taken, but an amateur who had set up his camera outside the window left a candid record of this "parade of beards" surrounding a somewhat rustic bride and her two or three bridesmaids.

The day had been spent in fabricating publicity slogans—"flash fables," as they were called at the time—using familiar lines of poetry; Willy never wasted time that could be used to make a bit of money. Gabrielle joined in eagerly:

"Here's one," I cried, "from Baudelaire: 'Be calm my pain, and be soothed/You wished for Le Soir *and it has come . . .' and it can appear on all six pages alongside serials by the most popular writers . . . will that do?"*

"Bravo, bravo," my husband replied merrily, "you're a real sweet little pal."[1]

All his friends at this time shared his love of punning, literary, ribald puns; they pursued them deliriously, and Gabrielle went along: *A childhood and adolescence spent with my two older brothers had . . . accustomed me to boyish diversions, among which I in-clude such forms of wit as irreverent parody, rebusses, puns, satirical acrostics.*[2]

So the day dragged on. *The long evening brought no break in the unseasonable heat. The new wife busied herself by enlarging the entrance to an anthill with the end of a stick,*[3] dizzy with fatigue and the discomfort of having been the center of all eyes throughout the day. "There is an obscene paradox," Simone de Beauvoir has written, "in superimposing a ritual ceremony on the brutal reality of an animal function."[4] Colette would always remember the hor-ror of her wedding night, of all wedding nights, along with her feeling that Sido had begun to reject her ever since the morning, that she "averted her eyes from me as from some scandal." She turned to fantasizing flight and homecoming: *Tomorrow I will put on my everyday dress, the one that suits me best, and I will take my fiancé to the station with my brother . . . tomorrow, tomorrow . . . we will go by Les Roches on our way home, because that is the pret-tiest way. We will take the milk jug.*[5]

During the wedding dinner, between the *brochet sauce mousse-line* and the sweet, the nougats and the Savoy cake on which trem-bled a sacrificial rose, she sought escape in a few gulps of champagne. Her head fell back against her chair and she dozed for a few seconds, watched over by Sido, who begged that she be allowed to rest for a moment:

"*She looks a little like Beatrice Cenci in the Barberini Palace,*" Willy said.

"*With her red carnations,*" said Paul Veber, "*she looks more like a stabbed dove!*"

"*Is that the best you can do, compare her with a decapitated woman or a wounded bird?*"[6] Aggressive, superstitious, Sido awakened her daughter by removing the unfortunate flowers from her bosom. Gabrielle ate her ritual portion of the wedding cake beneath her mother's concentrated gaze, heavy with meaning.

Sido knew, she knew more clearly than her daughter. Her ex-perience, her instinct, her maternal anxiety, made her more aware of what was in store than Gabrielle, whose sexual curiosity was at its peak and who had the comforting feeling that she was at last conforming, doing what everyone did. But despite her knowledge, Sido was powerless against the social conformism and socioeconomic predestination that forced every girl—and particularly if she were poor—into the arbitrary embrace of an institution, the institution of marriage, wherein the selection of her future master was made with an infinitesimal margin for error, and this margin containing the hope of her future happiness.

On the following day, *a thousand leagues, abysses, discoveries and irreparable metamorphoses seemed to separate me from the night before.*[7] It is impossible to calculate the psychological damage caused by the "wedding night," about which so much has been written and so little said. The bizarre combination of a girl's innocence and her solemn wedding ceremony "transforms erotic experience into a trial every woman anxiously senses she does not know how to overcome,"[8] a situation Steckel complacently translated by instructing males that they ought to put their anguished wives to soak overnight in a well. "Of course, she may harbor some vague apprehension. . . . 'Ah,' she may say, 'so this is marriage. This is why they've made such a secret of it.' You can douse her at length, frequently, without giving rise to any scandal among the neighbors."[9] So did some of our grandmothers expiate, passively and sometimes in insanity, the sin of having been born women.

The time came for the stout, bearded husband to return to Paris with his wife and his witnesses. Overjoyed, he leaped into the train compartment with a legerity that was amazing, considering his girth. Houdard sang, Veber amused himself by dismantling the alarm mechanism. As she was borne along toward the worldly, threatening City that was soon to take the form of her rakish husband's bachelor apartment, Gabrielle's thoughts were sad: her mind dwelled not on her uncertain future, but on her last glimpse of the person who had played the largest role in the great festival of her childhood, a person dressed in mourning: *My mother had not slept all night, and at dawn she was still wearing her black faille and her jade. In the kitchen, standing before the blue faience stove, Sido's face relaxed into an expression of awful sorrow as she pensively prepared the morning chocolate.*[10]

But it was now too late to escape her husband. The dream of marriage had become one of those nightmares in which one is forced to assist, powerless, at one's own execution. There is something funereal about Colette's evocation of her first wedding, written long after the event, it is true. It is not composed of raw recollection, nor is it merely a narrative. In retrospect, Colette was well aware that this was the border separating the land of childhood freedom, restricted only by maternal bonds, and the desert where sexual, economic, emotional and intellectual oppression would combine to turn the radiant girl into a crafty animal, trained to all kinds of compromise, too much at ease in its chains.

⚜ INGÉNUE AND LIBERTINE

" 'Willy is married!' The news spread like wildfire. It flew from theaters to concert halls, from editorial offices to café banquettes, to the Napolitain, Weber's, Pousset; it crossed the Seine and spread through the Latin Quarter and the terraces of the Vachette and the Harcourt." [1] Although the wedding had been discreet, practically private, it caused as much stir in Paris as though that city were a small town: the *enfant terrible*, the gay dog of Parisian high society, had captured a virginal goose from the country and turned her into a legitimate Gauthier-Villars spouse—thus the burden of the gossip. As society was preparing to receive her like some strange animal, Gabrielle arrived in Paris following her honeymoon in the Jura, *to the home of some man—some man I love, of course, but I'll still be living with some man.* [2] Gabrielle, however, was no longer Gabrielle. Having rebaptized her with her family name, her husband had given her his pseudonym, Willy, as her new family name. Until her fiftieth year, 1923, when she was finally to sign her works simply "Colette," she would be known as Colette Willy, in books and onstage. In the interim, she would have the public names Mme Henry Gauthier-Villars and Colette de Jouvenel des Ursins, and in literature Willy and Colette Willy. Today, when some women retain only their first names or their mother's maiden name in an attempt to maintain their identity, we are more conscious of Gabrielle's deprivation. Sido was to be the only person who would continue to call her "Gabri." The name existed only in the maternal line, and this line is severed with the umbilical cord; officially, she was now a woman and a wife.

During the years 1892 to 1895, the woman we identify with her fictional Claudine—who also had no other name—was to be merely Mme Willy, a young, unhappy wife living in a bachelor apartment in the Rue Jacob. *Bottle green and chocolate brown, furnished with dilapidated cardboard boxes, filled with bureaucratic gloom and disarray, the apartment had an abandoned air.* [3] There were clumps of dust under the sagging bed, piles of yellowed newspapers on the chairs, and masses of pornographic German postcards glorifying *garters, stockings, buttocks.* And Willy would not tolerate any alteration in his personal disorder. So began a monotonous period of utter bore-

dom; Colette appeared to adapt to her new life, but the inner shock
she suffered plunged her into a kind of withdrawal: her desire to
run away was replaced by a desire to die.

In the morning, her aversion to the apartment impelled her out
of bed, and she would accompany Willy to the Right Bank; a ten-
minute walk brought them to a modest dairy store where *the blue-
clad packers of the Belle Jardinière joined us in sustaining themselves
with croissants dipped in cups of mauve chocolate.*[4] Her diet was
unhealthy, consisting largely of sweets and food without nourish-
ment. She was short of clothes. When Sido came to Paris for a brief
visit in the middle of the winter of 1894, stopping at the Hôtel
Palais-Royal, she was shocked to discover that her daughter had no
coat. She said not a word, threw her son-in-law a savage look, and
took her daughter to the Louvre department store to buy her a 125-
franc black coat trimmed with Mongolian lamb; Colette thought it
luxurious. Willy was not poor; he was miserly, haunted by anxieties
over money. And since he was always short of funds, Colette dared
ask him for nothing. The only book Willy ever wrote all by himself, a book from which he was never parted, was his precious book
of accounts. And his hearty provincial wife, used as she was to food
being plentiful, even for the poor—milk, eggs, huge slices of bread
with fresh butter, walnuts, chestnuts—grew weak and holed up with
her books in her low-ceilinged apartment where the sun was replaced
by a kerosene lamp.

The couple soon moved to another apartment in the Rue Jacob, a
fourth-floor apartment between two courtyards; one of the rooms
overlooked the Rue Visconti. It was, as Willy said, "a dismal and
dreary house," with its salamander stove in the square salon, and a
gas fire in an alcove where Colette installed a tub, washbasin and
water jug.

The 14,000-franc apartment had been lived in for fifty years by its
former tenant, and he had decorated it in a singular manner: 175,000
pieces of confetti, according to the concièrge, lozenge-shaped, multi-
colored bits of paper, had been glued all over the doors, the cornices,
the columns, the niche behind the porcelain stove, the moldings, the
closet shelves, and large areas of the walls. Colette had the sensation
of being shut up in a dark and cheerless space over which brooded
the interminable energy expended by some madman. She was afraid
to go into her bedroom during the day because of a flaw in the
mirror of her carved walnut armoire which deformed everything
. . . and which reminded her all too vividly and unhappily of the

loss of the *armoire of her birthplace, rosewood and white tuya, with its provincial order, its sprigs of lavender and leafy red roses.*[5]

The Rue Jacob was full of the reassuring ghosts that inhabited its eighteenth-century houses. Mérimée, Adrienne Lecouvreur who had lived in the Rue Visconti, Laurence Sterne, were less compelling to the girl's imagination than the occasional "gust of spring hail blown in through the open window, the vague scent of invisible lilacs from a neighboring garden." In those days, she was unaware that this garden with its blowing leaves "marked the home of Remy de Gourmont and the garden of his Amazone, the American Natalie Clifford Barney," whom she was later to know. For the moment, her basic, her sole occupation was waiting. For what? For a miracle to take her back to her protected childhood, to the woods around Saint-Sauveur, to the presence of her beloved Sido. Meanwhile, she wrote to her daily, as she had written to Willy when he had been only her future husband. Yet she was unable to tell Sido the truths of which she herself was probably only dimly aware. The truth that the discovery of the abyss *between girlhood and womanhood, between life in the country and life in Paris, between the presence—or at least the illusion—of happiness and its absence, between love and this laborious, exhausting sensual diversion*[6] was one she could not bear. That she felt she was trapped, chained; that she was bored, literally to death; that the realization of her desires, what she was to call the "impure impulses of adolescent girls," had turned out to be frustrating and joyless; that there was a cruel dearth of people her own age. *I had new men friends, but no female friend. Girls may like the company of older men, but secretly it makes them sad.*[7] Aside from Willy, who was nearly thirty-five, there was Paul Masson, a facetious but melancholy man with a small, pointed graying beard. There was Marcel Schwob, thirty, but young only in his passion for knowledge. He shaved his head and had long mandarin moustaches.

The period condoned and even favored unions between older, bearded men and young girls. An older man is reassuring to an adolescent girl who may have a thousand reasons for feeling insecure. But there can be no doubt that Freudian analysis owes its birth to these socioeconomic factors and circumstances, and that machismo prejudices played a large role in the "Oedipus complex," a role that has yet to be examined. (Freud's *Investigation of Dreams* was published in 1900, the same year as *Claudine à l'école*.) One of Colette's critics, Claude Boncompain, has the following edifying words to say about the couple in that novel, Renaud and Claudine, who are based on Willy and Colette: "The fact that the man is considerably older than the woman, that he possessed her when she was still young and innocent, whereas he himself has the experience gained from age, further supports that natural law that dictates that the woman is a suppliant creature who relies on her husband, on his strength and his knowledge, and who rejects any friendship that weakens this unique love and is submissive to this law without even attempting to understand it." [8]

Just like a man! as Colette might have said. Some splendid vision of omnipotence is forced on women, who are thereby dominated in two ways: because of their sex, and because of their age. It is the old mirage of the anxious male, a deformed Humbert Humbert and his quest for a Lolita. Willy, obsessed with impotence, needed a dizzying proliferation of both women and books.

When we weigh the dream of perfect happiness promised innocent young fiancées against the reality of their demanding conjugal duties, something is very out of kilter. The more Colette was deprived of the company of younger men, the more she was fascinated by violent love affairs between young people. She did not consider sexual promiscuity, she was deeply monogamous, but she felt something akin to envy and she cherished a semi-innocent vision of fresh flesh and primitive lovemaking. The heroine of *La Vagabonde* says *I had . . . feelings, timid feelings, ordinary feelings, even common, shall I say? Happy in the habitual caress that assuaged them, timid about any licentious research or complexities . . . slow to catch fire but slow to quench—healthy feelings, in short.*[9] Like many young wives imprisoned by a certain image of virility, she vaguely hoped for savagery from a man, fierce jealousy, perhaps even physical brutality. But Willy, who was slightly effeminate, was more perverse than brutal, more complacent than jealous. His tastes ran to corsets, garters, titillating stages of undress, licentious byplay, rather than to chaste and passionate nudity. Of course, he was no Werther, but a young girl's upbringing led her to expect a young Werther; once her curiosity about the subtleties of licentiousness had been appeased, a young wife discovered that she was bound in married intimacy with nothing more than an old graybeard. She was forced to get over her deception as best she could, inventing or discovering imagined compensations: *This unknown and virile world of the young delighted me when I encountered it, and I did not complain if the encounter*

*gave me pain. To get around making too public an admission of my
privation, I created in* Claudine à l'école *the character of a little
pederast. In this way, while deprecating him, I could praise some
young man's looks, and in this oblique way I was able to protect
myself from the danger, the attraction. When I became friends with
Polaire later on and saw her crying because of some lover's quarrel—
her lover, Pierre L(ouÿs) was only twenty-five—saw her desolate
over a two-day separation or happy at the blows she had given and
received, she once told me, with her claws still bared in the abandon
of a cat in heat:*

"Ah, Colette! how good he smells, the rat, his skin and his teeth
. . . you cannot know . . ."

"No, I could not know!" [10]

⚜ BAPTISM

With regard to certain matters, however, she soon gained her freedom . . . and discovered one very sure way of relieving her boredom. Suffering, as young people suffer, is a full-time job, one that can
fill all twenty-four hours of the day: *I indulged my suffering with
an intractable pride and stubbornness.*[1]

One winter day in 1894, *I put on my lovely 125-franc coat, tied
up my serpentine hair in a new ribbon, and took a fiacre to the Rue
Bochard-de-Saron, where I rang the bell of a low-ceilinged entresol
apartment. Anonymous letters often contain the truth. I discovered
M. Willy and Mlle Charlotte Kinceler together, not in bed, but bent
over a book, and an account book at that. M. Willy was holding the
pencil.*[2] The drama, as usual, had its farcical side. Stupefied at the
sudden appearance of the outraged wife with her schoolgirl face
framed in her long braids, the lovers were speechless. Then Charlotte
grabbed a pair of sharp-pointed scissors to attack. Of the three, Willy
was the most uncomfortable. "Were you looking for me?" was all
he could find to say; recovering his composure, he shoved his wife
out the door with "magical celerity." Most embarrassing of all, he
had understood nothing, neither her silence nor her subdued reaction. Nor had she . . .

With time, humor won out over despair. Colette speaks of her first
rival with considerable feeling. There would be many more, and
adultery, like all of life's great experiences, has its own baptismal
ceremony and initiation rites which we remember with a pang of
something like tenderness. At a later period, Colette met Charlotte

again and became friends with her, as she made a habit of doing with many of the mistresses of her unfaithful husbands. A girl from Montmartre, the daughter of an alcoholic Communard, Charlotte, or Lotte, was a short brunette—almost exactly five feet tall—not pretty, but full of dash and grace; she had tempted Brieux, who based *Les Hannetons* on her, and had seduced Lemaitre and many other literary men with her glib tongue and her lower-class charm. She ran a herb shop to which she attracted clients with her talents as a fortune-teller, a seeress, a herbalist. She was converted by a priest to whom she had taken a liking when she glimpsed his face through the grille of the confessional, and afterward seems to have fallen into some kind of religious mania. One stifling afternoon, she put a revolver in her mouth and blew her head off. "She was twenty-five years old and had savings," Colette adds as eulogy for the girl who taught her so many things: *From her, I gained my doubts about the man I had trusted, and she did away with my stubborn, pretty, absurd girl's nature, from her I got the notion of tolerance and dissimulation, of making pacts with a female enemy.*[3] Now, however, the almost instinctive trust in women with which Sido had endowed her was being destroyed: she began to suspect every woman she met, to see in each overly affectionate woman friend another of her husband's potential or former mistresses; worse, she began to compromise. Her intimate respect for herself and for other women began to deteriorate, and the process was accelerated by her contempt for her companion. For contempt is an emotion with its own laws, with its own system of maintenance. It is not easily overcome.

There was still an ineradicable nucleus, some idée-fixe that impelled her to be more honorable in her own dissimulation. This was Sido. Suffering is an ignoble weakness, modesty bids us conceal it, particularly from those we love best; suffering is contagious. The most important thing was that Sido be kept ignorant. *I did not succeed in deceiving her completely, for she could see through walls. But for thirteen years, I did my best.*[4] In Colette's situation—and it was inconceivable to institute a divorce for sociological and obvious financial reasons (not that she wanted one at the time, for that matter)—her act of concealing her pain from Sido was the most heroic filial act she could perform, and it was also the only one that could enable her to overcome the humiliations and betrayal she was experiencing, the only action that allowed her to retain her vital self-respect. Here too, even though she was not present, Sido acted in spirit to safeguard for her, in spite of the ruin around her, some vestige of a positive image of her own femininity. Years later, when Colette relived this period in which she had repressed her tears and had managed to fight back the temptation to seek refuge in Sido's arms, to give in to her almost irrepressible need to unburden her heart and receive consolation, she could write with jaunty self-effacement: "After all, I wasn't all that bad off!"

However, stoicism, endurance, the indulgence of suffering, can take a physical toll. Unable to express her suffering, without any outlet for the problems and contradictions with which she was being forced to deal, she had recourse to the classic escape route and fell ill. During this year (probably 1894), she attended the annual Polytechnique ball on her father-in-law's arm, wearing a beautiful water green dress with a lace bertha. All eyes were on the "young girl," who was as green as her dress . . . a girl who was about to die. *There is always a time in young people's lives when dying seems as normal and seductive to them as living, and I wavered.*[5] Willy was busy with his own affairs. Dr. Julien tenderly attempted to give her encouragement: "*Come on, get well won't you? Help me, I'm doing all I can, alone as I am, to cure you.*"[6] Finally, the doctor wrote to Sido to tell her that he would probably be unable to save her daughter, and Sido arrived. *She concealed her feelings, she looked after me passionately, gaily, sleeping in the dark dining room. She only seemed a bit flushed and short of breath. But obviously she suffered continually as she pulled me back from a threshold she could not bear to see me cross. And so I got well.*[7]

The decision to get well is not arrived at all at once. It presupposes an acceptance of realities that were previously considered unbearable. Colette's illness represents her passage from adolescence to adult responsibility. In the subtle dialectics of one's life, acceptance precedes and leads to revolt. Once she had chosen to go on living, Colette had to spend twelve years in coming to terms with things, in learning. The time was both long and short. Years afterward, she made a precise summing up: *One can not care for ten years of one's life, so long as those years are in early youth. After that, one has to watch out.*[8]

❧ MARCEL SCHWOB, SACHA GUITRY, AND OTHERS

During the course of her partly psychological illness, while her robust nature—helped by Sido—was making the decision to live and not to die, Colette began to form her first friendships as a woman.

They were the first of many more to come, all of them faithfully kept throughout her long life devoted to the cult of friendship.

Sitting by her bed, Marcel Schwob would read from a book of American short stories, from Mark Twain, Jerome K. Jerome, Dickens or *Moll Flanders* (which he had not yet translated into French), in an attempt to help the "pretty secretary," as he was later to call her, forget her illness and the mustard plaster on her stomach. Born in Chaville on August 23, 1867, Marcel Schwob was one of those eccentric characters that thrived in the 1900s. Friendly with the greatest men—Verlaine, Maeterlinck, Gide, Valéry, Mallarmé, Henry Bataille and Anatole France, among others—he was a scholar and an admirable story teller, an English expert, a German expert, a devoté of slang and a medieval specialist. In 1894, the year of Colette's illness, he published *Le Livre de Monelle*, a work he had based on Louise, his former companion, a young and tuberculous working-class girl who had died on December 7, 1893, at the age of twenty-five, leaving him prostrate with grief. Schwob enjoyed ill-health and traveled constantly in search of some climate that might be kind to his frazzled nerves and body. He was later to become the companion and husband of Marguerite Moréno, at the time an actress at the Comédie Française, a slim young woman with an Egyptian profile who went on to enormous celebrity and to become Colette's dearest and lifelong friend. Marcel Schwob had met Willy, eight years his senior, around 1891; he was fond of him and appreciated his erudition, his sense of the fantastic. Most of all, however, he loved the "girl with the unforgettable hair" who teased him when they were alone together but "maintained a wild silence when there were people at the house, sitting on the floor." The Rue Vaneau where Schwob lived was a short walk from the Rue Jacob, and the two friends met freely and frequently, a situation remarked upon by Willy, who asked his wife not to allow her friend to see her all the way to her door, which might create talk.

Marcel Schwob's health continued to decline: up until 1905, his life was one long series of operations. He went from city to city, stayed in the Channel Islands for the climate; he translated Defoe's *Moll Flanders* into French and wrote an esesay on Meredith. In 1900, he married Marguerite Moréno in London. Schwob was enormously eccentric and cut a somewhat preposterous figure, going about everywhere with his Chinese nurse, the scholarly Ting, whom he had taken on after the closing of the Chinese Pavilion at the World's Fair and who acted as his manservant; they had drawn up a contract stipulating that Ting would shave him, and that in return Schwob would see to it he was repatriated when he died. He left the Rue Vaneau in 1896 and moved to the Rue du Bac with his Japanese furniture and his menagerie that included a dormouse, a squirrel, a Japanese dog given him by Robert de Montesquiou which slyly devoured Anatole France's kidskin boots one happy day, and a Belgian griffon. In October 1901, he set out with Ting for a voyage to the South Seas on a pilgrimage to the grave of Robert Louis Stevenson, recently dead in Samoa. He had many adventures and nearly lost his life on several occasions, all of which he set down in a notebook he wrote, full of jokes and puns on the order of "Claudine is off on a trip to the Polaire sea." In 1902, he moved to the Rue Saint-Louis-en-l'Isle and began to hold a salon frequented by his many friends.

Colette's entourage came to include Marcelle Tinayre, Paul Léautaud, Pierre Louÿs, Jean-Paul Toulet, Paul Fort, Anna de Noailles, Henri de Régnier, Paul Claudel, Jules Renard, André Rouveyre, André Allais and Pierre Champion. Sacha Guitry made his entrance at the Rue Saint-Louis-en-l'Isle in the spring of 1904 by sending up his visiting card: "Sacha Guitry, All Types of Specialties, President of the Mahogany Eyeglass Company." Still a young man, Guitry was trying to make his living as a draftsman and was accompanied by his very young wife, Charlotte Lysès, to whom he always referred simply as "Lysès." All at once, Schwob became very active, he returned to the Archives and the Bibliothèque Nationale, frequented theaters and music halls, and gave lectures on Villon that were highly appreciated at the Ecole des Hautes Etudes Sociales. In 1905, he caught cold and died.[1]

In addition to Robert d'Humières, the other friend who came daily to sit by Colette's bed and who remained faithful to her to the end, there was Paul Masson, the original of the character she called Masseau in her novel *L'Entrave*. A mad jokester, and devoted to puns like Willy and all the rest of the group, Masson adored pulling people's legs; he wrote erudite tall tales signed by a certain Mr. Rias (*Lemice-Térieux*) or entitled *Pensées d'un Yoghi*. Colette relates that he presented the Bibliothèque Nationale with the catalogue of an imaginary library consisting of nothing but puns. One of his fabrications was a forged "early diary" of Bismarck that brought France and Germany to the brink of war: "Go now, go later, what does it matter?" was one of the notations it contained. *Masson had been a magistrate at Chandernagor and had delivered judgments containing peculiar things described as "whereas having been found" that had fortunately not got back to Europe. "It was a pity," as he said himself. However, an account of the expulsion of the Jesuits he sent to* Le Gaulois *created such a stir among pious Frenchmen that the government called for an investigation. Paul Masson undertook it with immense zeal. . . . The most detailed of these reports reveals his immense application in his task and proves conclusively that no Jesuits had been present in French India since the days of Louis* XIV.[2]

The former colonial magistrate felt for the odd and unhappy girl an affection tinged with pity. When she was on the road to recovery and went to convalesce at Belle-Isle-en-Mer with her husband, Paul Masson went along. Colette was revived by this renewed contact with nature and her first experience of the sea, and she would drag her friend to the old fort on the Pointe des Poulains, where she would revel in the salt, the sand, the seaweed, the wriggling fish, and where she began to look more like Gabrielle again. A witness describes her at this time, "wearing blue sailor's trousers with a white stripe, with her lovely brown-velvet eyes and her two long braids falling below her knees, a woman who attracted attention . . . she would stroll along the front before the Palais with Willy." [3] And Willy, a confirmed Parisian and overwhelmed with work, would spend his time sending off letters and telegrams *the number and weight of which would have given any young wife cause for concern. . . . But I was already learning to avert my eyes.*[4] Colette and Masson, an odd couple, would search the western shores of the island for rocky caves where they could hear the music of the *great manes of foam the sea displayed as the wind drove it onto the rocky shore, a sound that made conversation impossible.*[5]

Paul would take from his pockets his notebook, his fountain pen and a little packet of cardboard cards.

"What are you doing, Paul?"

"I'm working. I'm working at my job. I'm employed by the Library Catalogue for the Nationale, I'm noting down titles."

"Oh . . . can you do that from memory?"

"From memory? What good is that? I'm doing better than that. I've noticed that the Nationale is very poor in Latin and Italian works of the fifteenth century. . . . So until the day when these lacunae are remedied by luck or scholarship, I'm making notes of

*highly interesting works that should have been written . . . so at
least the titles will maintain the Catalogue's prestige, the prestige of
the Khatalogue."*

"But," said I naively, *"you mean the books have never been
written?"*

"Ah," he replied with an offhand shrug, *"I can't be expected to
do everything."* [6]

A passage in a letter from Colette to Marcel Schwob sent from
Belle-Isle-en-Mer (August 1894) gives the flavor of the relationships
this young girl, still impulsive and mischievous, had with older
friends as she played at being a child. It also helps us to understand
why it was that Willy later had the idea of asking his wife to write
about her school days: *My God, Schwob, what odd places you've
been visiting! . . . Shut up! Well, I've just made Masson's wrist
bleed with my fingernails because he lost "Major Stede Bonnet" before I had a chance to read it! You'll pay for that! Yesterday we had
an admirable last outing in the boat, I was allowed to work the jib
and the sails instead of Willy or what's-his-name. . . . Oh! what
an ass you are Schwob! Not to have come to Belle Isle because—
what becauses can you give me? Fathead, sea louse, scoundrel, oakum
dripping, and so on! I'm not sure I wouldn't have hurt you as badly
as I've hurt Masson and I give him so much trouble that we've fallen
out for good.* [7]

We have already mentioned Schwob's premature death. Paul
Masson *made the classic end of a fun-loving man; standing on the
bank of the Rhine, he held a piece of cotton soaked in ether to his
nose until he lost his balance. He fell and drowned in a foot of
water.* [8]

⚜ A ONE-MAN BAND OF THE BELLE EPOQUE

Upon leaving Belle-Isle in September 1894, the Willys went to
Châtillon, where Colette wrote to Marcel Schwob: *I sometimes go
out in the carriage with my brother. . . . Maman fusses, settles her
pince-nez, waters and argues with Willy all day. This makes me
shriek with laughter.* [1]

Colette needed this respite between her illness and her imminent
enrollment in her husband's publishing factory, for the time was
approaching when she would be sat down before a blank page. Since
1893, approximately a year before their marriage, Willy had been
devoting himself single-mindedly to journalism and literature. He

was now only a sleeping partner in the Gauthier-Villars firm, and his partnership shares were to increase fourfold through an inheritance from his grandmother in 1904, shares he would be forced to relinquish two years later at the time of his separation from Colette. In the meanwhile, embroiled in his many projects, he had little connection with the family business.

The age was an age of newspapers: in 1900, there were 2,851 newspapers sharing the French market, 3,442 in 1904. Many newspapers had added gossip columns, and in these, alongside spicy tidbits about fashionable celebrities, one could find biographical notes, portraits of writers, stories and anecdotes, tales, news items, all written with the quick wit and elegant amorality, the cynical contempt for contemporary values, that is characteristic of the Belle Epoque. Willy wrote for dozens of newspapers and magazines. During these years, his signature appeared variously in *L'Action Française*, *L'Assiette au beurre*, *Le Capitole*, *Le Carcan*, *Le Chat noir*, *La Chronique parisienne*, *Cocorico*, *Le Courrier Français*, *Le Courrier musical*, *L'Ere nouvelle*, *L'Ermitage*, *Le Génie civil*, *La Grande Revue*, *Le Journal amusant*, *Mascarille*, and many others. He went from *La Vie Parisienne* to *Rire* and *Sourire*, which were more controversial, and above all to Juven's *Fantasio* where, alongside Maurice Barrès and Gyp, he was able to give free rein to his own particular brand of catty bitchery.[2] *Le Cri de Paris*, *Aux Ecoutes* and *Le Charivari* had staff caricaturists like Sem—who made dozens of caricatures of Willy—and Forain, Caran d'Ache and Steinlen.

The newspaper of the *demi-monde* was *Gil Blas*, founded in 1879; Maupassant, Richepin, Armand Sylvestre, had all appeared in its pages. *L'Echo de Paris*, in which "politics appeared cheek-by-jowl with typically Parisian articles, off-color verses, suggestive stories," had taken on Marcel Schwob and Catulle Mendès as literary editors in 1884. Willy succeeded Henri Bauer as its theater critic, and *L'Echo de Paris*, with the advent of Willy's great friend Barrès and Albert de Mun, went on to become a newspaper aimed at the Catholic middle class. The *Journal* was founded in 1892 with a brilliant team of collaborators, including Juliette Adam, Armand Sylvestre, Mendès, Mirbeau, Séverine, Theuriet, Barrès, Lorrain, Gyp, Meilhac, Lavedan, Allais and others.

The incredible upsurge in journalism included all genres, from sensational scandal sheets to "serious" papers such as *Le Temps*, on which Anatole France became the chief literary critic, taking over from Francisque Sarcey; he made frequent use of the talents of Paul

Souday, Léon Séché, Arvède Barine and Adolphe Brisson. *Le Figaro* was in direct competition with *Le Gaulois*. Jules Lemaitre, later replaced by Emile Faguet, was its theater critic. And to complete this brief survey, the great mass public was shared between two daily newspapers, *Le Petit Parisien*, strong in domestic politics, and *Le Matin*, specializing in foreign affairs. Many of these names are forgotten today, journalism being the ephemeral commodity it is, but in the Belle Epoque they were as well known as the "op-ed" writers and book reviewers we all turn to each morning.

Apart from his various other journalistic activities, Willy was generally considered to be the outstanding music critic of his day. The *Lettres de l'Ouvreuse* were the great success of *L'Echo de Paris*, and he also wrote articles on music for *La Revue Blanche* and the *Revue Internationale de Musique*. He was also a novelist and historian; among his books during these years were *Une Passade* (1895), *Maitresses d'esthètes* (1897), *Un Vilain Monsieur* (1898), and *Le Mariage de Louis XV* (1900). He was a great specialist in light, licentious tales and because of his life and the works he put his name to, he has a secure place in the sociology of literary life during the Belle Epoque, whatever his position in literature itself. Willy didn't give a fig about appearing in an academic periodical such as Brunetière's *Revue des Deux Mondes*; his goal was to reign supreme in the popular press, to make money out of writing. And in this, he was successful. The Belle Epoque, still pregnant with symbolism and impressionism, divided its favors between Willy and his kind, and men like Proust, Claudel, Mallarmé, André Gide or Guillaume Apollinaire, and the division was in no way a strict one. Alfred Adam, in a scholarly work entitled *Réflexion sur l'amoralisme du roman*, placed *Les Nourritures terrestres* of Gide and Willy's *La Maitresses du Prince Jean* on the same level. In the theater, too, which the Belle Epoque adored, the public's favors were indiscriminately doled out among Sardou, Lavedan, Hervieu, Bourget, Courteline, Labiche and Feydeau, after Meilhac and Halévy, before Flers and Caillavet, audiences were mad for vaudeville, the comedy of manners, plays about the eternal and adulterous bourgeoise triangle in all its forms; they couldn't get enough of sexual innuendo and inside jokes. Many critics were in complete accord. Yet at the same time, Antoine and his famous "*Théâtre Libre*," Paul Fort and his "art" theater were attempting to attract a more demanding public; there were daring experiments in theater, Alfred Jarry's *Ubu* among them. Later, during Willy's campaign to win fame in the theater for himself, he would remember that Feydeau meant cash at the box office, not Jarry.

In this period, the "one-man band" frequented every salon and literary café, he "haunted taverns, musicians' hangouts, clubs, studios, nightclubs; he courted performers and gave lessons in loose-living to even the most accomplished rakes." [3] We shall have occasion to note the price Willy paid for his widespread activities, a fraction of which would have worn out anyone else.

⚜ RUE JACOB: LA VIE DE BOHÈME

Colette had returned to the gloomy solitude of the Rue Jacob and to the company of her cat, Kiki-la-Doucette, to the bitter enjoyment of her unhappy marriage. Marguerite Moréno has described the ambiance of these years in Colette's life, the years when these two women who were to love and respect each other throughout their lives first met: "When I first knew you, Colette, you were living in an 'almost' old house in the Rue Jacob. . . . There was a gloomy courtyard, a vast chilly stairway, and a kitchen on the landing across from your apartment.

"Marcel Schwob introduced us. He loved you. He already foresaw what you were later to accomplish, he called you Lilith. We entered the room, and there you were. You were reading, your interminable hair was curled around you like a snake, and you turned to me that face which has only been made more beautiful by all you managed to steal from life. Life was depriving you of so much in those days!

"I can still see your eyes, your little pointed chin, your hair at once smooth and disheveled, I can hear your accent with its rolled 'R's' and your soft voice.

"The room was too big for you and you were hidden in the divan. After three sentences, we were friends. . . .

"One day your mother was there, sitting on the divan, in your kingdom. Her hair was gray, her complexion vivid, she was wearing a pince-nez on a black ribbon. Her hands, resting open in her lap, were begging for the things she missed, things Paris deprived her of.

"You are like your mother, Colette, 'Macolette' as I've called you for lo, these many years. . . .

"Everything else that is not she or you has been effaced from my memory.

"Oh—except there was also a gray cat prowling around." [1]

In the evenings, Colette would shake off her lethargy and turn into Mme Willy. She trailed after her husband as he led what has come to be called *la vie de bohème*, a way of life that "always suited me as badly as plumed hats and dangling earrings." Willy once told his friend Bonmariage that the *vie de bohème* was "the ideal life, provided you always have at least 100,000 francs in hand." He was devoted to it, both out of snobbery and predilection, and forced his wife to lead it with him until she *refused out of lack of aptitude, rejecting its lack of gaiety*.[2] The *vie de bohème* Willy condemned his wife to lead consisted first of all in spending part of the night in a corner of the editorial offices of *L'Echo de Paris* awaiting the proofs of his column, *L'Ouvreuse*. Trembling with lack of sleep, weakened by her unhealthy and irregular meals, worn out with disgust and boredom in *these old editorial offices where nothing defended or respected or facilitated mental labor*, where *no one was gay, worthwhile, young, or even cared about being so*.[3]

Fortunately, there were Catulle Mendès and Courteline to arouse her when they arrived. "Catulle Mendès never stopped writing, Courteline never stopped complaining. Catulle would greet the girls who always hung around him with high-flown salutations, 'Hail O bird, so dainty on the branch,' or '*Blancheur qui humiliez la neige*,' " when he was not holding forth on something, spouting the paradoxes of which he was so fond, generally anti-Semitic in content (it was in the midst of the Dreyfus *Affaire*), such as "Name me a single Jew who was a creative genius, just one!" Once someone said "What about Spinoza?" which Mendès got out of with the feeble response "Spinoza! Ah . . . I'm not too sure about his mother!" Once his proofs had been corrected, Willy would say "You must be dying of thirst," and they would find themselves walking down the dingy Rue du Croissant. Willy always spoke to Colette in the polite form, "*vous*," whereas she addressed him in the familiar, unlike the Claudine novels, in which Claudine says "*vous*" to Renaud, and Renaud "*tu*" to Claudine. There was obviously some ribald or social significance in this real-life reversal. In the Colette family, both parents and children had quite naturally used "*tu*." Perhaps it was a sign of Colette's refusal to conform to the high-minded and overpolite Gauthier-Villars family. "You must be dying of thirst." Colette would be dying of lack of sleep, above all, but they had to put in an appearance at the Brasserie Gambrinus or at Pousset, cafés packed with bearded men swilling beer. She preferred the Latin Quarter cafés like the Harcourt or Le Vachette, not so much because of the lemonade with currant syrup or the anisette and water she was allowed to have there, as because there, the clientele was younger. She could watch and listen to—for she never spoke in public herself —fresh young men, full of the grace and gaiety of their age: Pierre Louÿs, Jean de Tinan and André Lebey shared, among other lovers, the favors of *a girl named Loute, nineteen years old, who wore trousers and a cyclist's cap.*⁴ She would sit on Pierre Louÿs's knee while she ran her fingers through Jean de Tinan's hair that some other woman had perfumed. Another sullen girl caught a rabid case of syphilis and died in the hospital within a week, surrounded by oranges, bouquets of violets and friendly notes signed Pierre Louÿs, Jean de Tinan, Willy . . . and even Colette.

This dull bohemian life would sometimes be enlivened by radiant glimpses of the real world, and Colette's curiosity about this world could always make her forget her sufferings. Her invaluable curiosity was soon to be exploited by a "manager" who approached genius. The long lazy days spent alone with her cat, her letters from Sido, her books, the long evenings as a silent fixture in some café, were drawing to a close. One day, Willy said: "You ought to jot down some of your memories of your school days. Don't be afraid to put in spicy details . . . I might be able to do something with them. Funds are running low . . ."

⚜ "DE LA MUSIQUE AVANT TOUTE CHOSE . . ."

Behind the façade of Willy, the great music critic, the well-known novelist, was a man who was an accomplished exploiter of other people's talent. He applied his excellent mind to music criticism, but almost simultaneously, he was organizing his factory of well-oiled "machines" into a production line.

Although it is said that he raised the circulation of *L'Echo de Paris* by some 50,000 readers with his *"Lettres de l'Ouvreuse,"* his success was due less to his musical acumen than it was to his intuitive grasp of the commercial, of what the public wanted. He had noted that musical performances were rarely reported in the press, and that established music criticism was often deadly boring. "My notion was to devise a gay, mocking, witty music column that would make pleasant reading." Willy, who did have a certain taste in music, was no more a musician than he was an historian or a writer. And so much the better—there were already outstanding specialists in those mundane fields. The *Mariage de Louis XV* Willy published at Plon in 1900 was written by a schoolmistress in Sèvres; likewise, in his articles on music Willy was "assisted" by some of the best musicians and music critics of the day: Debussy, Fauré, Raymond Bouilhet, Pierre de Bréville, Alfred Ernst, Stan Golestan, André Hallays, Vincent d'Indy, Florent Schmidt, Eugène de Solénière, Emile Vuillermoz. He had quite naturally therefore become a supporter of Wagner and would publicize Chabrier, d'Indy, Fauré, Debussy, César Franck, Ernest Chausson, Henri Duparc.

Willy's battle for avant-garde music was probably inspired by sincere admiration, but it was also waged because of his desire to shock. Willy attracted readers with his sarcastic, cutting style and its myriad 'puns and neologisms, its outrageous technical jargon, its enthusiastic lyricism," [1] its barbed remarks on composers and conductors. And he was well aware of the publicity to be derived from scandals, quarrels, and duels. He attended every Parisian concert, and was prominent among the swooning hordes of French Wagnerites who attended, with tear-filled eyes, the annual Bayreuth festivals in Germany (Willy wept with immense alacrity). Perhaps the most famous of his altercations was with the composer Erik Satie, who became justifiably angry at the sarcastic remarks directed against him by l'Ouvreuse. One evening when Willy was entering the hall for a concert by the Lamoureux Orchestra, Satie accosted him:

"You are writing things about me that I can no longer stand for."

"What do you want me to do about it?" Willy replied. In answer, Satie hit him on the shoulder and they fell to, with Willy brandishing his walking stick and Satie his fists.

On the following day, the Ouvreuse noted in L'Echo de Paris: "I was distracted during the first part of the symphony, involved as I was in contemplating the sight of M. Erik Satie being beaten with a walking stick." [2] Colette had a good ear, she sang and played the piano, and she accompanied her vindictive and ventripotent spouse to his concerts, she tagged along to Bayreuth with the rest of music-loving, gossiping Parisian society. There was talk that she too had a hand in the Ouvreuse's letters and in the "Claudine at the Concert" series that ran in Gil Blas in 1903, the latter enabling her to attend Bayreuth at that magazine's expense. Debussy was also a critic for Gil Blas, and word went out—Willy himself most likely started it— that "Claude is worth more than Claudine." On the principle that all good publicity begins at home, Willy had articles written by or signed by Colette-Willy-Claudine reporting on his own activities as a music critic.[3] We cannot be certain today precisely what hand Colette actually had in these articles, and she herself never claimed to have written any of them.

What is certain is that during this period she gained a solid musical education and met many musicians, in particular Debussy and Ravel, both of whose portraits she would later write. Salons played a considerable role in spreading gossip and in disseminating works in the musical as well as in the literary world. The Willys frequented them all. Every Friday after dinner, Mme de Saint-Marceaux was at home to the musical world. In this relaxed atmosphere no one "dressed," and the huge shaded lamps, the tables stacked with magazines, newspapers, cigarettes, the warm rooms in the wintertime, the cool drinks and petits fours laid out in the adjoining dining room, all contributed to create a climate of "controlled freedom"—the mistress of the house "never forced anyone to listen to the music, but she would of course suppress the slightest whisper." This is the salon in which Debussy arrived one evening with the score to *Pelléas et Mélisande* under his arm, and where Fauré and Messager would improvise duets at the piano. In later years, Rouché, the impresario at the Opéra, asked Colette to write the libretto for a fairy-tale ballet; in a week she handed him the poem for *L'Enfant et les Sortilèges*. Ravel agreed to write the music and finished it . . . five years later. Initially written for her daughter, the opera-ballet was given its première in Monte-Carlo in 1925.*

⚜ A PROVINCIAL GIRL IN SALON SOCIETY

Colette met many Belle Epoque notables at Mme de Saint-Marceaux's salon: Louis de Serres, Pierre de Bréville, Charles Bordes, Déodat de Séverac, Vincent d'Indy, and Claude Debussy with his face like a satyr . . . *in moments of intense concentration, his eyes would cross slightly, like hunting dogs when they point their prey. He loved music as the crystal goblet loves the touch that releases its pure vibration.*[1] And in such surroundings, Willy could meet the people with connections and could polish the urbane aura that would help him create his reputation as a music critic, a reputation that

* After being booed at its horrendous first performance at the Opéra-Comique the following year, the work went on to achieve considerable success.

he actually owed to the musicians with which he surrounded himself. In literary circles, his strategy was the same, and he always dragged his socially inferior young wife along. She felt ill at ease at Mme Arman de Caillavet's dinners, in Mme de Saint-Marceaux's salon, only too well aware that they put up with her only because she was Willy's wife, a strange creature with a provincial accent, paralyzed with shyness, almost always silent.

People paid attention only to him. If anyone chanced to glance my way, I think it made them feel sorry for him. I was made quite well aware that without him, I didn't exist.[2]

Mme Arman de Caillavet, Anatole France's Muse (and a model for Proust's Mme Verdurin) held court on Sunday evenings. Before personal—and most likely political—differences caused her to break with Willy, the Gauthier-Villars couple was in constant attendance. Mme Arman, a woman of intelligence and savoir faire, wrote the preface to Proust's *Plaisirs et les jours* and had Anatole France put his name to it. In her home, Colette met Anna de Noailles and Proust himself, and it was there that Proust was introduced to Robert de Montesquiou, the model for his Baron de Charlus. Foreign authors such as D'Annunzio and Oscar Wilde, and politicians like Clemenceau, Poincaré and Léon Blum, also appeared from time to time.

There, Colette was to write, *the extraordinarily dull girl I was met famous men; I cannot say I knew them, because I was too timid to play more than a silent role on those Sundays, as I was at the Wednesday dinners for a more restricted guest list of twelve or fifteen. Silent as I was, however, I was better able to retain faces . . . the sonority and agreeable twang of Anatole France's voice, the slow-paced, marvelously menacing speech of Marcel Schwob, the so soft whisper of the adolescent Marcel Proust, the tenor of Capus, and Robert de Montesquiou, who would screech like a peacock at unexpected intervals.*[3]

The Willys were also in attendance at Mme Lucien Muhlfeld's and at the home of the poet Herédia, flanked by his three daughters, and at Philippe Berthelot's, whose Persian cats fascinated Colette as much as the poems Saint-John Perse showed up to read. Unlike his wife, Willy had a born gift for light conversation, along with an education and suppleness that made him able to adapt to a wide variety of circles, from respectable and even scholarly salons to more questionable surroundings. He was witty, affable, and could scratch sharply at unexpected moments. He could hold forth at the Comtesse Greffuhle's, at the homes of the Marquise de Saint-Paul or the Princesse de Polignac, with nary a pun or lapse in good taste, and then dash off to the low-life atmosphere of the Moulin Rouge, the Casino, the Folies, or to relax with his friend Rachilde in her apartment.

Rachilde's Tuesday gatherings at the *Mercure de France* were among the outstanding weekly events in Parisian literary circles; she was a most unusual woman. Descended from Brantôme, her real name was Marguerite Eymeri; she had been brought up in Périgord by a Jesuit and at the age of fourteen her father had engaged her to one of his officers. She had categorically refused to expatriate herself to Algeria and "unsuccessfully tried to drown herself in the lake" on the family estate.

A great admirer of Voltaire, Rachilde read her way through the three thousand volumes in her grandfather's library and published her first stories under a man's name in *L'Echo de la Dordogne* and other regional newspapers. At family gatherings, Colonel Eymeri would read his daughter's stories aloud, not realizing that the author was sitting beside him, skipping over the parts he considered unfit for a young girl's ears.[4] Rachilde waited until she was twenty-one before shaking the dust of gloomy Périgord from her feet and going off to Paris, where with difficulty she began working as a journalist, a playwright and a writer on fashion. *Monsieur Vénus*, her most famous book, was published in 1884 under the pseudonym Francis Talman, in Brussels; it was banned and confiscated. Five years later, the book reappeared with a preface by Barrès. At the *Mercure de France*, edited by her husband Alfred Vallette, whom she had married in 1889, she was a tough-minded critic; she was editor of the *Revue du Mois*, which covered newly published books, and later of the *Revue de la quinzaine*. She held open house in the Rue de l'Echaudé-Saint-Germain and later, around 1905, at the Hôtel de Beaumarchais, where the *Mercure de France* had moved. A great friend of Alfred Jarry, she wrote an enthusiastic volume of *mémoires* about this absinthe-sodden writer entitled *Alfred Jarry, or the Literary Superman*. She was friendly with Willy, but she was kind to Colette; she was an early admirer of her work, including the *Claudine* novels, and was one of the first to detect Colette's imprint on those books. Her Tuesdays brought many writers together—Henri de Régnier, Albert Samain, Charles Cros, Henri Albert, Léon Bloy, Pierre Louÿs, the Rosny brothers, Remy de Gourmont, Paul Léautaud, Laurent Tailhade, and Jean de Tinan, the latter of whom wrote cabaret reviews for the *Mercure* before joining Willy's stable of ghost writers.

⚜ THE SLAVE TRADE—ONE CHARACTER IN SEARCH OF AUTHORS

Any examination of the sociology of literature in France has to take Willy's "workshop" into account. There have been celebrated authors who were also "slave owners"—in French, unfortunately, ghost writers are called "niggers" (*nègres*)—and they were probably equally demanding. The exceptional thing about Willy was that he never wrote so much as a word himself, aside from telegrams, oceans of letters, a few pun-filled poems, some few articles he may possibly have actually authored—and of course, his famous account book. *Had he written a novel, it would probably have been far more clever than . . . many volumes whose titles I omit. But he never did write a novel.*[1] Sylvain Bonmariage, who most probably was forced to slave in the workshop himself from time to time, expresses surprise that Willy never wrote his *mémoires* when he was asked to later in his life. And they would have been a marvelous document on the Belle Epoque! But even his friends and his "niggers" were unaware of the true extent of his literary impotence.

Only his wife knew. Her awareness was based on her own past experience, as we know, since her husband shared her father's old urge, the urge to produce a printed volume, and they also shared the same almost obsessive impotence when confronted with a blank sheet of paper. Jules Colette, however, had concealed his impotence; he had written the titles of his imaginary books himself. Willy preferred to have his imaginary works written out by ghost writers. In the running of his factory, in which dozens of writers—often outstanding writers and men of unusual talent—were employed, Willy possessed several exceptional talents. He was endowed with *a gift for distributing work, for spotting ability, for giving stimulating criticism, an ability to encourage without overpraising.*[2] To this was added a rare gift for adding his own special touch to works written entirely by someone else. The puns, a certain light touch when dealing with serious matters, a kind of pomposity with regard to frivolous things, a kind of tasteful vulgarity, these elements combine to make the books to which he put his name appear somehow to be from the same hand, to share a common bond through similar characters in similar surroundings. In Willy's literary game, his "ghosts" wrote like Willy, and Willy wrote nothing. The complexity, the hierarchy of his workshop explain why his contemporaries were fooled and how he was able to carve out for himself a considerable position as a writer. He patronized good writers without patronizing them, *he who wrote nothing had more talent than those who wrote for him.*[3] And all this combined with a frantic, exaggerated, delirious bustle devoted to issuing orders and getting his demands executed managed to bring forth the things he wanted written. *A brief article of only a few lines would be the subject of ten pages of fevered correspondence along the lines "Construct some little bits of dialogue for me, as short as you can, fifteen lines, on some cheap spot. Use Marcel Ballot, Marquis de Chasseloup-Laubat, Frank Richardson, famous English essayist. Willy in company of sumptuous English women, one splits her swimsuit and makes the Kodaks click. Low-stakes baccarat, two-louis bancos, two rival casinos. Important: 'Her husband has gone off with a girl named Maud, she goes after him,' 'Bravo! a ménage à la Maud.' (Or, 'there's Maud in his eye!')"* [4]

Such collating, such prospecting for talent, so many catch phrases, combinations, and final assembling, and all to avoid that terrifying confrontation. "Everything seemed to be easy for him, everything was bestowed upon him, except being a writer." And of course this "freebooting hero of second-class literature" was himself a literary personality that begged to be put into a book. Yet Colette was never to write a novel about this character in search of authors.

And God knows he found them. "I did what everyone else has done," Ernest La Jeunesse was to say, "I began by calling myself Willy." [5] The list of his "collaborators" is endless; it extends from Christian Beck to Jean-Paul Toulet, it includes the famous Prince of Gastronomes, Curnonsky, it includes Francis Carco, once known as "Willy's Nigger," Fernand de Caigny, Armory, Charles Derenne, Jacques Dyssord, Félix Fénéon, Passurf—and my list is far from exhaustive, nor was Colette's. When Willy was short of cash, he was always in a hurry: *Quick, Pierre Veber, Jean de Tinan, Boulestin, Jean-Marc Bernard, Jean de la Hire . . . etc., turn out some novels. Quickly, Vuillermoz followed Alfred Ernest, André Hallays, Stan Golestan, even Claude Debussy and Vincent d'Indy himself had furnished the Ouvreuse with her letters, quick, Eugène de Solenière and Dussaresse, get to work; quick, quickly, I wrote the four Claudine novels, Minne, Les Egarements de Minne!* [6]

It seems the whole thing was not particularly unusual, "it was a common practice in literary production," Armand Lanoux wrote. Both Marcel Schwob and Willy himself—which astonishes us today

—had once ghost-written for Anatole France. In *Le Képi*, Lemice-Térieux/Paul Masson describes a woman to Colette who wrote a Hindu novel at one sou per line.

"A sou," I exclaimed; "why one sou?"

"Because she was working for a fellow who got two sous a line, who was working for another fellow who got four sous a line, who was working for someone getting ten sous a line!" [7] The nigger-ghosts' principal motivation was financial. Many of them were literary Rastignacs who, like Balzac's hero, had come to Paris to win recognition for their talents. After a short time, they would join the ranks of rejected writers at the entrances to publishers' offices. Willy's meager stipends and his glowing promises hooked the young author with his adolescent yearning to see himself in print, a yearning that has nothing to do with a thirst for fame or with mere temporary financial embarrassment. Willy had a keen eye for talent, and with the addition of his name, his tact and discretion, his connections, his genius for publicity, young writers who otherwise would not have been able to sell ten copies of a book under their own name were able to see their work printed by the thousands. There was also often a desire to shock, a mixture of exhibitionism and guilt, a feeling common to many who want to write, especially the young. Colette was to analyze with great perception the pleasure she had felt at being able to hold forth with impunity, protected by Willy's signature.

Willy, a typical employer, paid his workers as little as he could and pocketed the profit, the prestige, and of course the copyrights. He provided the means of production, i.e., publication, sales, distribution, publicity. As in any factory run on an assembly line, Willy's broke literary production down into various specific jobs entrusted to various specialists. A novel by Willy was turned out like a Renault. He hired experts: there were idea men (Jean de Tinan, Pierre Veber), landscape specialists (Jean-Paul Toulet), specialists in rhymed broadsides (Mazade-Rip), in stage scripts (Paul Acker, known as André Cocotte or Yves Mirande), and common laborers who were assigned to secretarial work and odd jobs (Paul Barlet, later editor of the Librairie des Lettres, who was to return Colette's *Claudine* manuscripts to her; Alfred Diard who remained Willy's faithful slave and later said things about Colette that were as full of macho contempt as they were untrue; Marcel Boulestin, who later became a restaurateur in London and remained on friendly terms with Colette—these were a few of Willy's "secretaries").

Willy would start out with a notion for an insignificant bit of work, some scenario to be worked up, an Idea. Accompanied with a handwritten note, the Idea would be sent off to the proper expert . . ."*Dear Old Cur [Curnonsky] how does this look to you? I've come upon the hereunto attached notion, rather sweet. Cast your experienced eye on this larva, sketch a future for it in fifty pages or so or stamp on it . . .*" Upon its return, the Idea would shed its new skin and all traces of a foreign hand and would be sent off to be typed, put in a new envelope, mailed to a new addressee: "*Help, Petipol! Here's my newborn. Could you within a month extract from it the elements for a light volume . . .*" The enigmatic Petipol, having precipitated out the aforesaid "elements" as requested and the manuscript having been retyped and dressed in a clean shirt, it would be dispatched to a third therapist with a letter: "*Dear Friend . . . you asked how my next book is coming along. Here it is. I'm a bit stuck. Only your adroit good offices, your light touch, your aptness of expression to which I pay such unjealous homage . . . etc., etc., it goes without saying you will be paid . . .*" etc. Notwithstanding all this communal attention, the work would often be subjected to yet another round of this honorable company, receiving a retyping and a fresh jacket at each stop.[8] Henry Martineau adds that it often happened that "chapters of the same work would be reworked simultaneously by various hands and readjusted afterward."[9]

Obviously, such an undertaking demanded absolute secrecy in all its phases. Communication between slaves separately employed on the same work had to be avoided at all costs. Everyone worked in the dark, in isolation, each unaware of the manuscript's earlier or future vicissitudes as it passed meteorlike through their hands, and usually unable to recognize their individual contributions in the finished product. Willy had reinvented that medieval system of labor toward which certain communal endeavors are leading us again today. Of course there was one huge difference: each person was unaware that he was part of a collective. There were a number of surprises, there are several amusing anecdotes: in 1907, Jean-Paul Toulet received a novel from Francis Carco entitled *Les Innocents*. In reading it, he experienced the same impression of "terror and complicitous pleasure" he had felt when summoned to "pretty up" a manuscript of Willy's entitled *Les Amis de Siska*. "Did you ever work in that factory?" Toulet asked Carco. As it happened, Carco had in fact originally written certain of the episodes Toulet had later reworked. At the time, each had been unaware of the other's collaboration.

Sometimes, Willy would purchase a fully completed work. At one juncture, Toulet had been going to sell him *La Tournée du petit duc*, but Willy had decided against it for fear the author would later lay claim to it—a lawsuit, perhaps—"so he had Toulet's manuscript reworked and destroyed rather than exposing himself to the accusation of having left it completely unchanged, of having taken over another person's work." [10] Having raw material reworked by several anonymous hands was cheaper than buying a finished product. Toulet had received 2,500 francs for *La Tournée du petit duc*, whereas he was paid 6,000 francs for tinkering with *Les Amis de Siska*; Curnonsky got half the royalties for *Maugis en ménage*. As a general rule, however, ghost writers were badly paid, paid late, or not paid at all. Willy's correspondence with his "employees" is replete with demands for payment followed by protests, promises and complaints. Toulet, who usually received three francs a page, was never confident he would be paid in full for work he delivered: "I was so weak, my dear Willy, as to rely on your promise . . ." "I suppose you find it amusing. You must send money . . ." Willy procrastinates: "Dear Toulet, please rest assured that in the end you, along with all my creditors, will be paid!" [11] Pierre Veber, who collaborated on *La Passade*, was thrown down the stairs by Willy, brandishing his walking stick, and stood in the courtyard in the Rue Jacob shouting:

"There are judges, Monsieur, for people who toss their creditors downstairs instead of paying their debts!" And Willy, impassive: *"Sir, I respect and honor my creditors. . . . But I will not give that name to a little prick who shows up twice a week on the pretext that I owe him thirty-two francs, but in reality just to pinch my maid's behind!"* [12]

And of course, Willy must have derived a certain pleasure from the whole thing. He was a man "who pretended to be poor all his life," who concealed his actual wealth, who went so far as to borrow from those poorer than he. Everything he owned was in another name, so that he could afford to be vastly amused at the bailiff's sequestering his "used flannel underwear, old pairs of trousers, worn collars."

Willy's slave trade took in everyone he knew. All of his friends, his acquaintances, his family, his son and his successive wives were dragooned into literary servitude to supply his monomaniac appetite for the written word. Upon hearing his son Jacques relate some of his pranks with his army companions, he told him to write them down, criticized the results at length, and concluded:

"I've read worse. Leave it with me. Your documentation may come in useful for me some day if I should run short!" And useful it was, as his son reports: "I discovered several of my anecdotes transformed in this way, just like an automobile frame is turned into a limousine." [13]

He urged Meg Villars, his second wife, to work up something on the lines of the *Claudine* novels; the result was *Les Imprudences de Peggy*, recounting the adventures of a pupil in an English girls' boarding school. The process was repeated with his third wife, Madeleine de Swarte, who produced a third generation of the same baleful family in *Mady écolière*.

And yet, Colette was to be his greatest discovery, his masterpiece the *Claudine* series. With them, he achieved his apotheosis. From then on, he repetitiously went downhill.

✣ WHITE SLAVERY: THE CLAUDINE NOVELS

It all began in the imperious tone Willy usually took with his wife: "You should jot a few of your recollections down on paper." Having grown used to her laziness over many long months, she was not overjoyed at the suggestion, but she was submissive to her master. In a stationery store she found some school notebooks that were very like the notebooks of her school days, *with rough paper . . . black cloth spines . . . called "Le Calligraphe."* She set herself to work as she would have toiled over a class theme, obeying the margins. She handed her husband a swollen manuscript of 656 pages.[1]

She had begun writing in October 1895 and she finished sometime in January of 1896, some twenty-nine months after her wedding, over a year after her illness. Her labors had been preceded by a visit to the source, Saint-Sauveur, accompanied by Willy, in July 1895.

According to the testimony of two former pupils at the school, this visit was almost exactly transposed into *Claudine en ménage*. It is all there, the popularity of this "Parisian" couple, the piece they played as a duet on the piano, Colette's braids, which she tucked into her belt or her pockets while jumping over the garden fence, all of it is there, even their visits to the dormitory, their good-morning kisses for each girl as she lay in bed, and the huge bag of sweets whose contents Willy "emptied into our washbasins, to our great delight." [2]

Indeed, it seems to have been more like an ethnological field trip than a vacation. In the following year, 1896, the Willys were to refuse Mlle Terrain's invitation to attend the prize-giving ceremonies and sent three bound and gilt-edged volumes instead. However, Willy wrote, "Colette was very sad." Perhaps his wife balked at making light of memories that touched her so deeply.

Once it was finished, in any case, the manuscript was received with little enthusiasm. "I was wrong, there's nothing in it," Willy said, and he tossed it into a drawer.

Free again, Colette returned to her sofa, to her cat, to her waiting, to her psychological balancing act between her various roles as a young wife homesick for her mother, the wife of a famous and talked-about figure in Parisian society, and her ungrateful position as the indigent daughter-in-law of her haughty and straitlaced in-laws.

That summer, while staying at Lons-le-Saunier at the home of her in-laws—who began by being shocked at her vocabulary and the enormous quantities of butter and jam she consumed—Colette went back to being Gabrielle, a little girl in a children's story. *I would listen to my mother-in-law, my sisters-in-law, my aunts and cousins by marriage, discussing Catholic matters. Leaning back in a wicker chair, I would let fall the female labor at which I was so clumsy and shut my eyes. Their patient voices spoke of dioceses, of fasts, of eggless pastry for Passion Week, of small fish and large fish, condemning the tolerant bishop who had allowed chocolate for breakfast, "made with water, of course.". . . Amid the aromas of ripened plums and pound cake I listened to the jaws of their scissors snapping at the cloth. . . . "When my girls are older," Madeleine would say, "I must teach them how to glaze men's shirts . . . what do you think, Mother?"* [3] Only the well-brought-up children in this exemplary family appreciated the old Gabrielle, the Gabrielle who knew how to start a fire with the bottom of a bottle, how to recite the magic words that would coax a snail to extrude its horns.

It was after one of these country visits that Willy decided to tidy up his desk. Two years had passed since the manuscript had been shoved into the drawer and forgotten. It was 1898.

"Well, well," M. Willy said, "I thought I'd thrown them out."

He opened a notebook and leafed through it.

"It's rather sweet."

He opened another notebook and fell silent, and then a third, a fourth. "God," he muttered, "what an ass I've been!" [4]

Thus Gabrielle became a writer.

But this was only the beginning. In the first place, the text was not spicy enough, not commercial enough. Willy would see to that. *"Couldn't you manage to spark them up a little . . . these childish things? For example, some unduly tender friendship between Claudine and one of her friends? . . . And dialect, lots of dialect . . . and kids' pranks. . . . Do you see what I mean?"*[5]

Many questions have been raised about the final form of *Claudine à l'école*, and the original manuscript has disappeared (probably thanks to Willy). It is probable that in line with the usual modus operandi, Curnonsky was detailed to turn the 656 manuscript pages into a novel, but he is said to have turned down the job. Yet the manuscript was cut and arranged. By whom? Colette's answer is categorical: *It was . . . entirely in my handwriting, with here and there another very small handwriting changing a word, adding a pun or delivering a harsh reprimand.*[6] Paul d'Hollander, in his thorough examination of this period of Colette's life, and after a lengthy analysis of those manuscripts that have been preserved *(Claudine en ménage* and *Claudine s'en va)*, concludes: "In my opinion, Willy personally made many corrections in the manuscript after he rediscovered it."[7] In any case, his must have been the guiding hand in fleshing out the episodes of unisexual love affairs between students and teachers and the latter with each other. The character of Aimée reveals his particular touch. On this point, Colette is quite firm: *When I married, I had no close adolescent attachments, the kind that imitate couples, to betray.*[8] Everything else relating to Saint-Sauveur/Montigny and to school life comes from Colette. Claudine has no mother, for obvious reasons; her father is based in large part on the Robineau-Desvoidy son, a relative of Jules, a man well known for his work in geology and entomology, particularly on the diptera and coleoptera, mollusks of the Frenois region.

Whatever Willy's actual role in the final version, Colette was henceforth relegated to the factory, and the factory became her prison . . . *a real jail, and that sound of the key turning in the lock, and being set free four hours later with "Show me your papers." What I was forced to show were papers well and closely filled up. I agree that such details of my daily incarceration are not greatly to my credit, I don't like looking like a dunce.*[9]

And this was only the beginning of her captivity. It was to continue for ten years.

Once her work was completed, Willy took over. Around 1889, he attempted to place *Claudine à l'école* with a publisher who turned it down. "I took my manuscript," he later related, "to various publishers, all of whom rejected it. Vanier, who owned my early *Lettres de l'Ouvreuse*, offered to publish it at my expense. Out! . . . Simonis-Empis, a childhood friend who ran a bookstore and was inclined to be receptive because of the success he had recently had with *Maîtresses d'esthètes* and *Un Vilain monsieur*, nevertheless told me he wouldn't be able to sell ten copies. One fine day, I handed it to Valdagne, a reader at Ollendorf's; his opinion was favorable. The book came out. Nobody talked about it and nobody bought it. Then an article by Maurras mentioned 'the unmentionable experiences hinted at in even the most reserved portions of these confessions,' and there were others. . . . I published a spicy little note in the papers that ended in the following mockery, not without its touch of bitterness:

Delagrave s'indigne, il crie à l'injustice,
Vanier en est malade, et Simonis . . . Empis! *[10]

The book came out in 1900 bearing only Willy's name and with a preface in which he explained, conventionally, that he had received the manuscript from an anonymous donor. "The modesty of my sex"(!), he wrote, "constrained me to make some cuts and to soften a few passages that were of an unduly peasant frankness." The most amusing element in all this is that Willy was telling the truth with the confidence that no one would believe it. He was later to admit that he had quarreled with Colette over the expression "belched apple," which he had found unbearably vulgar. This high-mindedness hardly stopped him from signing a book entitled *Suzette veut me lâcher*, an edifying work that began with the words "Marquise, why are you putting your panties back on?" His notion of vulgarity was fairly relative. And yet Willy allowed his wife's collaboration to be suspected, at least. When praises were showered on him for the book, he would lay his hand gently on Colette's head: "You know, this child has been precious to me. She has told me ravishing details about her school days." Thus Willy became known as the "Father of the Claudines," an offspring who, fortunately for him, had no mother. After favorable reviews by Rachilde and Gaston Deschamps appeared in the *Mercure de France* and *Le Temps*, respectively, the publisher sold 40,000 copies in two months.

Willy was on top of the world. Colette, with her adolescent and

* Delagrave is indignant and cries "Injustice!" Vanier is sick about it, and Simonis-Empis even more so—references to the publishers who had earlier rejected the work.

somewhat perverse penchant for mystification, and a certain irresponsibility that led her to relish her anonymity, played her husband's game—and he played his cards well—and helped maintain the deception. She was to write to Rachilde, who had proved herself more alert, or perhaps only more perspicacious, than her colleagues: "For years, you know, I've had piles and piles of notes in journal form, but I would never have dared believe they could be considered readable. Thanks to Belle Doucette [Willy], however, who pruned and smoothed over the overly Claudine-ish crudities, Claudine has become acceptable!" [11]

So, from slavery, Willy turned to white slavery. He was out to make his fortune, and with this in mind he set his wife to work under conditions that were infinitely harsher than those imposed on his other employees. The results were highly gratifying. In 1901, she produced—and he signed—*Claudine à Paris*; in 1902, *Claudine en ménage*; in 1903, *Claudine s'en va*; in 1904, *Minne*; and in 1905, *Les Egarements de Minne*. With *La Retraite sentimentale*, the concluding volume of the *Claudine* series, Colette began to rebel. But in the beginning, as shown in the following excerpt from a letter to Rachilde, she lent herself to her own exploitation with considerable alacrity: "God no, don't mention my name in connection with Claudine: family reasons, propriety, friends. . . . It's all Willy! Let Willy have the glory!" [12]

Colette had special status in the factory as the boss's wife. She was to be at once the most and the least exploited of all. In her case, the master-slave relationship tended to be more that of pimp-prostitute than boss-laborer. The exploitation of a woman by a man can never be reduced to mere socioeconomic factors; there are always added emotional and sexual variables that can affect it in other ways.

In the first place, unlike Willy's other ghost writers, hers was an unpaid "collaboration." One of Willy's string of secretaries, Alfred Diard, was later to remind her, nastily, "Madame Colette will allow me to recall that each *Claudine*, each *Minne*, was paid for in the form of a number of pearls added to her bridal necklace." [13] If we compare this "number of pearls" to the rivers of diamonds the cocottes of the period were able to amass for themselves, we have to agree that she was being paid at a cut rate. As a mere ghost writer, the same was true, if we compare the pearls to the subsidies Toulet and Curnonsky and their companions managed to exact. In the early days, her tools were minimal: a table, a lamp with a glass shade, a pen and school notebooks—and of course the necessary key, but a key that represented the opposite of freedom. When success came with its considerable dividends, the apprentice was promoted to master status in 1901, with *Claudine en ménage*, and was given a dazzling salary—300 francs a month, not including the idle summer months. The Popular Front had not yet made paid vacations the rule, but this trained female laborer was now earning nearly four times as much as her former headmistress in Saint-Sauveur, excluding the summer months. Colette grew more radical in 1902 and slowly began to become aware of her rights and to demand them—but the rights she sought were the rights of a powerless slave, compromises such as *quietly managing to bargain, to set terms, and finally, when I would be harassed with "Quick, quick for God's sake!" I managed to hint "Perhaps I might work more quickly in the country!"* [14] The boss, whose profits had reached considerable heights, agreed to improve working conditions as a means of improving his returns, and he purchased the house called Les Monts-Boucons in the Franche-Comté region, turning it to profit by using it as a special and private factory. In three years, by 1905, he had made back his investment.

1905 has generally been used by historians to mark the end of the Belle Epoque. It was also the year in which Willy's "belle époque" reached its end. The events were simultaneous, both on a personal and on a wider scale. Toward the end of his life, when war and twenty years of inner and world changes had made him a forgotten figure, he wrote: "Willy is an old joker I used to know well . . . He has been dead for twenty years now." Twenty years ago . . . the end of the *Claudine* series, the year of his separation from his best and most subservient collaborator. And for many, it was also the year that marked the end of an entire culture, the end of a society and way of life replete with frivolity and pleasure; for others, it was the political turning point, the moment in which France would experience a split that would last for decades: 1900, the Belle Epoque.

⚜ THE BELLE EPOQUE AND ITS CREATURES

The Belle Epoque—so *démodé* from our contemporary vantage point—was like a stage set; it didn't look quite the same from backstage. Made of cardboard and paste, it was largely show, artifice, decoration—behind its glittering façade was a vast emptiness. The Panama Canal scandal was just over, it was the year of the Paris world's fair, the Exposition Universelle, and Parisians, as always wildly eager to be in fashion, were overcome with a craving for novelty, for trumpery and fake exoticism. They couldn't have cared less about the Boer War, the first number of Lenin's *Iskra*.

Who cared! There were those who actually did have fun, and for years, people in France and elsewhere have enviously basked in the afterglow of their parties and diversions. For Jean Cocteau, the year of *Claudine à l'école* was always to be "the terrible year of Nietzsche's death, of a certain waltz that went 'You try in vain to understand me/By gazing in my distraught eyes/You want to know if love can be/But love's the thing that dies.'" [1] The Belle Epoque was kind to love affairs, if not love, and to love if not women. While consecrating an image of Woman triumphant, it treated women with contempt: "The Parisienne stands above the main entrance to an exhibition whose arts she seems to be protecting with her skirts. Statues of naked women ride horses and lead them in triumph atop the Grand Palais. A wave of Dostoevsky and Wagner flows in from Russia and Germany. Here comes another wave, this time Japanese, under the aegis of naturalistic and Cartesian France." [2] In the Palais de Glace, the afficionados in their olive green tunics and gold braid, their rakish hats and pointed boots, waltz endlessly: "Cocottes with names like 'Liane So-and-So' drape themselves over their instructor, clinging like the vines their names recall. Holding their muffs they glide forward, they turn, they dip, imitating the noble curlicues of the Métro entrances; they skim across the ice with lowered eyes. At intermission, with their silver skates still screwed onto their Louis XVth heels, they stagger to the washrooms or perch on the tables." [3] There is Willy at one of those tables, with "his huge mustache, his Tartarin beard, his glance lively under his heavy eyelids, his Lavalière cravat, his episcopal hands folded atop his walking stick," [4] and next to him sits Colette, "thin, thin. Like a baby fox in cycling costume," with her ever-present bulldog, Toby. "In the cloakroom our skates would be unscrewed and we would be jostled by serving girls. . . . We would risk getting home late for dinner to stay one more minute to watch the entrance of cocottes and actresses." [5]

Natalie Clifford Barney, the beautiful American famous for her wit, her parties, her sapphic love affair with Liane de Pougy, one of the celebrated *demi-mondaines* of the period, recalled the Belle Epoque as the time of carriages in the Bois de Boulogne, "when there was an opportunity to exchange long glances, half smiles, as one drove from the Tir au Pigeons to the Cascade, passing and passing again most of the fashionable courtisanes, actresses, society women and *demi-mondaines*; none of them had a glance as lovely as Colette's." [6]

Colette would walk her dogs, sporting high-buttoned shoes. In one direction was "the path of virtue on which the 'ladies of easy virtue' would descend from their carriages and indulge in what they called, ridiculously, 'footing,' mingling their perfumes with the scent of the acacia trees that rained showers of blossom at their feet to be crushed beneath their high-heeled shoes." [7] Each day, Willy would ride in the Bois, mounted on supposedly recalcitrant steeds, with Colette at his side, in riding costume and wearing a huge gray felt hat with a plume.

For Sylvain Bonmariage, 1900 was the year of "great scientific discovery, the first automobiles, Rostand's plays, artist's studios." A package of Hungarian cigarettes—the cheap cigarettes of the time—cost seventy centimes, and "one could lunch marvelously on fifty sous in any ordinary restaurant, while at Larue's the usual meal never cost more than ten francs. The meter of a cab hailed on the Place de l'Etoile would read less than three francs when you got out at the Gare du Nord. An apéritif in a fashionable café cost seventy-five centimes, three sous at the Café Briard. . . . At the Abbaye de Thélème, the poshest late-night restaurant, a bottle of Pommery sec cost twenty francs. 'Ah!' one sighs, 'you could really enjoy yourself then. . . .' As a result, we are considered monsters merely because we have retained our souls, our personalities, because—skeptical where faith and trust in democracy are concerned—we have avoided becoming nothing but statistics." [8] Willy would most likely have subscribed to such a statement.

How can we evaluate such witnesses? They speak with some conviction, recalling for us the unique atmosphere that surrounded a few people in their twenties at the time, a time when it is probably true that for the privileged members of a social and geographical minority, life had never been more wonderful. Colette would probably have been more inclined to agree with Nizan's despairing cry: "I was twenty too, and I will not let it be said that it was the most wonderful time of my life." [9] Even for her, however, looking back ten years later, there were picturesque, if not nostalgic, memories: *There was nothing nomadic about the vie de bohème. . . . Between 1897 and 1900, outside of Montmartre and Montparnasse, Bohemia barely knew Paris. It did employ the bicycle, which later the Bohemians in 1930 regarded with contempt. M. Willy rented a bicycle for "picnicking." I rode a little blue-enameled racing bike innocent of brakes or mudguards that Willy had won in a raffle celebrating a hundredth performance.*[10] With its taste for dress-up, the period was particularly fond of cycling costumes. Dr. Delarue-Mardrus, translator of the *Thousand Nights and One Night*, insisted on his wife Lucie being married in such a costume, wearing a boater and zouave trousers.

The Belle Epoque had strange fads—*pétomanes* who farted popular tunes were but one, and punning was another. Everyone had this mania, from Aurélien School, "The Last King of the Boulevardiers," to Tristan Bernard, André Allais, Maurice Donnay, Capus, or any of the habitués of the defunct Chat Noir, who gathered at the Café Tortoni until 1893, or the Napolitain. Willy was addicted to the practice to an immoderate degree, in the *Lettres de l'Ouvreuse* he described himself as "beset by the degrading mania for puns." His readers proved to be so avid for them, however, that they sent new ones in by every post; on some days, Willy would receive as many as forty letters. Puns, of course, are nearly always untranslatable, but one that went the rounds and helped make Willy famous has been handed down over the years; it concerns Mme Lili Lehmann and her husband, Herr Kalish: "We have drained," Willy remarked, "the kalish to the Lilees." It is marginally better in French. His particular humor can be adjudged from the following anecdote. His secretary Marcel Boulestin, a young homosexual who was the model for Marcel in the *Claudine* novels, had written a book on the subject of what was in those days called "Uranism," entitled *The Frequentations of Maurice*. The book was also translated into English and created a scandal, being slapped with legal proceedings on both sides of the Channel. Willy suggested the problem might be got round by distributing the English version in Paris, and vice versa, since, as he said, "Judges are never polyglottal, faggots always are."

For that matter, these same "witticisms" have been attributed to various other people; no one was ever really sure who had first come out with them. But they are part and parcel of the Belle Epoque, during which the craze for the novel and the bizarre went hand in hand with an immense conservatism in particular areas. Heterosexuality was "in," women and "faggots" were regarded with contempt, and wild xenophobia took the form of spiteful and aggressively ethnic jokes. Many clichés have been used to express the snobbery of the period, but the elegant term "dandy" was the favorite.

Dandyism, the cult of eccentricity, entailed a taste for animals less banal than the everyday domestic varieties. We have mentioned Marcel Schwob's menagerie. Over the years, aside from ordinary dogs and cats, Colette kept a veritable zoo ranging from a squirrel to a wild panther. Jarry lived with two owls (he also appears to have used his flower pots as toilet bowls). Léo Paillet arrived for an interview at the home of the famous Rachilde and was stupefied to witness the daily outing of Kyrie and Eleison, two black sewer rats "the good hostess clasped to her bosom, caressing, petting and kissing them." [11]

And there were picnics in the countryside reminiscent of Renoir, Sunday canoeing parties on the Marne or the Seine, around Mantes-la-Jolie. Copious *déjeuners sur l'herbe* or in the local restaurants would be followed by long siestas for Willy and his cohorts, *the sons of printers or ink manufacturers, ex-sublieutenants from the 31st artillery regiment who had turned into lawyers or notaries, strangers with artistic leanings emulating the still-fashionable Maupassant type with his tan and his muscles, and his paunch, and his fondness for post-prandial betting.*[12] Left to enjoy the snores of her flushed companions, in their "blue and white sweaters, their shirt-sleeves," the young woman who had once been Gabrielle would go off alone, *to indulge homesickness that returned so acutely under the poplars, with the odor of the river.*[13]

Colette mentions Maupassant, and it is he who perhaps best portrayed this frantic search that combined pleasure and bourgeoise vulgarity, its deep underlying *malaise* that was to lead him to madness, others to a boredoom impelling them to ever more desperate attempts to attain that sacrosanct pleasure. The most important thing in this society with its rabid pursuit of women was seduction: "To please women," Maupassant had cried, "is nearly everyone's most ardent wish. To be in Paris on the basis of one's sovereign talent . . . someone adulated, loved, able to harvest at will the fruits of living flesh for which we all hunger." [14] Willy's dizzy success with women was also based on the Don Juan complex: "Around 1900, there was a kind of erotic interplay between art and lovemaking. The better writers paid homage to this trend, the more willingly because it was a sure way of winning a large public." [15] Systematic eroticism in celebrating women and the pleasures of the flesh entails a marked element of contempt for the objects that must be abased in working out such libidinous fantasies. The widespread adulation of women was also an implacable way of subjugating them. Women had never before been so described, evoked, painted, parodied, worshiped, caricatured, dressed, undressed, photographed, veiled, revealed, and they had never before been so overtly despised and ridiculed. The playwright Henry Becque created a female type, the Parisian woman, that was to become a mythic figure: a tiny, elegant woman, a flirt, open, witty, ardent in lovemaking, she would wreak havoc; today's Frenchwoman still bears the burden of this stereotype.

The public looked upon the *grandes cocottes* and the famous boulevard actresses as incarnations of the Eternal Female. As a rule, they were lower-class girls or middle-class women whose beauty, temperament, finesse, willpower—and luck—had earned them admission into the *demi-monde*. All these dancers and singers, music hall artistes, the *grandes horizontales* La Belle Otéro, Liane de Pougy, Granier, Cléo de Mérode, parceled out their favors among the crowned heads of Europe, from Alphonse XIII to Franz-Joseph, from Léopold II of Belgium to Edward VII of England, and still managed to carry on their private love affairs or write their *mémoires*. Many were called, but few, unfortunately, were chosen. For those who were lucky enough to catch a son of some well-to-do family and lead him to ruin, to the consternation of that family, there were hundreds who failed in the attempt and were forced back into their lower-class poverty after a few second-rate appearances on the boulevards, to sordid dwellings and to a life that was a far cry from either the "great" world or the scandalous *demi-monde*.

These were the days when *men admired the ample and even the bosomy woman*,[16] a time when a woman was valued by her weight; and the Parisian woman was a slave to fashion, it turned her into a glittering slave tortured by a wasp-waisted corset, her feet crushed into her narrow shoes, her head weighted with her flowered hat and its thick veil, its aigrettes and ostrich plumes. Chignons were heavy, skirts had trains that swept the ground, blouses had leg-of-mutton sleeves with ruffles that matched one's jacket, one's stiff high hat. Nothing was functional, everything was for show. Colette was among the avant-garde; she cut her hair, she shortened her skirts, she wore sandals. Fashion decreed all, even the manufacture of automobile bodies, where "advice was humbly sought from the great designers and allowances were made for the height of women's hats." La Belle Otéro's blue Mercedes was so high and narrow that it frequently flopped on its side going around curves. As for the vast corsets that raised the breasts, drew in the waist, crushed the stomach, it was impossible to sit down in them. *Germaine Gallois . . . refused to play any part in which she had to sit down. Confined in a corset that began at her armpits and ended around her knees, with two flat iron supports down the back and another two down the thighs, with a "fastening" that went between her legs and kept the contraption in place, all of which required in addition some six meters of lacing, she would remain standing from eight-thirty to midnight, including intermissions.*[17]

The crushing luxury and the heavy hand of fashion were no more lenient when it came to interior decoration. *One was smothered in furniture. The atmosphere at receptions would be stifling. . . . There were "Arabian" boudoirs that didn't have windows.*[18]

The homes of these *demi-mondaines* were stuffed to overflowing with monkeys, yapping little dogs, vases, plants, portraits by Ferdinand Humbert, Prinet, Roybet, Antonio de la Gandara . . . with *cushions for the chaise longue, Spanish shawls flung over the baby-grand piano, statuettes, bibelots on the mantel, boxes of chocolates and fondants, Chinoiseries, lion skins.*[19]

Colette's memory collected pictures of the *demi-monde* like a magnet collects iron filings; it was so much more fascinating than the other world, in which she was never really recognized and accepted. In passing, she may mention a few things about Mme Arman de Caillavet's salon, not many, but her works are haunted by the *demi-mondaine*, that great figure of the 1900s. Her gaze caresses them, she searches out the real women inside the dolls. Above all, she was fascinated by aging cocottes (Léa in *Chéri*) and by the apprentice courtesan (Gigi). Her keen investigations into the beginnings and endings of the *grandes horizontales* left her with memories of some key figures, such as Caroline Otéro. Already an old woman when Colette was young, "Lina" had her extracurricular diversions, like those that would later comfort Léa in her old age: her family, gossip, other people's love affairs, gluttony.

"My child," she said, "you don't look to me as though you've had much experience. Remember, in a man's life, even the most miserly man, there always comes a moment when he really puts out and opens his hand."

"You mean the moment of passion?"

"No, I mean the moment when you twist his wrist." [20]

Still beautiful at an age when other women have to begin to forgo indulgence, Caroline Otéro would serve huge meals to one or two of her contemporaries and *me, who was not old, but colorless,* as Colette remarks. After having helped herself to her fifth serving of *puchero,* a kind of Spanish stew that was her favorite dish, Caroline Otéro would slip on her castanettes and dance from ten in the evening until two in the morning.

This recollection of La Belle Otéro in her declining years was so full of meaning for her that Colette set it at the beginning of *Mes apprentissages*, the book in which she evoked her life in the Willy era, the era that had hardly been her own "Belle Epoque." There is a kind of symbolic gap between the myth and the reality of the 1900s.

To measure this gap, we can use two referents: on the historico-political level, the Dreyfus Affair; on the socioeconomic level, the status of women.

⚜ CLAUDINE AND THE "AFFAIR"

In the literary circles in which the Willys moved, it was hard to avoid taking sides with regard to Dreyfus. The "Affair" grew to such proportions that, in Sartre's view, anyone not involved was automatically against it. Colette, who appears to have become more of a minor at this period than she had been at ten years of age, had many other things on her mind and blindly followed her husband's lead. Willy's political and ethical background had hardly prepared him to become a Dreyfusard. Sylvain Bonmariage, a literary hack of the day and a rabid defender of Willy, waited until after Colette's death to publish a revolting book [1] in which he drags her through the mud —though even he admits that she had rejected his immoral proposals. Willy is supposed to have told him "I have my own politics, and you know what they are. My basic principle is never to argue with people I agree with, but, to relieve the monotony, I sometimes discuss with people who think differently. This is my real intellectual pleasure." It was also a way to confuse people.

Bonmariage's book, although beneath contempt, still has its uses. He depicts himself and his friend Willy in a much more favorable light than he does Colette, and his own words are revelatory of the type of men surrounding Willy. For that matter, Bonmariage makes no secret of his own political views, he does not refrain from apologizing for Pétain, "who saved France by his actions," for Bonnard, a cabinet official during the Occupation "who helped Colette keep alive and was viciously attacked by her afterward," or for Paul Chack, whose "sincere anti-Semitism and rabid anti-Bolshevism" come in for high praise. He expresses sorrow that men whom he admired—Jean de La Varende, René Benjamin, Sacha Guitry—had flouted the expressed wishes of Edmond de Goncourt ("No women, no Jews") by making a second exception in Colette's favor and admitting her into the Académie of the same name—mistaken all round, Bonmariage contends that the first exception was Bergson, a member of the Académie Française. In Bonmariage's pages and his admiration for Willy's "acute attack of nationalism" in 1914, we can glean some notion of the deep-rooted opinions both men shared, opinions that were fairly typical of the age: anti-Semitic, antidemocratic, anticlerical, nationalistic, dandiacal and amoral, strongly rooted in class consciousness: "With our backgrounds, my dear friend," Willy confided to Bonmariage, "we are permitted to commit moral errors, of course, but never errors of breeding." Added to all this was their contempt for women, fed by the licentious lives they led, and their amused disdain for inverts: "As far as I am concerned," Willy was to note in his *Souvenirs littéraires et autres*,[2] "I will never be the prey of the homosexual octopus, whose tentacles are abhorrent to me. I am an old inveterate pistol, and why should I aim at another target? Woman is worth more than some substitute. Not that I think she's worth much!"

Willy would naturally have been spontaneously hostile to Dreyfus. This is evident from the anti-Semitic touches slipped into all his "works" during this period, and particularly in the *Claudine* novels. Colette had her share of responsibility for this, and she does not deny it; she readily expressed her shame about this time in her life when her husband had flaunted his personal hatreds and political opinions through the medium of her own pen. In *Mes apprentissages*, she writes: *I blame myself for the fact that the Claudines are so careless about hurting other people.* The two are often inseparable. The bilious sarcasm with which Mme de Arman de Caillavet is sketched in the guise of Mme Barmann, the Jewess "Barmann with her hooked nose," also enabled Willy to attack two targets at once.

To understand better the connotations that even an apparently harmless narrative with anti-Semitic overtones could have at this period, we might recall a few dates. On October 15, 1894, Captain Dreyfus, an attaché in military intelligence, was arrested following the discovery in a wastebasket of the famous *bordereau*, a list of secret documents being offered for sale to the Germans. The handwriting on the *bordereau* resembled that of the Jewish Dreyfus. On December 2, on the basis of a forged document fabricated by Colonel Henry, Dreyfus was sentenced to life imprisonment on Devil's Island in Guyana, where he was to remain for the next four years. The matter aroused little comment until a certain Colonel Picquart discovered that the handwriting of a French officer of Hungarian birth, Esterhazy, closely resembled the handwriting on the *bordereau*. After reporting his discovery to his superiors, Picquart found himself transferred to Tunisia, his career momentarily in shambles. In November of 1897, however, the Affair exploded into the open: Dreyfus's brother Mathieu denounced Esterhazy and circulated a facsimile of the *bordereau*; Clemenceau in *Le Figaro* called for a revision of the trial. But on January 11, 1898, Esterhazy was acquitted by a military tribunal; it was at this juncture that Zola's open letter, "*J'Accuse*," was printed in *L'Aurore*, in which he accused the army general staff of having knowingly condemned an innocent man.

The effect of Zola's article was of course resounding and the French public was split into two camps, Dreyfusards and anti-Dreyfusards. The day following the article's publication, a petition of intellectuals that included the signatures of Proust, Anatole France, the Halévy brothers, Jacques Bizet, Robert de Flers, Léon Yeatman, Louis de la Salle, Albert Bloch, Jules Renard, André Gide, and many others, called for a review of the trial.

By the end of that month, the petition contained more than three thousand names. From February 7 to 23, Zola stood trial for libel. In his journal for February 17, Jules Renard mentions a protest in support of Zola in *La Revue Blanche*. Willy, who had written an anti-Zola article, refused to sign this petition. "It was the first time," Veber wittily remarked, "he had balked at putting his name to something he hadn't written." Zola was found guilty and forced to flee to England. On August 7, 1898, Colonel Henry's fabricated document that had been used to convict Dreyfus was uncovered, and a review of the first trial became unavoidable. Henry committed suicide, whereupon the anti-Semitic newspaper *La Libre Parole* opened a subscription for his widow that rapidly took in over 130,000 francs; Willy was one of the subscribers.

Owing to the circumstances attendant on a remission of sentence, Dreyfus's situation gradually improved, but it was not until July 12, 1906, that the Court of Appeals overturned the sentence of the military court martial at Rennes and Dreyfus was rehabilitated. He was reinstated in the Army.

The Dreyfus Affair—1894 to 1906—extended more or less throughout the entire period of Colette's first marriage, 1893 to 1906. Thus, all the books written under Willy's aegis were composed and published during the Affair. At the time, the literary salons were divided along strict partisan lines, so much so that many hostesses who couldn't have cared less about Dreyfus found themselves forced to come down on one side or the other or risk seeing half their guests leave the house before it became a battlefield. Thus the famous salon of Mme Arman de Caillavet, where Anatole France held sway, had followed Proust's lead in 1898 and wholeheartedly supported Dreyfus—this is one of the salons upon which Proust later drew for Mme Verdurin's.

Mme Arman, née Léontine Lippmann, born a Jew, had married Albert Arman in 1868; he was later granted permission to add the name of one of his properties, Caillavet, to his patronym. Their son, Gaston, was to make the name famous on the stage. In 1886, Mme Arman weaned Anatole France away from the influence of her close friend of ten years' standing, Mme Aubernon de Neuville, whose salon was famous at the time. Following his divorce in 1893, the distinguished academician, who had already been Mme de Caillavet's lover for years, moved in for good. He was the star turn in the literary salon she ran in her mansion at 12, Avenue Hoche. During the early years of their marriage, the Willys went there often, and it was in this salon that Colette was to meet Marcel Proust. She gives a glimpse of him—probably much colored by Willy—in *Claudine en ménage*: the "pretty young man of letters" is seated next to the short-haired Claudine at dinner and showers her with compliments, comparing her to Myrtocleia, to a young Hermes, a Prud'hon Cupid, to so many hermaphroditic works of art that he nearly ruins her enjoyment of *a divine cassoulet, a specialty of the house. . . . Sunk back in a Louis XV armchair, I listened to his literary meanderings. . . .*

"Ah, you are dreaming like the child Narcissus, your soul too is full of bitterness and delight."

"My dear Sir," I told him firmly, "you're quite wrong. My soul is full of nothing but baked beans and thick little strips of bacon!"

With that crushing blow, he fell silent!

Colette was later to pay an homage to Proust based more on her reading of *Du Côté de chez Swann* than on actual memory. She recalled Proust as she had known him in Mme Arman's salon, *singularly young, younger than all the men, younger than all the other young women.*[3] They corresponded, but were to meet infrequently before the death of that *tottering young man who was fifty years old!*[4]

During Colette's illness, Mme Arman was extremely kind to her, visiting her, depositing fruits and a huge scarf full of candies on the bed. Shortly after this, around 1895, Willy picked a quarrel with her. There is a letter from Proust to Louis de Robert that throws some light on the personal motives behind the break.[5] Mme de Caillavet is supposed to have accused Willy of attempting to seduce her daughter-in-law, the former Jeanne Pouquet (who is the model for the girl called Rose-Chou in *Claudine s'en va*, and also one of Proust's models for Gilberte Swann); worse, the attempt had occurred in the hostess's own home, and she had taken it upon herself to inform Colette. Furious, Willy accused Gaston de Caillavet's mother of having attempted to turn his wife against him. Somewhat naively, Proust told Willy that if his wife's view of him had changed, he knew of an excellent oculist. By 1896, Proust would have had to conceal the fact that he had not completely broken with Willy from Mme Arman—we are in the midst of the Dreyfus Affair. In the novel *Un vilain monsieur*, Willy managed a cruel caricature of Mme Arman, calling her Barmann, and three years later came *Claudine à Paris*, where he enlisted Colette's help in attacking her. She was a "horrible old mole," a "bitch among bitches," that "woman who is keeping Anatole France," and in an elaborate pun he referred to her husband as the "conservator of the Collage de France," *collage* meaning "living in sin" as well as referring to the august Collège de France.[6] Willy was not entirely without inspiration. Mme Arman appears in the *Claudine* novels as the mistress of a certain Gréfeuille (Anatole France) wearing a stuffed screech owl in her elaborate coiffure—"screech owl above, screech owl below, a great hook nose . . . marbled with broken veins." *Claudine à Paris*, written in 1900 and published in 1901, in the midst of the Affair, contains passages such as the following:

"My dear Renaud," Tante Coeur said, "do you really think a race course is the proper setting for this dear child?"

"My dear Madam, he'd see some eminently suitable people, and a great many Jews," he said softly, with a sidelong glance at Mme Barmann.

It was marvelous. I was seething with suppressed delight.[7]

In his own list of the persons who had served as models for characters in the *Claudine* novels, Willy wickedly noted "the *rose-chou* [cabbage-rose] is the silly but amiable wife of [Gaston] Arman de Caillavet whom Colette detested even as a young girl [Jeanne Pouquet]."[8] We now know why!

Such was the position to which Colette had sunk through her alienation, the totality of her submission. Prostituted by her lord and master, her literary work was not only taken from her, it was intimately altered and manipulated by him. According to her husband,

160   WILLY

Colette is supposed to have written unconsciously, almost at his dictation. The extraordinarily sad thing is that he didn't even need to be present. He exercised an inner censorship and control that extended all the way to the physical act of writing. Freedom and equality of women at the turn of the century! True, Colette at this time in her life is far from being a good example. But as the companion of a man who lived licentiously, who preached license for himself and for his mistresses, the way in which she was made a writer illustrates for us the enormous gulf that separated myth and reality in this area as well, the contrast between emancipation and oppression; it reveals that a certain freedom for women in the sexual and moral spheres must not be confounded with true liberation, with real access to any equal status.

⚜ Some women

Although the Parisian woman, her image, her escapades, dominated the period, although there were a few society women or *demi-mondaines* who went to the theater, took lovers and openly flaunted female liaisons, although the mistresses of literary salons welcomed famous actresses or celebrated courtesans into those salons for decorative purposes, although there were a few female journalists, a few women who wrote shocking novels, although—finally—there were a few pioneers engaged in national and international feminist movements with avant-garde goals and demands, it is nonetheless the fact that at the turn of the century the status of the average Frenchwoman was legally, professionally, and economically a minority status. She may have been a haunting presence in the privacy of her own home, in the theater, or in society, but when it came to serious matters she was totally shoved aside. Her only existence was as a corseted and young—preferably—female. Should her thigh in its fetching garter wither and yellow with age, should her adorable face begin to show signs of fatigue, or the onset of menopause, the female became a non-being, odious in every respect. Unattractive women were the most unfortunate of all. Many great beauties of the period were to commit suicide when their fiftieth year rolled by. Some, calling on reserves of wit and cleverness, or on the protection of an influential man, survived. What would Mme Arman have been without Anatole France, or Rachilde without Alfred Vallette, Colette without Willy? Not to mention other *"femmes de lettres"* like Judith Gautier, the poet's daughter, Marie-Louise de Herédia, daughter of a famous father and wife of Henri de Régnier, Mme Catulle Mendès, and so many more.

The cultural heritage of the defunct nineteenth century lay heavy upon them all! It is painful to recall some of the commonly held opinions of that era: Lamennais, that theocratic philosopher, watch in hand, stated that he had never met a woman who was "capable of following fifteen minutes of logical discussion." Joseph de Maistre maintained that "Science is extremely dangerous for women," Proudhon that "women who exercise their minds become ugly, mad and frightful." Auguste Comte's idolatry of Clotilde de Vaux did not prevent the father of positivism from writing that the female sex was condemned to a "natural inferiority nothing can alter, one that is even more pronounced in the human race than it is in the higher animals." In his *Histoire de la littérature féminine en France*, Jean Larnac notes that in 1872 the famous Bishoff, a professor at the University of Saint Petersburg, had declared that women were incapable of intellectual activity because their brains were too small. In an attempt to prove this fascinating theory, he instructed that his own brain be weighed after his demise. To everyone's stupefaction, it turned out to be five grams lighter than the average female's!

Barbey d'Aurevilly, undeterred by this setback, made up an anthology of articles on female writers entitled *Les Bas-Bleus (The Bluestockings)* in 1879, and maintained that female writers were not real women at all. "They attempt to become men, at least ostensibly, and since they fail, they become bluestockings. . . . Even when possessed of wit and talent, women can never achieve lasting success, and fate has rightly decreed that women were not brought into the world to accomplish what we [men] can accomplish!"

Jean Larnac, who was interested enough in the female writers of his day to write a book about them in addition to a biography of Colette, expressed an ingenuous astonishment at women's propensity for "dwelling on their childhood and adolescence. It almost seems that youth is their most precious possession . . . that the upbringing of our female writers was in every case deplorable, so eagerly do they indulge in describing tomboy delights in the garden, in the woods, at the seashore, without a thought for anything but their own sensual gratification in pure air and the beauties of nature."[1] Larnac was shocked to note that the fate to which they were promptly condemned upon reaching a marriageable age did not seem to inspire them to even greater raptures, and he expressed indignation at the fact that they did not sufficiently—at least to his liking—hymn the blessed state of maternity.

Albert Cim caricatured educated women in a particularly vulgar way in *Les Bas-Bleus* (1891) and *Les Emancipées* (1899). Paul Hervieu presented his play, *Les Tenailles (The Pincers)*, in 1896, and Eugène Brieux's play, *L'Evasion*, dealt with young girls. In 1898 came Maurice Donnay with *L'Affranchie (The Emancipated Woman)*, followed by Marcel Prévost's *Les Vièrges fortes* in 1900. Even some women writers severely criticized female "rebels," most likely in an attempt to gain credit with the public.

In 1900, nevertheless, there were many French feminists participating in suffragette movements, inspired by women's groups in England and America, and taking part in social and political struggles. At the end of the nineteenth century, French feminism had its own great figures and martyrs created by the events of the Paris Commune during its short months of existence. Women had organized labor, set up cooperatives, introduced new teaching methods, and had fought for public, free and compulsory education. Nursery schools had increased in number, workshops had been opened guaranteeing equal pay.[2] Female prisoners—the most famous of whom was Louise Michel—had been cruelly treated by their jailors, who made no distinction between the women and the men in their charge. The government, maintaining that women had set fire to certain districts of the city as the loyalist troops were advancing from Versailles, held a propaganda trial of the *"pétroleuses"*—a nickname with connotations of wild harpy and hysterical bacchante that was henceforth attached to any woman with militant or revolutionary leanings. The period that followed the Commune and lasted up to the First World War in 1914 was a period of great procrastination within the labor movement between Proudhonist thinking, hostile to competition from female labor, and anarchist or socialist thinking favorable to women's participation in the labor force. This was also the period during which the female role in journalism was being kept subservient to Catholic factions desirous of maintaining the female-oriented sectors of the press in their role as upholders of traditional family values.

In 1881, Hubertine Aucler founded *La Citoyenne*, the first suffragist newspaper, with its slogan "We Dare Resist." She editorialized for the winning of political rights as more pressing than the gaining of civil rights. Problems of sex hygiene and sex education were dealt with for the first time in *La Femme et l'Avenir (Women and the Future)*. Talk of birth control was in the air. In 1892, Marie Hérot declared a boycott on pregnancy, but her proposals were wildly attacked by the Church, leaders of industry, and even militant labor union leaders and political radicals. Many feminist newspapers began publication, aimed at the female labor force and dealing with unions and working conditions. The first daily put out entirely by women was *La Fronde*, an ominous title for those with long memories, founded by Marguerite Durand, a former actress at the Comédie Française, in 1897. It was advertised as a "daily political and literary newspaper edited, administered, written and printed by women" (from the masthead of *La Fronde*). Among her collaborators were Mme Catulle Mendès, Judith Cladel, Clémence Royer, Daniel Leseur, Hermine Lecomte de Noüy, and Séverine, who reported the Zola trial, took part in political struggles and supported Dreyfus. "If we do not demand justice for a condemned man we have reason to believe is innocent, what right have we to seek justice for ourselves!"

In 1900, three female congresses were held, the most important of which, the Congress on the Status and Rights of Women, was chaired by Maria Pognon. Women's demands were submitted to the Chambre des Députés in 1901, 1906 and 1911, and were rejected on each occasion. In 1900, "seating laws" allowing salesgirls to sit down, were passed. That same year, the first woman was admitted to the Bar. The Church began to change its position on suffragism when it began to see it as perhaps another tool for fighting secular education. At the same time, the number of women studying law, medicine or the natural sciences at the University of Paris remained extremely small. Yet there were a few, often ephemeral, magazines for women, a few women's groups; feminism had gained a few victories.

But at what a price! In reality, the feminist movement affected few women, the majority of whom feared the disapproval and ridicule that were attached to it in varying degrees. The coolness and hands-off policy adopted by some of the most daring women writers is striking. "So you don't agree with feminist notions?" Léo Paillet asked Rachilde, when she remarked that she had made a mistake in being born a woman. Her reply: "I've turned this famous problem over and over in my mind, and I still can't find it of the slightest interest." This was a view shared by Colette and by most of the female writers at the time. And the others? Successful female writers acted like men in skirts and regarded their less fortunate sisters with a contempt equaling that of men. Many took male or asexual pseudonyms: Rachilde, Gyp (the Comtesse Martel), Gérard d'Houville (Marie-Louise de Herédia), Arvède Barine (Mme Vincens), Daniel Leseur—all were attempts to conceal the infamy implicit in being a woman. "When Madame Sand is in the Académie Française, Madame Stern in the Académie des

Sciences Morales et Politiques, and Madame Rosa Bonheur in the Académie des Beaux-Arts," Barbey d'Aurevilly joked, "we will have the whole so-called *triumfeminat* thinking they're a *triumvirat!*" They were fooling themselves. Obviously, trying to pass as men did not earn them any greater favor. The brotherhood never really accepted them; they were like blacks in the days when attempts were still being made to pass as white, rejected by both sides. The doors of the Académie Française were closed, and have remained so. Much later, as already noted, Colette was admitted to the Académie Goncourt. In an attempt to redress the imbalance in prize-giving, the magazine *Vie Heureuse* established a female academy in 1904 along the lines of the Goncourt, and offered an annual prize of 5,000 francs—the origin of today's *Prix Femina*—a prize not restricted to women, however.

Anna de Noailles, Renée Vivien and Lucie Delarue-Mardrus were Colette's friends. Some of her other friends are certainly ripe for rediscovery; many of them were famous at a time when the name Colette Willy stood for no more than the submissive spouse of Henry Gauthier-Villars. We might mention Gyp, Marie Bashkirtseff, Séverine, Juliette Adam, Colette Yver, Gabrielle Reval, Judith Gautier, among others. Even the cocottes, Sapphos and muses of the Belle Epoque were quick to set pen to paper. "Who would believe," Colette was to write in her mémoires, "that when Liane de Pougy's novel *L'Insaissisable* appeared in 1898 it was a sensation?" Liane even wrote another book, *Idylle saphique*, describing her liaison with Natalie Clifford Barney, herself the author of poetry, pensées and recollections.

Thus, despite these brilliant individual or social exceptions, the actual status of women improved very slowly, both on the legal level and on the level of actual fact and mental attitude. Divorce, forbidden under the Restoration in 1826, remained so until 1884, and even after reinstatement the only grounds available, with minor modifications, were based on dereliction of conjugal duty (*séparation de corps*);[3] "adultery on the part of the male, and only if his concubine was maintained under the same roof," "female adultery, brutality or serious injury; and conviction with death sentence, penal servitude or public disgrace."[4] Petitions for separation were automatically followed by divorce after three years' delay. In this regard, it is interesting to note that for the year 1895, "out of 8,497 petitions for divorce, 3,131 were brought by the husband, 5,366 by the wife. Out of 2,446 petitions for separation, 391 were filed by men, 2,055 by women."[5] Also interesting is the fact that between 1885 and 1895, the number of petitions based on immorality, brutality or serious injury—covering the vast majority of petitions filed by women—almost quintupled, from 1,635 to 7,473. At the same time, petitions based on adultery on the part of the wife merely doubled, from 526 to 1,127. Petitions based on the husband's adultery rose from 192 to 606.[6]

A law promulgated in 1804 and still in effect at this time stipulated that women had no right to pursue a profession or to select the family domicile without the permission of their husbands. Even when legally separated, a woman could not "give, remove, mortgage or acquire" possessions without her husband acting for her or giving his consent.[7] She did not enjoy the control of property acquired through exercise of her profession and was unable to open a bank account in her own name. Not until 1900 was the working day reduced to ten hours for women; the granting of one free day a week became obligatory in 1905. Until 1893, the year of Colette's marriage, a working woman received half the salary paid to a man for the same job. Her earnings were turned over to her husband, and indeed, women were not granted control over their own earnings until 1907, after Colette and Willy were separated.

So is it surprising that Colette was put under lock and key each day in order to turn out work for her husband to sign, or that he pocketed the profits? Her situation was not much different from that of any of her contemporaries. And not many women had husbands who earned their daily bread from the often meager and always ephemeral harvest provided by fame.

⚜ THE SCANDALOUS CLAUDINES

"He looks like somebody famous."

"I guess only God and maybe Alfred Dreyfus are as well known."

"In the same way that when very old people die, we're always surprised, having thought them dead for years, Willy is so famous that we're beginning to wonder if he really exists. Willy has become a manner of speech. Still, he invented Claudine, who is a naughty, charming and universal character. . . . He invented his famous hat, still firmly settled on his head. Ah! if he would only publicize himself just a little. But he is determined not to!"[1]

Willy was so fond of exhibitionism for business purposes, so intoxicated by fame, that during the years of his greatest renown, 1900 to 1907, he shrank at nothing in their pursuit. He paid newspapers to print publicity about him, even derogatory criticism, he provoked scandals, he had a passion for eccentric clothes and he forced his wife to follow suit, dressing her up and exhibiting himself with her and another woman as a purported ménage à trois; he wrote and caused to be written dozens of articles about himself; he disseminated questionable photographs, medallions, daguerreotypes and caricatures of himself, with or without Colette, with or without other women in filmy garments. His desire—first and foremost and above all—was to be talked about. It didn't matter what people said, so long as they were talking. He spent all his time living up to the stories evil tongues spread about him. He was among the first to exploit the taste of a certain sector of the public for intimate details and spicy gossip about the private lives of celebrities. He was at one and the same time the producer, author and propagandist of his own personality. He had mastered, with the effectiveness of a precursor, all the devices of publicity—shock value, repetition, a keen feeling for the collective subconscious, brainwashing, anything to do with the blatant exploitation of public taste. In a consumer-oriented society, he would have been a genius at "marketing," at "advertising." In addition, he had a "fiendish facility for making the public believe what he wanted it to believe, and for concealing the truth. Willy would have been able to pull the wool over the eyes of even the most perspicacious historiographer." [2]

Although one or two duels and other altercations had made him fairly well known at the time of his marriage, he cleverly managed to create his first real scandal with *Claudine à l'école*. There was nothing puritanical about the age in which he lived—far from it. There were abundant lewd books, particularly books dealing with lesbianism. Willy's coup was in combining the "unisexual" love affair with an evocation of adolescents in a girls' primary school, the whole thing resting firmly on Colette's experience and her talent. To worldly Parisian society, a village public school was a highly exotic setting, an ethnological curiosity. The heroine's fresh innocence, so like that of the young Gabrielle, set off those scenes inspired by the "boss." And there had been a real scandal at Saint-Sauveur, a scandal rife with politics and local color, involving the burning issue of lay education. Of course Mlle Terrain was never able to forgive her "former pest" completely, even when Colette sent her an inscribed copy of *Sido* in an attempt to "soothe the irritated nymphs of Puisaye." "These school secrets caused a revolution in the Département de l'Yonne, ruined Deputy 'Dutertre'—that *marlou* [pimp] of a Merlou—and gave some of the local rags an opportunity to look on me as an adversary of lay education (a mere nothing!)" [3] Thus Willy. And of course, no charming description of so-called unnatural practices between teachers and pupils in a public school in all its questionable morality could have failed to make an effect at a time when the battle for lay education was still being waged. The Catholic factions were torn between their pleasure at seeing their rivals destroyed and their virtuous indignation at the book's indecency. This reflects Willy's own character, which was both antidemocratic and anticlerical. "The clerical party wavered. Jacques Bainville opined that the book was less likely to corrupt than a Zola novel, but I was excoriated by *La Croix de Reims*. . . . And the socialists were no more united.

"They went off in all directions.

"Deputy Mirman, who was small potatoes, screamed bloody murder, but Léon Blum, who was editor of *Droits de l'homme* at the time, strewed rose petals on my balding head." [4]

The publication of *Claudine à Paris* in 1901 brought the scandal home to Paris and into *mondaine* Paris society. Willy's disguises for actual people were surrounded by intentionally transparent "clues." People were less shocked by descriptions of Marcel's "uranian" love affairs with his high school chums or by lewd descriptions of Luce, the perverse country girl who sells her favors to an old protector and plays out his sexual fantasies, than they were by the caricatures of Willy's enemies—and even his friends—who seemed like a parade of distorted marionettes creating an exact picture of a thin slice of Parisian society when seen through Claudine's perverse and wicked eyes.

Mention has been made of Willy's tactics for settling accounts with those against whom he bore grudges. In later years, he was to draw up a methodical list of all his "clues," punctuated with nasty remarks on each: "Léon Payet . . . a physical portrait of Barlet, known as Paul Héon, some sort of writer and . . . once sort of my secretary. I fed him when he was lying low in Brussels as a deserter, and later on in Paris. He stole letters from me and then sold them to Colette." [5] Indeed, he never forgave Barlet for having sneaked off with the *Claudine* manuscripts that were still in existence and returning them to Colette, who was after all their legal owner.

Circumstances surrounding the composition and publication of *Claudine en ménage* gave rise to further scandal. In it, Colette and Willy had described an episode in their private life involving a certain Georgie Raoul-Duval, on whom the character of Rézi is based. *Claudine en ménage* had begun life as *Claudine amoureuse (Claudine in Love)*, and in it the relationship with the aforesaid Georgie was described and transposed in a very transparent manner, one that was extremely insulting to this woman, with whom Willy had ended by quarreling. In a letter to Jeanne Muhlfeld, Colette referred to this: "My dear Jeanne, I was in such a state of moral deliquescence yesterday owing to fatigue that I was unable to talk with you as I would have liked. Even though he is chronically in a state of exhaustion, Willy sat up late when he arrived home and since he's been out all morning I've been able to find out why—from 'Claudine.' The spiteful lad, who has had a serious falling out with G.R.D. (I mean it), is in the process of turning Claudine's Rézi into Georgie by making some fairly brutal changes. It's very like her, and she will be awfully recognizable. This is wrong. It's unworthy of him, of almost anyone, for that matter. I have reasons that make me less interested in . . . Claudine's girl friend. My dear friend, you know that one word from you or from Lucien or both of you would be enough to keep Willy from doing this." [6]

But in fact, nothing was to prevent Willy from "doing" *Claudine amoureuse*, which was published by Ollendorf. Before distributing it, Ollendorf advised Willy through Valdagne, his reader, that certain third parties were protesting the book's being issued. Lucien Muhlfeld, Jeanne's husband, was called in to arbitrate; he was also employed by *L'Echo de Paris* and was friendly with both the Willys. At this juncture, Colette wrote to Lucien Muhlfeld—whether because certain details had been changed to her satisfaction or under pressure from Willy is not clear: "Dear friend, Valdagne has just left, having brought extraordinary news. Ollendorf is refusing to publish *Claudine amoureuse* because it is too racy. This is incredible, and Willy got very angry. . . . Now, as you know, I have my own reasons for knowing what's in *Claudine amoureuse*. There's nothing awful in it at all, and not a word that can be attacked. You'll see for yourself." [7] What in fact happened was that Georgie Raoul-Duval got wind that she was abused in the book and bought out the entire edition before it was distributed to avoid scandal. For some unknown reason three or four copies were saved, either by the lady herself or by whoever had been entrusted with pulping the book, or by someone involved in the arbitration who wanted to retain some evidence in case the affair came to trial. In any event, after Georgie's freebooting initiative, the couple went back to work; they were out of pocket for the costs. The rewritten manuscript finally appeared in the *Mercure de France* in 1902 under the title *Claudine en ménage*.[8]

Despite the alterations in the book, the critics were aroused. A husband willingly relinquishing his wife to a woman, which woman is then revealed to be his mistress, this scabrous tale in which poor Claudine is doubly deceived by both husband and female lover, the whole thing went far beyond what the public was willing to accept. Impervious to sexual prudery, Rachilde showed great discernment in perceiving the really subversive element in the female viewpoint that was expressed in the book for those with the ability to read it. Her review in the *Mercure de France* began with a quotation from Claudine herself: " 'All the same, if I had spoken of taking a girl friend instead of a lover, he would have gone along with my wishes. For Renaud, adultery is a matter of gender.' These words of Claudine embody the Gospel of conjugal—modern conjugal—morality. And Claudine further says that 'Vice is the evil we do without pleasure.' You might have added, my spontaneous Claudine, 'or for any reason other than pleasure.' Then you will have completely summed up all the elegant attitudes some pretty and honest female creatures take when confronted with the gross, dishonest gestures and solemn words of certain men who purport to instruct their companions in the dignity of socially acceptable love." Rachilde maliciously adds that for her, the miracle is that "Claudine has sprung from a male brain, for she is the great and eternal enemy of man."

Rachilde was not a committed feminist, but, subtle woman that she was, she had recognized that behind Willy's name there lurked, unseen by all, a rebel whose voice ultimately drowned out that of the man who was supposedly speaking. Like Willy himself, however, all the male critics were completely fooled, along with the public; they saw only the licentious elements in what was actually a fairly serious and already mournfully clear-sighted text. "The *Claudine* novels are overtly unhealthy, perverse, scabrous and scandalous books. A charming artistry often overlays licentiousness," wrote E. Charles in *La Vie littéraire*. "In society, we are shocked, we hide our faces," La Hire wrote, "with our ten fingers spread wide apart the better to read between them; some shout scandal, others clamor for censorship; older women confess they don't really understand . . . some publisher faints, families we all know attempt to find out clues to their identities. In short, *Claudine en ménage* is a book no husband can permit his wife to read, unless it is rather a book wives would prefer not to see their husbands reading. Everyone is whispering, hinting, repeating: it's the *Liaisons dangereuses* of the twentieth century."

Claudine s'en va (*Claudine Goes Off*, misleadingly translated as *Claudine and Annie* in most English editions) was published by Ollendorf in 1903. In it, the focus shifts somewhat to another character, Annie; this shift in fact betrays the conflict that was taking place in Colette's own subconscious, but public and critics joined in seeing it as a ploy to retain interest in a series everyone was growing a bit bored with. Some jokesters wished the departing Claudine a good trip and no return ticket. A few years later, *La Retraite sentimentale* would, however, bring her back, twice as old and half as interesting; Renaud is killed off in the book and Willy did not sign it. *Claudine s'en va* did, however, result in its "father" fighting a duel with a certain Jean de Mitty, a Romanian writer he had lampooned, or had had Colette lampoon, under the transparent and pungent name Jean de Quatorze Heures (Jean Afternoon, we might say), a character endowed with "uranian" predilections.

In the meanwhile, Willy's gamble had been successful. Claudine, "the embodiment of the modern woman," and her "father," Willy, became enormously popular. On January 22, 1902, *Claudine à Paris*, having been turned into a three-act play by Willy and Luvey (a nom de plume concealing the joint work of Lugné-Poe and Charles Vayre), was presented at the Bouffes-Parisiens.

This play—the text has never been published—and its eventual prologue, *Claudine à l'école*, enjoyed a run of 123 consecutive performances. One of the main reasons for its success was the appearance of the first in a long series of actresses who played the role of Claudine: Polaire.

⚜ POLAIRE

She was a true star of the Belle Epoque: Polaire, tiny, exotic, with huge eyes and an incredibly narrow waist. When Willy rebaptized her and made her famous, she was pursuing an undistinguished career on the variety stage. The same age as Colette, she had been born Emilie Zouzé Bouchard in Algeria in 1873. She was to become Willy's interpreter, and Claudine made her famous; she went on to appear in his *Le Petit Jeune Homme* in 1903, and in *Le Friquet* in 1904.

At the Palais de Glace, wrote Jean Cocteau, "a creature suddenly appeared whose name was singularly apropos in such surroundings: Polaire. Her flat, yellow serpent's head was balanced by her Portuguese-oyster eyes glittering with mother-of-pearl and salt, like a fresh umber fish. Her features were drawn back tautly by her massive knot of hair caught at the back, like a Percheron; with her felt hat pushed back above her bangs, a Lalique ring as a belt, a slinky skirt revealing her stockings and her tiny boots with their cruel skates, the actress, violent as a Hebrew insult, stood straight and stiff at the edge of the rink, tense as a raw nerve." [1] Colette describes her astonishing wardrobe, her inimitable mixture of modesty and cheek: *I once saw her erupt onto the stage madly jumping rope, turning "red-hot-peppers," catch her foot and fall flat with a loud "Oh, shit!" Whereupon she leaped to her feet . . . and like a frightened child advanced to the footlights, her hand over her mouth, stammering in her odd accent, "Messieurs, Mesdames, I beg your pardons, zat just zlipped out. I beg zat you will overlook it."* On another occasion, *Willy had occasion to speak sharply to his star, who was nervously shifting her weight from one foot to the other in her white morning-glory dress. "Please, Polaire, stand still! You look like a flower that has to pee!" Polaire choked, blushed to the roots of her hair: "Oh, Villi, zat's not a nice word! You should say 'go potty'!"* [2]

She gave a superb performance and made the play a success, dressing—with an utter contempt for reality—the sixteen-year-old character she was playing like a street urchin in socks and a black smock, changed in the second act for *an equally unsuitable frothy white frock.*[3] But no matter what she did, the public was mad for her, and Polaire was equally mad about Claudine, totally identifying with the character.

After the evening performance and dinner in a late-night restaurant, she would begin to feel depressed at abandoning Claudine:

"Good-bye, Colette, good night!"

"Sleep well, Polaire!"

"Oh, I hardly sleep a wink, you know . . . I just wait!"

"Who do you wait for?"

"Oh, not for anybody. I wait for tomorrow's performance." [4]

She carried things to the point of forbidding Pierre Louÿs, with whom she was having an affair, from coming to the theater at midnight to pick her up after the performance: *"It doesn't look right zat a man should come to fetch me here,"* she would say indignantly, *"it looks like I do something naughty!"* [5]

When she went on to play other parts, she missed Claudine; when the play was revived, she waxed mystical: "I'm to be reunited with her," she sighed. To the end of her life, which was a gloomy and unhappy one, she always spoke of Claudine as a friend who had died. Colette was only too happy to yield up the character of Claudine, the witness to her own "enslavement," to Polaire, and did so gracefully: *"Her faith, her certainty, were such that listening to her, I secretly withdrew, and thanked Polaire for having invented Claudine.*[6]

There were to be many interpreters of the role—redheads, blondes, brunettes, tall, short, healthy and "consumptive," even one who had a beard inherited from her mother, the bearded lady in a sideshow, and who was obliged to shave every evening before putting on her stage makeup. However, Polaire had stated firmly upon first reading the play, even before she had played the part, *"No, Monsieur Vili, I am ze real Claudine."* [7]

The script of *Claudine à Paris* has disappeared; however, in it Willy had greatly developed and enlarged his favorite character, one he regarded as his double: Maugis. In this play, a "collective" undertaking, even if the purported author had confined himself to exercising remote control and autosuggestion, there were two views of Willy. There was Colette's Willy, refined, elegant, with a touch of melancholy: the character of Renaud. Willy's Willy was the rotund and voluble Maugis. In the course of the novels, as Willy's Claudine became too different from her own concept, with her unisexual affairs, her complacency toward infidelity, her unnatural conjugal submission, Colette created her own Claudine, calling her Annie in *Claudine s'en va*. Maugis, predating Claudine and the *Claudine* novels, was to outlive Renaud and his touching death in *La Retraite sentimentale*.

⚜ MAUGIS THE KING

In creating the gross Maugis, I think that Willy was in the throes of one of his attacks of megalomania, obsessed with the idea of portraying himself, with his passion for self-contemplation. . . . If he hadn't had such a writer's block, I think he would have been able to make his name and his novels known without having had to exceed the bounds of commercial opportunism as he did.[1]

Maugis, like Willy, wore a distinctive wide-brimmed hat; he was a music critic and inveterate punster, "filled with fatherly vice," a great afficionado of women, exotic liqueurs, and plays on words, full of bravado, thin-skinned and unscrupulous. Like his original, his creator, Maugis *called women in their slips "baby," he preferred half-*

dressed women to naked women, he preferred socks to silk stockings.
Onstage, elaborate makeup made the resemblance between Willy and
Maugis startling when the character made his theatrical entrance in
the middle of the second act; his presence in the play was completely
gratuitous, aside from fulfilling the iron whim of his creator. Not that
the character was flattering, far from it, but Willy was caught in the
toils of Narcissus: *His double's entrance would throw Willy into a
state of actual intoxication. This man, in the midst of his growing
success and fame, worshiped his own attributes even as he exploited
them. As soon as the witch doctor begins to believe in the effectiveness of the noxious medicine he is concocting, one begins to tremble
for the witch doctor rather than for his patient.*[2] Indeed, but can the
remedy really work if the witch doctor doesn't believe in it himself?

So Willy was on top of the world. Because of his reputation as the
"Father of the Claudines," he was showered with letters from all sorts
of women. Young working-class girls would come to him with tales
of their sapphic love affairs, there were hordes of adolescents, young
and not-so-young, each of whom was convinced she was the "real"
Claudine; they thronged to his bachelor dwelling to offer themselves
to their incestuous "father."

Since he was always in financial deep water, he augmented his
activities by launching a line of commercial products inspired by his
"works": Claudine lotion, Claudine ice cream, Claudine perfume, the
"Claudinet," a low-collar and striped cravat for women and children
(April 1903). There was a second Claudine perfume, followed by
the Claudine hat. There was Willy face powder, durable and invisible. There were Claudine cigarettes. There was a device with
sensitized paper for making "Claudine photographs."[3]

At the same time, Willy's mania for self-display took a wilder
turn. There were caricatures by Sem and Cappiello, statuettes by
Widhopff, pencil drawings by Léandre, a portrait by Jacques-Emile
Blanche, versions of Willy were produced by Léal de Camara: *I
recall one of "L'Ouvreuse" by Rip, a Vallaton . . . drawings by
Rabier and fifty unknown hands, a very dignified portrait signed
with a Slavic name, innumerable figurines. . . . The Boldini portrait
was a high point as far as publicity was concerned. . . . After Boldini, we fell into a vortex of photography, not to mention miniature
full-length statues, cardboard cutouts, rubber figures, wooden sil-
houettes, froglike figurines, inkstands in the shape of Willy hats,
sculptures, postcards, stamps for stationery.*[4]

In 1903, Willy was indicted for an "offense to public morals" because of "La Maitresse du Prince Jean," a story published in *La Vie en Rose*. The ensuing trial created even more talk about the "author," recalling former famous trials, the *Madame Bovary* trial and the proceedings against *Les Fleurs du Mal*. Willy played it for its full value. He persuaded Huysmans to be a witness on his behalf, he got Catulle Mendès and Jules Renard to support him and Joseph Paul-Boncour to take charge of his defense. In the end, however, he was found guilty and sentenced to pay a fine of 1,000 francs. "But what was a fine, compared to the incredible publicity the trial provided him!"[5] The scandal and publicity increased. Ernest Charles, a man whom Willy detested, wrote an article in *La Vie Littéraire* in 1905: "He doesn't make a move that will not serve to increase his notoriety. . . . Need we mention the countless advertisements in all kinds of publications depicting the sad and lovely features of Mme Willy between the round, intelligent features of M. Willy—not overly gay himself—and the likeness of Mme Polaire, whom I shall pass over in silence. . . . Willy devotes more time to publicizing a book than he does in writing it."[6] (The last sentence was a low blow.) Despite articles about Willy by such people as La Hire or Henri Albert, the translator of Nietzsche, all of which were dithyrambic, it was beginning to be whispered about Paris that Willy was in actuality little more than a literary pirate. Ernest Charles quotes a current epigram:

> The sermons Abbé Rochette preaches
> They say he steals without remorse.
> But I know he pays his scribes,
> And so in law they're his, perforce.[7]

⚜ THE VICIOUS TRIANGLE

Meanwhile, in the full flush of their success, Willy and Colette had moved in 1903 to an apartment at 93, Rue de Courcelles, an atelier with a "small studio, a corridor, a tiny salon," and then to number 177 in the same street, where they took over half of a private house. They attended every reception, every vernissage, every concert, every sporting event, every society function. "The Rue de Courcelles, when its inhabitants were not in Monte Carlo or Bayreuth, at the races at Auteuil or Longchamp, was overrun with gossip columnists, violinists, piano tuners, all keeping Willy abreast of events and intrigues in the music world. He was, after all, a person who could ensure success or demolish, using either incense or picric acid, who could put together a winning combination or put over an opera."[1]

Willy was totally drunk with power and he began to indulge in even more excessive behavior. He determined, authoritative and feared as he was, that he would actually turn the author of the *Claudine* novels into Claudine herself and pair her off with the actress who had become Claudine's incarnation on the stage. The "Father of the Claudines" thus gave birth to the "Twins."

Around 1902 or 1903, Willy forced Colette and Polaire to have their hair cut—it was a fashion to which Claudine had already sacrificed her fictional hair in *Claudine à Paris*. This innovation was wildly applauded by feminists and by hairdressers—although for different motives—and it assumed enormous symbolic significance. Many Parisian women embraced the style, usually to the immense chagrin of their husbands and their conservative families. *Lucie Delarue-Mardrus also had her abundant brown hair cut off, those massive tresses she had worn coiled round her head for so many years. My own hair, nearly five feet of it, the silvery shock of the Amazon [Natalie Clifford Barney], what a crop was sacrificed to the caprice of fashion.*[2]

Like her contemporaries, Colette experienced a vivid sensation of release and liberation, somewhat mitigated by a letter from Sido, who never forgave her son-in-law. She was still thinking of it in 1911 when, in a letter to her daughter, she wrote: "I've always thought it was Willy who made you cut it, out of jealousy. You can tell me now, come on, I was so upset when you destroyed my twenty years of accomplishment."[3] In the years before 1914, as Jacques Gauthier-Villars wrote, "This hair style, like that of a Florentine page, was still shocking, and Colette, in explaining it to her parents-in-law, muttered something about a kerosene lamp that had been clumsily and unfortunately knocked over onto her loosened hair."[4]

But whether it was done because of a bald man's jealousy, or that of a suspicious husband, or whether it was done solely for publicity, once their hair had been cut off under pressure from Willy, Colette and Polaire suddenly seemed to look alike, with their broad faces and level eyes. Colette felt liberated, contentedly reveling in being able to *feel the breeze blowing on my scalp*, but someone else had further plans. Willy was working toward his "Twins." The time was particularly ripe because *Claudine en ménage* described a ménage à trois, and his new trio would arouse all kinds of speculations and triangular fantasies: Willy ordered three identical changes of costume made up for his Twins. There was a plaid jacket and skirt, a white dress, and another suit in bluish gray. And then the Father of the

Claudines escorted his "dressed-up animals" out to restaurants, to theaters, to any fashionable public place where society might notice them. This raised Willy's popularity to such a height that Sylvain Bonmariage was able to report the following anecdote:

"You hail a cab. 'Driver, 93, Rue de Courcelles!'

" 'Right you are, Mister—to Willy's!' "

Of course the cab driver didn't know Willy apart from his famous flat-brimmed hat and the two similarly dressed beauties he escorted around, Colette and Polaire. Street urchins called him " 'the man with the monkeys,' but the monkeys were what attracted attention." [5] On a certain evening, at either the Moulin Rouge, the Casino or the Folies, Papa Willy had ordered the presence of his daughters, specifying the white dresses. *When we three entered our stage box, the audience turned to us so fixedly, silently, unanimously, that Polaire's sensitive antennae quivered and she drew back, as though scenting some trap.*

"What is it, Popo?" asked the ringmaster.

She clutched the door to the box with both hands and attempted to withdraw. "No, no . . . I don't want to . . . please, I can hear what they're all thinking, it's ugly and frightful." Of course, she gave in. But sitting beside me in the glare of the lights, she sighed under her breath, *"I am zad, so zad."* [6] What Colette does not mention is her own suffering, the suffering of a mistreated animal put on display. Her own skin had grown considerably thicker. *I was over thirty, so I had been in training for over ten years.*[7] There is a photograph from this period showing Willy, the bourgeois proprietor, in his opera hat, with his two daughters beside him, both dressed alike, both looking rather grim. Here, as in other photographs—and as in Pascin's great portrait—we can detect in Colette's expression something at once submissive, shut in, half gentle and half guilty; there is *something about which I was vaguely ashamed.* Indeed, around this time her face began to reveal that sorrow all her contemporaries mention, the sorrow we see on the faces of children or young people who are being forced to perform, the sorrow of a circus animal. In ten years, Willy had managed to turn a young and vibrant woman into a woman in chains.

⚜ VOLUNTARY SERVITUDE

"We humans can resist forever if we know how to yield," Colette wrote, unaware that Lenin was speaking in much the same terms of revolutionary strategy. What strikes us first about the slave is the burden of his chains; only afterward are we astonished at his ambivalent and shameful attachment to them. And yet, history has taught us that this condition is actually the forerunner and often the accompaniment of an irreversible urge to resist.

In these early days, one has to listen carefully to catch a hint of resistance in a discourse that seems to be exalting the pleasures of the chain. So in this passage, in which Claudine, in love, speaks of her complicity in the manner in which she is being manipulated: *For a year and a half now, I have felt the slow inner growth of the agreeable corruption I owe to Renaud. I see through his eyes the denigration of great things, the belittling of serious things; futile, silly things assume a vast importance. Yet how can I protect myself against this incurable, seductive frivolity that controls him, and me with him?* [1] This complaint is tinged with an undeniable albeit vague disgust. The attraction of her chains, here called "corruption," is clear, but her conscience intervenes. Contempt is a language, Colette knows its grammar; she also is aware that its structure can be altered while leaving its basic meaning unchanged. Her contempt for the world, learned from Renaud's contempt, logically turns into contempt for herself, and at a given moment it all becomes one. Contempt is contagious, just as love was in Sido's time.

This darker side of the pleasure of enslavement cannot be explained solely by pleasure taken in suffering. Although part of everyone's complex psychological makeup, masochism may be particularly significant in women because of their historical status. And it is exacerbated by the secondary benefits women have gained by becoming comfortable in their lack of responsibility, their idleness. The part masochism plays in erotic experience, in love, is also based on a delight in "corruption," in becoming a part of someone else's fantasy world, and on the taboos that are thereby violated. Here, too, Colette's hyperactive curiosity also played its part, but even curiosity has limits as to what it can be curious *about*. With the infinite repetition of actions that had once fascinated her, the boundaries of the unknown were reduced, the other person became all-too familiar; once satisfied, erotic yearnings arouse a more primal emotion: disgust.

And the part played by fear should not be underestimated. *There are still three or four women who tremble at his name*, Colette wrote of Willy, *three or four that I myself know of. They have gradually stopped trembling since his death. When he was alive, I must confess there was some reason for it.* [2] Like contempt, fear creates ambivalent feelings that underlie its effectiveness. *I know women who went on to lead happy lives after they got over him. They were almost like some lover of fine music mistakenly transported to Gounod's paradise, "Too many harps, Eternal Father, let us have some triangles and clarinettes and a few sharp discords, out of charity!"* [3] Moreover, fear is a powerful force in the implacable dialectic of resistance. If, that is, fear does not destroy its object and turn its force inward to self-destruction, it must finally lead to revolt.

Beneath the attraction of her chains and her suffocating and wide-ranging contempt, boredom and disgust were working away in Colette's subconscious, gradually building up a resistance that exploded into open rebellion. One fine day, we discover that the ground one treads has been mined and that one false step will blow everything to pieces.

⚜ THE ISOSCELES TRIANGLE

After the first shock of the early Kinceler episode, Willy pleaded guilty and begged forgiveness. *The first forgiveness is the one that makes a difference . . . he quickly learned that I was a member of the better race, the female race. The woman who forgave him the first time became, through a clever process, the woman who would submit to it, and who would finally accept it all.* [1]

One imagines that afterward he began to take precautions and to act discreetly. And as the years went by, he gradually lost all respect for his wife. Colette was jealous, the feverish jealousy that invades the entire mind, that affects one's health, that becomes an obsession leading to homicidal thoughts. Jacques-Emile Blanche, who was painting her portrait at the time, described the attacks he witnessed: "She would jump up from the dais where she was posing whenever a car stopped at the door and run to the window to spy on her torturer's farewells to the fine lady whose crested automobile had brought him to Auteuil. On several occasions, the woman betrayed had real convulsions, crying jags, she had to lie down on the couch and have her forehead bathed with eau de cologne." [2] Was her jealousy natural to her, or was it caused by her husband's infidelities? Whatever the case, it tortured her and she waged a determined struggle to overcome it or bring it under control. Her success was, as shall be seen, partial at best: sometimes she would accede to the sisterly feelings and deep affection for women with which Sido had endowed her and she would strike up with her rival an almost narcissistic friendship with strong homosexual overtones; sometimes this relationship would be based on a shared contempt for men. At other times she would have fits of rage, fighter's fatigue, times when, half-crazed, she would try to calm herself with a kind of magic ritual: on these occasions the thought of her rival's wax image stabbed through the heart would become an obsession. Most often, however, her sense of humor saved her, banishing the trite and tempting reprisals, the murderous Othello-like fantasies of jealousy.

Willy on occasion found himself duty bound to play the jealous husband: following the classic formula, he took umbrage only at males; where friendship was concerned, he objected to any relationship with a young person of either sex where mutual esteem and familiarity based on age might have undermined his own omnipotence: *In Paris, I frequently had occasion to note that he was careful to curb my enthusiasm for friends of my own age, male or female, enthusiasms that were for that matter fairly infrequent, but which he would thwart with great skill. . . . "The friendship is unworthy of you," he would say, muttering under his breath, and not omitting to mention the reasons that made it so. . . . He seemed aware that friendship would be a more powerful adversary than love.*[3]

Colette was left to make do with "safe" friendships with young homosexual men, *none of whom excluded me, none of whom loved me,*[4] with a few old friends, and with "unisexual" liaisons. It is clear that Willy's own erotic tastes, aided and abetted by prevailing Parisian fashion, led him to encourage his wife's entering into homosexual relationships; the capacity for such relationships exists, often repressed, in all of us. Such things excited Willy, who did not regard them as threats to himself. The triangle fantasy, voyeurism aimed at sapphic lovemaking, is fairly common among men. The prevailing contempt for women buttressed the belief that such things were unimportant, negligible, a point of view Sylvain Bonmariage was expressing when he wrote: "I maintain that two women joined in a fondness for the embraces of Gomorrah cannot be compared to a pair of normal lovers. Their union is episodic, temporary, passing, and in most cases need not necessarily exclude a man's participation."[5]

When Claudine tells Renaud of her puzzlement at his contradictory reactions to his son Marcel's love for his young friend Charlie —which makes him highly indignant—and to his wife's activities with her intimate friend Luce, which he views with complacency, he replies: *"It isn't the same . . . not the same at all . . . you women can do anything you want, it's charming, and unimportant. . . . I might—but of course I don't—almost go so far as to say that some women need another woman to keep up their taste for men." He was right*, Claudine concludes, with perspicacity, *I could not regard what my husband had just told me as other than a paradox with which he flatters and conceals his somewhat voyeuristic tastes.*[6]

The Georgie episode undoubtedly illustrates Willy's own erotic philosophy. Was the triangle described in *Claudine en ménage* entirely fictional? Willy was to give a waspish description of it that allowed him to settle accounts with his former wife and his former mistress, with both of whom he had broken. He doles out a drop of venom for each of them: Colette— "It was quite natural, granted, and I did not prevent her from allotting herself the noble role in this disturbing story, from describing her worried hesitation, her second thoughts, her gradually weakening refusals . . . lies, lies. In fact, she was the one, almost from the beginning, at their first meeting at the Muhlfelds, who subjected Rézi to an ardent, brutal and tenacious courtship." As for Rézi-Georgie, "Her great pleasure (among a thousand others) was to arrange to have a rendezvous with both Colette and myself in the same room, one after the other, an hour apart. One day, recognizing the conjugal perfume still lingering on her neck, I said:

" 'If my wife ever discovered your tricks, she'd be quite capable of shooting you.'

" 'What's that?' she exclaimed, her eyes widening in fright, 'you mean she carries a gun?'

" 'Always!'

"It was not true.

" 'And why wouldn't she shoot at *you?*' The dear child! How indignantly she said it! I could have wept with joy!"[7]

Colette never mentioned this story, and the texts in which Georgie appears are contradictory. The triangle is clearly described in *Claudine en ménage*, but in *La Retraite sentimentale*, Colette creates a character named Suzie, an American like Georgie, to whom Renaud is attracted and who accompanies the couple to Bayreuth. Claudine does not have an intimate relationship with Suzie, but she is wildly jealous of her. She is overjoyed when the pretentious and flighty Suzie is humiliated by a gaffe she makes that reveals her total ignorance of *Parsifal*, thereby destroying any attraction Renaud might feel toward her.

We do know that in 1901 Georgie was present with the Willys in

Bayreuth from an unpublished letter to Jeanne Muhlfeld written from that town, where the Willys went in 1895, 1896, 1899 and 1901, in search of Wagner and other less lofty distractions. (Proust's Mme de Guermantes's friends consider Odette the kind of woman who "was entirely capable of going off to Bayreuth, for a little fling, that is." [8]) Willy also confirms this: "The trip to Bayreuth is based on memories of an absurd and charming peregrination to Germany and Austria (Carlsbad) made by Colette, Rézi, and Renaud-Maugis, at the latter's expense, of course, following which the trio disbanded." [9] ("At the latter's expense" is apparently not true, since this is the year in which Colette was sent to Bayreuth to represent *L'Echo de Paris.*)

Whether the trio was in fact a triangle is not too important. We should beware of attempting to distinguish in the texts between what is fiction and what is memory, between what may be only subjective and what her inner censor allowed her to reveal of the actual truth.

⚜ A LA SUIVANTE!

What is certain is that throughout this period, Willy had increasingly frequent encounters with all sorts of Claudines. *There are two, three, four of them hanging onto Him, cooing to Him, writing to Him, "My darling, you will marry me if She dies, won't you?" Wouldn't he just! He's already "marrying" them, one after the other. He could pick and choose; he prefers merely to collect. He acquires—and they are only too willing—blotchy, music-loving women of the world who can't spell, eager virgins who write a thousand unprintable things to him in their placid, upright hands, tawny Americans with sinewy thighs, and a whole procession of silly purported minors all wearing flat collars, all with bobbed hair, who rapidly succeed each other, their eyes cast down and their behinds quivering, "Oh, Monsier, I'm the real Claudine, I am . . ." The real Claudine! Minor, my eye!*

And all of them wish me dead, they all invent lovers for me.[1]

This passage inserted into the *Dialogues des bêtes* in 1904 reveals Colette's exasperation. Later, *La Vagabonde* would reflect her relief when she at last got over regarding every woman she met as a former, present or future mistress of her husband. For the time being, however, Colette was consumed with defiance, repressed anger, wild jealousy. *These sinister adolescents were a tide that invaded the very domicile I was still determined to regard as conjugal.*[2]

After the studio, in which the cat, Kiki-la-Doucette, ignoring her owners' torments, had delicately nibbled at peas one at a time, Colette had moved again to a new home in a private house on the Rue de Courcelles. *When it came to decoration, my taste still ran to the eccentric.*[3] One item was chosen with a purpose, however: this was a painted wooden balustrade she had erected down the middle of the salon, dividing the room in half and giving visitors the suffocating feeling that they were penned in. *I kept promising myself to remove it*, Colette recalled, *but I never did.*[4] The balustrade served a symbolic function, separating her from territories she had not yet consciously begun to regard as foreign, enemy land.

Her work room, her own restricted domain, was plainly furnished with a solid table and an Art Nouveau lamp with a green glass shade, an exact replica of one she had glimpsed at her neighbor's, Prince Bibesco. This room was on the far side of the salon, which had to be crossed to reach it. *One day I chanced upon M. Willy and an unknown woman sitting very close to each other. With the casualness of habit, I merely paused for a second and hissed urgently, "Quick, be quick, you poor thing, the next one's been waiting for fifteen minutes!" What did I have to lose? A year earlier, this would have cost me . . . a great deal. But now, M. Willy was flattered, if you can believe it!*[5]

A woman forced into the role of deceived spouse cannot always manage to act with humor or wit in such circumstances. Often, she will give way to her sense of offended dignity. On another occasion Willy saw fit to bring home one of the painter Léandre's promiscuous models, the notorious Fanny Z., who made herself comfortable by tossing her beret on the conjugal bed, opening her dress down the front out of force of habit and offering her voluptuous charms to all comers. "Madame Colette's daughter's blood boiled," but her only course was to "ignore" the intruder; Willy attempted to cozen her, as if she were a child unwilling to greet a grown-up visitor with the proper respect. And in the end, Willy himself began to lose track of his myriad conquests. He would leave his wife to entertain one of them while he was dealing with another. Without raising his voice, *thrusting his redoubtable top-sergeant's chin at me, he would inform me of this new selection: "I hope you will be good enough to wipe that expression off your face when she comes," or he would suggest offhandedly, "Weren't you supposed to be going to spend a couple of days at your mother's this week?"*[6] In the end, the apartment in the Rue de Courcelles harbored a live-in companion, and the slave was exiled to Monts-Boucons to work on her master's next novel. Where was her life leading her?—this was a question she must have been continually, unhappily, turning over in her mind. Still she waited, passively expecting some miracle to turn her husband into a virtuous spouse and save her from the final, terrifying decision to leave him.

⚜ THE STUBBORN CHINA REPAIRER

In fact, Willy's tyranny involved more than his chronic infidelity; he was an authoritative and demanding husband about every detail of their private life. Natalie Clifford Barney—Flossie in the *Claudine* novels—met the couple at the Comtesse Armand de Chabannes's and noted that neither of them "indulged in the luxury of any kind of private life." It was at this party, which Colette recounts in *Mes apprentissages*, that Natalie Barney asked Willy's permission for Colette to perform at one of her garden fêtes in Neuilly: "Willy was kind enough to lend me Colette," who was to recite Pierre Louÿs's *Dialogue au soleil*. "At the end, the audience's attention was distracted by a spectacular apparition: a naked woman riding a white horse with a turquoise harness appeared through the shrubbery: it was Mata Hari."

A later party, Natalie continues, "was planned for a more restricted gathering. And on this occasion I witnessed a painful example of Willy's control over Colette. When I arrived at their house to invite Colette to this little fête I was giving at my property in Neuilly, a rather hastily organized one at which Mata Hari had promised to give an encore performance of her Javanese dances in the all-together before a limited audience of women only, Willy took umbrage at being excluded and refused to give his consent without setting certain scabrous conditions. On the way, Colette confided to me, 'I'm ashamed you were given such a close look at my chains.' "[1]

Colette had been parted from Sido for ten years, yet she wrote to her almost daily, letters in which, out of love for her mother, she omitted mention of the central facts of her life. With the modest allowance Willy meted out to her—she thought it was dazzling—she sent Sido frivolous presents, bars of pure cacao from Hédiard, a quilted bed-jacket, fine woolen stockings, books. But her principal gift was her own duplicity, her picture of a false happiness.

To all outward appearances, nothing had changed, but beneath the surface her resistance was slowly building up.

At first she had tried to get accustomed to her jail, she had suppressed her yearning to escape. *After all, the window was not barred, I had only to slip my tether.* She had learned to compromise to hold her life together; she had become a *china repairer*, as she glumly noted. She learned that domestic art handed down by women over centuries of apprenticeship, the art of waiting, *of dissimulating, gathering in the broken bits, reconstructing, regilding, making the best of a bad thing, losing and seeking all at once the frivolous taste for life.*[2] Her resistance manifested itself only in her infrequent refusal of her master's urgings to appear in society. No, she would not have a "day," she would not become a literary hostess, she would not go to this opening, she would not sit silent through that elegant supper party. A young woman's resistance often takes the form of refusal or inability to adapt. In the Rue Jacob, she had run to lock herself in the bathroom when the bell at the door announced a visitor, she had been silent and touchy—she who was so alive, so full of fun—in gatherings that placed a high value on conversation; she refused to get rid of her rough Burgundian accent, even though it often grated on sensitive ears. She refused to change Gabrielle into Colette. It doesn't seem like much, but the force of inertia requires immense energy. In the presence of her husband's multifaceted and changeable personality, his diabolical ability to adapt, Colette struggled with the ruthlessness of a born peasant to preserve a few shreds of her own identity.

⚜ THE CLAUDINE EPIC: FROM THE CAGE TO THE DOOR

Whether or not her love affair with Georgie was really encouraged, or whether she was doubly deceived in it, she was in fact dressed up and exhibited in company with Polaire, she was rejected as a wife, exploited as a writer. Her revolt was not an open one; it was slipped into the *Claudine* novels. If we read the books in this series through their author's eyes, they reveal the development of her revolt through its various stages. Claudine at school is a sweet schoolgirl, homesick for her village but submissive and romantic, ripe to fall into the clutches of the first Willy-Renaud who comes along; Claudine in Paris determinedly does so. *To obey, to obey, it was a humiliation I had never been subjected to. I almost wrote "enjoyed"* . . . Claudine writes in Paris. *My freedom weighed me down, my independence wore me out; what I had been seeking for months, for even longer, was obviously a master. Free women are not really women.*[1]

Claudine married begins to feel a bitter resentment: the heroine, doubly deceived, flees from the couple that persecutes her, breaks the triangle her perverse husband has complacently constructed, and goes "home" to the country in an attempt to recover her integrity; she writes to Renaud *I am more beautiful, more tender, more honest here*.[2] Her further painful progress toward self-awareness occurs in the guise of Annie in *Claudine s'en va*. The character of Claudine, appeased, finds happiness with Renaud, who has now become faithful to her, but although a part of Colette hopes for an ideal couple, her innermost self finds expression through Annie, who starts off as the submissive wife of a dreaded master and gradually gains an awareness of her enslavement. *He gave me . . . a cage. And for a long time that was all I wanted. . . . Free! What a strange word. There are birds who think they are free because they are allowed to leave their cage, but their wings have been clipped.*[3] Foreshadowing Colette's own future decision, Annie decides to run away: *I would be the solitary traveler . . . that's what life is—time passing, the hoped-for miracle at each turn in the road—and seeking that, I am running away.*[4] The book's title expresses Colette's own confusion, since actually it is not Claudine who goes off, but Annie. *La Retraite sentimentale*, which serves as a kind of epilogue to the symbolic film of the *Claudine* novels, entails the execution of Renaud-Willy: we find Colette's anxiety and ambivalence with regard to her inner struggle set forth in the disturbing character of Annie, wildly preoccupied with her body, pursuing clandestine albeit liberated sensual pleasure, and Claudine in mourning for Renaud, seeking in solitude and in a return to the countryside of her youth some reason for continuing to live—seeking, that is, her own identity. Willy was not blind to the subconscious motives that had dictated Renaud's death; following the publication of *La Retraite sentimentale*, after their separation, with the signature "Colette Willy," he began to refer to his exwife as "my widow."

⚜ THE CHRYSALIS

In Colette's step-by-step evolution in the year 1901 to 1902, the move to the Rue de Courcelles with its divided salon marked a considerable advance. This way station *was the place for shy experiments in breaking the shell. Such attempts*, Colette wrote long afterward, *seem as devoid of significance as the twitchings of an inhabited chrysalis*.[1] Beneath the apartment there was a little room down a narrow stairway in which Colette set up a crossbar and some exercise equipment. This gymnasium was her domain; she worked out her pent-up aggressions in physical activity, building up her muscles for the hard times that lay ahead; *I felt I was exercising my body as prisoners do, not really thinking about escape, but cutting up and braiding their sheet, sewing gold coins into their clothing, hiding chocolate under the mattress.*[2] She was in fact investing capital. For what purpose; how and when? This, she would not discover until afterward.

In the meantime, her private territory was established and visitors to the Rue de Courcelles had to make choices. If they were there to see Colette and not Willy, they would skip the second-floor landing . . . and a growing number of them began to do just that. Robert d'Humières came through the studio and found himself standing under the trapeze; Marcel Boulestin camped out for a few weeks in the small adjoining room; Paul Barlet, an eternally timid young man, one day announced, "Madame, all of your manuscripts that I could salvage are safely at my home in the Rue Fontaine." Another of the "colored people"—Marcel Boulestin, who spoke English, always referred to Willy's "niggers" politely in this way—bravely whispered to Colette one day: *"If M. Willy mentions another project to you, don't get mixed up in it!"* [3]

When the outside world begins to feel sympathy at the slave's plight, when that world begins to grow fond of him, the master begins to lose ground, the spirit of revolt begins to grow. None of all this escaped M. Willy's eye; he began to feel that the ground was slipping from beneath his feet, he felt the first gusts of a wind of independence. And it affected the laborer as well as the wife. Colette had learned all that prison could teach her, and the time had now come to begin thinking of escape. In her earlier manuscripts, the boss's marginal instructions, his reprimands, had been direct, curt, sarcastic as the notes on the theme of a recalcitrant but gifted schoolboy: "Unclear," "Too soon," "Was this agreed between them?" "Yes," "Get on with it!" "Am I married to the last of the lyric poets?" Willy would scoff, with his low opinion of the dubious values of lyricism; he always kept for himself the passages dealing with his favorite character, Maugis. With *Claudine s'en va,* however, his apprentice protested, stood up for her rights, and demanded total responsibility, complete control: *"If you need me for Maugis," Willy said, "leave blanks." I left no blanks. My own way of doing it worked*

very well, my Maugis too spoke pure, authentic Maugis. . . . "Bravo,"
Willy coldly remarked.[4]

Claudine s'en va was published in 1903. Colette had already conceived the idea for a book that would free her from the demanding
Claudine, a book that would be conceived, executed and—sacrilege!—
signed only by herself. She *exuded the Dialogue des bêtes drop
by drop.* It was to be a fundamental turning point in her life as a
woman more than in her life as a writer. In *Dialogues des bêtes*, she
awakened to the notion of a duty toward myself, to the possibility of
writing books other than the *Claudine* books; she allowed herself the
indulgence—*not a wild one, but an honorable one—of not talking
about love. . . . I did not go back to putting love into my novels
with any pleasure until I had regained my esteem for it, and for myself.*[5]
Willy was not interested in her *Dialogue des bêtes*; she knew that it
would not unduly affect him financially to make a munificent gesture
and allow his apprentice to have ownership of a text he could not
reasonably expect to be more than a *succès d'estime*—and in fact, it
was regarded as an innocuous, female production. The book appeared
in 1905; the text has an ambiguous dedication that speaks volumes:
"To amuse Willy"! E. Charles found the work "unbearably pretentious," but Colette was given her first real thrill as a writer by
having her very own preface, written by Francis Jammes: "It falls
to me, living as I do in Orthez, to teach Tout-Paris who you are, to
introduce you to all my acquaintances, I who have never laid eyes on
you. . . . Madame Colette Willy is a living woman, a woman for
all seasons, who dares be natural, who is more like a village bride
than that perverse creature, a female writer." This was an immense
step forward for Colette. She was not to have the same success with
Minne. In its earliest form, *Minne* was a short story that resembled a
fairy tale based on a news item. It contained both a recurrence of the
fantasy of abduction and a tale of the "fortifications." At the time,
these old fortifications at the end of the Boulevard Berthier and the
Rue de Courcelles were a fairly rough area. It was here that *apaches*
hung out, petty crooks and underworld figures whose crimes and
exploits Colette followed in *Le Journal*. This was not yet the day of
the "Brothers of Belleville," or the "Aristocrats of Levallois-Perret,"
but there was one gang, the "Belleville Bombs." In the year 1903,
the newspapers were full of stories about a girl named Deslandes,
known as *"Casque d'Or."* Colette wrote a short, curious story inspired by this locale and wanted to publish it under her own name.

*Willy didn't want that. After an endless struggle and a siege that
would have weakened anyone's resistance, I gave in. I expanded*
Minne *into a novel. In* Les Egarements de Minne *I made her heart-
lessly unfaithful.*[7] (Both works were later combined to form *L'Ingénue
libertine.*) Willy boldly put his name to *Minne* in 1904 and to *Les
Egarements de Minne* in 1905. But that was the end. And, Colette
wryly noted, *it is a good thing for the reputation of the French novel
that the end of my cowardice marked the end of the series, nipping
in the bud Lord knows how many* Minne in Hades, Minne's Daughter,
Minne's Divorce.[8]

The great year of decision was 1904, the year in which both
Minne and the *Dialogues de bêtes* were published. Colette seems to
have spent a great deal of time at Monts-Boucons working away under
orders at *La Retraite sentimentale.* The beginning of her "recalci-
trance" she dates from *La Retraite sentimentale;*[9] she was undergoing
a change: *I had not yet reached the point of wanting to escape from
the conjugal roof, nor from my work, which was the more conjugal
of the two. But I was changing. It doesn't matter if it's slow, the main
thing is to change.*[10]

In 1905 came the *Sept dialogues de bêtes* with Francis Jammes's
preface, and *Les Egarements de Minne.* On September 17, Captain
Colette died. Was it her own sorrow and her mother's sorrow that
made her continue to cling to the flotsam from her foundered marriage, that caused her to hesitate? Such a rupture is never an easy
decision. With her usual openness, Colette admitted that the final
initiative had not been hers. Evidently, she had been made increasingly aware of its imminence.

She made a lucid interpretation of a prediction by Freya, a fortune-
teller:

She gazed at my palms in astonishment:

*"It's . . . oh, it's very strange. I'd never have believed . . . you
must get out of it!"*

"Out of what? You mean I should move?"

*"That too, but that's only a detail. You've got to get out. . . .
You've waited too long as it is!"*

*With that, despite the sibylline terms she used, I was in complete
accord.*[11]

⚜ GETTING OUT: THE POETRY OF EXPULSION

But how was she to get out of it? Envisioning a future without a
husband caused her to hesitate prophetically: *My improvident father*

had left me no sense for the future, and Sido, ever trusting, had cast no more than a frightened glance down the narrow paths her children would follow toward death.[1] She was without money, she had no profession, no training of any sort. Willy had collected both her royalties and the recognition due her as a writer. As far as everyone else was concerned, she was Willy's wife; and she had written the *Dialogues de bêtes.* She had been tainted by the scandals in which her husband had implicated her; she had few if any friends. *Willy knew a great many people, more in the mass than personally. We went out a great deal, but not often by invitation. What upstanding society would have wanted us? . . . As a couple, we aroused curiosity; alone, I aroused none at all. I couldn't have recognized two hundred people by name!"*[2] A separation, a divorce—and Sido would have to be told—were terrifying prospects—like prostitution or an illegitimate child—to bourgeois families like Colette's; they were awful things that happened only to other people. *We others, country girls, had a fearful and unmanageable notion of marital desertion in the 1900s, a notion entailing police, round-topped trunks and thick veils, not to mention railroad timetables.*[3]

Willy doubtless had his own misgivings as well. He was bored with the wife but anxious to retain the employee. And he was sufficiently alert and aware of his own self-interests to have sensed that the goose with her golden eggs was beginning to elude his control. He reacted to the earliest signs of subversion. In the year in which he first began to sense rebellion, 1905, he sold Monts-Boucons. *The house, the little farm, the five or six hectares around it, M. Willy had made a show of giving it all to me, "All this is yours." Three years later, he took them all back: "It no longer belongs to either of us."*[4]

Once again, the trauma of Saint-Sauveur was repeated, perhaps made easier by repetition: Gabrielle had grown stronger in the interim. She made up an imaginary bouquet by which to remember Monts-Boucons: *yellow leaves and cherries half-preserved by the ferocious Comtois summers . . . a bunch of speckled feathers, the plumes of my five goshawks who charmed lizards and snakes.*[5] Before Monts-Boucons, nothing had mattered to her aside from her natal Puisaye, that bouquet of sweet flag, sorb-apples and medlars, water chestnuts and red, pink and white heather. With these two imaginary bouquets, the emblems of her indomitable vitality, Colette turned twenty-nine, thirty years of age. *Already the age at which the forces that will ensure a long life coalesce and organize themselves, the age for resisting diseases, the age at which one no longer dies for any-*

one nor because of anyone. Already this hardening that I compare
to the slow deposits laid down by mineral springs.[6]

And Willy stubbed his toe on this hardened deposit he should
have sensed in his wife as she became less and less "the child," less and
less submissive. In addition, their "business" had fallen on hard
times. The public had grown bored with Claudine, the magnificent
Twins had run their course. Polaire began to refuse to appear in the
threesome, and Willy turned to other, substitute Twins who gave
less satisfaction. Gradually, Colette began to hear indirectly about
these others: *"M. Willy's daughter bought a hat just like yours,"* a
milliner told me one day.[7] Indeed, M. Willy had other plans and
other loves on his mind. The problem was to get rid of his difficult
wife without too much fuss. And he began by coming up with a
way for her to make a living without his help.

Colette was supple, she had kept herself in good physical condition through exercise; she was clever and had a mobile face. At
Natalie Clifford Barney's, she had recited Pierre Louÿs's *Dialogue au*
soleil couchant in the garden with a redheaded American named Eva
Palmer. The author, entranced by his interpreters' Burgundian and
American accents, reported *"I have just had one of the great emo-*
tional experiences of my life."

"Oh, my dear Louÿs!"

"But it's true! I've had the unforgettable experience of hearing
my words recited by Mark Twain and Tolstoy!" [8]

Colette's disappointment and the attention of the gathering were
both distracted by Mata Hari's entrance. On another occasion, however, she had performed in the same garden in an amateur performance of *Le Faune*, a verse play attributed to Willy. And she had
also gone on once or twice as Claudine in Polaire's place.

Obviously, her Burgundian accent presented a handicap to any
possible career as a classical actress. Around 1905, Willy had arranged for her to take lessons in mime with Georges Waag, known
as Wague. Willy had met him at the Cercle de la Plume, where
Wague had created his "Cantomimes." He became Colette's teacher,
and later her partner.[9] He was approximately the same age, having
been born in Paris in 1874, and had been a student of Dupont-
Vernon, a professor of declamation at the Conservatoire. For many
years, he had been playing Pierrot in various short-lived companies,
and had partnered Félicie Mallet and Caroline Otéro. In 1898, he
had married Clotilde Maringuaux, also a professional mime, known

by her stage name Christiane Mendelys or Kerf; she was to be his interpreter, along with Colette, on and off up until 1912.

As usual, Colette went along with her demiurge's wishes. At the same time, the signs and messages being sent by fate—by her subconscious—became increasingly urgent. She was offered a job working as trainer with thirteen greyhounds, but she let the opportunity slip by; perhaps greyhounds would have been too fast for her as yet. The greyhounds escaped; she was caught in another way. M. Willy had met an avid fan of the *Claudine* novels, one more persistent than the rest. One day she dropped by to obtain the autograph of the famous Father of the Claudines. Marguerite Maniez, later to become Meg Villars, managed to supplant Mme Willy. She was some twenty years of age and had been raised in England; most likely she flattered both Willy's Anglophilia and his "paternal vice." After considerable difficulty, she managed to make him marry her, only to divorce him before the First World War.

Willy was so taken with her, however, that one fine day he offhandedly remarked to his wife: *"If it would amuse you to act in a real theater, I have a little prose piece. I'm sure you wouldn't have any trouble getting up a series of suitable performances . . . a tour. . . . It would be a good opportunity to get rid of this horrible apartment, for us to work out some more adequate arrangement for a somewhat different way of life. Oh, just a bit different, there's no rush!"* [10]

Willy's words were carefully chosen, he was attempting to maintain the special ties between them; Colette reacted like a wife dismissed. A breakup is very like a duel: someone has to be the first to draw. And it is always a shock. *While I was only dreaming of escape, the person beside me was figuring out a convenient way to show me the door, my own door.* [11] The gap between thought and deed is a wide one. She was dreaming of flight, of escape, as she had in Sido's day, an imaginary escape guaranteeing her both the intoxication of leaving and the solace of returning. He spoke of separation, of moving out, of changing their lives, of a real separation that would give him liberty to pursue a new love affair along with security in their profitable collaboration. He said "No rush," but she understood "Everything is over." Her plans were all frustrated; there would be no great scene with *loud voices, gestures hitting the ceiling*, no floods of tears or threats of homicide, not even the pride of having been the first to say "It's all over." Yet she had written it in her books— although at this time no one identified her with either Annie or

Claudine. *Since I had not said it, I could only remain silent. . . . I still clung to what I had been plotting to break up.*[12] So she hung on, waiting, *shamefully . . . knowing that I would not be the one to put an end to my misery, but the man who had been the first to have his way with me.*[13]

Exploited, oppressed, deceived and rejected, she was also to be thrown out. Her plaint is not without humor: *It's not easy to make something lyrical out of expulsion.*[14]

Years later, she was to find a way, soberly, in quiet tones, tones much more considered than tones that glorify departure, haughty abandon. How many men have the courage to say publicly, with such simplicity, "Ah yes, I was thrown over," or how many women, for that matter?

When she was cast out of the Rue de Courcelles, Colette left behind her a long period of captivity. The Years of Contempt! At the same time, she took what she had learned away with her: My Prisons or My Apprenticeships.

The new beginning would be difficult, but it would be better. She was embarking on self-discovery, the exercise of a new freedom. For Willy, it was the beginning of the end, the end of his personal Belle Epoque. Time has been the judge.

III
COLETTE WILLY—
COLETTEVILI
Free and Fettered

Solitude . . . freedom . . . my work . . . the new duty of earning my own bread, my clothes, my rent. . . . This was the result of my condition, but also of my wild defiance, my disgust for the world in which I had lived and suffered, a stupid fear of men, of all men, and of women too.

COLETTE, *La Vagabonde*

The illusion of freedom is the same as freedom. . . . La Vagabonde, L'Envers du music hall, L'Entrave, evoke a certain time of my life, six years and surroundings in which nothing seems vile or bitter to me.

COLETTE, *Paysages et Portraits*

November 1906. She was thirty-three.

Willy had showed her the door, "her door" . . . in the beginning, thinking it was only temporary, Colette took refuge with the Marquise de Belbeuf, who welcomed her into her house at 2, Rue Georges-Ville, near the Etoile. She also rented a nearby ground-floor apartment at 44, Rue de Villejust, into which she would move officially following the Moulin Rouge scandal. The Marquise de Morny, or Missy, her nickname, a famous figure in Parisian society, was to be linked with Colette throughout this entire period, up until 1911, when they separated temporarily. Mathilde de Morny, Marquise de Belbeuf, Missy, was through her father the youngest granddaughter of that Duc de Morny who was Napoléon III's illegitimate brother, the great-granddaughter of the Empress Joséphine, and descended through her mother from Louis XV. At the time Colette first met her in 1906—at either the Cercle Victor-Hugo or the Cercle des Arts et de la Mode—she was notorious for the affair she was currently having with one of the Poniatowska princesses and she was one of the leading figures in the Lesbos of the Belle Epoque.

Ten years older than Colette, the Marquise had played the part usually taken by a male lover in the Willy-Colette separation. Colette was fundamentally monogamous, and Willy had hurt her so cruelly that she had conceived an enormous distrust for the entire male gender. For reasons already noted and that were exacerbated by his growing desire to get rid of her, Willy had thrust his wife into female arms that could provide for her the material support he was so eager to avoid. Bonmariage: "On the day of the Departure for Gomorrah, Willy joked and remarked, 'Well, at least no one can call me a cuckold!' "[1] So Missy plied the oars of the pleasure craft, and Colette escaped from conjugal storms into calmer waters. Missy's emotional and probably her financial support were necessary. Colette had not chosen this woman by fluke; she had a very explicit maternal side that made the passage possible. Female freedom was a rocky coast, the approach to it terrified more than one woman less radically alienated than Colette. A guide was needed to extend a helping hand, someone like Sido; so Colette took the plunge, she made the crossing.

Colette's letters in November of 1906 refer to both her addresses. If she is not in her apartment in the Rue de Villejust, she is at the Marquise's, Rue Georges-Ville—"a seven-month-old child would have been aware of that much." In her writings during this period and in later evocations of it, however, her memory retained only the solitude of her ground-floor apartment for "single ladies." *When one is a single lady, that landlord's bête noire, his terror and pariah, one takes what one can get, one beds down where one can, experiencing the coolness of bare floors.*[2] Set aside for lovemaking—clandestine or not—and for work, the ground-floor apartment in those days traditionally meant a comedown in the world, the frequent shelter for the loneliness of old age. Here, Colette moved all her worldly possessions; there were not a great many, since she left most of them to her husband—rented them to him, bad risk as he was. She took the cat, the dog the couple were later to leave with a third party to spare it the difficulties of divided custody, a large black trunk; with these she set up house in her new home, along with her bust by Masson, *my portrait by Ferdinand Humbert, a lithograph by Forain showing me with only one eye, the photograph of a portrait of Renée Vivien by Lévi Dhurmer, a fish service that had never encountered a turbot of equal quality in my home, a small gouache depicting me in all the glory of my twenty-eight months, my glass paperweights (which I still have), books, and my lamp with its lilac flowers in mauve-colored crystal . . . a dwarf Japanese tree that didn't like to be moved and that died after its change of domicile.*[3]

Thirteen years of married life, more than half of which had been spent in apprenticeship, had left this dowryless young woman with very little, although she had worked to repay her husband with six successful novels. The house where she lived would later be replaced by a luxury apartment building; at the time, she enjoyed *its modest amenities, its slummy charm.* Colette had never before lived on her own; like so many women she had moved straight from her father's and her brothers' house to the home of her husband. *On the first night I spent in this ground-floor apartment, I left the key outside in the door. It wasn't absentmindedness, it was trust. I never trusted any shelter as I was to trust that one which cost me 1,700 francs a year.*[4] There were three rooms, one of which was flooded with sunlight. In the mornings she could hear the carriages as they slowed down outside her window before turning onto the avenue. Separated

from them by her tulle curtain and the windowpane, she felt close
to these *dear human beings* passing by so close to her. *I dedicated
to them my passionate unsociability, my lack of experience of human
nature, my shyness that was part of my nature and had nothing to
do with cowardice.*[5] On the edge of the tub before the wood charcoal fire stood a pitcher for cold water, a pitcher for hot. *This kind
of comfort could have suited me for years.* She would have been
happy to live there forever, walking her animals in the Bois in all
kinds of weather, watching from her window men and women go
by on horseback, other *human beings.*[6] But the building was about
to be torn down; the invisible American owner let it be known that
she would pay a tidy sum to recompense her for moving out.

Colette long cherished the memory of this ground-floor apartment
because it was the place where she served her apprenticeship in living
alone, a solitary, laborious apprenticeship that taught her self-respect.
In the beginning, however, things were hard: *I had brought with me
my ancient, faithful fear that was not soon to leave me. I would leap
to my feet at each ring of the bell . . . often merely announcing
that someone had just slipped a letter under my door.*[7] Afraid of a
letter full of affection and demanding she return to her husband, at
the same time half hoping; but the only letters he wrote were business letters, demanding compliance: *"I am made in such a way that
Rancor has always been an ardent part of gratitude." "See here, my
dear . . ." "Your farcical ploy of not returning my manuscript to
me," "We have been business partners, don't let us become enemies.
I promise you'll gain nothing by it . . ."* But none of his letters
ever asked me to retrace the path that had taken me from the Rue
de Courcelles to the Rue de Villejust. In my tiny ground-floor flat,
therefore, I became accustomed to the thought that here I was and
here the flavor of my life would have to change, like the bouquet of
wine changes according to the slope on which the vines are planted.*[8]

⚜ The Moulin Rouge scandal

Colette had been taking lessons in mime in the Rue de Courcelles
from Georges Wague, a follower of Debureau, since 1905; on
October 1, 1906, at the Olympia Music Hall, she had appeared in a
mimodrame entitled *La Romanichelle* with Paul Franck. On November 8, 1906—that is, very shortly after her "expulsion" from her husband's domicile—Colette wrote a letter to her instructor asking him
to come to give lessons to the Marquise as well: Missy was eager to

play Franck's role at the Cercle (either the Cercle des Arts et de la Mode or the Cercle Charras, it is not clear which). Wague's account book indicates that on November 16, he was paid 120 francs for six lessons. Everything still seemed to be going along swimmingly between the two couples, Willy-Meg and Colette-Missy. An article by Fernand Hauser dated November 17 describes the very "Parisian" ambiance that surrounded the two couples at the time.

"It was whispered around Paris: Have you heard the news? The ex-Marquise de Belbeuf is going to perform in pantomime with Mme Colette Willy!" The journalist paid a call at Rue Georges-Ville: " 'Here's the gossipmonger,' the author of *Dialogues de bêtes* exclaimed as I was shown in. 'What business is it of yours if the Marquise wants to appear onstage with me? We're performing at a private club and it doesn't concern the newspapers.'

"A man dressed from head to toe in velvet and carrying a palette came into the room: it was the Marquise in costume for her role in *La Romanichelle*, by P. Franck and E. Mathé, a role she was to perform that very day. In her low voice, the Marquise announced, 'I'm performing at the Cercle tomorrow. . . . One amuses oneself as best one can. But why should you tell your readers this? I can't allow . . .'

"At this point Willy, the author of *Claudine à l'école*, entered the room:

" 'Marquise,' he said, 'since a reporter for the *Journal* is here, you might as well give in; he'll get it out of you in the end.'

"After the rehearsal, Willy congratulated both the Marquise and Colette, and when the latter gave him a flirtatious look, he remarked: 'When Madame was married to me, she never looked at me like that!'

"Whereupon the assembled company shrieked with laughter." [1]

A few days after this, Colette wrote a letter to the *Cri de Paris*, dated November 25 and published on December 2, complaining about gossip writers in general, and reproaching the editor for an article he had printed under the title "All in the Family." "This article," she wrote, "makes us all—my friend Willy; the Marquise; myself; and the calm and gentle English dancer Willy chooses to call Meg—look like some kind of salacious commune. . . . You ought not link together so . . . intimately in your readers' minds two couples who have arranged their lives in a completely normal way, one that suits them and is entirely to their liking."

On November 28, Colette appeared at the Théâtre Marigny in the role of Paniska in *Pan*, a pantomime by Charles Van Lerberghe with music by Robert Haas. The Marquise de Morny, according to *L'In-transigeant*, was to have played the role of Pan, but at the last minute she had withdrawn in favor of Georges Wague. Intimidation? In any case, many thought she had been the one playing the role, and Wague noted that people turned away with a smile when he went by. "Everyone takes him for the Marquise de B.," a reporter noted in *L'Intransigeant* on December 17, 1906. "One of my girl friends murmured this sentence, which says it all: 'And of course, she does *look* like a man!' " [2]

But this was no more than a skirmish. The scandal occurred on January 3, 1907, fed by sensational reports in the press and by gossip that had for years, thanks to M. Willy's public flaunting of his private affairs, been repeated all over town. For once, this man who had become the leading expert in this sort of self-publicity, who had all along been a willing accomplice, ended by becoming a victim. The actual scandal was fomented by people in Missy's circle—aristocrats didn't condone scandal when it included one of their own.

Theretofore, the Marquise had been content to restrict her appearances to amateur performances in private clubs; now, however, she had written the scenario for a pantomime entitled *Rêve d'Egypte* —*An Egyptian Dream*—and it was to be given a series of ten performances at the Moulin Rouge. The scene was set in the Egypt of the Pharaohs; a mummy awakens from her eternal sleep, divests herself of her wrappings and, almost naked, mimes the tale of her former loves. The posters were designed to arouse as much curiosity as possible: "Yssim? / And Colette Willy / in *Rêve d'Egypte* / a Pantomime by Mme la Marquise de Morny." It took no great intelligence to recognize the enigmatic "Yssim"—particularly since the Morny family crest was printed directly below it on the poster. The first performance was scheduled for January 3. Missy's husband, the Marquis de Belbeuf, was no more pleased than the Morny family by the Marquise's public exhibition of herself in a theater; there was still a smell of sulphur surrounding women on the stage. He made plans to attend the performance in the company of friends from the Jockey Club; the Morny family filled the house with hired thugs. Willy also planned to be there in a stage box alongside his new companion, Meg Villars.

The performance began. At the moment when Colette and Missy were to exchange a long, rapturous kiss onstage—a kiss that was obviously not simulated—the audience, seeded with the Marquis de Morny's hirelings, began to shout protests and to boo. Willy then stood up in his stage box and began to applaud ostentatiously. The public's fury was thereupon diverted to the complacent husband and he was forced to depart in a roar of booing while the other husband, the Marquis de Belbeuf, slipped away out a side door. "It is almost impossible to describe to respectable readers," Felicien Pascal wrote in *L'Eclair de Montpellier* on January 7, 1907, "the revolting scandal created by the comportment of Mme La Marquise de Belbeuf, dressed as a man, and Mme Colette Willy, in her husband's presence, a scene so repugnant that the audience was forced to intervene and demand order. . . . M. Willy, the husband . . . was so amused and complacent at a pantomime that could just as well have been a reproduction of scenes from the private life of the three persons involved and it presented a spectacle of such audacious immodesty that the entire audience rose up against them."

Willy saw fit to reply in the same paper on January 15: "It is not true that I was forced to leave my box; I left of my own free will because the pantomime was over (an entirely innocent one, I can assure you); whereupon, 150 or 200 men then made as if to attack me, true, but since I had a half-dozen strapping and determined friends to protect me, the 150 or 200 knights-errant, evidently feeling there were too few of them, and perhaps insufficiently paid for their work, abandoned the fray. It is true that they made a lot of noise, but noise does not make right, and I am still waiting for an explanation of the attempt being made to hold me responsible for the actions and behavior of Mme Willy, from whom I am separated *de facto* and expecting this separation to become *de jure*.

"If you deem me wrong (and this is the sole wrong that can be imputed to me) for having attended the first performance of *Rêve d'Egypte*, here is the explanation for my presence. A few hours before the performance, I received a bravely anonymous telegram couched in highly insulting terms, containing threats that my 'filthy face' would be smashed in and forbidding me from going to the Moulin Rouge on that particular evening. Obviously, therefore, I went."

Willy was clearly not prepared to stand up for his wife. Another letter, this one from Meg Villars to Willy's son on February 10, 1907, gives further news of the scandal, and some insight into the woman who wrote it: [3]

"To begin with, the Moulin Rouge was filled to overflowing with the most elegant people in Paris. All Prince Murat's friends were there, all the Bonapartists, and all scandalized at one of the Morny's taking to the boards. When Papa and I arrived, the entire audience stood up and turned to our box with a low growl. The pantomime began. There were forty musicians in the orchestra, and even when they were all playing it was impossible to hear a note for the noise. The whole audience was booing, blowing horns, yelling 'Down with dykes!' I stood up all alone in the box and applauded—Papa couldn't do this, of course, since it would have looked like he was still living with her. I did it, not because I think Colette is a a good actress (she isn't) and the Marquise is just *awful* . . . but . . . I enjoyed showing I wasn't afraid of them. . . . Then they began throwing seat cushions and candy boxes onto the stage . . . neither Colette nor Missy were struck. The curtain came down at last, and then everybody turned on us and yelled 'Cuckold, Cuckold!' screaming at Papa, who naturally hit the first person who got to him with his walking stick. . . . The duty police dashed up and stood around Papa, and four hefty boxer friends, and you know I'm pretty strong myself. . . ."

Following this memorable evening, the prefect, Lépine, had the play banned upon the urgings of the Morny family. *Rêve d'Egypte* was replaced by *Songe d'Orient*, and Georges Wague, to whom Mayrague, the proprietor of the Moulin Rouge offered 300 francs a performance (actors received only 5 francs on the average), took over the Marquise's role. Despite an announcement by the management, however, audiences continued to believe that Missy was still playing the part, and there was continued booing: Willy was challenged to attend the performance. The impassive artists performed as though oblivious to the hullabaloo and were in the end applauded for their courage. There was one more performance on January 5, after which the pantomime was taken off the bill; it was to be performed again in March, but this time in Nice.

For once, scandal had turned against the interested parties. Willy was fired from *L'Echo de Paris*. Colette was forced to take refuge in her ground-floor apartment and to stop living openly with Missy. A campaign of denigration, gossip and caricatures was aimed against the two outrageous couples and their provocative "understanding." There was a caricature by Sem entitled *"Claudine en ménage"* that showed a scantily clad Colette in Egyptian costume clasped in the arms of the Marquise, who was wearing a riding habit with a top hat. Another, dated 1907 and entitled "After the Races," was a cartoon strip showing Paris society on parade, with Willy, "the cab-driving Usherette," holding the reins and Colette and the Marquise behind him in the fiacre; it was entitled "The Morganatic Marriage."

Colette put up a dignified front. When questioned by Paul La-gardère on the event all of Paris was talking about, she gave a jaunty and plucky reply: "My impressions? . . . very dim. I'm a bit dis-gusted by the cowardice of those who saw fit to hurl insults at me yesterday evening, such gallant knights who acted so bravely . . . because it went that far, and I only avoided getting hit in the face with a chair because I was able to shield myself in time. . . . Do you call that nice?

" 'Forget it, Colette,' the Marquise de Morny whispered, 'forget it. . . . My dear sir, last night we saw gentlemen acting like lackeys. Let them be and let's forget about it. . . .'

" 'So long as they leave us alone,' Colette Willy said, a bit nervous nonetheless. 'You asked me a while ago if I had stage fright. No, that's not in my nature. Look, I'm not trembling. I assure you that such displays don't frighten me, and I will go on again, if my en-gagement for this evening isn't canceled because of them, and if I am not forced to leave the country to practice my profession.' " [4]

Willy and Colette presented a united front to the attacks of "gentlemen" who had their enemies beaten up by hired thugs, just as in the eighteenth century. The tenor of Willy's letter to L'Eclair de Montpellier has been noted; his dismissal from L'Echo de Paris made him furious. For once, scandal had not paid off. The end of Meg Villars's letter to Jacques Gauthier-Villars seems to hint at a growing coolness in that couple's relationship. Meg Villars herself was also affected: "The terrible aftermath of Colette's scandal is that Papa has lost his job at the Echo de Paris. You can imagine what that means to us, especially since we've lost our money. Yesterday evening, he told Colette she had been terribly selfish, but her only reply was 'Oh, sorry!' and she went on talking about her own affairs. And she knows that everything is her fault; I'm completely disgusted with her, and even the Marquise seemed a bit put out at seeing her so changed!" Willy applied for a legal separation on January 23, 1907, some two weeks after the scandal, probably on the urging of his new companion who, according to Jacques Gauthier-Villars, threatened suicide to make Willy marry her—which he eventually did on June 15, 1911. Willy's divorce petition states that Colette had not been domiciled with him since November 1906, and that she had publicly and insultingly demonstrated her firm in-tention not to return to the conjugal roof.

Colette instituted a countersuit on January 31, 1907, through her lawyer, Maître Mignon, claiming blatant infidelity.

⚜ DIVORCE

Having "shown her the door," Willy now accused Colette of desertion. Still under the spell of her long years of servitude, Colette attempted to patch things up and wrote a very tender letter to him in February.[1] It gradually became clear, however, that Willy was far from willing to give up Meg and that he had no intention of ever living with Colette again. On February 13, 1907, they both appeared in court with their separate petitions, which were deemed reciprocally supportive and which the court accepted; they were filed in the First Chamber of the District Court of the Seine. The legal process ground on, and three years later, under the Law of 1884, they were automatically divorced. Legally, and in their affections, since relations between them had continued to deteriorate during the three years of their separation.

The break did not occur all at once, however. In the summer of 1907, both couples were in Crotoy, living in neighboring villas. Jacques Gauthier-Villars went to stay with his father and reported that "their relations appeared to be excellent, and their literary collaboration continued as in the past." [2]

The Marquise gave a New Year's Eve party in 1907 attended by Willy, Colette and Meg Villars. This is the period when Colette was writing what became *Les Vrilles de la vigne*. On April 27, 1907, *La Vie Parisienne* published *Toby-Chien Parle*, a short story included in a collection of stories the following year. According to Bonmariage, Charles Saglio is supposed to have asked Willy's permission to publish *Les Vrilles de la vigne* and *L'Envers du Music Hall* in *La Vie Parisienne*. The magnanimous Willy granted his permission: "Tell Saglio I must thank him for demonstrating that his author has profited from my instruction." In *Les Vrilles de la vigne*, there is a section addressed to Willy, one for Meg Villars, and several to Missy. And during these years, Willy tried to repeat with his new companion the same process that had turned out so successfully with her predecessor: he got her to write *Les Imprudences de Peggy* in 1911, a novel containing attacks on Colette as well as the spicy adventures of some fairly vicious English schoolgirls. He also sent Meg off on a vaudeville tour as a singer. Colette however, who mentions Meg's new career in a letter to Georges Wague as early as the summer of 1908, refused to indulge in disparaging remarks about Meg and continued to see her on and off over the years, even after the latter's divorce from Willy in 1920. She was to make only one bitter-sweet reflection in this respect, in *La Vagabonde*, and even this she disguised as fiction; the character of Renée is a picture of Colette only in part (she is the divorced wife of a famous painter, Adolphe Taillandy, who is very like Willy): *Sometimes I dream with luke-warm commiseration of his second wife. . . . Is she still blissfully happy and in love, enjoying the fruits of what she regards as her vic-tory over me? No, by now she has probably begun to discover, ter-rified and powerless, the man she married . . . is she merely at the edge of the abyss, or has she fallen to the bottom, her flesh bloody from the same thorns that left their scars on me.*[3]

Willy did not willingly relinquish the slave he had promoted to the rank of partner when she began to show her independence. For his next novel, Colette turned out some twenty pages of description for which he was forced to pay the astronomical sum of 1,000 francs. *A thousand prewar francs, a thousand francs after our separation, a thousand francs for twenty pages, when for the four Claudine volumes . . . I was sure I was dreaming.*[4]

So gradually she ceased to harbor any illusions about a possible rec-onciliation; she lost any desire for one. Her new freedom had its underside—solitude, anxiety about the future—but it was also a tonic that gave her strength to go on to continual discoveries. At the same time, the experience of her marriage was transmuted into a new awareness, awareness of its abnormality, awareness of the man she had married. She was continually uncovering new betrayals, new lies. The final blow was dealt when Willy, short of funds, sold the rights to the *Claudine* novels to various publishers, the first two and the fourth to Albin Michel for 5,000 francs, and the third to the *Mercure de France* for 4,000 francs. The contract with the *Mercure de France* in fact bears only Willy's signature, which confirms the version contained in Colette's letter to Léon Hamel of February 28, 1909. In *Mes apprentissages*, on the other hand, she suggests that her signature was coerced out of her, but Colette may have been con-fused about details after so many years. To Hamel, she wrote: *In short, you should know that without my permission he sold all the* Claudines *to the publishers for next to nothing, and that these books that (morally) belonged entirely to me are now forever lost to us both. It's almost as though, given the conditions under which he turned over the four* Claudines, *he not only wanted to be paid a nig-gardly sum, but that he wanted to ensure that even after his demise I would never be able to gain possession of these books that are mine.*

I was terribly upset by it, my dear friend, and wrote to him. He re-
plied to my despairing cry with a very cold, threatening letter, and
I think that after the necessary explanation that will have to occur
upon his return from Monte Carlo, everything will be irrevocably
over between us.[5]

After this, the couple's story entered its final phase: an ugly divorce, during which the protagonists' typically Parisian notoriety
and the aura of scandal that surrounded them—added to money problems and literary rivalry—all combined to kill an already deteriorated
relationship.

Willy was a miser and carefully concealed his wealth; but then
his wife had come to him without a dowry and there was no question
of her making any financial claims on him. Colette was in real need.
Without Missy's assistance and generosity, she would have had to
share the poverty and insecurity of the other music hall singers who
were her comrades on the vaudeville stage.

Willy had always pretended poverty; he habitually refused to pay
his bills. Colette, for example, had agreed to leave all their furniture
for Willy in return for a monthly rent. She was forced to sue for
this unpaid rent; a judgment was handed down by the *Cinquième
Chambre* on May 3, 1911.[6] On two occasions, Willy referred to
this "filthy lawsuit underhandedly brought against me by my ex-
wife." [7] According to him, she was trying to crush him, to destroy
him with the help of some of their mutual friends such as Marcel
Boulestin. Willy brags about having dissuaded Boulestin from testify-
ing by employing some kind of fairly vicious blackmail, most likely
something to do with his homosexual books and life-style (which
were, we will recall, a frequent target of legal proceedings). "Were
I to relate," Willy had the gall to write to his friend Jules Marchand,
"all the ignominious things I have been subjected to, I would be
accused of exaggeration." [8]

He joked to Bonmariage that Colette and the bailiffs both seemed
to favor the same shade of blue notepaper. This man who had stated
that "truth is one's personal view of events," and that "morality consists of a group of conventions that are needed for the peace and
protection of society, adherence to which is in no wise obligatory,"
could also tell his friend: "I have creditors, and every day my 'ex'
passes on to me bills she ran up when we were living together and
which she imputes to me. Well, I am refusing to pay them. I am
having my royalties from the theater collected by trusted collaborators who pass them on to me under the table, and I am going to

sell all my rights to my publishers for a lump sum. In this way, I will lay my hands on some 25,000 francs, maybe 30,000, whereas if I got 2,000 francs in royalties I wouldn't be able to touch it because of the garnishees. This way, I'm home free!" [9]

Colette's letters during this same period reveal her real financial need: *You think I'm staying in Paris on the 26th just to get out of it. . . . If it weren't for the lecture at La Femina, I would arrange to do it, but the lecture will bring in fifteen louis* (Letter to Georges Wague, fall of 1908). *I got the two biggest fees of my life, which is always welcome* (ibid., September 1, 1908). *I'm shocked . . . at having been paid 973 francs for two performances* (ibid., September 1908). *If the Alhambra can't let me have as much as the Gaité-Rochechouart, then so much for the Alhambra! It's one theater that could at least pay me a reasonable fee. And then, do I always have to put up with never getting more than five louis, when I have a name and I bring in the customers? When will I be able to raise my prices—when I'm as old as Otéro? . . . Outside Paris 200 francs, in Paris 150 francs. They should be able to pay that . . .* (ibid., April 29, 1909).[10] After the breakup, Willy realized that he would be unable to retain his partner and discard his wife at the same time. So he removed his mask and ceased to treat her with any consideration. Poverty and vaudeville turned Colette into a *hard and honest businesswoman. It is a profession even the least-talented woman can learn, if her freedom and life depend on it.*[11]

From this point on, Colette abandoned her role as an obedient and submissive wife; she insisted, she fought, and in the end, she won. She began by seeing to it that future editions of the *Claudine* novels would note the dual authorship of Willy and Colette Willy and contain the following foreword, signed by her exhusband:

"The Willy-Colette collaboration having come to an end, it has become necessary to give each his or her due and to replace the original signature to this work with that of Willy and Colette. For typographical reasons, my name is placed before that of Colette Willy, whereas for strictly literary and for other reasons, hers should come first."

Future books would be signed Colette Willy, *La Retraite sentimentale* in 1907, *Les Vrilles de la vigne* in 1908, *L'Ingénue libertine* (a reworking of the two *Minne*'s) in 1909; in the latter volume, Colette forced Willy to insert the following dual notice: "By mutual consent, the authors of *Minne* and *Les Egarements de Minne* have deemed it necessary to rework these two volumes. This reworking having been the labor of Mme Colette Willy alone, the two collaborators have felt that she alone should sign it. Signed, Willy." To this, Colette added: "It goes without saying that by accepting sole responsibility for this volume, I have out of basic literary fairness included in my alterations the suppression of those portions of the work owed to the collaboration of the preceding signatory." This "collaboration," as has been noted, consisted of a number of innuendoes and nasty remarks which Willy, as was his habit, had aimed through her at his personal enemies. For example, Lucien Solvay, who is called "Solvey" in *Minne* and "Sioney" in *L'Ingénue libertine*, had been insulted in the former book as "Solvey, known as Pipi la Vipère, a Belgian bookie, [was] seriously wounded and called Frisé to help him." Colette wrote to Lucien Solvay in February of 1909:

Dear Sir, during the days when Willy did me the dubious honor of signing my novels, he would often insert into my books phrases designed to satisfy his personal grudges. He called this "collaborating." In Minne, *this collaboration consisted in endowing various crooks with the names of honored colleagues, notably your own. . . . My first concern has been to remove these unfortunate epithets.*[12]

Colette was unfortunately unable to "purify" the *Claudines*, to which she had no legal right. (Willy's name was removed from the *Claudines* in the collected edition of Colette's works in 1949, but had to be replaced on his son's insistence in 1955.)

When we realize that Colette was devoting equal attention to both her stage and her literary activities at this time, the list of her books published during these years, which includes a play, *En Camarades*, written and performed in 1909, reveals the effort and discipline she must have exercised to write as she did, whenever she had a free minute, between rehearsals, on tour, in her dressing room. *Writing, the pleasure and the pain of the idle. The fragile story I am constructing crumbles to bits whenever the delivery man rings, whenever the bootmaker presents his bill, when the lawyer telephones, and the attorney, whenever the theatrical manager calls me into his office for some performance.*[13] It would not be until 1910—with *La Vagabonde*, published in installments in *La Vie Parisienne* beginning on May 21 of that year—that her own literary talent, separate and apart from Willy's influence, would gain public recognition and praise.

La Vagabonde, however, is still full of Willy; it shows very plainly Colette's view of him when it was written. (M. Raaphorst-Rousseau had examined a copy in the possession of Maurice Goudeket; the characters' real names are noted in the margin, with comments, by Colette herself.) Renée Néré, ex-Taillandy, is a former *femme de lettres* who has turned to performing in vaudeville. Renée's new-found freedom in her work and her rejection of her lover are haunted by her memory of the nightmare of her marriage, her fear of her former husband.

⚜ THE FARCICAL BARONESS

Taillandy is obviously a portrait of Willy, and although the character is largely an unsympathetic replica of the heroine's first great love and the pain he caused her, he is fairly innocuous com-pared to the base caricature Willy confected—or caused to be con-fected—of his ex-wife in his novel *Lélie fumeuse d'opium* (*Lélie the Opium Addict*), published in 1911. The novel had been commis-sioned from Toulet, but Curnonsky seems to have had a hand in it as well, and when Willy's personal spite was not sufficiently vented by his low collaborators he obviously added his own touches. Set in Paris with a strong odor of opium in the background, a setting with which Toulet was very familiar, the characters included a young and fair English girl in a secondary role, very like Meg, a girl fond of wearing socks and no underclothes, and the Baronne Gousse de Bize (a scurrilous name one might render as "Lumpy Dyke"), an inveterate "amphibian"—Willy's word for homosexual or bisexual—who is vicious, crafty and avid for young bodies of both sexes, whose heavy Burgundian accent and sayings, along with her pretended passion for "nature," made it impossible for even the most ignorant reader to mistake the original.

Willy sent Toulet a draft of *Lélie* with the following: "As you said, embroidery won't do. It must be completely rewritten. I im-plore you to undertake it, at any price you name." [1] Willy was obviously ready to pay money to get his revenge on his ex-wife. He goes on to state his desires to his "nigger" quite baldly: "The Baronne de Bize, I want her to resemble—blatantly—(and for 'reasons,' as Verlaine stammered) Mme Colette Willy, both physically and in her predilections, with the exception that that poor perverted peasant girl was never able to find what she was after, *id est*, a companion-able cat and a human she could get along with rolled into one. And of course, unless you are of a different opinion, there can be no question of imputing to the Baronne Gousse de Bize the least smidgen of literary ability, can there?"[2]

Willy spared nothing in venting his bile on the character of the Baronesse; Toulet may have toned her down too much to suit him. He wrote again: "I'm working full tilt. Bastienne has been fixed up. It had to be done! And Lélie! You know, my dear Paul-Jean Toulet, why it had to be done. It was necessary!" He added: "Right or wrong, I've put in a lot of myself I didn't want to keep."[3]

The text is a combination of Willy and a kind of talent owed to Toulet (or Curnonsky). The combination of their cynicism and peculiar style of humor led to passages and bits of dialogue in which each seems to be taking turns.

Willy's main interest was in the portrait of Bastienne Gousse de Bize (Colette), and it is vile enough to be the work of that mean-minded author whose signature was never any guarantee of the slightest authenticity: "Not that Mme de Bize was any spring chicken. Her forty years were all-too evident from the bitter creases in her sunken cheeks left by her perpetually commanding smile; her exaggerated hips that had in bygone days been praised by friends of both sexes for their arrogant curves were now, unfortunately, turned to fat. Her short, thick waist revolved above those hips, reminiscent of a gourd rather than an amphora, and a network of crows' feet creased her Kalmouch temples, her gray eyes and her eyelids smeared with Kohl, crafty eyes like a peasant's, and made an amusing contrast with her mouth, which was always held childishly open in a way she had carefully practiced before her dressing-table mirror. . . . Thus—not to mention the way her sweat-frizzled curls concealed her high and masculine forehead whose nudity she hid with considerably more care than she concealed that of her rear end—Bastienne dreamed. For a time, she forgot . . . her everyday worries, always hidden beneath a false and obtrusive gaiety, her fear of approaching age, fixing her lust on ever-younger prey, on Lélie who was still but a child, on gigolos whose mother she could easily have been . . . her hidden terror of the reprisals she knew her infamies deserved, reprisals that she sensed were patiently being planned in the dark, reprisals she knew would be horrible."[4]

Insult and defamation were followed by threats. Willy was the wrong person to have as one's enemy, but it must have been worse to have him as one's husband. The terror he inspired is easily understandable. At the end of the book, the "baroness sent a ridiculous letter from 'Casamène' "–Colette's name for Monts-Boucons in the *Claudines*–a letter written in Colette's style: "On the nearest of the rounded and monotonous flanks of the Jura one can count the trees in the pure air . . ." After eight pages of these landscape musings, Lélie learns that the Baroness, tired of her "disjointed life, as they say in my belovèd Frenois" refuses to return to Paris and is determined never to abandon her dear little property where she is held captive by "the insidious voices of the spring." "Bastienne felt it was useless to reveal . . . that [the Baroness] was really spending her leisure hours in sharp deals having to do with vaguely illegal sales of furniture, for which she demanded commissions that shocked the employees of the Banque Tierry." [5] This ultimate perfidy on Willy's part was based on a shadowy "affair involving the properties in Auteuil," as we learn from a letter from Colette to Léon Hamel of June 1, 1909: *By an inspired stroke of luck and Missy's intervention, I managed to get some of this back, and I think Missy and I will actually receive some recompense for our labor in the near future. . . . You should be pleased with your capitalist, your capitalists.*[6] Capitalist indeed! Willy's nasty acts were never totally without effect. The novel was published as part of a series entitled "Successful Novels," and sold well to a certain segment of the public. But this last vengeance was, like its perpetrator, mediocre. Almost without anyone's noticing, Willy disappeared from Colette's life and from her literary work, and then from literature itself. This man, who had so adored the glare of the spotlight, died in the dark.

⚜ A ROUGH LIFE

Colette suffered because of Willy, she suffered from her sensational divorce, when her most private scars were laid bare before the public. Through it all, she controlled herself, she displayed an unclouded brow and dry eyes. *Two habits have enabled me to restrain my tears, that of concealing my thoughts and that of using mascara on my eyelashes.*[1] *Tout Paris* took sides for and against. There was endless gossip about their private lives. "At Sacha Guitry and Charlotte Lysès's where they were tearing Willy apart with their teeth, Toulet took a violent stand in his defense and found himself cast out as a partisan of his." [2] He obviously deserved it. Willy had enemies who were delighted to blame the whole thing on him, and Colette had a few friends who sprang, albeit discreetly, to her defense. But by and large, public opinion was on the side of the husband; prejudice

tended to favor him. There was his social position, for one thing, and
the power he had managed to acquire in literary and artistic circles;
and then, above all, he was a man. Colette reverted to her former
state, a poor unknown girl from the country, a girl who was forced
to appear half-naked on stage to earn a living. *During our divorce,*
Renée Néré bitterly comments in La Vagabonde, everyone as much
as held me completely in the wrong and held innocent "the handsome
Taillandy," who was guilty of merely having given pleasure, of having
deceived. And I almost began to agree with them, intimidated as I
was and relegated to my usual submissive role by all the talk going
on about us. . . .
    "What? But he's been cheating on her for eight years, and she
hasn't complained before! . . ."
    I received calls from superior, authoritarian friends who "knew all
about life"; I was visited by older relatives whose most telling argu-
ment was:
    "What did you want, my dear child?"
    What did I want? At bottom, I knew very well. I wanted out![3]
With all the humiliations to which "society" subjected her, a
divorcée forced to turn to vaudeville for a living, Sido's daughter
gritted her teeth and accepted her life with that taste for provocation
persecution often gives to very shy people: *I had had enough . . . I*
wanted, I want to do what I please . . . I want to perform in panto-
mimes, in plays. I want to dance naked if tights hamper me and
destroy my pose. I want to retreat to some island if I so desire, or to
frequent women who live by their charms, as long as they are gay
and full of fantasy, or melancholy and wise like so many femmes de
joie. I want to write sad books and chaste books in which there will
be nothing but descriptions of landscapes, flowers, sorrow, pride,
and the straightforwardness of charming animals that shun men. . . .
I want to smile at every kind face and turn away from ugly, dirty and
evil-smelling people. I want to cherish those who love me and give
them what I have to give: my body that hates to be shared, my tender
heart, my freedom.[4]
Haughtily, proudly, her first impulse was to reject any *blame,*
advice, consolation, even congratulations, and to turn away from the
friends who, in defiance of public opinion, rang her doorbell; public
opinion, so *sacrosanct, sovereign, ignoble.*[5] A few friends stuck by
her, three, four . . . *They were the stubborn ones, the inseparable,*
determined to put up with my rebuffs. How badly I received them,
but how I loved them, and how afraid I was when I watched them

leave that they would never come back.[6] One of these friends was
Léon Hamel. "The Silent One," as Colette called him, was born in
1858, fifteen years earlier than she, in Fontenay-aux-Roses. "Tall,
slim, very distinguished looking, he waltzed well and played tennis,
a man of the world, a dilettante by choice, all made possible by a
personal fortune. He traveled in Europe and in the Far East (Cochin
China, Tonkin, Haiphong), and had lived in Egypt from 1888 to
1905, where he had been an inspector for the Deirah Sanieh, a
body that looked after the properties of Ismail Pacha, the former
Khedive. . . . Upon his return to Paris, he took a ground-floor apartment in the Rue de Florence and formed many friendships in the world
of letters and the theater. It was in this way he met Colette, whose
friend he remained until his death in April 1917." [7] The letters in
Lettres de la Vagabonde are addressed to Hamel for the most part,
along with Georges Wague. The Silent One, with immense tact,
destroyed Colette's letters "so that the originals would not fall into
unfriendly hands, but not without first copying them out into a notebook." [8] The character of Hamond in *La Vagabonde* is obviously based
on Léon Hamel and gives some notion of the relationship these two
extremely shy creatures, both somewhat wary of life, enjoyed: they
would meet in one or the other of their apartments to share modest
and somewhat glum meals spiced with the bitter memories they
shared; after dinner there would be long sessions of bezique.

Colette was to retain her youthful affection for undemanding older
male friends like Masson or Hamel, independent, cosmopolitan, cultivated, utterly faithful. In later years, she was to have many friendships
with younger, not necessarily homosexual, men, and with women.
During this period of her life, however, she felt the need for friendships that made her feel secure, and aside from Missy, her companion
and protector, and Missy's homosexual circles, she does not seem to
have had any friendships that compare with her later friendships
with female friends like Marguerite Moréno (who was away in
Argentina from 1907 on), Hélène Picard, Renée Hamon, Annie de
Pène, Germaine Beaumont or Germaine Patat.

Sido, the irreplaceable Sido, was still alive, and she and her daughter
corresponded regularly when the latter was not visiting her in Châtillon.
How did Sido react in her old age to these events in her daughter's
life, to these unhappy experiences Colette had repressed for so long
partly out of consideration for her? There are no documents containing her precise comments, but it is safe to say that she would have
accepted them with the same equanimity and lack of conformity that

had always been characteristic of her. Her maternal intuition, we can be sure, was not misled by her daughter's white lies about her married life, and we gather she was not overfond of her former son-in-law. Speaking about her mother in a radio broadcast in 1937, Colette related that at the time of her first marriage, Sido had exclaimed: "I adore you, I will pine away if I can't see you often, but nothing in the world could make me live with my son-in-law!" And she had added, "And you can be sure, Minet-Chéri, that I would be even more upset if I were *fond* of your husband! A mother-in-law who doesn't like her son-in-law is a normal thing. But one that is fond of her daughter's husband, that's unnatural, and it doesn't make things easier, quite the contrary!"

On July 31, 1908, Sido wrote: "You're going full time into the theater, so it must be because you want to, and of course you're being paid for it. Well, I would never have supposed you particularly suited to it, you were always somewhat unbendable, and for the stage you have to be supple, physically as well as morally, and I never really thought you had those qualities. You must have become supple in both respects, that's a fact." [9] Sido was well aware that harsh realities had made her stiff, stubborn adolescent daughter more supple. However, along with tender advice, Sido's letters contained love: "That's all for today, my treasure. I'm better, and that's all I ask. As for yourself, try not to come to grief in doing pantomime. Training your torso and your legs, you might cause some pain in your knees." [10]

Apparently she followed her daughter's activities closely. With regard to "Claudine" onstage, she wrote: "Minet-Chéri, you're going to act the Claudine you created, and as you say, it won't be easy. I saw it when Polaire played it, and I was not satisfied with her understanding of it . . . there are certain scenes that should be glided over with a light touch . . . but since you created the literary version, perhaps you will be able to act her." [11] Colette wrote her mother constantly when she was on tour, on the edge of a table, in a restaurant, in her dressing room or her hotel room; she sent her a Sem poster of herself during the Baret tour. Sido was quick to reply (May 1, 1909): "I got the poster, it's very like you, he's even captured your way of holding yourself, tensing your left buttock and thrusting your pretty bosom forward. This is a criticism I am making, and you should profit from it. To stand straight, you have to hold your head level between your shoulders, shoulders back, and all without being stiff or affected." [12]

⚜ Another step down in the world!

Though she was still as precious to her, Sido was older, she was now relatively poor, she lived some distance away. Colette knew that she had to endure the isolation forced upon her by public disapproval alone. In 1906, she wrote to Francis Jammes, a man she had always admired and whose preface to the *Dialogues de bêtes* had given her such pleasure, to thank him for some books: *Dear Sir, I received* L'Eglise habilée de feuilles *and* Pensées du jardin. *I haven't written because I had begun to work in the theater, and I was afraid this would lower me forever in your eyes. You see how I know my place.*[1]

Around 1907 or 1908, she was writing to Robert de Montesquiou-Fezensac: "I have so few friends, dear sir. This is in no way a complaint. Oh, no; certainly not! But I am told that my life is so 'unusual,' and I know many people disapprove, especially since I haven't bothered sufficiently to explain my motives for breaking with everything proper, or that passes for being so. However, let me assure you that I am not really bad, and that there is not a single base motive for anything I have done." [2]

It took courage for "My-Friend-Valentine," a woman of the world, a member of high society, to remain on friendly terms with an "errant femme de lettres," a divorcée, calumnied, impoverished, living off her vaudeville earnings, a woman who, to top it all off, flaunted her bisexuality. It is difficult, and probably nugatory, to try to relate the character My-Friend-Valentine to a particular person; she may be a composite of several of Colette's friends during this period of her life. In any event, she reflects the complex of conflicting attitudes some of her former friends had with regard to Colette. Valentine prefers to say that Colette is "dabbling in the theater," rather than that she is an actress. My-Friend-Valentine is the "proper friend" of Colette and Toby-Chien, a survivor from the former world of Willy, a world *full of traps, duties, prohibitions . . . so far behind me that I can barely remember it.*[3] Torn between her amused irritation and her vague, worried gratitude toward My-Friend-Valentine, Colette acts as a confidante for the minor and unimportant events that agitate her friend's artificial social life. *In the days when I was in pantomime or the theater, My-Friend-Valentine almost disappeared from my life, discreet, in the background, modest. This was her courteous way of condemning my mode of life. I am not offended. I bear in mind that she has a husband in automobiles, a lover who is a fashionable painter, a salon, weekly teas, dinners twice a month.* She turns up anyway, *at the risk of compromising her upstanding position as a wife with a husband, a lover, with an affectionate persistence approaching heroism.*[4]

Valentine is drawn to the "actress's" ground-floor apartment because it fascinates her; she comes into contact with low society there, but she is also attracted by desire for "something different," for something forbidden. Even though regarded with contempt, Colette has become free. And Valentine is made aware by a thousand small details that she herself is a prisoner of her social code. Her friend can indulge in the luxury of lying in bed late in the morning; Valentine sighs and yawns, her eyes are tired:

"Love? Oh, la-la! No time! What with opening nights, dinners, suppers, lunches in the countryside by car, exhibitions and teas . . . this month is terrible."

"I guess you get to bed late?"

"Alas . . ."

"Well, you'd better sleep late or you'll lose your looks, my dear!"
She gives me a look of astonishment.

"Sleep late, me? It's easy for you to say. What about the house, orders to give, all the bills for the provenders? And all the rest of it? What would people think?"

"Oh, I don't know . . . they'd think you were a woman in need of rest!"

"That's easily said . . ." she sighs with a nervous yawn. "You can afford it, you're . . . you're . . ."

"On the outskirts of society . . ."

She laughs heartily, suddenly younger. Then, melancholy again:

"Yes, you can do it. We others, we're not allowed to!" And Colette considers class consciousness: *We others . . . that mysterious plural, that strict free-masonry of those whom the world holds in thrall, exhausts, disciplines. What demi-mondaine could stand up under the daily comings and goings of certain women in society, or even mere mothers of families!*[5]

When Valentine, who still has some vestiges of real feeling beneath her mask, is jilted by her lover, she comes for consolation to the outcast, the experienced woman on the outskirts of society. Just as lying late in bed is denied her, however, so are tears. The real world is a demanding place. *I think of the fact that for three weeks she has been dressing each day out of habit, minutely constructing*

*her fragile crown of hair. . . . For three weeks, for twenty-one days,
she has protected herself against her betraying tears, has darkened
her blond eyelashes with a steady hand, has gone out, received visitors, gossiped, dined. It's the heroism of a doll, but heroism nonetheless.*[6] Colette has more respect than she is willing to admit for this
kind of heroism.

For every "My-Friend-Valentine," however, still kind to her beneath her makeup, there are all the dirty old men who revel in her
seminude performances, and all the virtuous and envious bourgeoise
women who indignantly disapprove of her and snub her when they
meet. The narrator of *La Vagabonde* confides to My-Friend-Valentine:

*"One day at a concert I had to leave, to the great relief of my
neighbor on the right, the 'lady wife' of a municipal councillor."*

"Were you upsetting her?"

*"I made her uncomfortable. She no longer recognizes me, I've been
so altered by my divorce action. Every time I blinked an eye, she
trembled for fear I was about to do something to embarrass her."*

"Ah, I can understand . . ."

"Yes, you can understand. I am very sure of it. You would understand that!" [7]

The tone of voice, the emphasis, both are bitter. Who can understand who has not experienced such things themselves? In her books
told in the first person, Colette maintains a detached tone, but in a
narrative such as *La Vagabonde* she is more frank; it is as though
novelistic fiction somehow protects her modesty, just as the footlight
trough veiled her nakedness on the vaudeville stage. Colette has her
ostrich side, as do so many novelists and actors. She reserves the most
humiliating aspects of her brushes with her former life for her fictional works. Renée Néré, dancer and mime, is persuaded by her
partner Brague (Wague) to perform at a society function. There is
a description of her inner conflict between her desire to earn a handsome stipend and her terror at having to face the society in which
she formerly lived: *To see them again, them . . . those people I had
abandoned with such violence, those people who called me "Mme
Renée," making a point of never calling me by my husband's name.
Those people, those women! Women who deceived me with my husband, women who knew I was being deceived. . . . I still have a silly,
superstitious horror of those salons where I might encounter witnesses, accomplices, of my past misfortune!*

Arriving late in the evening at an address in the Avenue du Bois,
Brague and Renée are ushered into a sumptuous private house by a

supercilious butler who takes them to the *room reserved for the artists*, where Renée refuses to allow him to take her fur coat. *Did he think I was going to wait on the pleasure of the assembled ladies and gentlemen wearing nothing but four blue necklaces, a winged scarab and a few yards of gauze?* Renée's only hope is that she won't be able to see them. *"If only there were going to be some kind of footlight trough between us!"* Brague said. . . . Alas, there wasn't even a stage! *"No matter what I do, I'll be able to see them. . . . Dancing, groveling, twirling, I will see them, and I will recognize them! There in the first row is a woman, still quite a young woman, who was my husband's mistress for a time . . . my sudden appearance has brought back unpleasant memories for her, this woman who suffered because of Adolphe, who would have given up everything for him, who cried bitter, imprudent tears and wanted to kill her husband, to kill me into the bargain, so that she could run off with Adolphe. . . . And behind her I can recognize another woman . . . and another. . . . When I was married they came to tea every week. And perhaps slept with my husband. It's not important. They all preferred not to know me, but I can tell they recognize me. . . . And along the walls, at the back of the room, men stand in the darkness. They all draw near, lean forward with the cynical curiosity men of the world have for a woman who is 'declassée,' a woman whose fingertips they once kissed in her salon and who is now dancing on stage, half-naked."* [8]

Is this the memory of a real event, is it colored or deformed, exaggerated? The narrative contains impressions of actual events, along with things that were perhaps only sensed, events that are condensed or out of context. Whether it is based on anxiety or on actual experience, this nightmarish scene translates better than any lengthy analysis Colette's perceptions of the opinion "proper" people had of her. In using her body to earn her living, in one way or another, she had removed herself from that society. Any woman who is not a part of society but who nevertheless manages somehow to live off it is looked on as a prostitute; she is regarded with an equal contempt. And society left such women no other choice. *What was I to do*, asks Renée Néré, a woman, a writer whose husband too has stolen her work, *sew, type, go on the streets? The variety stage is the profession for women who have never learned a profession.*

Through her divorce and Willy's various underhand maneuvers, Colette learned not only social opprobrium, but also the harsh dictates of necessity, of need, *of bartering for hard cash my move-*

ments, my dancing, the sound of my voice.[9] A woman's position was more affected by contemptuous scandal than it was by any problems she might encounter through being divorced, an actress, even a lesbian. Separated from her husband, dressed in her men's clothes, Missy was still the Marquise de Morny. She could even appear on stage, provided it was in an amateur performance for some theatrical club. Even the Moulin Rouge scandal for which she had been at least equally responsible had damaged the Marquise far less than it had Colette. Sylvain Bonmariage writes about her with a certain respect, despite his contempt for her morals. As for Colette, she experienced the dual misfortune of being poor and of having no social status. A poor divorcée from a common background had the same status as a girl from a modest family without a dowry: both were regarded by class-ridden society with nothing but contempt and could look forward to nothing but poverty. People in need always appear vulgar, sordid, to those who enjoy opulence and security. Such people do not want to face such basic want; they turn away from physical, material description. Anything can be talked about, so long as it is not detailed. The image of Colette gracefully dancing onstage in her veils might have been acceptable if no one had been forced to follow her into the wings. This backstage view is contained in her letters about salary and contracts, in all her writings over these years in which she describes, modestly and harshly, but always with precision, the fluctuations in her economic status: not altogether poverty, but rather "hard times," financial straits.

The barrier to any kind of mutual comprehension between the world of ease and the world of need can be examined at those points where the two worlds almost meet. In *La Vagabonde*, Renée Néré contemplates her rich suitor, Maxime, and is rather shocked at what she sees, *a man with nothing to do, who always has money in his pocket. . . . He has no profession, no sinecure to camouflage his idle freedom.* Renée's lover, even as he is courting her, treats his idol's sordid professional concerns with the offhand casualness of a rich man who is above such things. One day, Maxime arrives early at Renée's home and finds her discussing the details of her forthcoming tour with Brague. She is uncomfortable at Maxime's being there, as the poor are in the presence of the wealthy; *my music hall matters were poor, dry, commercial things in which I had no desire to involve my friend, my dear, lazy lover.* Brague, however, with his blindness to the true situation and with the professional single-mindedness of his class, does nothing to spare her embarrassment, the embarrassment of a woman who has come down in the world:

"On the last tour," Brague began, *"in September if you recall, we had ten to eleven francs in excess baggage, as though we were Carnegie!"*

"Not all the time, Brague."

"What will you be taking as luggage aside from your suitcase?"

"My black trunk."

"The big one? That's ridiculous, I can't allow it!"

Max coughed.

"Here's what we'll do. You can share mine. In the bottom, stage costumes; second compartment, your underthings, slips, panties, stockings, and my shirts, my underwear, etc." [10]

Shocked, her worldly suitor contains himself with difficulty, and as soon as Brague leaves *I was greeted with a torrent of protests, complaints, reproaches.*

"It's monstrous, Renée, and it's impossible! You must be out of your mind! Your slips, your intimate underclothes and your poor little panties, oh, my darling! all pell-mell with that person's underwear. And your stockings mixed in with his socks, I suppose? All just to save a hundred sous a day. What folly, what poverty!"

"What do you mean, poverty? It comes to 200 francs!"

"Oh, I know that! But how shabby!" [11]

Where could this spoilt child have been expected to learn that money, the money one earns oneself, is something serious and respectable, that it has to be carefully husbanded, discussed with solemnity.[12] Embracing his belovèd a few minutes later, Maxime whispers all-too typical endearments to her: *"To hell with your profession. . . . Ah! when you're all mine, then I'll shower you with all the first-class trains and flowers you want, and dresses, dresses! and everything I can find that is most beautiful, everything I can think of!"* [13] Half-flattered, half-believing in this universe being laid at her feet, Renée is still Sido's daughter; she hears a small, sane and very realistic voice telling her, ironically: *What do you want deluxe train accommodations for? They won't get you there any faster than the others!"* [14]

⚜ THE FEMALE CAVALIER

So not much was gained from Willy: revenge, contempt, double-dealing, indifference at best. Women were arrogant, men were envious. But Colette also began to become aware that "Society" was not the entire world; in her exile from it, she found another world, other worlds. Distressed, abandoned, she found human tenderness: *I was quite right to trust in what I barely knew: those in my own position, human concern . . . if one day I write my recollections of that "other side," I think that the grunt of effort, the cry of sorrow, might even become a sound expressive of happiness, and that I would have to lament with a joyful face.*[1]

This final paragraph of *Mes apprentissages*, the book that describes her captivity, is the overture to marvelous days Colette was always to remember with delight. At the moment, however, she was just beginning her familiarity with two circles that proper people disapproved of; she was just beginning to meet new acquaintances who aroused her curiosity, took her out of herself and her narcissism, helped her to recover from her vanished dream of love, her unimportant sorrows: these circles were Lesbos and the variety stage. The human warmth she received from these outcasts of both sexes helped her to regain a lost passion Sido had earlier encouraged, the passion for living. A love of life, ambivalent, full of overtones, also has its accompanying sorrow, but despite the overwhelming disgust with which Willy had contaminated her, her "cry of sorrow" became a "cry of celebration."

After her breakup with Willy, Colette sought refuge in Gomorrah, the unisexual city—one that Proust, according to its inhabitants, described incorrectly. The Marquise de Morny was one of its leading citizens. Through the character of La Chevalière (the Female Cavalier) in *Le Pur et l'Impur*, Colette told fragments of her story. Detested by her father, ignored by her mother, Sophie Troubetskoy, who loathed both her husband and her offspring, Missy had been one of those aristocratic children handed over by noble parents to the care of servants. *Like their brothers, they had trembled in the servants' hall, but they had also loved. A child has to love. . . . What was better for them, a hired tormentor or an immoral accomplice? The women who told me these things did not judge them. They had no need to invent when they could tell me true stories of orgies in the servants' hall, of alcohol served to drunken children, of that disastrous servants' care that overfed nurselings one day and neglected to feed them at all the next. . . . They had no need to color their stories with journalistic sentimentality. None of them claimed to have been martyred, not even the daughter of the Duc de X, who from six to fifteen years of age had never worn anything but the worn-out shoes "handed down" by her older brothers and her sister.*[2]

Married to the Duc de Belbeuf, whom she loathed as much as her mother had hated her own husband, Missy obtained a separation from him in 1903. At last free to indulge her basic feelings, she rarely dressed in anything but male attire, her hair cut short like a man's.

Seen from a distance—by Willy's friends, for example—Missy was a sexual deviate, tolerated only because of her noble background. "I had the 'honor' to be acquainted with Mme de Belbeuf," Bonmariage writes; "she was a woman of breeding, of an exceptional intelligence, and even when dressed as an automobile mechanic she was reserved, her manners polished." [3] Referring to the Moulin Rouge scandal: "Willy, who knew her well . . . was always of the opinion that Colette had coaxed her into it. Mme de Belbeuf went onstage with her because it was a way of appeasing Colette's jealousy, and because she wanted to help her to abandon the idle life that was so bad for her." [4] (It is hard for us not to respond.) "Mme de Belbeuf was noted for her total commitment," he continues. "From her wedding night on, she had erected an impassible barrier between herself and men out of disgust, it was said, for her husband, who had botched it up. I have difficulty believing this. Women who suffer this kind of misfortune always go back to men as soon as they are lucky enough to meet some nice lad who understands them." [5] Unfortunately for Bonmariage's complacent assurance, the Marquise never encountered any of his friends who could understand her.

For his part, Willy felt no need whatsoever to speak well of her and preferred to indulge in his usual gross witticisms. One of his favorite games was to travel in train compartments marked "For Women Only." When someone would finally complain of his presence, he would reply, "But I am the Marquise de Belbeuf." [6] "The Marquise's apartment was furnished in a mixture of Art Nouveau and Second Empire, with pink and yellow silk hangings. She received guests in two connecting salons . . . a curious mixture of people, her brother Serge's friends from the Jockey Club, real society women and hordes of females like Emilienne d'Alençon and Clémence de Pibrac; Jean de Lorrain (a notorious homosexual writer and pornographer) was an intimate of the house . . . and Liane de Pougy.

"Even with such a hodgepodge of guests, however, manners were always perfect, and a stranger would have thought himself in real upper-crust society." [7] Bonmariage's wicked, monotonous narrative is largely devoted to reciting the Marquise's affairs with a girl who worked in a Parisian copper foundry, the origin, according to him, of the mechanic's overall she wore when "machining bathroom fixtures."

He describes Missy's suits and neckties with many pornographic-pedantic pleasantries of doubtful humor. "Poor at spelling, she always mixed up masculine and feminine, Lesbos and Cytherea." The whole passage betrays the view a small, pretentious and self-important segment of society took toward a subculture it sought only to vilify, never to understand.

Colette's text has quite a different tone. She evokes her companion of *uncertain or dissimulated sex; filled with anxiety, always veiled, never naked, the androgyne is a wanderer, perpetually wondering, always a supplicant. . . . Man, her half-likeness, is quick to take fright, to abandon her. She is left with her own half-likeness, woman. And yet, she is duty-bound to be unhappy. . . . Incurably, she displays her seraphic misery, her glittering tears. She moves from tender yearning to maternal adoption. . . . 1 am referring still to La Chevalière, she who is so often hurt by other women. . . . One day, someone was describing an ugly woman to her:*

"That one, if she didn't have those eyes . . ."

"What more does one need, besides a pair of eyes?" La Chevalière asked.

But 1 knew that she was actually wildly partial to transparent green eyes, and when 1 told her that she shared with Jean Lorrain an obsession with green or blue eyes, she bridled:

"Oh, but it's not at all the same thing. Jean Lorrain, he uses green eyes as a pretext to . . . you know. Nothing is too low where he's concerned."

The remark is worth its whole epoch and the literature of 1900,[8] Colette concludes.

❖ In Lesbos

The fact is, the period was rife with sapphism: "Purporting to represent Diana Bathing, Semiramis and her court, painting and sculpture were devoted to female couples. Courbet's girl friends are intertwined as tenderly as the nymphs in those plaster allegories that decorate office buildings and banks." In literature, there are countless novels featuring governesses who—not content with seducing the master—succeed in troubling the mistress of the house. Zola boldly described Nana and Satin kissing. In *Amants féminins*, Adrienne Saint-Agen states flatly: "Such love spares no one, it affects the duchess and the working girl. Gomorrah is continually extending its borders."[1]

Caricaturists were devoted to the subject. Forain portrayed two girls holding hands and sighing, "And of course, men are so ugly!" [2]

Encouraged, almost esteemed, female homosexuality was asked only to retain a modicum of reserve. They were still women, even if they were homosexual. Prefect Lépine banned the wearing of men's clothes in public. Discreet, forced to be real women, at least on the surface, these stubborn aficionadoes of the *pleated shirt, the starched collar, often even a vest and always a silk pocket handkerchief . . . would never venture into the street, never leave their phaetons, without donning with palpitating hearts a large plain cloak, like that of a mother superior, to conceal their masculine jackets and their embroidered vests.*[3]

Unlike their counterparts in Sodom—super-virile, often avid for violence and vicious degradation, if not for power—these women could forgo futile provocation because as a group they were partially accepted. They kept to the shadows, they could spend sleepless nights, could turn their idleness to advantage as long as they played the game. Their meeting places reflected their need for discretion, for darkness, reflected their wariness of intruders and the idly curious: they congregated in cozy hangouts, in small neighborhood cinemas where couples would go in groups, in back rooms in out-of-the-way and smoke-filled restaurants, in Montmartre cellars where they could revel comfortably at their ease *in low-ceilinged rooms under the rough supervision of the proprietress, one of their own, amidst the delicious crackling of a real Vaudoise fondue and the harsh contralto of a sister singer crooning ballads by Augusta Holmès.*[4]

In this feminine antiworld, the most common form of relationship was built on the protective-maternal model. *These Empire Baronesses, canonesses, cousins of Tsars, illegitimate daughters of grand dukes, elegant Parisienne bourgeoises, these aged horsewomen born Austrian aristocrats with eyes and hands of steel . . . gazed longingly in the protective and jealous shadows at younger women, at knowledgeable young actresses, at the next-to-last true demi-mondaine of the day, at some variety star. . . . Protectress and protégée would whisper together, their conversation disappointing to the curious eavesdropper: "How did your lesson go? Have you got it down, your Chopin Waltz?" "Here, take off your furs, you'll catch cold and this evening you'll have no voice." "Of course, you know better than I about everything, that goes without saying. But I'm the one who studied with Nilsson, my child." "Tsk, tsk, darling, you're not supposed to cut a baba with a knife. Take the small fork." "You have no sense of time, and if you didn't have me . . ." "What good can it do to upset your husband by getting home late all the time?*" [5] Unlike Sodom, there was no cynicism in Lesbos. In speaking, *they made do with circumlocutions. Only one of them, a German princess with the ruddy face of a plump butcher, boldly introduced her girl friend one day as "My wife," upon which my staid gentlemen in skirts sniffed and pretended they hadn't heard.*[6]

Lesbos was a mixed society in which sex consciousness apparently replaced class or caste consciousness. By "sex consciousness" we should understand a sense of feminine community, rather than feminist self-interest. A more detailed analysis might bring out more clear-cut divisions. Bonmariage employs the term "salmagundi," a medley, a potpourri. Such a salmagundi obviously must have been constructed on an implicit social code. Homosexuality does not wipe out any and all social differences, especially when it is not combined with any ideological commitment. The most obvious social division was between protectress and protégée, between real princesses and their *demi-mondaine* or actress girl friends. The Marquise de Morny and Colette Willy were a typical example. We have noted the extent to which their implicit status singled them out in the eyes of public opinion. But the horsey types from the Austrian aristocracy could in practice rub elbows at the Marquise's receptions with married women like Proust's friend Mme de Clermont-Tonnerre, with Yvonne Sabini, wife of the Italian commercial attaché, with militant feminists such as Anne Wickham, the English suffragette, or with courtesans like Liane de Pougy or Emilienne d'Alençon relaxing from their professional duties.

The provisional bisexuality prevalent in Lesbos brought together the fanatic homosexual, the tolerant heterosexual and the more or less asexual androgyne.

⚜ THE AMAZONS

The Marquise's circle of acquaintances had contact, through lesbianism, with a more intellectual, cultivated and talented group of women dominated by Natalie Clifford Barney, Lucie Delarue-Mardrus and Renée Vivien. Colette expressed her astonishment at these cultural interminglings, *termitariums devoted to curaçao over ice, café cognac, multivolume novels and the drama, beneath which lay another, much more subterranean, much more literary kinship.*[1]

The kinship, however, was less subterranean that it appeared. The courtesan Liane de Pougy, Natalie Clifford Barney's lover, wrote and published with prolific abandon a whole series of novels, *L'Insaissisable Mirhille, L'Enlisement, Idylle saphique*, which was about Natalie. The latter, a rich young American, also inspired another book by another lover, *Etudes et préludes* by Renée Vivien. Natalie had been the model for Flossie in the *Claudines*, for Evangeline Musset in *Ladies Almanach*, a book attributed to Djuna Barnes, for Laurette in Lucie Delarue-Mardrus's *L'Ange et les Pervers*, and for Valérie Seymour in Radcliffe Hall's *Well of Loneliness*. She was the *Amazone* to whom Remy de Gourmont addressed his famous *Lettres*. And she was herself a writer, a poet; she assembled a freedom-loving and passionate group of intellectual and "marginal" women of all kinds, from Anna de Noailles to Mata Hari, along with some men, all of whom met in an atmosphere of partying, novelty, freedom. The *Comœdia* of May 23, 1909, noted: "the festivals of chaste nudity in the shadows of her Neuilly gardens. Miss Eva Palmer, whose marvelous red hair can be seen flaming in the paintings of Aman Jean and who has just married the poet brother-in-law of Raymond Duncan, performed with Mme Colette Willy." [2] In his secret journal, Comte Robert de Montesquiou noted a remark made by one of the inner circle: "People call it unnatural—all I can say is, it's always come naturally to *me*!" [3] A further proof that such literary sapphism among young, pretty and talented women was deeply ingrained in the customs and fantasies of Tout Paris.

Along with Natalie, "the wild girl from Cincinnati," with her "feminine figure, golden hair, [her] pastel-colored skin, steely eyes, a biting smile, and a sudden blush," [4] there was Lucie Delarue-Mardrus, a "languorous, dark-haired beauty who was a seductress like Natalie. In Provins in 1898, she had added Captain Philippe Pétain to her conquests; he proposed marriage. Lucie and her parents turned him down. As consolation, the rejected captain received a farewell poem ending 'I shall not weep, I shall not weep.' And for good reason; Mlle Delarue was about to marry Dr. Mardrus, much in the public eye since his translation of *The Thousand Nights and One Night*," [5] a work whose impropriety and strange orthography was to shock the mother of the Narrator in *A la recherche du temps perdu*. "The Almond Princess," as Lucie was called, because of "the paleness of her totally hairless body," and her husband, the black-bearded Dr. Mardrus, known as "The Caliph's Eye," were among Natalie's frequent visitors and Colette too saw a great deal of them. For Lucie, Natalie had feelings that "wavered between love and friendship for years, finally resolving into a lasting friendship." [6]

And there was Renée Vivien, a poetess who was to die prematurely, with her tumultuous love affairs on which she based her poems. During Colette's years in Lesbos—from 1906 to 1911—she was fast friends with Renée Vivien; her house in the Avenue du Bois could be reached from Colette's in the Rue de Villejust through two interconnecting gardens separated by a gate; on the way, Colette could stop at the courtyard apartment of Robert d'Humières and his cat, Lanka. Colette includes in her evocation of the Parisian Lesbos at the beginning of the century in *Le Pur et l'Impur* a deeply felt and attractive portrait of Renée Vivien, using her real name, Pauline Tarn, a "blond young woman with discouraged shoulders," [7] who left behind lovely French poems inspired by sapphism. Excitable, passionate, childish, generous, unpredictable and unequaled at downing impassively her own horrific cocktails, Renée Vivien was more like a citizen of Gomorrah than of Lesbos, Gomorrah being the country of mad romantic disorder of both mind and senses. Having planned to appear at a costume ball being given by Robert d'Humières at the Théâtre des Arts dressed as Lady Jane Grey on her way to the block, Renée discovered with dismay ten days before the event that *"the greatest possible misfortune has befallen me,"* she had *inadvertently put on ten pounds.*[8] She set out to lose them in the required time, ingesting nothing but tea and alcohol and, in this state of fast, taking long, exhausting walks in the woods. Despite her love affair with Natalie, she was in the toils of a domineering protectress whose very name terrified her half to death; she burnt herself out in vertiginous bouts of alcohol and passion. What a contrast between the earthbound Colette, healthy, avid for life and light, and the moonstruck Renée with her miasmas, her morbid premonitions. One evening, suffocating in the incense-laden darkness of Renée's apartment, Colette brought with her *a huge impermissible, offensive, kerosene lamp and set it lit up before me at the table. Renée cried huge tears like a child, but, like a child, it is only fair to add that these managed to console her.*[9]

Renée was an alcoholic, and she had worked out a system that enabled her to drink in public without being caught. *The intemperate child taught me, with naive competence, "There are fewer ways of making love than they say, but more than they think,"* [10] and this blond child with her dimpled cheeks, her soft, laughing mouth, and her gentle eyes, was to die before she was thirty, in 1909. After her death, Natalie Clifford Barney moved from Neuilly, too full of the memory of her lover, and took a house in the Rue Jacob, the same house the Maréchal de Saxe had built for Adrienne Lecouvreur, a

house with a leafy garden in which Racine and his mistress La Champ-
meslé had strolled together. Hidden away in an interior courtyard
was a small temple with three Grecian columns known as the
Temple de l'Amitié, which became the symbol of all these friends
for whom the feminine element played so preponderant a role, and
where, along with Valéry, Rilke, Ezra Pound, T. S. Eliot, Bernard
Berenson, D'Annunzio and Pierre Louÿs, Colette, Lucie Delarue-
Mardrus, Anna de Noailles and Marthe Bibesco all congregated.

⚜ GOMORRAH AS SEEN FROM SODOM

Colette's Lesbos was Gomorrah without its myth. Natalie Clifford
Barney too found, when reading Proust, that "Albertine and her
Gommorrean friends were not so much charming as improbable, and
grimly declared: 'Not everyone is able to infringe these Eleusinian
mysteries.' "[1]
Although she admired Proust in so far as his attention was turned
to Sodom, Colette took issue with him when he turned to *a
Gomorrah of inscrutable and depraved girls, denounces an entente,
an entire group, a fury of fallen angels . . . for despite Marcel
Proust's imagination or error, there is no such place as Gomorrah.*[2]
This is a very flat way of saying that Gomorrah is a male fantasy, a
heterosexual fantasy that does not at all correspond to reality. In addition, in an unequal society where virility is given pride of place in
the hierarchy of values, a female subculture will not be regarded in
the same way as a male subculture. The best proof of this is the different treatment meted out by society to lesbians and to pederasts.
At a time when sapphism was openly being dealt with in literature
and the arts, works treating male homosexual themes were being
censored, their authors brought to trial. Male homosexuality was regarded as a threat to society as a whole: its persecution was an indica-
tion of fear. Tolerance of female homosexuality was not due to any
special indulgence; it was simply considered harmless. Lesbians,
Painter notes, were spared "the unjust stigma which condemned the
natives of Sodom to a furtive or defiant criminality . . . they
seemed to the world, as indeed they were, an innocent, proud, eccentric, indispensable leavening in a monotonous society."[3] His choice
of words is revealing. Female homosexuality was seen as something
"innocent," in other words, harmless. The lesbian was never seen as
"rebarbative," but rather as the victim of some disease. Her choice
was not regarded as the result of freedom, but of frustration, of her

attempt to compensate. In the eyes of public opinion, the lesbian was not so much preferring women as she was fleeing from man, a different matter altogether. Popular feeling has not changed very much in this respect. As for the bisexual woman, she is even more readily accepted by men who regard her homosexuality as a charming caprice, a sensual vice from which he too may profit: *Two women in each other's arms are regarded by him as something off-color, suggestive, never as the melancholy, touching sight of two weak creatures who must seek refuge in each other to sleep, to weep, to escape men who are so often cruel, to enjoy—more than mere pleasure—the bitter happiness of knowing they are the same, both weak, both neglected.*[4]

Here, Colette is indicating for us her own path toward homosexuality, a path that had led through Willy. "A woman can devote herself to women because a man has deceived her, but sometimes the man has deceived her because she was seeking a woman in him," Simone de Beauvoir has written. "For these reasons, it is a mistake to establish any radical distinction between heterosexual and homosexual women."[5]

In addition, there is the notion of communion, of the oppressed in league against their male oppressor, a factor lacking in male homosexual relationships. Colette's Lesbos is more a comforting womb or a mild eighteenth-century convent than it is a debauched Gomorrah. It is placid, even cozy, a refuge where the notion of power is less predominant than with homosexual males. "The Lesbian is no more like a male homosexual than the latter is like a woman."[6] And the different ways in which they are perceived reinforces their specific characteristics. Individual reactions to homosexuality are based on the institutional differences we have mentioned. Faced with homosexuality in the opposite sex, heterosexual men and women are equally ignorant, but in men it is a complacent ignorance, in women it is fraught with anxiety. *Women unfamiliar with pederasty adopt when they encounter it an attitude that is forced on them by instinct,* Colette writes.[7] If the man with whom one is in love is involved, the attitude is terror. *The wife of a man who deceives her with another man knows that all is lost. . . . She is completely unable to assume the mockingly salacious attitude of the man who catches his wife embracing another woman: "Oh, I'll get you back again!"*[8] Society seems to fall prey to collective panic when confronted with pederasty, as if it were some contagious disease. It must be awfully attractive for mere contact with it to carry such a powerful toxicity. And yet, despite all the taboos, male homosexuality manages to flourish. Written about, described, evoked, stigmatized, half-admitted, fought against and even repressed and persecuted, male homosexuality is the object of an insidious and continual attention that demonstrates the immense interest it arouses. Female homosexuality, once voyeurism is set aside, seems to be regarded principally from a macho point of view: as nonessential. Lesbos remains a mysterious region because it is regarded with contempt, at best a suburb of Sodom. In its attention to variant life-styles, our society's official approach has been toward widespread assimilation, toward reducing the unknown to the familiar. The bourgeois has imbued class society with his own system of values; the West has bleached the black and made him homogeneous; early in our century Freud coupled Electra and Oedipus, sidestepping the problems of femininity by positing the effects of historical accidents. At best, man forces the woman to be a reflection of himself, his shadow. But Lesbos was never and is not now Gomorrah, the shadow of Sodom. It institutionalizes not only a sexual preference, but a social status. In both the unisexual city and the heterosexual city, women are still women, their virilization exists only in the imagination. Both these cities are located on the edges of the "dark continent" of femininity, a region into which Freud at the end of his life confessed he had never penetrated.

⚜ The Ladies of Llangollen

Women who prefer women become extra-feminine, not less so, and in so doing they are regarded with additional contempt for having cut themselves off from that male desire for which they were purportedly created. In the luxury society of Tout Paris at this time, however, they reveled in being the innocent and eccentric leavening of which Painter speaks. Whence their vogue, and whence too the misunderstanding with regard to them.

Wondering about the secret for success between two women in love with each other, Colette mentions *the noble season of a female passion;* she endows female homosexuality with specific traits, emphasizing its femininity and distinguishing it from male homosexuality. Two women come together in a complete and clear-eyed acceptance of their femininity, not as some ridiculous parody of men. It is their instinct of *industrious females, destined to build and populate a home, that leads them to collect what they need to construct a sentimental hideaway, a rickety and immaterial roof sup-*

ported on embracing foreheads, clasped hands, joined lips.[1] Heterosexual passion always has to deal with mutual ignorance, which can be
both an attraction and a threat: *A woman given to a man, a loved and
demanding man, can never separate from the happiness she feels her
intermittent foreboding of eventual loneliness: "One day when He
is gone . . . the bench where I will wait for Him . . ." But it is
different when the couple does not include a man. Two women
totally absorbed in each other do not fear, they do not imagine
separation any more than they would be able to bear it.*[2] No modesty
contaminates the hours spent sleeping, swimming, being ill, nothing
separates *two twin bodies with the same afflictions, needing the same
care, the same enforced chastity.*[3] Passion may be less strong, for passion is the creation of difference. *Passion is not what creates fidelity
between two women, but rather a kind of kinship. "Oh, my sisters!"
Renée Vivien constantly sighed . . . close resemblance can even
assuage desire. The female lover takes pleasure in the knowledge she
is caressing a body whose secrets she knows, whose preferences her
own body indicates to her.*[4] Such love, in its best manifestations, when
it is fully accepted, eludes the *seasons and declines of love.*[5] For a long
time, obviously when she was with Missy, Colette mused on the
romantic story of two aristocratic Welsh girls who ran away together in May 1778. They loved each other for fifty-three years,
hidden away in their Welsh village, and according to the older
woman's journal no shadow ever came between them; it was a serene
understanding that had been proved by scandal but which finally
won respect and approval for the "Ladies of Llangollen."

❧ MISSY, THE GOOD FAIRY

To these generalized homosexual considerations, we must add
special factors. Colette, deeply wounded by Willy, discovered in
Lesbos what she had learned from the pederasts in Willy's circles,
that *the antipathy of one sex for the other has nothing to do with
neurosis.* Since then, she adds, *I have not noticed, moving in other
milieus, that the behavior of normal people is much different.*[1] She
also began to feel a vague desire, one that had never left her, to come
again into contact with that part of herself that had remained the
best: Sido. Only another woman can restore the verdant paradise
represented by the mother's body. To Colette—and particularly during this period—the male represented otherness, separation, jealousy,
suffering, slavery, emotional alienation; the female was relationship,

contact, fidelity, independence, emotional harmony. The call of the springs again began to draw her back to her mother, backed up by her yearnings for independence in which the maternal siren acted both as a model and an obstacle. Like Sido, Missy protected Colette's freedom with her material and emotional gifts. Colette Willy played the vagabond, she went on tours of the vaudeville circuit, she danced naked beneath her veils for modest fees; she traveled, rehearsed and toured with her fellow troupers, but in coming back to the Rue Georges-Ville in Paris, to Crotoy in the summer, it was to Missy that she returned to regain her strength. The hard life of her profession, the vulgarity of the audiences, the contempt of the straitlaced, the fatigue of endless rehearsals, all that mattered little *as long as when I returned, tossing my hat onto the bed, a belovèd, somewhat husky, voice would murmur, "I hope you're not too tired, my love?"* [2] While Wague and her colleagues were forced to stint, to count their money, Missy's generosity allowed Colette to travel first class, to eat better meals, to wear a warmer coat. In *Lettres de la Vagabonde*, Missy is always in the background, often with her darling child on her travels, comforting her, soothing her, caring for her. *Profiting from Missy's presence*, she wrote to Léon Hamel on November 21, 1908, from Brussels, *I have treated myself to a fine case of the flu, sudden and violent. When Missy is here, I allow myself every luxury*.[3] And of course, set free by Missy, Colette was not totally free from Missy. No more than she was from Sido. Can anyone be free from the person they love? As in the past, when Sido had made her a gift of the blue springs at dawn, Colette Willy journeyed from town to town, from theater to theater, holding in her hand an invisible slender string by which she was attached to Missy. "Colette had two failings, she was sensitive to flattery and she couldn't bear to be alone. But of course, she never was," as Natalie Clifford Barney told Jean Chalon.[4]

She obviously had a hard time living through periods when she was without a lover; she needed to love and be loved, and also, perhaps, to have the approval of those she loved. In this regard, Sido had spoiled her. However, her weakness also constituted a strength, an inexhaustible reserve of strength. Her relationship with Missy occurred at the same time that Colette began seriously to ponder the question of freedom. Missy does not appear to have been a hindrance or an alienating factor. On the contrary, she—as had Sido—offered the love necessary for the forces of life to triumph over the forces of death, and this reciprocal love did not create disequilibrium; it was not oppressive. "A whole part of herself," Simone de Beauvoir wrote about the lesbian, "is always ready and hoping for the acquisition of a treasure analogous to the treasure she gives a male. . . . The lesbian and the mother are similar to the extent in which they break down this barrier, caressing in their child or in their lover their own extension and reflection." [5] In Colette's writing throughout this period we find the same association being made between motherhood and homosexuality. Renée Néré in *La Vagabonde* speaks of Amélia Barally, the ex-operetta star and actress who is on tour with her: *In her I enjoy this protective feeling, this capacity for caring, this delicate maternal touch, which is the attribute of women who sincerely and passionately love other women: it gives them an indefinable attraction, one you men can never appreciate.*[6]

A passage in *Les Vrilles de la vigne*, a book deeply imbued with Missy's presence, almost echoes Simone de Beauvoir's words: *I know that then you will hold me close in your arms, and that if being rocked in your arms is not enough to calm me, your kiss will become more profound, your hands more loving, and that you will bring me bliss for succor, like an immense exorcism, driving out the demons of fever, of anger, of care. . . . You will give me pleasure, and you will gaze at me with your eyes filled with maternal concern, seeking in your passionate lover the child you never had.*[7]

The passages in *Les Vrilles de la vigne* devoted to Missy are free of hypocrisy, of any attempt to arouse; they are modest, but explicit: *They who enter here cannot know that every night the weight of our united bodies makes deeper beneath its shroud of delight this valley no larger than a tomb! Oh, our naked bed . . .*[8] For Colette, and in this she never changed, there was but one kind of love: physical love. She would have been in complete agreement with the phrases Remy de Gourmont wrote for his Amazone: "Love is physical, all love is physical, because only the physical exists, and the soul is an invention . . . but it exists in so many bodily guises . . . so many that other chapters are needed." [9]

⚜ MALE-FEMALE MIRAGES

Colette's life with Missy drew to a close around 1910. Her letters in which the person sharing her life was always included in the closing phrase, a changing symbol of her profound monogamy, cease to mention Missy; they begin to contain the name of a sad "little companion" who sends best wishes from Italy: Auguste Hériot. They

had met at Polaire's, whose lover—according to Bonmariage's un-
trustworthy testimony—he had been. Rich and well-educated, Auguste's family owned the Grands Magazins du Louvre department
store; he was madly in love with Colette, but she did not return his
feeling. Was their relationship an intimate one, as contemporaries
thought, or did Colette reject Auguste, as Renée Néré rejects Maxime? It is hard for us to know. In any event, Auguste—like Maxime—
proposed marriage, and Colette's friends, including Missy, favored
the match; Missy probably hoped that Colette would settle down
with a stable man with a house of his own. Colette, however, coun-
tered her friends' attempts at her rehabilitation with a stubborn and
active resistance; it is reflected in *La Vagabonde.*

Lesbos had distracted Colette, but it did not retain her. Was this
because of social pressure, or did her irrepressible need for a man
cause her to separate herself from it? Clearly, although she was bisexual as all human beings are to some extent, the facet of her sexual
life devoted to the male was the more highly developed. And although she was to remain wary of men until she became an old
woman, although she continued to form special attachments with
women, some of whom were her rivals, her homosexuality had been
a temporary maternal substitute for which she had felt a vital need;
it had reconciled her to women, and it had enabled her, paradoxically,
to come to terms with her own femininity which men, so easily
mistaken as to appearances, had denied her. If vestments do not make
a priest, clothes have never made a man: *I was not misled for very
long by those photographs showing me wearing a stiff collar, a straw
hat, a short jacket and straight skirt, with a lighted cigarette between
my fingers.*[1] In fact, they only deceived men, a few men, men fond
of women. One of her friends Colette calls "Damien" in *Le Pur et
l'Impur,* an inveterate Don Juan: *During the time when I was—or
thought I was—unattracted to Damien, I suggested that we should
take a trip together like a couple of courteously selfish, easygoing
men friends, fond of long silences:*

"I only like to travel with women," he replied. *His soft tone allowed his harsh words to pass. . . . Fearing he had offended me, he
"made up for it" with even worse:*

"You a woman? You might try . . . ?"[2]

*The words hurt. I never had the opportunity to admit to him that
just then I would secretly have liked to be a woman. . . . I was
then hoping to get rid of this ambiguity, with all its shortcomings
and its privileges, and throw myself living at the feet of a man to*

whom I could offer a fine and wholly female body with its perhaps fallacious vocation for servitude.[3] With her air of a naughty boy, with her sailor's kerchief from London, she still felt that beneath her masculine short hair she was truly a woman. *Who mistook us for women?* Colette wonders, *certainly not other women. . . . They were the only ones who were never fooled.*[4] And Simone de Beauvoir: "In order for her to display her lesbianism, a woman must reject feminism, or her femininity must be best satisfied in a woman's arms . . . especially for the woman who is attached to her own femininity, the sapphic embrace is the more satisfying."[5]

What did the expression "to be a woman" mean to Colette? Was it a synonym for "servant," for "female animal"? Her awareness of how artificial her dressing-up as a man was, her knowledge that in no way was she really the boy she was copying with her clothing? The somewhat puritanical provincial girl had been perverted only in appearance. Boldini, the painter, was not at all misled:

"You're the one who goes about in a tuxedo in the evenings?"

"I may have done . . . for some costume ball."

"Aren't you the mime?"

"Yes."

"And you're the one who doesn't wear tights. You dance così, così, *naked?"*

"I beg your pardon, I've never appeared on stage naked. People have said so, and in print, but the truth is that . . ."

He didn't even bother to listen. He gave a knowing laugh and patted my cheek, murmuring:

"What a proper little bourgeoise . . . a proper little bourgeoise."[6]

Colette was ambivalent, torn between fairly provocative behavior and dress and her old petit-bourgeoise background, torn too between the desire to separate herself from men and her profound desire to be a woman. Her awareness of her own contradictory feelings led her to reflect that what we call virility or femininity is not really a clear-cut distinction where biological sex is concerned. Her anxiety at not being entirely female led her to a concerned examination of the preconceptions that underlie so many misleading clichés. What did it mean to be a man? To be a woman? Colette felt that *somewhere impossible to situate precisely*[7] she was virile; perhaps it was only her awareness of her own autonomy, but at the same time she worried lest her virility might repel men. *"You have no reason to think so," Marguerite Moréno said to me one day. "Why don't you just bear in mind that for certain men some women represent a homosexual threat?"* [8] The discussion turned to a man's "femininity," his "weakness," his "vulnerability" in more everyday language.

Colette, however, went beyond this confusion of categories. She arrived at a particular concept of androgyny in which everyone was predisposed to discover within himself, herself, and in other people, a subtle mixture of male and female components. *Once the precious tresses are cut, the breasts, hands, bellies, hidden, what is left of our female façades? In sleep, an incalculable number of women approach the form they would probably have chosen had their life awake not made them ignorant of themselves. And the same for men. I can still see the gracefulness of a sleeping man! From forehead to mouth, behind his closed eyelids, he smiled, nonchalant and sly as a sultana behind her grilled window. . . . And I, who would have in my stupidity "really liked" to be completely a woman, I looked at him with a male regret.*[9] A statement of great import in its ambivalence, its pertinence. Colette would have gone along with the title of a novel by one of our own contemporaries, *I Wanted to Be a Woman.*[10] But woman, the woman so many force themselves to become, mourning their failures, that woman does not exist. Neither Colette nor anyone else has ever succeeded in becoming that woman. A myth, a lie, unrealizable, she is nothing but a figment of the collective imagination. Every woman has briefly pursued this female chimera, at least for the man she desires, but once that man shuts his desire away behind his closed eyelids and drops off in angelic sleep, the old confusion rears its head again. Who is the woman, he or I? Who is the man? Angels have no sex. Aside from biological facts like blood, sperm, milk, womb, aside from the common desire that turns a production into reproduction, man and woman are ambiguous entities dictated by History. Who knows what History will end up with?

⚜ THE END OF THE BOULEVARD

The years 1905 to 1906 were a turning point, and not only in Colette's life. André Billy fixed 1905 as the last year of the turn of the century, the *fin de siècle*: "The first symptoms of the Great War, the debarcation of the German Kaiser in Tangiers and the resignation of Delcassé unified against the Dreyfusism that was in power a nationalist-reactionist opposition by the supporters of Maurras and Barrès, by neo-Catholics and academics—foretold in Paul

Bourget's *L'Etape* as early as 1903—and completely altered the climate of moral freedom and artistic independence that had prevailed for thirty years." [1] In the minds of those who had lived through it, the Belle Epoque was always to seem a paradise of freedom and pleasure, made even more attractive in retrospect by a new prudery.

Billy writes of the *Boulevard*, the center of Paris, an area full of excitement, of life, of novelty: "From 1905 to the War, the decadence of the Boulevard became ever more evident; its most outstanding representatives were Catulle Mendès, Courteline and La Jeunesse, barely hanging on. Many newspapers were still headquartered in the area or on the Boulevard, *La Libre Parole*, on the Boulevard Montmartre, *Le Figaro*, Rue Drouot, *Le Gaulois* on the Carrefour Drouot, *Le Journal* in the Rue de Richelieu, *Paris-Midi*, Rue Louis-le-Grand, *Le Temps*, Boulevard des Italiens, *L'Echo de Paris* in the Rue Taitbout, later on the Place de l'Opéra. . . . The Boulevard gradually changed its appearance with the increase in taxicabs, but its death blow was dealt by the disappearance of the Olympia and the Théâtre du Vaudeville, replaced with a cinema, the disappearance of the last section of the Rue Basse-du-Rempart and the Pavillon-de-Hanovre, with the substitution of mechanical vehicles for the horse-trams on the Madeleine-Bastille line. When the Boulevard Haussman was cut through, it was evident that the life of the former Boulevard was over; the Taverne Pousset, the Flammarion bookstore, the Rey, the Passage de l'Opéra so full of life, all were no more than memories, and the literary cafés made famous by Courteline, Mendès, La Jeunesse and their group experienced the same fate. Only the Napolitain and the Cardinal remained, and their clients had moved on." [2]

In February 1905, Colette's first friend from her earliest days in Paris, Marcel Schwob, died in his house in the Rue Saint-Louis-en-l'Isle. He caught cold; in a few days he was gone. "I saw him lying in his coffin, thin and stiff, his arms laid straight alongside his body, his face on the little pillow very peaceful," Paul Léautaud wrote. "On his breast, they had placed a tiny branch of white lilac. . . . We looked at him one last time. Then they shut him away."

On the day after his death, Colette wrote to Marguerite Moréno: *I am sorry I didn't see Schwob again while he was still alive, still wicked, with his affectionate contempt I found so delectable. You know how much I particularly loved Marcel.*[3] On February 28, 1909, Catulle Mendès also died; he was taking the last train from Paris to Saint-Germain and fell asleep; at one of the stops, he woke up and thought he had reached his destination. He jumped from the train just as it was starting up again and was thrown against the embankment. His death and Schwob's marked the end of an era.

1905 was the year of Red Sunday in Saint Petersburg. One hundred thousand people were massacred while attempting to present a petition to the Tsar; the massacre set off a series of revolutionary acts. On July 8, the crew of the battleship *Potemkin* mutinied at Odessa; repercussions in Paris were fairly feeble. There, these great historical events were felt in small ways. Having crossed the border, this mighty upheaval that was to mark our century so indelibly took for Tout Paris the form of a passion for the Ballets Russes. It was revolutionary enough, to be sure. The Imperial Opera had supported the Saint Petersburg riots in its own way—Fokine, Pavlova, Karsavina, Serge Legat had each taken part. "The latter slit his throat in remorse for having betrayed his comrades. Shortly afterward, Fokine took over as ballet master. . . . In 1908, Serge de Diaghilev organized several performances of *Boris Godonov* in Paris; he then got the idea to put on an entire Russian season." [4]

The Ballets Russes were to inspire a whole generation. "Each new season of the Ballets Russes was impatiently awaited by writers and artists prominent in Parisian society. . . . *Le Sacre du Printemps* created as much dissension as had the quarrel of the Bouffons. The success of *Shéhérazade* spilled over into literature." [5] Jean Cocteau, later one of Colette's great friends, was closely linked with Diaghilev and his Ballets Russes and acted as an intermediary between him and new movements in poetry and painting.

The Russian ballet had an important influence on Parisian dandyism and snobbery before 1914. The "dandy" was defined thus by a young writer: "He owns a Russian wolfhound and exercises this fascinating pet; he writes good French often redolent of the eighteenth century, novels in a pure style, free of lasciviousness, at least two chapters of which are set in a foreign city; he is well-dressed, wears his hair parted in the middle, is clean-shaven, and nonchalantly despises literary competitions while secretly engaging in them; he replaces his older mistress who has acted as his protectress with a ballet dancer to whom he gives nothing, attends all the exhibitions of new painting, lives in a bachelor apartment with Louis XVI or Directoire furniture upholstered in soft pastel materials, and hangs on his walls prints by Brissaud, Taquoy and Boutet de Monvel; despises equally Romanticism, lyricism and all true poetry, knows how to choose hosiery but nothing about foreign literature, is moderate in all things, including imagination and courage, has no intellectual interests, hates history and philosophy, frequents literary salons but never recites his own poetry, and may on occasion, if need be, accept a post as secretary to some minister." [6]

Colette played little part in this prewar Parisian literary world. Less than she had earlier, as Willy's property, a minor figure in Parisian literary circles; less than after the war, when she began to gain recognition as a woman of letters. But her marginal position and a few of her former friends helped her to sharpen her antennae; we have a few sketches describing the snobbery that prevailed in these years. Her friend Valentine, *since the Ballets Russes, wears fashions that the softest Oriental grace might barely excuse. She perfumes herself with rose and jasmin, swears by Teheran and Ispahan, in her Byzantine robe set off with a Marie Antoinette fichu and wearing a cossack cap and American sabotlike shoes, she boldly exclaims: 'How can anyone not be Persian?'* [7]

❧ OPIUM DENS—THE LAMENT OF THE NIGHTINGALE

She knew some of the dandies of the day simply because they had worked with her in Willy's "factory." Paul-Jean Toulet, one of the more famous of them, had actually written *Lélie, The Opium Addict*, a novel that did him little credit. When he was not ghost-writing, Toulet produced work of his own; *Mon amie Nane*, a light and misogynistic work revealing considerable talent, was his chief claim to fame. He published regularly in *La Vie Parisienne* from 1899 to 1907. His apartment was on the Place Laborde, in the same building as Curnonsky, who had moved in following a trip they had taken together to the Far East; they had returned with the opium habit. All Parisian literary society was fascinated with opium and opium dens; they are described in many books (among them Jarry's *Les Propos des assassins*). This explains the background of *Lélie*, in which the Baroness Gousse de Bize and many other characters are addicts.

Passages in *Le Pur et l'Impur* indicate that Colette herself frequented clandestine opium dens, hideaways so obscure that one never knew precisely who owned or ran them. She was not a smoker, and purportedly came "out of professional duty." But it was a pleasure foreign to her: *A somewhat low albeit harmless pleasure, a pleasure derived solely from a particular kind of snobbery, a spirit of bravado, a curiosity more feigned than real.* In actuality, she was seeking human contact, but she found nothing but *well-concealed and rest-*

less grief, frightful passivity.[1] She was fascinated by the human types she encountered, by the naked reality that emerged from their deliriums, exhaled in discreet moans or shared confidences throughout the sleepless nights. Above on a balcony, Charlotte, a solid, Renoir-like woman of around fifty, once began to emit roulades in the throes of lovemaking, the song of a nightingale. *Above, some woman was struggling against her mounting pleasure, urging it toward its climax, its destruction, with a calm and initially harmonious rhythm, regularly cadenced, and I inadvertently began to follow . . . that cadence, perfect as the melody*.[2] Later, drinking maté and pale Chinese tea, the smoke rising from the bowls of the pipes, Charlotte imparts to Colette her secret, the secret of a *clear-eyed genius at deception and tact*.[3] Her twenty-two-year-old lover is incapable of satisfying her, but for love of him, to spare him pain, Charlotte emits her nightingale lament. In public, in these exotic surroundings where they make love together, she simulates her pleasure to make her lover happy with his orgy, to deceive the other smokers he is trying to impress. In the sordid and somehow pathetic opium dens, Colette sought out people like the down-to-earth Charlotte with her pitiable self-abnegation, examples of unhappy people attempting to conceal their innermost secrets. She seeks others; she finds herself.

The rancorous Bonmariage, who was also an addict, did not comprehend such subtleties; they were probably not refined enough for him: "Colette never had much interest in any artificial paradise. The powerful spiritual content of such places attracted her not at all, immune as she was to any spirituality, without any urge to achieve such a state for herself. She even saw fit to scold me for my penchant for the drug."[4]

Aside from opium addiction, Toulet was a member of a group known as the "Fantasists," opposed to other groups such as the Abbaye and Unanimism and to the serious-minded *Nouvelle Revue Française* writers. Under the influence of ultraright Barrèsian nationalism and Maurrasian neoclassicism, they were convinced that they were restoring uniquely French qualities to a place of honor. Along with his friend Curnonsky, Toulet hung out at Weber's in the Rue Royale, at Vachette on the Boulevard Saint-Michel where Giraudoux held court, "but his favorite place from 1910 on was just off the boulevards in the Bar de la Paix on the Rue Auber, two long, narrow rooms with the same decor as the stuffy café whose name it bore." [5] Toulet had sided with Willy—we have already noted to what extent—and Colette of course no longer saw him, but another member of the Fantasist group, Francis Carco, became over the years one of her intimate friends. Along with Dorgelès and others, he helped turn Montmartre and the Lapin Agile into a legend.

✤ From the Lapin Agile to the Semiramis Bar

"The artists' Montmartre," Carco wrote, "began halfway down the Rue Ravignan where Max Jacob lived, veered left toward the Rue Caulaincourt, climbed up the Rue Lamarck to the Place du Tertre, and then descended a steep street to the Lapin Agile. This Montmartre had no sharply defined boundaries, of course, but its soul was contained in two favorite spots, Frédé's famous cabaret [the Lapin Agile] and the Bateau-Lavoir." [1]

If Colette's name is only peripherally linked with this group, it is owing to the rancor left over from her time with Willy. She was not to become close to Carco until 1918. Her separation from Willy also cut her off from literary circles, most of which were misogynistic to boot. A basically uncomplicated woman with a vast reserve of common sense, she was skeptical and quizzical with literary men who took themselves too seriously. She called Moréas, "considered by the Left Bank as the greatest living French poet," by the deflating epithet "Matamoréas," an untranslatable pun that neatly pricked his conquering-hero ways (*matamore*: swaggering braggart).[2]

Although Colette did not frequent the Montmartre of the Lapin Agile, the Montmartre of artists and poets, the literary Montmartre, she had her own bohemia. To find it, one descended one of the streets parallel to the Rue Lepic; not far from the other, separated from it by the Pont Caulaincourt, this bohemia had almost no contacts with the "higher," elitist version. Across the bridge, there was another world. In the Place Blanche was the restaurant run by Palmyre, a locale Colette refers to in her books as Semiramis (*Paysages et Portraits*) or Chez Olympe (*La Vagabonde*). In a letter to Léon Hamel dated February 28, 1909, she mentions it by name: *We always eat at Palmyre's, she smothers us in maternal care, cooks little steaks for Missy; yesterday she made us go to inspect the three pups her bulldog Bellotte had just whelped.*[3] The bar at the Olympe was more than a favorite restaurant for Colette, however; it was a symbolic crossroads rich with discoveries: discoveries of other ways of life, of circles vastly different from those that had condemned and rejected her. Palmyre's restaurant and bar, like the opium den, under whatever name she gave it, represents in her books a focal point on which new roads converge, roads that represent new choices; it is the central point of her freedom, if by freedom we mean a change of perspective. To My-Friend-Valentine, the symbol of the world she has left behind, she explains: *"Well," Valentine was huffy, "if it's only a question of dropping in when you're in the neighborhood. . . . But to become a regular, that's something else again. If you only went sometimes in a group. . . . But to sit there alone in your corner, with your newspaper and your dog, with all those people saying hello to you, those little gentlemen with their rings and their ankle bracelets . . . and then . . . they say that the food there is dreadful!"*

"I know, Semiramis tells me . . ."

"She . . ."

"Of course, she's a good sort, Semiramis. Her leek soup is very cheap, so is her chicken with sausages and her veal cutlet. She even gives food away free to all the jacketed bums, to poor girls all dressed up with nothing to eat; she feeds them and gives them a bit of cash. . . . She knows all her clients by name, the names of all their friends. She dislikes newcomers, if anyone happens to drop in she yells, 'You won't get anything to eat here!' Since I often have to eat out, I go to Semiramis's . . . who speaks her own colorful language to her long-haired young men and her short-haired young women."

"That's just the kind of people I'm talking about. . . . There are scenes, orgies, even fights every night in that bar."

"That's got nothing to do with me. The orgies at Semiramis's bar are like all orgies—they're so dull that even the wildest person would turn virtuous. I'm just interested in the people who eat there. . . . Yes, most of the young men aren't interested in women. When they eat there, they feel at home, relaxed. They gather strength for later on. There, they don't have to camp, to shriek, to wave an ether-soaked handkerchief or dance together. . . . And Semiramis stands with her hands on her hips and yells at a tall boy with dazed blue eyes who refuses a full plate of food, 'So you've been taking morphine again, have you! What does your mother mean by letting you ruin yourself like that?' . . . Semiramis doesn't ask for respect. What good would respect do her? You can't eat it, sell it, it takes up space. . . . 'What do I owe you, Semiramis?' a skinny

customer asked her one evening, anxiously. 'I don't know, I haven't figured it up,' Semiramis growls. 'Do you think you're all I've got on my mind?' 'But tonight I've got money, Semiramis.' 'Money, money, you're not the only one who's got money!' 'But Semiramis . . .' 'All right, that's enough of that. It all evens out in the end. The client down at the end table just paid me a louis for his stewed chicken. Monsieur didn't like my menu! Monsieur asked for special dishes . . . Monsieur must think he's in a restaurant!' " [4]

Between her cabbage soup and her *boeuf bourguinonne*, Colette would examine the young neighborhood toughs, the models, the second-rate variety artists, as they danced together, *lewdly, voluptuously*. And as she prepared to leave the Semiramis Bar, its proprietress would stop her at the door with a *gesture of complicity*, *"Shhh!" she whispered the other evening as she slipped the string of a bulging package onto my finger, "Don't say anything, it's apples I found for you, old reinettes like you like them, wrinkled as a poor man's behind!"* [5] These evocations of a proprietress with a heart of gold and salty language remind us of Georges Brassens and his songs about his own Semiramis bars, bars where those who are cold and hungry come to be fed and warmed, no questions asked. And like Brassens, Colette evokes the habitués of the Semiramis Bar—homosexuals of both sexes, drug addicts, neighborhood prostitutes—without any tender pity, without any street romanticism. Such girls gave her courage to resist. One icy February night, a local whore made an attention-getting entrance *wearing only a kind of cape in blue Liberty fabric embroidered in faded silver. . . . She was frozen, stunned from the cold, and her quick-tempered gray eyes rejected sympathy, compassion; she was prepared to insult, to scratch out at the first person who said "Oh, the poor kid!" . . . They are not a rare type in the land of Montmartre, such girls, crushed beneath their poverty and their pride, beautiful in their awful destitution. I would run into them here and there, trailing their flimsy rags from table to table, at late suppers on the Butte, gay, drunk, raucous, bitchy, never soft, never tender, always complaining about their job and always at it nonetheless. Men, with complacent and contemptuous laughs, call them "Dirty little sluts," because they never give in, they never admit hunger, cold, or love, they will die insisting "I'm not sick," they bleed from blows but they give as good as they get. . . .*

Yes, I know them, those girls, I dream of them . . . as if they had given me some undefinable education, had set me an example against any and all weakness. [6]

✤ HIDE AND SEEK WITH THE AUDIENCE

Colette's motives for going on the stage were mainly material; as already noted, she had to find some way to make a living. But complex psychological motives also guided her to a career on the variety stage. The decision to act or to write is never entirely innocent: although Colette was modest, her decision nonetheless translates a desire for self-exhibition. At the same time, her exhibitionism made her feel somehow guilty, a guilt manifested in her need for protection, for some kind of barrier—whether the barrier of the footlights, a sheet of paper, or the fictions, the lies of writing. Here too, she was ambivalent, she was both a naked dancer and a "hidden woman," which is the title of one of her volumes of collected pieces. In justification, she was to remark on several occasions that the best part of herself, her most real, innermost self, were her secret treasures she shared with no one. This is what she calls modesty. Yet she betrayed herself, all her texts betrayed her and her desire to expose herself. A defensive sentence in *Gribiche* reveals her subconscious association between her two professions: *Months went by, years went by during which I displayed* myself here and there on the stage, *thereby forfeiting* my right to keep silent about myself.[1] (emphasis added) Even in texts in which she spoke most explicitly about herself, she obviously avoided any direct confidence. But is a person's innermost secret self really revealed by anecdotes, fragments of his or her private life? Colette was well aware that this is not the case; her indifference to scandal, the very uninhibited way in which she exhibited herself naked onstage, demonstrate this. Although she herself never makes any flat statement, every writer, every actor, is an exhibitionist; the desire to write or to act is almost always accompanied by a certain amount of guilt. As a private person, this same need to "seek out and preserve," to be an "avid spectator of life and of herself," dictated her investigations of love. *"One has to have grown dreadfully old,"* Margot tells Renée Néré, *"to forgo the vanity of being alive through someone else's eyes."* Later, when she feels she is weakening under Maxime's persuasive pressure, Renée will recall, *I gave in . . . to the desire to keep him not as a friend, not as a lover, but as an avid spectator of my life, of myself.*[2]

Critics have noted the importance of mirrors, the importance of the act of looking, in Colette's work, but this is not the classic narcissism Simone de Beauvoir describes as a process of alienation in which the "ego is posited as an absolute and the subject is subsumed into it." [3] The power of the mirror in Colette's imagination, according to Yannick Resh, arises from the fact that "the image of a body glimpsed in the mirror is not simply a reflection, it is an image that reconciles the viewer with his concept of himself, it restores his equilibrium." The woman in the mirror is allowed to "see herself as others see her." [4] The mirror fulfils the same function as the audience's attention in the theater, it is a "tool for knowing the self." [5] The mirror and the Other's Eyes, each has interchangeable functions; they come together in an act in which a woman, beforehand, in her mirror, controls her image and prepares it to *confront the gaze of other people.*[6]

The variety stage perfectly embodied both types of self-knowledge for Colette; the preliminary mirror stage in her dressing room with its makeup table, its costumes, prepared her as an actress for the second stage, her confrontation with the public eye. For Colette, self-examination is a preparation for examination by others, preparing oneself to be looked at by other people is already a step toward looking at others oneself. Far from limiting her, far from making her self-complacent, self-absorbed, vaudeville enabled her to escape from herself. For the first time since the days of Saint-Sauveur, she was able to quit her personal emotional suffering, her complacent, coddled grief, and encounter other kinds of distress. The variety stage was probably the most valuable of all her apprenticeships. In a profession where the main thing was to be looked at, Colette learned to look at other people; separated from the audience by the blinding footlights, she diverted her eyes from them, she looked into the wings, not into the auditorium. She described the "backside" of the music hall, not the music hall itself. And as she learned to look, she also learned to listen. In daily contact with popular speech, rich, imaginative, direct, as her companions spoke it, her own style was purified; she eschewed the rococo preciosity that make many works from this same period by other writers unreadable today.

⚜ "LET OUT A BREAST!"

Colette began replacing the traditional tights with actual nudity in her earliest mimodramas, *La Romanichelle* and *Pan,* dressing only in the tatters of a gypsy maid, the draperies of Paniska. Scandal was also created by Colette's avant-garde naturalness; she was always more comfortable naked than when wearing some social disguise.

Colette's nakedness, however, was not entirely her own choice; it was also due to the pressures of her profession, to the urgings of her employer with his eye on the box office returns. She describes the scene in *Les Vrilles de la vigne* with a good deal of humor: Mme Loquette (Colette) and her partner W. (Wague) are in the midst of a rehearsal with the theater director in attendance. Mme Loquette's costume is being discussed, while *Mme Loquette averted her eyes and said nothing, devoutly wishing for a ham sandwich, or perhaps two—or three, with mustard.*

"Well," the boss sighed, *"let's see it . . . Go on, W., begin the scene where you tear off her dress."*

He rushes toward the famished Mme Loquette with dagger drawn, and she suddenly turns into a pursued and panting child, claws bared . . . for an instant, they struggle, the dress rips from top to bottom, and Mme Loquette is revealed half-naked, her bosom bared to the knife.

"Oops! stop there, my dears. It's a fine effect, but, wait . . ." The boss meditates, smacks his lips, mutters.

"Of course, of course it's not . . . it's not naked enough there!" The bored filly jumps as though bitten by a wasp.

"Not naked enough! What more do you want?"

"Well, I'd like . . . I don't know . . . I'd like . . ." Inspired, he steps back a few steps and stretches out his arm; with the voice of a pilot taking off, he says:

"Let out a breast!" [1]

Nudity onstage, however, turned paradoxically into extreme modesty off; Colette, like her fellow actresses in the theater or on the vaudeville stage, maintained *a singular and professional modesty that enabled them to stand confidently naked before the footlights, but protected them on the streets with buttresses of severe taffetas, opaque wimples.* Lovely Bastienne, covered up to the eyes in a dinner dress, her bosom covered with a triple layer of muslin, *struck her concealed breasts and exclaimed, "That, my dear sir, is the business solely of my profession and my lover!"* [2]

Critical opinion at the time was very divided as to Colette's stage talent; we cannot know, since there is no film, no trace that would help us to form an opinion. The *Album Comique* of October 1908 notes that "The characteristic thing about Colette Willy's acting is that she follows no hard and fast rules but, on the contrary, has a total sincerity of expression, almost impulsive, almost like actual emotions. She gives all of herself to her character, she lives it more than she acts it."

André Rouveyre's judgment, full as it is of the standard prejudices of the day, testifies to the way she was viewed by certain of her contemporaries: "She danced pantomime, and she danced naked. It was a sorry sight. Although Colette already possessed wings of the spirit, they were not in evidence on her body in the theater. . . . She gamboled about, but there was nothing aerial about her. . . . After each jump, her naked feet would hit the floor with a thud, heel and sole would strike the cold stage and her legs would unsteadily absorb the shock. . . . Colette's nakedness, although daring at the time, and her frantic attempts to dance and to perform in pantomime were obviously a mistake, but it did enable us to discern with even greater advantage, perhaps, the exclusive and inviolate genius of her writing." [3] Rouveyre does not tell us why Colette's nudity was "obviously a mistake," nor does he explain the precise relationship her stage nudity had with the "exclusive and inviolate genius" present in her books. With his comment, we can compare a description by Rachilde dated December 1, 1913: "I can still see in the half-light of a stage night a tiny faun, a reed flute at its mouth, spying on the nymph's frolics. Malicious, clumsy, yes—but the line was so pure, the gestures so chaste, such a poetic rhythm guided its every move, that one sensed it to be a flesh and blood creature against the cardboard scenery, one believed in it despite the rays of the electric moon. He did not dance, he lived his dream, creating a beautiful nature amid the most factitious surroundings." [4] Rachilde had also made a clear-sighted evaluation of the *Claudine* novels when they appeared. Indifferent as she was to the scandals about the dancer's morals, or her nudity, might she not also have been equally clear-sighted about her stage performances in which Colette, for the pleasure of her contemporaries, "was living her dream"?

⚜ TRAVELING COMPANIONS, ENFANTS DU PARADIS

Colette's career in the music halls, from the time of the Moulin Rouge scandal to the year of her daughter's birth, was a continuous occupation. In November 1907, the year of the scandal, she performed in a pantomime at the Apollo entitled *La Chair* (*The Flesh*), partnered by Georges Wague, and enjoyed an enormous success. In 1908, the year of her first tour, she was in Geneva on August 23, performing in a play by Xanrof and Guérin. From November 18 to 29, she played the eponymous heroine created by Polaire in a series of fifteen performances of *Claudine à Paris* at the Alcazar theater in Brussels, accompanied by Missy. She performed the same play from December 19 to 27 at the Scala in Lyons. Early in 1909, she was performing in a play she had written herself, *En Camarades*, at the Comédie Royale, along with her dog, Toby-Chien.*

In February, she was again in Brussels in *La Chair*, and appeared in the *Claudine* plays in the South of France; she was to appear in *La Chair* again at the Gaité-Rochechouart in Paris, in December in Brussels, in February-March 1910 in Grenoble and Nice, and in September in Dijon. She was back in it again in April 1911 at the Gaité Montparnasse, and in June–July she took the play to Geneva, Lausanne and the Etoile-Palace. In August, she performed in a new pantomime entitled *Bat' d'Af* at the Ba-Ta-Clan in Paris, and another entitled *L'Oiseau de nuit*, a title she had suggested to the Gaité-Rochechouart. In April 1912, she returned to the Ba-Ta-Clan in *La Chatte amoureuse*, which was one of the acts in a revue entitled *Ça Grise* (*It's Intoxicating*). Before the war, on July 3, 1913, Bel-Gazou her daughter was born, and for a few years her activities as a mime and a dancer had to be suspended. And at barely forty, her music hall days were over. She was always to recall them, with emotion, as "the most peaceful years of my life, just like being on retreat in some convent!" [1]

During these years, Colette Willy—"Colettevili" as her fellow performers called her—came into contact in her performances and on tour with a vast number of "artists," a very small minority of whom managed to win out over poverty, need, and become well known; most of whom did not. There is only one really important figure in her life throughout this period, Georges Wague, who is called "Brague" in *La Vagabonde*, *L'Envers du music-hall* and *L'Entrave*, and "W" in *Les Vrilles de la vigne*. Georges Wague was simultaneously Colette's teacher, partner, associate, friend and model. All her books about this period treat him with affection and kindness: a uniquely Parisian personality, kind, churlish, a hard worker, exacting with himself and others, efficient, fun-loving, fair, pitiless

---

* Toby-Chien, after the Willys' separation, had ended up being given to a third party; at this time, Colette had two dogs, a bulldog named Poucette and a German shepherd, Belle Aude. In her later recollection of *En Camarades*, Colette was obviously mistaken in attributing this role to Toby-Chien.

and unrivaled in the difficult world of pantomime or *"pantoche,"* as
Colette calls it.[2] They often toured as a trio with Wague's wife,
Christiane Kerf, or Mendelys, who was also a mime. *For Brague, I
had no need to powder my nose or exaggerate my eyelids with a
blue line. . . . The only time Brague pays attention to me at rehearsals is to say:*

*"Don't do that, it's ugly. . . . Don't lift your upper lip, it makes
you look like a fish. . . . Don't blink your eyes, you look like a blue
rat. . . . Don't wriggle your behind when you walk, you look like
a brood mare."* [3] Quick to make fun of himself, tolerant of others,
Brague/Wague respected his friend's privacy. Inspecting Renée
Néré's meticulous home, he asked sarcastically, just like a man:

"And who's all this for?"

"What do you mean? It's for me."

*"For you? Only for you all by yourself? Forgive me, but I think
that's kind of . . . dumb. . . . You broads are all alike."* [4]

Although his disapproval was expressed in silence, he believed that
for women, undue continence where men were concerned was a
mistake, and was of the opinion that a good dose of male companionship was just what his colleague needed. However, he was strict
about maintaining a separation between professional and private life.
*"I really like a nice tour with a bunch of friends. You know me, as
I've always said, love and work don't mix."* He himself was fond of
a bit of adventure on tour. Bordeaux: *"a nice town, I laid a pretty
girl there . . . tiny little thing, nice tits, short legs, plump little feet,
just the kind I like."* [5]

Wague was fond of using lapidary phrases to sum up his professional experience, such as "Wet weather, dry pockets." He was always ready for a joke; one of his favorite pastimes was to play at
being a dirty old man on public conveyances: he would choose a
victim, some shy girl or tough old maid, sit down across from her,
and stare at her lasciviously, lewdly scrutinizing every feature of
her face, until she blushed, coughed, adjusted her clothing, turned her
head, or fled from the apparent sex maniac: *"It's an excellent facial
exercise,"* Brague *would remark. "When they set up a class for me
to teach pantomime at the Conservatory, I'll make all my students
rehearse it, together and separately."* [6]

And surprisingly, he finally got his class, partly thanks to Colette.
When interviewed about his former partner after she had gone on
to become famous, he recalled her obsession with time: she was always early—he had nicknamed her "What time is it?"—her discipline

at work, her habit of frittering away her salary on tour on useless objects, a basket for her dog, lace-bordered writing paper.

Maurice Chevalier recognized himself in the character of Cavaillon in *La Vagabonde: Young, already well known in vaudeville, everyone envied him. They said "Dranem is afraid of him," "he can name his own price." . . . He was always saying "I'm killing myself." All day he looks forward to the time for his performance, during which he forgets himself, has fun, becomes young again, entertains the public. He doesn't drink, he doesn't carouse. He invests his money and he's dying of boredom.* [7]

A singer named Frehel served as model for "Jadin" in the same novel. She sang like a seamstress, a streetsinger. The public adores her in *her overlong dress without any pretense to style, her chestnut hair hanging loose.* But it is possible to be misled by Colette's game of condensing many real people into one fictional character, giving traits of one person to another, collating, altering personalities, names and places. Keys often open the wrong doors, in the end. The people who most interested her were "unimportant" people, stagehands, accompanists, wardrobe mistresses, cashiers, dressers, second-rate artists, comedians, tightrope walkers, choristers, all the changing and indistinguishable characters of her backstage world.

She dwelt very little on the audience, aware only of its omnipresent, mocking picturesqueness. She wrote that *the minute I step onto the stage, I no longer belong to myself,* [8] which simply means that the only important thing was not to fall down when dancing, not to catch her heel in the hem of her dress. The audience was a popular one, easily amused. It consisted for the most part of children of paradise, the public of the upper balconies. Dressed in sweaters, colorful collarless shirts, their hands thrust into the pockets of their tight jackets, berets on their heads, unlit cigarettes hanging from their mouths, "pimps" filled the Empyrée Clichy on weekends.* Saturdays were always sold out, *but as Jadin rather crudely put it, "What the hell do I care—I don't get a percentage of the take."* [9] *Some shell out 2.25 francs to reserve one of the cane-bottomed chairs close to the stage. These are the faithful, passionate fans, the ones who talk back to the artists, who boo them or applaud them, who make scatalogical remarks or shout obscenities that break up the entire audience. Sometimes, they get carried away, they go too far, and the*

---

* This is the name Colette gives to the Parisian vaudeville house in *La Vagabonde* where Renée Néré performs. She herself played in the Gaité-Rochechouart, the Moulin Rouge, the Ba-Ta-Clan.

whole thing turns into a real brawl. . . . The artist onstage had best wait with deadpan expression, stock-still, until the storm rolls over— unless he wants to become a target for the oranges, rolled-up pro- grams and coins flying through the air. [10]

Fortunately, the head cashier is there to maintain order.

She presides over the box office and is able to wither any tough guy or real *apache* who tries to purchase a ticket to one of the spe- cial cane-bottomed seats:

"Keep your forty-five sous and get out!"

"But why, Madame Barnet? What did I do?"

"Oh sure, 'What did I do?' You think I didn't see you last Satur- day—you were in number one in the gallery, weren't you?"

"Who says so?"

"You're the one that stood up during the pantomime and yelled, 'She's only showing one tit, I want to see both of 'em—I paid two bits, one per tit!' "

"Me? Come on, Madame Barnet, I behave myself, I don't do things like that. I swear, it wasn't me."

"Don't give me that. I saw you, didn't I, and that's it! You can't have a seat for another week. Put away your money and get out!" [11]

At the Empyrée Clichy, in Paris as a rule, there was some pro- tection. But in the country there were old-fashioned *cafés chantants* and music halls where one had to pass through a section of the audi- torium to get onto the stage. There were touchy moments when *we were nudged and elbowed and the way was purposely blocked so that they could get a better look at us.* [12] Fingers and furtive hands would explore, shawls were surreptitiously pulled, or the hems of dresses. *Heads held high, we had to face the contempt and con- cupiscence of this excited mob like proud prisoners.* [13]

For the first time in her life, Colette was made aware of the im- portance of her body as a tool of her trade instead of merely a sexual object to be adorned. She had neglected her body when she was unhappy; now she began to care for it zealously. *Realizing the value of health, the anxiety of losing it, I began to take care of myself, to worry about my bowels, my stomach, my skin, with the tetched vigilance of a devoted landlord.* [14] One had to be strict: it was a rough life.

On tour, she returned to the hotel after midnight weighed down with a heavy makeup box. The exhausted woman would wait in the damp night, leaning against the door until the night porter finally roused himself to let her in. It was a long way from Gabrielle to

Colettevili! Her hotel room would be cold, the sheets damp, the pitcher of hot water would have cooled off. And there were other even more unpleasant nights on the train, sleeping on one's hat and crushing it, arriving at dawn in some hostile little town to eat a heavy breakfast in a smoky brasserie, overcome with drowsiness. Wague was a hard taskmaster:

"Eat up! Rehearsal at two o'clock!"

"To hell with that! I'm going to the hotel and get some sleep. And don't use that tone of voice with me!"

"Oh, excuse me, Your Majesty. I merely intended to humbly beg Your Majesty to be so good as to get the lead out!" [15]

Her Majesty made a rapid mental calculation: *An hour and a half or two hours of orchestra rehearsal, that gets us back to the hotel at seven . . . a rehearsal scheduled for two hours always took around four and a half . . . then dressing, dinner, back to the hall at nine, dressed again at quarter to twelve, just time for a quick lemonade at the bar. . . . My God, if all goes well I might be in a bed within ten hours.*[16]

And in those hours, the work was demanding. Wague was a ruthless and difficult director. His advice was rough, full of invective: *so many harsh words for one delicate gesture. . . . How many attempts and failures were written on the faces of these three mimes, what barely masked fatigue! Hands forced to speak, arms fleetingly eloquent . . . forced to land without pressure, like mutilated statues. . . . We struggled to remove from our mute dialogues all speech, all vulgar obstacles to our silence, our perfect silence . . . proud that we could manage to express everything . . . without any hindrance, any support other than music.*[17] This is an odd praise of silence, coming from a writer—and this is not the least of Colette's paradoxes, the author of a body of work that extends to sixteen volumes praising silence in the higher beings. Her profession of pantomime taught her her profession as a writer. Her eye became more keen, she learned how to create out of a few gestures an entire ten-line novel. For example: once upon a time, backstage in the music hall, there was an English girl named Glory and a skirt-chasing French tenor named Marcel. Neither could speak the other's language. There was a lengthy flirtation, the usual thing, in which Glory acted the coquette, *an almost mute idyll, like a pantomime. No music other than Glory's cheerful voice, scarcely a word other than her loving "Mass'l." First it would be joyous, slightly nasal, and then slower, "Mass'l" would sound flirtatious, coaxing, demanding, and*

*then one day a "Mass'l" so tremulous, so defeated, so full of suppli-
cation . . . this evening I heard it I believe for the last time, for at
the top of the stairs, huddled on the very last step, I found Glory all
alone, her wig askew, weeping humbly through her makeup and repeating in a low voice, "Mass'l."* [18]

❋ THE CAF' CONC'—TOTAL EXPLOITATION

Colette was placed—by circumstances, by her talent—in a position
that enabled her to make a profound study of her surroundings;
performing and playing at being an actress on the surface, she was
both an observer and a participant. As a protected bourgeoise accustomed to having others provide her basic comforts, she descended
in the social scale when she began to perform in vaudeville. Just as
in her school in Saint-Sauveur, she found herself in a lower social
position among the lower-class, then rural, now urban. Her comrades were the proletariat of the theater, and she was not one of
them; they never let her forget it:

"Gribiche isn't a member of the union."

"Neither am I," I said.

*"I would have been surprised to be told otherwise," Carmen re-
marked, overpolite, cold.*

*"You're young," Lise Damoiseau said. "Young in the trade, I
mean."*

*I said nothing. Their cruelty, apparently based on protocol, left
me speechless, as did their perspicacity in sensing—beneath my inex-
perience—my bourgeois past, in discovering that beneath my youth,
my apparent youth, there was really a thirty-two-year-old woman
who didn't look her age.*[1] (And Colette has taken off a few years in
this passage; at whatever time she is situating the action of *Gribiche*,
she herself was at least thirty-three when she began working in
vaudeville.)

She turned to vaudeville as she would have gone to work in a
factory, not to join her proletarian sisters and brothers like Simone
Weil, as a humanistic intellectual, not for professional reasons, to
gather material for her writing as Zola had done in the mines, but
out of necessity. Her evocations of music hall life are not made from
the outside, as if it were some kind of zoo; she is narrating her own
life. These men and women were her comrades, forced upon her as
well as chosen by her; their problems and anxieties are her problems,
her anxieties; the conflicting or harmonious relationships she describes

are real relationships. Neither an ethnologist, a sociologist nor an historian, Colette simply relates "her" music hall. Yet the distance created by her different social status, her intimate experience of other ways of life, the temporary nature of her stay in vaudeville, all combined to give her a particular detachment that made for creative perspective. *L'Envers du music-hall* describes one of the fundamental experiences of Colette's life: it was a glimpse into a working-class world more varied than the usual proletariat, one in which the female element was considerably more important. In a certain way, Colette lived as a working-class woman. She did not approach her life as a militant, she had no ideological prejudices, but from it she gained a clear realization of class and sex consciousness. The rapidity with which she moved from one stratum of society to another also makes us realize how socially mobile women are, and how fragile that mobility is. Yesterday, she had been a respectable middle-class woman; today, she is a semiworking-class actress; tomorrow she will be a baroness. Women were less strictly tied to one social class than men, to an almost unalterable hierarchy. The wheel of fortune could drop her in an instant from the heights to the bottom of the rickety social ladder.

Although she does not formulate her insights in class terms Colette nevertheless became aware of the twofold alienation of the working-class woman. In all her writing from this period on, she will unforgettably describe the minor performer from a working-class background who must bravely face up to the threat of poverty. At once outside and in this class, she is in the same position as the "accompanist" in *L'Envers du music-hall* who remarks: *Here you only see the trouble people have to take. The lights, the spangles, the costumes and makeup faces, the smiles, that's not what I see. . . . I can see the training, the sweat, skin that is sallow in the light of day, disappointment. . . . It's as if I alone see things from the back and everyone else sees them from the front.*[2]

L'Envers du music-hall is both a revelation and a demystification of the whole inglorious backstage world of the variety stage. It is like Lesbos. Colette's entry into these two milieus occurred at the same time, and both were populated in their different ways by women. To both, her approach is the same; she penetrates their mystery, she takes them out of the shadows and examines them in the light. In this way, she is able to examine herself, her position in both worlds. It is a way of freely exercising her own freedom. And her ambiguous position, not belonging completely to either of these worlds, her eternal status as an outsider, are what give her her creative breadth, unhappy as her life must have been at the time.

From force of inertia—the weighty contact of her feet with the stage—the dancer acquires her spectacular elevation, her wingèd grace; Colette, in her own sweat, her fatigue, her daily struggle against cold, hunger and anxiety, finds the words to describe the harsh life of her colleagues, her troupe. And since she is both an exile and an inhabitant of both Lesbos and the music hall, she finds freedom outside her former cage. What would freedom mean if there were no fetters? The music hall world, which might have been a traumatic experience both socially and economically, became a school for fantasy, for the imagination—despite its rigors and its discipline—and Colette, with her curiosity inherited from Sido, was continually awake to her unending discovery of its countless "demons and marvels."

⚜ Miseries

There were not many love stories in the music hall world. The story of Gitanette is very like the story of Glory. Gitanette loves Rita, but Rita does not love her as much. They occupied the dressing room next to Colette's, the door between them was always open; *they were content to be working together, to seek refuge in each other, each protecting the other from the desolation of prostitution, from often-cruel men.*[1] Then one day, Rita left Gitanette for Lucie Desrosiers, a *big redheaded broad* who also made off with part of the couple's savings. Many years later, when Colette met her again, Gitanette was still brooding about it: *"I guess you're right when you say time cures everything, but it depends on the person, too. You see, I didn't know anyone but Rita, it just happened to be that way. I never had a boyfriend, I never knew what a child was, but when I'd see a pair of lovers who were happy together, or married people with little kids on their laps, I'd say to myself 'I've got everything you do, I've got Rita.'"* [2]

Unhappy love is a luxury. The main concern was always the most basic: eating. *"Eating well," Brague says, "eating. . . . People who have always had enough don't appreciate it. I can remember a time when I had a bill at the bistro and not even enough for a piece of bread . . . I'd drink a glass of red wine and almost cry at the thought of a little fresh crust of bread to dunk in it." "And me," beautiful Bastienne chimes in, "when I was only a kid, fifteen or sixteen years old, I almost fainted one morning in dance class because I hadn't been eating enough. The ballet mistress asked me if I was sick, but I was a real trouper, I told her 'It's my lover, Madame, he's worn me out!' A lover! As if I knew what that was! She threw her hands up, 'Ah, my child, you won't have your marvelous posture for long at that rate. But what's got into you all!' I know what hadn't got into me—a nice bowl of hot soup!"* [3]

On tour, Gonzales, one of the extras, would go without eating in order to have enough to subsist on for a couple of months afterward. He concealed his poverty as if it were a crime, and Colette, suspecting the true state of affairs, would set childish traps for him:

"Aren't you having any coffee, Gonzales?"

"No thanks, I don't drink it . . . nerves, you know!"

"That's not very friendly, today's my turn to buy. You can't be the only one to refuse."

"Well, if you put it that way . . . just to be friendly." [4] In the end, Gonzales confided in her: the son of a bookbinder, he had left home to go on the stage. Since then, he had literally been starving. *"You've got to have the stomach for it, and I don't any longer . . . we're paid so little. I haven't got a name, no wardrobe, no profession outside the theater . . . no savings. I don't think I'll make old bones."* [5]

Another *child with the remains of mucous membrane fever,* a sickly singer wilting in the hot weather, keeps going on iced absinthe. Another one who will not make old bones.

Bastienne is seventeen, a lovely girl, startlingly so, tall, *expensive to feed* as she says, whose diet is insufficient for someone five months pregnant.

No word from the child's father.

"The man's just bad, that's all," Bastienne says. No more. She doesn't want to be coddled, *she rejects help, bridling indignantly.* *"I'm not sick!"* She accepts the burden that pushes out her belt, treating it roughly with the insouciance of her seventeen years:

"You—I'll make you behave!"

And she tightens her belt . . . she laughingly scolds her burden, slapping her stomach with her hand. "Boy, does he make me hungry." . . . Without an evil thought in her head, she commits all the heroic follies girls without a sou commit; having paid up her hotel bill, she often goes to bed without either dinner or supper, she wears her corset all night to "cut the hunger." [6]

Gribiche, who is one of the "French soldiers" in the revue, has chances even slimmer than Bastienne's. Her mother is a fortune-teller who isn't exactly "like that"—the familiar crossed fingers—with her daughter, who is pregnant. Arriving to present Gribiche, who has "fallen down the stairs," with the fruits of a collection to which her colleagues have all chipped in, Colettevili and two other "artistes" find her and her mother, Mme Saure, in a slum tenement room with holes in the roof, furnished with a single bed on which the terrified girl lies bleeding.

"What would hurt less," Carmen said, "would be a bowl of really soapy water, and then you run around as fast as you can for fifteen minutes."

"Do you think, Madame, that maybe she should see the midwife?"

"So she can get herself cut up," Mme Saure replied with bitter disdain, "like all the rest of them! They get a kick out of that, obviously, curtain rods in a rubber tube, and they poke you and poke you." [7]

Colette's recollection of Gribiche—or Mlle Ourika, "who cashed in her chips in Cochin," as they say—is of a *tiny martyred being, lying flat on her bed beside her small-paned window.*[8] No one ever saw Gribiche again after she tore her French military trousers on the stairs and was fined twenty francs; even in the throes of abortion, a variety chorus girl had to obey the rules. Her disappearance probably caused less of a sensation than did the fine. Her sagacious and hardened companions, *passive and prudent when faced with the dangers of childbirth . . . spoke of monstrous things in casual tones.* Hospitals were closed to girls who had had abortions. There were "encounters," *threats I knew nothing about, some kinds of criminal behavior made them discreet.*[9] Colette was stunned by Gribiche and those like her. When the time came to tell her story, she hesitated, replacing it *with a blank, with elisions, with an asterisk . . . as I tell her story now, I am naturally concealing her real name. . . . On Gribiche's memory I bestow all the attributes of silence, including the conventional signs in music that signify an interruption in the melody, the poor mute swallow perched on the five black wires of the staff, the rest hooked like a sigh onto those wires, the pause like a staring pupil beneath a huge and terrified eyebrow.*[10] Against the world's sound and fury, only the rhetorical devices of silence can honor the memory, the long history of aborted women.

And others must risk their ill-paid skins each evening, twice on matinée days: the little black trick cyclist struggling against the centrifuge, the Human Snake who forces himself to suffer such tortures that sometimes his face refuses to obey him and takes on the expression of someone suffering in hellfire, the female target whose temples are constantly grazed by the knife-thrower's blades. Is it today that he or she will be killed? And yet they go gaily on, they eat their meager midday meals, children, animals, women, adolescents, men, all in the same boat, not friends but companions, together in a comforting promiscuity.

In the great brotherhood of the music hall, all sexes, ages, statuses, are equal. There are no real children. Princess Lily was a child prodigy, the daughter of a seamstress, with the good fortune to look young for her age and who was taking advantage of it for as long as possible. The "Queen of Gall," as the others called her, continually complains to her mother that she is growing too fast. " '*Couldn't you have seen to it I was born a dwarf?' that's how she reproached me!* '*But I'm your mother, after all. What if I were to grab you by the hand and stop you from going on with the theater . . .' And she laughed. 'Stop me from going on? I suppose you're going to get up there and sing Chiribiribi to pay the rent?' For four years now,*" *her mother sighed, "I've not heard her talk like a child.*" [11]

While Princess Lily's success is evanescent, the "Reject," a frail adolescent raised on abuse and suddenly abandoned by her hysterical "sister," a Russian chanteuse and Spanish dancer, is old enough to get along on her own. "*Eighteen!*" *Jady barked, in the throes of a hangover and bronchitis, "Eighteen! and she expects me to feel sorry for her!*" [12] Poverty makes hard bedfellows. Colette's own past had been a sheltered one. Yet when confronted with a child without a childhood, with a rejected child, a tuberculous adolescent or an aging comedy actress who must lay out all her savings to pay for a bad winter attack of bronchitis, she never waxes sentimental. If she feels emotion, she is silent about it. She respects the reserve of suffering, both her own and others. Only the "miniature circus" number forces her to avert her eyes: *I no longer could stand to watch them up there, captive, well behaved, the sight of their resignation had become unbearable. I knew that the little martingaled horse tried in vain to toss its head and pawed with its foreleg in an ataxic motion. I knew that the ill and melancholy monkey would childishly lean its head on its companion's shoulder and shut its eyes . . . that the bear, especially the little bear, would clasp its head between its paws and whimper and whine softly because the narrow strap buckled around its muzzle was almost cutting through its lip.*

I would have liked to forget this miserable group in their white leather harnesses and their bells, adorned with ribbons, to forget their panting jaws, the harsh breathing of these starving animals, I never wanted to see or pity again that animal pain I could do nothing to assuage.[13]

❦ THE VARIETY GIRLS: FACTORY AND LAUNDRY

Although Colette makes no conscious effort in her depiction of the backstage life of the music hall to single them out, women—children, girls, adults, old women—appear with a frequency that is more than statistical. Just as she will show a predilection for the female in the animal world—dogs, cats, even panthers—so women play the principal roles in her inside picture of the theatrical world. Women played a preponderant role on the stage, particularly in the spectacular revues that were so popular during this period, entertainments in which the display of women was given pride of place, women covered with feathers, naked under gauzy draperies, powdered with gold and azure. Already an inhabitant of Lesbos, Colette enters this female universe with considerable pleasure, a world where *one sex nearly obliterated the other, dominating by its monosexual number, odor, electricity. A world of women in which sadness rose and fell like a barometer. . . . I was not affected, but because I had spent very little time with women and suffered from only one man, I welcomed it.*[1]

When Colette evokes the variety stage and her companions, particularly the women, she very naturally regards them as hired labor. Not at all bohemian, quite unlike the racy picture of this world so prevalent in bourgeois minds, particularly where its female population is concerned, the world of the music halls is more like a factory than a temple of the arts because of the social background from which most of the artists come, their salary, their working conditions. And further unlike the legend, so are the morals and education of its inhabitants. *"Don't talk to me about your travels,"* Ida, the Fat Lady, says in *Ida et Hector.* *"All cities are just alike! First off, there's always a vaudeville house to work in, a Munich brasserie to eat in, and thirdly, a bad hotel to sleep in!"* Exoticism is a cultivated bourgeois taste. Ida finds the Tunisian souks *"ill kept," "full of filth . . . rugs that aren't even new, broken pottery, everything's second-hand, right? . . . And as for the men! Fine-looking men, Madame, who mince along holding little bouquets of roses and violets . . . and no one says a word!"*[2] Bastienne's universe is summed up by the

Five Parts of the Globe, one of the acts she has danced in, uniting *"America, terra-cotta makeup; Africa, black tights; Spain, fringed shawl; France, a white tutu; and Russia, red morocco boots."* [3]

Homey, domestic, these are two of the adjectives she employs in describing these young, working-class artistes, and Colette includes herself. Between dressing, undressing, makeup, dashing up and down the stairs and making forlorn appearances on the stage, five chorus girls slowly asphyxiate in their cramped dressing room whose single window looks onto an alleyway; and yet they are always busy at something, sewing feverishly whenever they can find a free minute. Childbearing Vanda always pulls from her pocket a child's sock with a hole, or a flannel vest on which she surreptitiously stitches away. A veteran performer pays for her bus trips home on Sundays and Thursdays by knitting for a hosiery shop. Beneath the layers of makeup, Colette's attentive eyes discern the reddened wrists, the hardened hands that cook and scrub and sweep; she imagines the laddered stockings, the flimsy-soled shoes, the damp staircase leading to some unheated room with its feeble candlelight. Exhausted, neither wicked nor flirtatious, they move from hotel to train, from train to theater, racked with hunger and lack of sleep, concerned about the future, returning home at all hours to heat their man's soup, a man who gets up when they go to bed and goes off to his job after sending the children to school.

And after rehearsals, before the evening performance, they have just enough time to dash home *to a peevish mother, to wash their hands, retie their hair band tight around their foreheads, make sure the kid hasn't fallen out of the window or burnt himself on the stove, and then rush off again. They jump into busses, subways, trams, along with all the other workers, the dressmakers, the seamstresses, the cashiers, and typists, who are ending their working day!* [4] One of them never has time for a hot meal; she lives too far away, she is always on the run. *She doesn't earn her 180 francs a month by the performance, but by the kilometer!* [5] And another: *Had she perhaps fallen into the habit of perpetually complaining because of her husband, a consumptive bookbinder? She has more than enough to do out there near Château d'Eau with her man and her two kids.* [6] And as they wend their way home at dawn after their long night's work they are very like their sisters and mothers returning from work on some laundry boat moored in the Seine, these women in their makeup, their tawdry and tinseled costumes.

Bastienne is on top of the world; she has been eating her fill every day since *a nice working boy, dazzled and full of pity, brought mother and child home one Christmas Eve when Bastienne was celebrating on four sous' worth of roasted chestnuts.* . . . *For Bastienne, now flourishing, once impoverished, life meant dancing first, then working, in the humble domestic sense females use that word.*[7] Hélène has been made bitter by her hard past, and Colette is almost frightened by her forthright common sense. She plasters her face with makeup: *"I know I'm of an age to do without all that muck. . . . But it's useful. You see, I'm making up for the future. When I'm twenty years older, I won't have to add anything. I can afford to be sick, to have bags under my eyes. It's useful, it's a disguise. I have a good reason for everything I do."* [8]

However, they don't all manage to get along like Hélène and Bastienne. There are "Mary Badluck," the "Reject," who return exhausted to their hot, small rooms around Caulaincourt, overlooking the Montmartre cemetery. Men wait for them after the performance and follow them through the dark streets on summer nights, whispering propositions, obscenities, threats. At home, they make a meal on a few cherries while sitting in their slips in front of their narrow windows to catch the feeble breeze. *The thin walls stay warm throughout the night, the breeze carries in the fumes from some factory.*[9] From her sojourn in this land of working-class women, from her knowledge of other circles, Colette gained a lifelong admiration for the ability of women to resist:

"She's made of steel!"

"No, she's just a woman!" [10]

And she includes herself and her own small daily victories over time, over her body, over poverty and contempt, over suffering, victories that are the fruit of a specifically female heroism. Colette believed in these things for the rest of her life, combining naive, superhuman bravado with a passive, durable and effective resistance, without fuss or furor, a resistance that, in the end, was to become totally impregnable.

⚜ STRIKE

When such female resistance, obscure and stubborn, runs up against male resistance, which is more securely fixed in History, the result can sometimes lead to strike.

And Colette's occupation was much more insecure than had she been a laborer. The lives of working artistes were lived between two extremes: "Everything's coming up roses," or "Things couldn't be worse."

Colette understood their discretion, their restraint. Although they displayed their bodies, these working girls were strangely reticent, *their silence about their personal lives was a polite way of saying "that doesn't concern you."* [1] At times, however, these exploited women could revolt; in the theatrical world there is generally not the same struggle for social betterment that exists in the world of the factory, but there were some with combative spirits, some who demanded the minimum due them.

Wilson, a chorus girl, *lifted the blond fringe of hair covering her forehead and revealed a badly healed scar:*

"You can't imagine how it still hurts!"

"Good enough for you!" Anita interrupts dryly. "So you let some scenery fall on your noggin, and since the manager is disgusting enough to fire you rather than cough up for 2 sous of ether on a cold compress, not even 40 sous for the cab or 100 sous for the doctor—when you're laid up at home half-dead for a week—and you don't even have the guts to sue the management, you don't complain, you just take it! Ah, if it had been me . . ." [2]

One day the word goes out—strike! At the end of a long day of rehearsal, unpaid rehearsal, a mime with the same fatalistic patience as Colettevili—a patience taught them by their profession—watches the "Great Concubines of History" go into their pavane for the umpteenth time, *"Another day down the drain for the rest of us. . . . Look at them, the 'Great Concubines'! And to think they're grinding away for free!"* . . . *"Strike—oh Lord! a strike!" Everyone had the idea, everyone was muttering it in corners; the chorus girls in the next revue, the "canaries," all talked of nothing else, each after her fashion: some loudly whisper "Strike!" "Paid matinées and paid rehearsals!" and some wave their muffs like flags, their handbags like weapons. . . . Unlike the men—singers, mimes, dancers, acrobats—who tried to voice their demands in courteous, man-to-man, calm discussions, my comrades, the caf' conc' girls, are immediately fired up. . . . Emotional Parisiennes, they have a confused picture of rushing out into the streets at the word "Strike!"—of riots and barricades. . . . They don't do it often. The simple and rigorous discipline that controls their lives allows for few infractions. . . . They were so easy to regiment, these poor honeyless bees. The lowliest milliner's apprentice in the Rue de la Paix made more than they. They had been as ready to yell "Strike!" as to say "We're going to win the lottery," without any real belief in it. Now that they are beginning to believe in it, they are trembling with hope.*[3]

⚜ CARNAL SIRENS

Oddly enough, the "caf' conc' girls," "my comrades," dealt with the strike in the same way Colette had earlier dealt with her own revolt—clumsily, but courageously. When one has been alienated for so long that alienation had turned into voluntary servitude, it is hard to proceed to greater freedom without setbacks, without pain. Colette always recognized the conflict between her desire to be completely autonomous and her desire—to which she was tempted by those demons who flaunt the age-old image of the ideal woman—to be submissive and calm; she describes this conflict in *La Vagabonde*. The novel contains a complete dialectical history of female freedom.

Colette had met Auguste Hériot, the young and wealthy dandy, around 1910; she may well have had an affair with him. In that same year—the year in which *La Vagabonde* was published—she met Henry de Jouvenel at the offices of *Le Matin*. She was living through a period of change, and the novel describes the elements involved. The plot is simple: Maxime, who is Renée Néré's "suitor," not her lover, offers her love with marriage, material comfort, emotional security with a man whom she feels, this time, will be faithful to her. In addition to offering her the sensual pleasure she is seeking, Maxime himself suits her. And despite all this, this "disreputable" music hall performer, this déclassée caf' conc' performer, allows herself the luxury of refusing him. The text clearly describes her motives, detailing with considerable subtlety the specific contradictions inherent in female sexuality. Of course, Renée could sleep with Maxime without marrying him. She refuses not out of coquetry, not out of calculation or modesty, but out of prudence. She does not trust herself, she feels that the act of love, for a basically monogamous woman, is a dangerous and dangerously simple way to bind herself to her lover. This problem was to be resolved with Henry de Jouvenel, and in *L'Entrave*. Intellectually, Colette wanted pure pleasure, voluptuous lovemaking, passing adventures with no future, the perfect embrace that *will not leave a trace*. At the same time, however, she realizes that pleasure can bind her to a man, that love furtively creeps into any pleasure, and love terrifies her. *The most abandoned license doesn't faze me, but I don't like the word "love."* . . . *If I had lost a child I loved, I don't think I would ever again be able to speak its name.*[1]

"When a man leaves her," Simone de Beauvoir has written describing the woman in love, "she feels rejected by the world, lying on her bed in the light; she regains her own name, her own visage, she is someone vanquished, prey, an object. It is then that she needs love. . . . Any woman in love recognizes herself in Andersen's Little Mermaid when she trades her fish tail for a woman's legs and, out of love, walks on needles and burning coals." [2]

Aware that she must part from Maxime, Renée experiences a renewal of her keen desire for him. *My exhausted body illogically suffered pangs of intolerant chastity during which I was thrown into a brazier lit with all those pleasures I had not experienced, the flames consumed me, immobile, my knees pressed together as though the slightest movement would increase my pain. There was no delirium like the delirium of my senses,*[3] she adds soberly, rejecting this image of herself, this *naked undulating shadow agitated by pleasure like a blade of grass in a brook.*[4] Intermittently, the temptation becomes too great and she almost gives in to devoting herself entirely to Maxime; she spontaneously intones the discourse of voluntary servitude: to accept love is to become love's "slave," the slave of a man, *Maxime remained on the bed, and his mute appeal won him that most flattering response, my gaze like a submissive bitch, sheepish, whipped, but cherished, accepting everything—the leash, the collar, the place at its master's feet. . . . He decides, he gives the orders, and along with the homage of my freedom, I tender him my pride.*[5] And in the expectation of becoming her lover and her husband, Maxime, happy and passive, *lets himself be waited on. . . . I had been a female before and I was a female again, suffering from it, enjoying it.*[6]

Linked with this carnal desire and the powerful impulses that assuage it is social conformity, the solid grounding in provincial bourgeois standards that Colette never completely forgot. This is sublimated in her dread of solitude. *So here I am, Renée sighs in her solitary and lugubrious ground-floor apartment, alone, probably for the rest of my life. Already alone.*[7] She embodies the entire traditional social system that condemns single women to lonely and penniless old age, as it also condemns "fallen women"; the same material and moral curse is uttered against both virgins and prostitutes. Colette was almost forty, and she was fraught with anxiety for the future in a period when there were no social security, no pensions.

How long would I have to wander from vaudeville house to theater, from theater to casino, trailing the talents that were politely regarded as "interesting . . . very nice, even more than we're looking for." *But where will it all end?* [8] Solitude too can be ambivalent, sometimes *an intoxicating wine making you drunk on freedom,* sometimes *a bitter tonic,* sometimes, on other days, *a poison that makes you bang your head against the wall.* [9]

Along with her relative isolation and her financial insecurity, Colette was also obsessed with growing old, much more strongly now than later in her life. This may be an anxiety that especially torments women at this age, between thirty and forty, at a time when they are still in full possession of their physical powers, at an age when deterioration is scarcely perceptible. Recalling one winter day the winter mornings of her childhood, Colette suddenly shudders: where had Gabrielle gone while she was dreaming? In the mirror, she then sees an image very like herself, but *marked with light fingernail tracings delicately engraved on her eyelids, in the corners of her mouth, between her stubborn eyebrows,* and she murmurs, alone, *one must grow old. No use crying, clasping your hands in supplication, no use to revolt. One must grow old. Repeat the words not as a cry of despair, but as a summons to a necessary departure. Look at yourself, your eyelids, your lips, lift your curls off your forehead—you're already beginning to retreat from your life, don't forget, one must grow old.* [10] On other days, however, when she is waging the hard struggle with her senses, against the sirens of love, she thinks of old age as a kind of liberation, made up for by the absence of desire; she fantasizes old age as a lovely desert in which one never feels thirsty. An austere paradise, but how preferable to the compromise in which fresh water is doled out as payment for servitude!

"You're made to be devoured like me," sighs Margot, Renée Néré's pessimistic sister-in-law; *"I'm a fine one to preach to you: 'a scalded cat always goes back to the pot.'"* [11] The pressure to conform also comes from outside herself; all her closest friends conspire to throw Renée into Maxime's arms. Even Missy took Auguste's part. Renée becomes irritated at her old friend Hamond's naive attempts to influence her as he plies his "dirty trade of go-between"; and she flares up: *"What do you really want? Do you want me to go to bed with this man? . . . Just say so. You want me to be like everyone else. You want me to make up my mind. What's the difference, after*

*all, him or someone else! You want to disturb my hard-won peace,
to divert my life from this bitter, fortifying, natural course of working for my own living. Or maybe you think I should take a lover for
reasons of health, like a laxative!"* [12]

And there are even moments when carnal desire vanishes, moments in which one has the illusion it has disappeared and given way
effortlessly, without a struggle, to freedom. *Don't fool yourself that
you're dead, cleansed, unburdened. The beast you are forgetting
hibernates and gains strength from its long sleep.*[13]

And face to face once again with Maxime's physical, flesh-and-
blood presence, Renée trembles at the temptation. *And could I peacefully end my life in his vast shadow? Will his faithful eyes still love
me when my charms have faded one by one?* [14]

⚜ WILLFULLY FREE

Her dream of secure tenderness is destroyed by the thought of the
"Other." *Ah, what a difference . . . with the Other . . . save that
he too spoke as a master, he too was made for saying under his
breath, grasping me in a tight fist, "Walk straight ahead, I'm holding
you." I suffer . . . I'm sick of their differences, I'm sick of how
they resemble each other.*[1] After Willy, Colette saw every man as a
master, in every embrace she saw marriage. The first man! *That's the
one that destroys you,* she was later to write, *and after that married
life or something very like it turns into a habit.*[2] Calm, unlike other
men, Maxime sometimes allowed the beast to surface: speaking of
future motherhood, he adds, tellingly, *"and then at least you won't
be able to leave me and get along alone in the world, right? Then
I'll have you for good."* [3] Food for thought. Colette is no longer
Gabrielle; she has learned from her apprenticeships: *What did I
know about this man I love, who wants me? When we have got over
the first brief pleasure, then we will have to start living with each
other, through each other!* And such married domesticity *that turns
so many wives into nursemaids for grown-ups* was all too familiar to
her.[4] *Marriage means "Help me with my necktie," "Dismiss the
maid," "Cut my toenails," "Get up and make me some camomile
tea," "Run my bath!" It's "Get out my new suit and pack my suitcase, I'm going away with Her." Governess, nurse, nanny, enough,
enough enough!* [5] Then her friend Hamond drags out all the arguments she herself had used in earlier days: *"You have to say love, not*

marriage. Love is the one thing that makes all the things you're talking about easy, joyous, glorious, all the servitude. Remember when you were so miserable. I used to shudder with indignation seeing you go about with Taillandy and his girl friends, like some madam, but when I lost patience and spoke my mind, you told me, 'Loving is serving.' " [6]

Those days were over. Colette replaced her former, alienated concept of love with her desire for freedom, for unfettered love. *From love I wanted nothing but love.*

Yet there was a worm in the bud; "freedom" was a paradox fraught with contradiction, with mutual desire, male desire. If there was no "happy love" for a man, there was no free love for a woman. Things have not really changed all that much since. In the earliest days of their relationship, even before there is a question of their going to bed together, Maxime controls Renée, he chooses her friends, becomes jealous of her profession, upsets her serenity, vampirizes her inner peace: *You are offering me an ardent, young, jealous and sincerely attracted lover? Yes, I know. That's called a master, and I don't want a master. . . . When he touches my lips with his, I am no longer myself. He becomes my enemy, a thief robbing me of myself.* [7] If she is not strong enough to deal with the temptations of her flesh, she must abstain. Renée does abstain, she speaks for Colette, but Colette did not abstain. This was not the first time that one of her characters had outdistanced her, nor was it to be the last.

Renée writes to Maxime: *I miss you, and I am choosing . . . everything that is not you. I have known you before and I recognize you. You think you give, but are you not rather a person who takes? You came to share my life. . . . Share, yes; take your share! You want to become half of my actions, to enter the pagoda of my mind whenever you want, isn't that it? But why you and not another? So I've closed it to everyone.* [8]

She rejects him. Colette was to reject Auguste's proposal of marriage; she wanted to go on rejecting, *to be a real vagabond,* refusing to be taken in by Gabrielle's unmasked prince. Away from her enchanted palace, she can then achieve anything she wants, but in return she will see *the masters of the earth pass wandering by. . . . I have no equals, I only have traveling companions.* [9] Nor does Renée retain any illusions about this other chimera. *Yes, a Vagabond, but one resigned to going around in circles like everyone else, my companions, my brothers.* [10] The voyage is an intoxicating one, forever bringing one back to the starting point.

⚜ THE SPRINGS OF WRITING

Her starting point was not this affair, nor even her love for the Other. It existed long before Willy, before Auguste—before Taillandy and Maxime. Colette and Renée discover it together. The latter goes on tour, her mind full of Maxime, having decided to marry him when she returns. But the tour is really an escape. Each turn of the wheels takes Renée further away from Maxime and brings her closer to her familiar countryside where she had lived as an independent child. *Is there still one last little ghost very like myself that sits dreaming in the chimney-corner like a good child, bent over the book she forgets to read? And to this ghost one must add the rest of it: My countryside enchants me . . . lovely perhaps only because I have lost it. . . . No, nothing keeps me here—or anywhere else—no beloved face will emerge like a fresh flower from the mist, rising from the dark waters to beg me tenderly, "Don't go away."* [1] Blindly, the little ghost goes back to the dark source from which so long ago a clear flower—her mother's face—had emerged. The image that haunts Renée's thoughts as she moves ever farther away from Maxime is a familiar one. It is the *cord that tirelessly pulls me back.* On an earlier trip, leaving Rennes on a May morning, Renée had seen from the train window the figure of a child standing on the edge of a woods: *A girl of twelve looking strikingly like myself; serious, frowning, her tanned cheeks like mine once were, her hair slightly bleached by the sun, holding a leafy sapling in her hand as I once did, her hands bronzed and scratched as mine had been. And her wary stance, her ageless and almost sexless eyes that seemed to be taking everything so seriously, they too were mine. . . . There, on the edge of the copse, my untamed childhood watched me pass, dazzled by the rising sun!* [2]

The ageless, almost sexless eyes, the free child, and behind it all the image of a clear and tutelary flower emerging from the water to beg, "Don't go away." On the brink of departure, Renée again hesitates. She is almost at the springs, but something or someone has blurred the outlines of the landscape, ruffled the transparent water. Has it been Time? The man whose flesh has aroused her flesh has grasped the end of the cord once held by the tender maternal hand. She had managed to break that first cord, the more resilient cord. When Gabrielle had run to the spring at dawn, she had ignored Sido's voice summoning her home. "Where are the children?" Now that same dawn is rising over Sète and the Mediterranean, and Renée opens her eyes in her train compartment. *The seven o'clock sun, low on the horizon, did not penetrate the sea, the sea refused to allow itself to be possessed, retaining in its half-awakened state a splendid and nocturnal tint, like velvet blue ink, tinged with black. . . . And I savored one of those perfect moments of unexpected memory, an image, a name. . . . How long had I forgotten Max, for the first time? Yes, forgotten him . . . as though the greatest need of my life was this search for words to tell how yellow the sun was, how blue the sea, how brilliant the jade-white fringes of salt. . . . Yes, forgotten him as though the most urgent thing in the world was my need to possess with my eyes the wonders of the earth. And in this same instant an insidious spirit whispered to me, "And what could be more urgent than that? What if everything save that is only ashes?"* [3]

And thus the encounter with freedom that seals the pact to write is infinitely repeated: the search for words in which to express the wonders of the earth, of oneself: *To write, to pour out passionately all one's own sincerity onto the tempting paper.* [4] The element of Colette's freedom was always liquid, spring water, sea water. At the other end of the cord, her Ariadne mother, her lover, her husband—the cord is so tightly stretched at times that it almost prevents her conquest of her liquid realm. At such times, the ego that sees the face emerging from the spring, the face from which it flees, becomes confused. At other times, the hymn of servitude is sung gladly. And yet, in the dialectic of her freedom, the decision to write is the one irreversible term. Gabrielle escaped from Sido's love to possess the spring at daybreak; Renée flees from Maxime to arrive at the sea, *La Mer(e)*; Colette will flee from the imperious demands of love by returning to Sido, to the source, as her writing will testify.

One of the fetters from which her writing will free her will be her reliance on men. In her alienated state of female servitude, she will resolve the problem of freedom only in her writing, always by a return to the maternal springs, a symbol that varies only in form: Annie leaves Alain, Claudine becomes Renaud's widow, Renée rejects Maxime; Colette, discarded by Willy, assisted by Missy, may perhaps have shared herself with Auguste before giving herself to Henry de Jouvenel. Her next novel, *L'Entrave*, was to be her novel of desire and alienation, the antithesis of *La Vagabonde* and, paradoxically, its continuation. Is it any wonder that the novel is generally considered a failure? Yet at the same time, Colette's encounter with Henry de Jouvenel, the inspiration for the book, was a "success" as such things go, and throughout the time she was restrained by Henry's love, she was silent on the page. There would be no novel between *L'Entrave* (1913) and *Mitsou* (1919).

A life is not a machine. In *La Vagabonde*, a certain route to freedom was envisaged; symbolically, the novel received three votes for the Prix Goncourt. Her decision to become a writer was recognized by authority. Despite her fetters, her increasing freedom would begin to be manifested more and more at the expense of her everyday life. Although Renée refused to enter a cage, Colette was about to return to one. Her text tells us something different than her life, but biography is also a text, and the airy song of freedom is so much more powerful than any earthbound facts. Perhaps the truly and completely free can exist only in books; freedom is a circle and the desire to square it is a delusion life reveals to us. Everything must be grounded in reality, and at forty, Colette had landed on her feet.

IV
COLETTE
DE JOUVENEL
Sharing at Noon

---

*Tell the truth, yes. But the whole truth, one cannot,
one must not.*

COLETTE, La Vagabonde

*A woman has as many countries as she has had
happy love affairs. She is born under any skies
where she has recovered from the pain of loving.*

COLETTE, La Naissance du jour

Colette had written "One only dies from the first man," but the second was also to kill her. She survived them both. In the meanwhile, she had been free, she had thought she was free, she wrote books about freedom. But clearly, her striving for freedom, her renunciation of possessions, cannot be dissociated from her fascination with the act of possession, with possession itself. Perhaps she was less attracted to servitude than to the fate that impels women to love. There is such charm in self-damnation when one is a woman in love. Guided by age-old example, by myths from the dawn of time, a woman—particularly a lucid woman—senses the trap, understands and feels trickery, and yet almost in spite of herself she steps into the abyss. And particularly so if she is sensual, in love with life, and if it is the year 1910.

Even in *La Vagabonde*, that hymn to freedom, she wrote *Freedom? . . . pooh! Freedom is only dazzling at the beginning of love, first love, when it can be offered to the person one loves while saying "Take it! I wish I had more to give you!"* [1]

She made a success in a hard profession, the variety stage. She had begun to gather the first fruits of her labors as a writer. She had learned the lesson of captivity for herself and in *La Vagabonde*. She was once again comfortable with herself. And Auguste Hériot, young, handsome, wealthy and faithful, came into her life. She rejected him and threw herself into the arms of a seducer. At the same time, she also threw over everything she had built up, had respected, for six long years: the stage, literature, the circles in which she had lived her hard and honorable life as a free woman. She was overcome by a mixture of social conformity and passion, emotional insecurity and the security of social status, by contradictory feelings and impulses. Her friends worried and protested, "Colette! Not again!" Missy tried to force her to accept Auguste; she became angry with her. Sido softly preached to her. Others may have given her more discreet counsel; who knows? Colette sent them all packing. From the outset, however, she was unable to shut her ears to the small, clairvoyant voice prophesying to her the unthinkable . . . prophesying what she already knew. Oracles are nugatory things. They can predict apocalypse, epidemics, conflagrations—is anyone the less burned in the flames? One part of Colette was a clear-sighted woman whose candle cast light before her, and in that light she wrote. The only thing to be learned from experience is that life is a perpetual beginning . . . "A scalded cat always goes back to the pot," as Margot tells Renée Néré.

And while all the conditions that had forced Colette into a kind of alienation in love were reproduced, so too were the conditions that impelled her toward independence, toward that inalienable part of herself expressed in her writing. It is futile to look for the "why" when the answer is contained in the "how." Human actions cannot often be traced back to causes; they can only be understood as they progress, and this progression always occurs following the same models.

It did little good for Colette to attempt to save herself, to tie herself to the mast and plug her ears like the sailors of old; the song of the sirens was being sung from within. Although at forty she knew much she had not known at twenty, she willingly embraced a woman's fate nonetheless, a fate few women at that time were able to resist.

She played out all the scenes in the commonplace scenario: alienating desire, mystifying possession, loss of freedom, self-contempt, jealousy, servility, disdain for the other person and for oneself, vengeance, a spiteful divorce suit, scandal, resentment, bitterness. But there is a more pleasant side to the story, one of carnal well-being, of the ambiguous feelings of maternity, the mastering of immense daily suffering. She would have been unable to describe the common abyss in which so many women founder had she not herself been to the bottom and risen again to the top.

⚜ THE BARON

The years 1909 to 1910 were busy and apparently serene. Colette performed frequently in Paris and on the road; Willy persisted in his final perfidies but gradually faded into the shadows. Colette worked on La Vagabonde, begun in 1909. She was greatly disappointed when La Chair was performed at the Manhattan Opera House in New York without her, but this was a minor matter. In the fall of 1909, she took an automobile trip through Brittany with Missy looking at country houses; the two women wanted to settle down. In

1911, they found a house at Rozven on the Cancale coast near Saint-Malo. In December of 1909 they moved together to the Rue Saint-Sénoch and later to the Rue Toricelli near the Place des Ternes, a neighborhood that was then being built up. The Rue Toricelli was in the area between the Boulevard Pereire and the Place des Ternes and boasted *an heroic sergeant, a canonized Sénoch, a Bayen abutting the Château des Ternes with its famous garden. In the spring, violets sprang up beneath its ancient trees. . . . A street was cut through and destroyed it. And then they put up twenty more buildings on what was left of the park. . . . And along with the trees they destroyed nest after nest . . . and I set up my own in the midst of this devastation: a brand-new ground-floor apartment.*[1]

In 1910, she was still busy on the stage with *La Chair*, which had a long run. From May 21 to October 1, *La Vagabonde* was published in serial form in *La Vie Parisienne*. On June 21, her divorce from Willy became final.

Colette spent October in Italy with Auguste Hériot. On November 14, Willy's operetta based on the *Claudines* was premiered at the Moulin Rouge.

On December 2, *Le Matin*, the large-circulation daily newspaper, began publishing a series entitled "Music Halls" in its *Thousand and One Mornings* column. Instead of a byline, the following notice appeared: "The story *Le Matin* is publishing today is signed by a mask. Behind this enigmatic domino one of the foremost woman writers of our time has chosen to conceal her identity, a woman whose talent—a combination of exquisite sensitivity, keen observation and playful fantasy—has recently been newly revealed in a sentimental novel that is a current best-seller."

The mask remained in place until January 2, 1911. "It's me, Colette Willy." Of course, Colette was no newcomer to journalism; she had already published several short stories, beginning in April 1907 in *La Vie Parisienne*, Charles Saglio's newspaper (*Toby-Chien Parle, Le Semiramis Bar, La Baptistine*), and also in the magazine *Akadémos* ("Une Clarière dans la forêt" and "Le Passé").

The decisive reason for her hiring by *Le Matin*, however, was undoubtedly the three votes *La Vagabonde* had received in the first round of voting for the Prix Goncourt, alongside Apollinaire's *L'Hérésiarque et Cie.*, which also received three votes, and the two given to Marguerite Audoux's *Marie-Claire*. In the end, the prize was given to Louis Pergaud for *De Goupil à Margot, Histoires de bêtes*. Sido wrote a consoling letter to Colette, who had been building castles in the air in the expectation of winning; less than a month later, Colette made her first appearance in *Le Matin*.

One of *Le Matin*'s editors-in-chief was a man named Henry de Jouvenel. The fairly common story can be told in a nutshell: the masked pantomime performer was in search of a name. The editor offered the anonymous woman of letters his own. A thousand and one mornings became a thousand and one nights, and the debutante journalist became the public Colette de Jouvenel. Such sleight of hand is not uncommon where female identity is concerned.

The facts, however, were a bit more complex. The year is 1911. Colette, who had officially ceased being Madame Gauthier-Villars several months before, was still Colette Willy, actress and author of *La Vagabonde*, published by Ollendorf. While Missy was setting up house in Rozven, Colette was off in Nice with Auguste Hériot and a woman named Lily de Rême, who was perhaps the model for the character of May in *L'Entrave*. On the 14th, Colette wrote to her old friend Léon Hamel from the south of France: *These two infants, both in love with me, are worth noting for that reason. I spoil them, I put them to bed. My own ego derives maternal satisfaction from their appetite and their fresh complexions. However, I'm a little worried about the Hériot child. . . . I'm afraid he is taking this adventure too seriously, I am not morally threatened.*[2]

In March she went to Tunis with Lily, leaving Auguste behind, and on the 21st she wrote: *Missy tells me Auguste Hériot has turned up in Rozven; the little lovebird is billing and cooing around Missy. I've not written to him since I left, and it's all for the best.*[3] The end of March found her in Rozven, where *Missy has done wonders in creating a room for me out of the chaos, and one for herself. Alas, there is still a great deal to be done. . . . We eat where we can, but the stove is working. . . . I'll tell you all about my trip and how impossible Lily was in Tunis, in Marseilles, everywhere—it was awful! Can you imagine, she's suggesting we go to India together. I'd rather die!*[4] The rest of the spring was spent performing in *La Chair* in Paris, Geneva and Lausanne.

Things blew up in July. *There's been a bit of an upset,* Colette wrote to André Rouveyre on July 22, as always a mistress of understatement: the man who was to play the principal role in her life for the next fifteen years had come onto the scene.

The Baron de Jouvenel des Ursins, born in Paris on April 5, 1876, was three years younger than Colette. According to the article devoted to him in the *Dictionnaire des parlementaires français*, he was "a *grand seigneur*. He was a born aristocrat, descended from the famous Juvénal des Ursins, and prided himself on being related to the princely Roman Orsinis. His bearing and manner was aristocratic, as was his character. After joining the staff of *Le Matin* at the age of twenty-six, he quickly rose to editor-in-chief and helped the newspaper to reach a wide public by recruiting outstanding talent. His friend Anatole de Monzie remarked that 'journalism afforded him the opportunity to disseminate his nobility with a prodigal hand. In addition, he had an undisputed talent for speaking and writing, and rare powers of persuasion.' " [5]

Gossip might well have added another trait to the official dithyrambs, a talent that Henry de Jouvenel possessed in plenty: his love of women. When he met Colette in 1910, he was a handsome man of thirty-five, tall, dark, well built, with a distinguished mustache. He was already notorious for his past and for his passivity, both sentimental and conjugal. During the Dreyfus Affair, as a young, active liberal Henry de Jouvenel had fought for Captain Dreyfus alongside his friend Anatole de Monzie and other aristocratic youths, to the great dismay of their conservative families. He had frequented the home of Alfred Boas, at 35, Rue de Châteaudun, a Jewish journalist and active Freemason with close connections among left-wing republican politicians. Boas had managed to marry his daughter, Sarah Claire, to the youthful baron. From this union was born a son, Bertrand de Jouvenel, in 1903. But the marriage soon fell apart.

Unfaithful and fickle, it was said that Henry de Jouvenel rarely took time to say good-bye. Colette may have had this in mind when she had May make the following remark in *L'Entrave*: *Jean treated me no differently than he did Marthe Byse, great star that she is, nor than Madame. . . . He decamped, that was the awful thing about it. When someone's jilted, it's usually after a good scene—you know— or a gradual breakup. Well, my dear, he just leaves in the middle of a sentence, shutting the door behind him, or he goes out to buy cigarettes and is never seen again except for a farewell letter, very well written, very impressive.*[6]

⚜ THE CAT AND THE PANTHER

When Colette met Henry de Jouvenel at the offices of *Le Matin*, he was the official lover of Isabelle de Comminges, the "Panther," who had borne him a son, Renaud de Jouvenel, now six years of age.

A series of episodes far too confusing and romantic for any Colette novel was to mark the beginnings of her liaison with Jouvenel. The meeting had been preceded by one of those petty Parisian furors: an anonymous remark in *Le Journal* on June 26, 1911, was felt to be insulting to *Le Matin*, and Henry de Jouvenel had fought a duel in the velodrome in the Parc des Princes with Georges Charlet, an assistant editor on the former paper. Both adversaries were wounded in the forearm at the first shot, and the battle had been called to a halt.[1] As with Willy's duel long ago, Henry de Jouvenel's altercation created considerable talk. In a letter to Léon Hamel from Rozven dated July 31, Colette relates the outcome with great excitement:

Dear Hamel, I am overcome with sorrow and remorse that you have been worried. For that matter, I have worried right along with you, and have upset my mother, you, and everyone else who loves me by leaving them in ignorance regarding my fate.

Dear Hamel, so much has happened! I've been hurt, but it was worth it for the happiness (touch wood!) or something very like happiness that I can see glittering within reach (I am frantically touching wood!).

I got to Rozven this morning after a fairly busy month spent almost entirely in Paris in this deadly heat. You know I was performing in Geneva and Lausanne (end of June, early July). But do you know that the day after his duel Jouvenel * turned up in Lausanne, wounded, his arm in a sling and declaring that he neither could nor wanted to go on living without me? And do you know that at the same time Hériot was planning to join me in Switzerland and that I stopped him only with panicky telegrams full of lies and contradictions? Do you know that when he got back to Paris Jouvenel informed the Panther that he was in love with another woman? Upon which she swore she would kill the woman, whoever she was. Jouvenel, distraught, communicated her threat to me, whereupon I said "I'll go to her!" and off I went. And I told the Panther, "I am that woman!" Whereupon, she fell on her knees before me. Her moment of weakness was short lived, since a few days later she announced to Jouvenel that she intended to stab me. Again distraught, Jouvenel had Sauerwein collect me in his car, and he, along with Sauerwein, took me off to Rozven, where we found Missy chilly and disgusted, having just got the news from the Panther. Then my two guards left and Paul Barlet stood guard over me with a pistol in his hand. Still chilly and disgusted, Missy went

---

* In the printed text, the protagonists are designated only by their initials. It is time to lift a disguise that has long ceased to fool anyone.

off to Honfleur. Shortly (three days) after that, Jouvenel telephoned for me to join him and Sauerwein came to pick me up in the car because the Panther was prowling around the neighborhood looking for me, also armed with a revolver. So I began a period of semi-sequestration in Paris, guarded like some precious reliquary by the police and by Jouvenel, Sauerwein and Sapène, the three pillars of Le Matin. Believe it or not, this period had just ended with an unexpected, providential, magnificent event. Tired of stewing at Gastinne-Renette's, M. Hériot and the Panther have taken off in the yacht Esmerald for a voyage of at least six weeks, after having shocked all of Le Havre with their drunken orgies. Isn't that great? Isn't it like a play! Isn't it almost too much?

In the meanwhile, Jouvenel has been absolutely outstandingly proper, earning Missy's contempt since she basically adores Hériot—she had prepared a room for him here and was planning to force him down my throat conjugally. What else can I tell you, my dear Hamel! Jouvenel is getting his house ready for me. He has no money, he has Le Matin (around 40,000 francs) and I am making a decent living, so we'll get along.

Need I tell you again that I love this tender, jealous, unsociable, incurably honest man? I have no need to. I would love to see you, if you want to, since Jouvenel has already told me that he will allow me only "Hamel and Barlet." Ah . . .

Missy has bought Princesse. That's the villa that's only three kilometers from here. This news is like an epilogue, don't you think? Day after tomorrow, I'm off to Castel Novel, Jouvenel's château in Corrèze, and I'll send you a picture of it. . . . Paul sends his best. Missy is still acting cool and disgusted, and nothing I do gets a reasonable response. I assure you. It's not wickedness on my part, I have enough troubles.[2]

This letter says it all: Colette's giddiness; Missy's fury, very like jealousy but also very like well-founded caution; the commencement of Jouvenel's over-all control.

Colette, however, ignored it all, and fifteen years afterward she still recalled her arrival at Castel Novel on a summer evening in 1911: *A Limousin summer, compared to which July in Provence is all coolness and dew; nightfall, the towers dark against the sky, the ground floor lit with candles and kerosene lamps, some polished silver, a tall butler in a whitish livery, a huge untrimmed rosebush; everything was dark and crumbling and charming. In the Lion bedroom I left the doors and windows open all night hoping for a breeze, and the bats frolicked back and forth between the columns of the bed-posts. I was dazzled for more than one reason!* [3]

In August, Colette moved into the Hôtel Meurice; on the 25th, she wrote to Rouveyre: *You will never see Missy with me again, my friend. We are no longer living together. You will be told all whenever you want. It's really so simple.* [4] On August 28, she wrote to Christiane Mendelys: *You ask for news of Missy. I have none, she is still holding onto everything that belongs to me. I like this special treatment; I will be the first woman the "marquise" has asked to give her money after she has left her!* [5] In the end their quarrel was made up, and in later years Colette saw the woman who had filled an entire period of her life fairly frequently.

⚜ SIDI: PRELIMINARY SKIRMISHES

The first weeks of her liaison with Henry de Jouvenel were weeks full of activity. Her work on the stage was at its peak: in August she created the mimodrame *Bat' d'Af'* at the Ba-Tan-Clan; she appeared at the Etoile Palace in *La Chair*; she created another mimodrame at the Gaité-Rochechouart entitled *L'Oiseau de nuit*. In October 1911, she moved from the Hôtel Meurice and into 57, Rue Cortambert, the home of the man she was henceforth to refer to as Sidi, the "Pasha," the "Sultan," because of his oriental tastes for display and luxury. The chalet on the Rue Cortambert was a *kind of bungalow built above a wooden gallery with a balcony. It overlooked a 3,000-square meter garden filled with old trees, wild roses, hazelnuts and rife with cats. . . . The chalet that unfolded before me* like a trap *was small, like a Swiss stage set. . . . When I first stepped through its heavy street-door, it was a luminous June night, the acacias were in bloom, shaded red lamps glowed behind the curtains. . . . The surrounding gardens hid the walls. I hesitated on the brink of this enticing spot, this overcharming place, this ambush. Was there still time to turn back? But the owner was already coming toward me.* [1] (emphasis added)

It was already too late—for the stage, for literature, for freedom—when Colette moved into the Passy chalet with Sidi.

In the same month of October, Henry de Jouvenel ordered *Le Matin* to print his companion's signature every week. The order did not go unopposed. Upon being told by Charles Sauerwein, the news editor, that Colette Willy would be providing *Le Matin* with a weekly story, Stephane Lauzanne, the co-editor-in-chief, laid down his pen.

"If that person is put on the paper, I will leave on the spot!"

"On the spot is a bit strong," Sauerwein replied. *"You know her!"*

For the first time in his life, Stephane Lauzanne blushed.

"Me, acquainted with that . . . tumbler . . . that . . ."

Charles Sauerwein, who was fond of me, held out his hand to Lauzanne.

"Farewell then, my friend. I say farewell, because Colette's first story is coming out tomorrow!"

Despite his threat, Lauzanne did not leave Le Matin *until thirty-five years later, the year of the Liberation, 1944. But that's another story.*[2]

With new heart, Colette saw everything through Jouvenel's eyes. *Who says I am neglecting my exercise? I've got a new method, that's all. The Sidi method. An excellent one. No public classes. Private lessons. Terribly private!*[3] But Sidi went out more and more on his own; he began to be away frequently, to lunch with "Aunt Delcassé" leaving Colette to play interminable games of bezique with Léon Hamel . . . waiting. In May 1912, the couple was in Normandy. Their happiness was apparently unclouded. *I can see myself getting fat, and I don't cough. Sidi is already very tan and revoltingly young.*[4] On June 16, however, she mentions a "rare argument" with Sidi; on the 26th, she recounts an odd quarrel with Jouvenel to her old friend in the following Coward-like dialogue, with no explanation:

Four days of conversation might be condensed as follows:

J: *We must separate.*

C: *Yes.*

J: *Life together . . .*

C: *Is impossible.*

J: *But it won't stop us from being good friends!*

C: *Of course not.*

J: *So, we're going to separate?*

C: *Right away.*

J: *Oh, there's no hurry.*

C: *Yes, yes, it's urgent, absolutely.*

J: *Absolutely's not the word.*

C: *Absolutely. July 1st, the end! Each will go his own way, and as for me, if something happens to change my feelings, if I meet someone beddable or whom I can love, out of loyalty I will have to . . .*

  J: Of course. But in the meantime . . .

  C: In the meantime, I'll go to the Rue la Fontaine [Barlet's home].

  J: That's unnecessary, even silly. You're better off here.

  C: No. Good night, Sidi.

  J: But . . . where are you off to?

  C: I have things to take care of. You said yourself . . .

  J: Oh, don't pay any attention to what I said. Don't you want to play a hand of bezique?

  C: For money—with pleasure.

  J: 4,500!

  C: Bravo. And now, farewell, Sidi.

  J: But . . . what you are doing this evening? If you'd like to eat Chez Laurent, out of doors . . . It's fine weather, I want to be with you! . . . etc . . . etc.[5]

Thus Colette's version, the comic version. The other version appears in *L'Entrave*, with the difference that in real life, Colette brazened it out, whereas her fictional character breaks down. Between June 26 and August 17, Colette's letters are full of bitterness, nostalgic disenchantment, real material anxiety, but never despair. Her suffering was concealed: *I am not feeling too well, but some awful rancor is beginning to grow within me, and I am counting on it to comfort me. . . . I am physically exhausted but I can't sleep, and I am unwilling to go on feeling so low. Alas, I miss so terribly the presence of a certain unworthy person, his warmth, the sound of his voice, his lies, his childishness, his jokes.*[6] On July 20: *Yes, I know I must get a place of my own. At the moment, however, it isn't really possible to manage it. . . . Jouvenel is supposed to give me 1,000 francs on the 31st of August, but that's August 31st. Until then, I will earn only another twenty-five louis. And I owe Hamel money for some time now. It's all so silly, isn't it? . . . So, until further notice, I'll be living at Jouvenel's.*[7]

Apparently breakup and separation were two different things, and Jouvenel and Colette continued to live together and see each other. *On his part (I'm telling you everything) there is even a certain carnal tenacity that is fairly singular; and since I suffer too from the same tyranny, I guess we're in for good moments and awful quarter hours.*[8] At one point, Jouvenel seems to have left for good. On August 6, there is mention of pawning a pearl necklace, an event

Colette may have been recalling when she wrote *Julie de Carneilhan.* Jouvenel was in Brive: *I've pawned my pearl necklace through the only person who can discreetly provide me with a large enough sum at the present time. I picked Auguste Hériot. . . . So at least I have the wherewithal for instant freedom. I could leave in two hours if I wanted to. However, I don't want to. I'm still waiting. I'm going to write a long letter today to the Baron, who seems to be putting on the dog and getting into debt down there. But don't worry. This money's not for him.*[9]

The last sentence is food for thought, particularly in the light of the plot of *Julie de Carneilhan.* Before her marriage to her second husband, Julie pawns a diamond necklace and gives him the money. In return, *angrily, jokingly,*[10] he gives her a receipt on which turns a novel that lights up dark corners, perhaps the economic relationship between the future couple. Colette braves it out and conceals her defeat; she waits . . . waits patiently at Sidi's house for him to come back to her. Like Julie, who knows that she has, *without appearing to, laid down her arms . . . to how many men had she humbled herself at their command!*[11] Like Renée, who not only waits for Jean but even telephones him for the pleasure of hearing his voice before she hangs up, who does a thousand foolish things, who pretends to go out, writes she is going away on tour and then lies in wait for her lover, hiding *in our room, in the middle of the night, with all the lights out.*[12]

"He" came back on August 17. *Jouvenel returned Monday noon. . . . I am enjoying an ephemeral animal pleasure, a pleasure worth all the trouble; you know what the presence of the person one needs means after the dark hours and weeks. He arranges "our" future just like he arranges the articles on the dresser, with the same emotion. I keep quiet and wallow in it, at least I have the comfort of my stupid stubbornness, the persistence that everyone condemns me for.*[13]

An "unworthy" person has become a "needed" person. What a woman wants . . . But she wants the wrong thing. Their reconciliation was sealed by a treaty under whose terms Colette—as far as we can tell—surrendered to him . . . not only her weapons, but the entire country of herself, all she held most dear. In the fever of reunion, she wrote to Georges Wague on August 26:

I can tell you at least that I am leaving for Châtillon, that much is true, where my blessed mother is being extremely difficult, not that she's seriously ill, but she has an attack of "I want to see my daughter." Sidi has allowed me a "maximum" of three days.[14] A month after this letter, Sido was dead in Châtillon. After these "maximum three days," Colette probably never saw her again.

⚜ Sido's death

Clairvoyant Sido. She had looked down the new path her daughter was embarked on with distrust, with her usual tenderness. As early as October 27, 1911, she had written: "Minet-Chéri, you'll be writing a weekly column for *Le Matin*. That's a lot of work, and I don't approve because journalism is death to a novelist. It's a pity you're doing it. Protect your talent, my darling, be sparing of it; it's worth the trouble." [1]

In December, Colette sent her an article that would later become the nucleus of a book dedicated to her mother, the book she would call *Sido*. "I got your letter and the article," Sido replied, "and was very pleased. I see that the old house and garden still haunt you, my darling. That makes me happy and it also makes me sad. I can still see your graceful little body strolling there, dreaming of so many things, with Mine-Belle at your heels. Ah, if only de Jouvenel had seen you in those days! What memories those are. When I think of you then I see you most often in a pale blue dress, the one that you looked so pretty in and that Mme Paul Bert was so enraptured with when we would go for walks together. How long ago it all seems! Yes, you were my golden sun. And when you would come into the room where I was sitting, I used to tell you that the room would grow brighter." [2]

Was it during this last visit with her mother, about which she never spoke, that Colette had the conversation she transposes in *La Naissance du jour?*

"You like this Monsieur X a lot?"

"But Maman, I love him!"

"Yes, yes, you love him . . . you don't need to tell me that you love him."

She thought a bit, trying to hold back what her celestial cruelty was forcing her to say, and then burst out:

"Ah! I'm not pleased!"

I lowered my eyes with false modesty, trying to shut out the image of the handsome, intelligent, enviable man with his bright future, and answered softly:

"You're being difficult."

"No, I'm not pleased. . . . I'd have preferred the other one, the boy you're now treating like dirt."

"Oh, Maman! He's an idiot!"

"Yes, yes, an idiot! . . . Exactly."

I can still recall how she bent her head, squinting her gray eyes to focus on the flattering, dazzling image of the "idiot." *And she added:*

"What beautiful things you would write with the idiot, Minet-Chéri. With the other, you'll spend all your time on him, you'll give him everything that is most precious to you. And what if he makes you unhappy, to top it all off? It will probably come to that."

I laughed aloud: "Cassandra!"

"Yes, Cassandra if you like. If I told you everything I can foresee . . ." Her narrowed eyes looked into the future. *"Fortunately, you're not in too much danger!"* [3]

Sido's last years, her final months, were spent with her eldest son, Achille, the one she had loved best—after Colette—with her possessive and worried love. In her daughter's memory, Sido's only flaw was that *to bring her back to me again I have to refer to the time when my mother dreamed dramatic dreams during the adolescence of her eldest son, so handsome, so seductive. I remember that in those days she was always wild, full of false gaiety, full of curses, ordinary, plain, always on the alert. . . . Ah, if only I could see her again, diminished as she was then, with her cheeks red with rage and jealousy.* [4] Sido was as lucid as her daughter, however, and saw into the "tumult of her heart." *Yes,* Sido wrote, *I also find Madame X much changed and very sad. I know there is no mystery in her private life, so it's a good bet that her grown-up son has taken his first mistress.* [5] Later, she grew calm and certain. *Of course at least you others—I know you—will miss me. Who will you write to twice a week, my poor Minet-Chéri? For you it's nothing, you escaped, you built your nest far away from me. But your elder brother . . . Yes, yes, of course you love me, but you're a woman, a female animal like me, my rival. But as for him, I never had a rival in his heart.* [6]

There came a time when Sido began to grow weaker, but she refused to acknowledge it; her capacity for wonder was endless and she continued to commit "sins" she concealed from her doctor son and confessed to her daughter, her "likeness."

"Believe it or not, I fell down the stairs."

"Were you going too fast?"

"Too fast? What do you call too fast? I was coming down fast. At seventy-eight plus, do you think I have time to descend a stair-

way like Louis XIV?" [7] Sido burned herself on the old boiler; she planned to move the old oak armoire, as wide as it was high; she drew water from the well and scrambled up the extension ladder attached to the attic window; she began to rise in the morning at ever-earlier hours to indulge in all her forbidden pleasures before anyone else was up.

It was not until one morning when I saw the stove was cold, the blue enamel pot still hanging on the wall, that I felt my mother's end was near. Her illness often abated, and then the fire would leap up again on the hearth and the smell of fresh bread and chocolate would creep through the door with the cat's impatient paws. These remissions would lead to unexpected crises. Once she was discovered on the stairs with the huge oak armoire while secretly attempting to move it from one floor to another. . . . One morning, returning from a visit to a patient before the sun was up, my brother caught my mother red-handed in her perversity, dressed in her nightdress and her outsized gardening sabots with her little gray seventy-year-old braid of hair standing up on her neck like a scorpion's tail, one foot on the X of the beechwood sawhorse and her back bent like a busy construction worker, rejuvenated by her pleasure and her unconcealed, palpable guilt; despite her promises and the freezing dew, my mother was sawing up logs in the courtyard.[8]

La Naissance du jour begins with a letter from Sido, reworked by Colette. The letter tells us that when Henry de Jouvenel invited her to visit her daughter, Sido declined the invitation, despite her maternal feelings. Her pink cactus, the one that bloomed only once every four years, was in bud. Sido's original letter was simpler, in its ordinary way more moving than the "literary" letter: she accepted Jouvenel's invitation: "Your kind invitation has persuaded me to accept for several reasons, among them one I can never resist: seeing my daughter's dear face and hearing her voice. And then to get to know you and try to find out why she so enthusiastically threw caution to the winds for your sake. As for me, I will abandon for a few days the things that rely on me—my cat Mine, who gives me all her trust and tenderness, a sedum that is ready to bloom and is magnificent, a gloxinia whose gaping chalice enables me to watch it seeding at my leisure. They will all have to make do without me, although my daughter-in-law has promised me to look after them. And of course she will, since she's overjoyed to be getting rid of her mother-in-law for a few days.

"So I guess I'll be seeing you soon. But tell Gabri to write to me.

Do you know who 'Gabri' is? There's worse, her name is Gabrielle. Did you know that? And I'm called Sidonie Colette!" [9]

Is Colette's transposition only another example of her propensity for putting into her writing the "abnegation" and renunciation she found so difficult in her life? Or is it an unconscious desire to make it appear to be her mother's decision not to see her, a decision that was in fact her own in Sido's final days?

In the event, Sido probably did not come at Jouvenel's invitation. On September 27, 1912, Colette wrote a brief note: *Dear Hamel, Maman died the day before yesterday. I don't want to attend the funeral. I've told almost no one and I'm not wearing any outward mourning. For the time being, everything's all right. But I am tortured by the stupid notion that I won't be able to write to Mother now as I used to so often. My brother will be very unhappy. I'm still appearing in* L'Oiseau *and life goes on as usual, needless to say. However, as happens whenever I am truly grieved, I have got an attack of swelling . . . inside that is very painful.*[10]

That is all. Achille must have been very unhappy. He was to die of cancer a year after his mother, on December 31, 1913.

In the meantime, he destroyed the approximately 2,000 letters Colette had written to Sido. Was this destruction perhaps partly the reason for her later decision to embark on a search for the past, her past, in which her mother is the principal character? However it may have seemed on the surface, deep within her a drawn-out period of mourning had begun. It was to result in the books she explicitly dedicated to Sido, the books of her old age, or in that strange parable of loss, *La Fin de Chéri*. Apparently, for the moment, there was nothing. Her understatement, her need to bury her grief so deeply that it could not touch her, at the time prevented Colette from sending out any signal of distress when she lost the one person she was never to replace.

And by one of those strange coincidences, one of those "objective chances" that life sets up with so much more abundance and complexity than literature, Colette conceived a daughter shortly after her mother's death. From Sido to Bel-Gazou, the cord was again to be stretched in its unbroken continuity.

⚜ A REAL BARONESS

Her letters during this period of her life are very frank: they express the blind happiness of a woman in love. As she herself was to have Masseau say in *L'Entrave: There are two kinds of love, unrequited love that makes you hateful to everyone, and satisfied love that turns you into an idiot.*

Jouvenel's love literally changed her life. She devoted herself to his craft, journalism; she ascended in the dirigible *Clement-Bayard,* reporting the *grand prix de l'aviation* . . . and she made plans to give up the theater. On September 17, she wrote to Léon Hamel: *Tomorrow evening, I'm going back into* L'Oiseau *at the Ba-Ta-Clan. This time it's more a question of duty than of pleasure, and it will be no hardship to give up the caf' conc'. This is just to tell you that everything is going well within and around me.*[1] In other words, "I'm prepared to give it all up." Her new allegiance to Jouvenel and her sorrow at Sido's death both touched her lover; he treated her very kindly. In October, although unaware of it, she was already several days pregnant. To comfort her in her mourning, Sidi took her to Castel Novel, where his mother welcomed her as his wife. With both "Mamita" and Henry's brother, Robert de Jouvenel, Colette was to have a long-lasting friendship. In December, on the 19th at four-thirty, Gabrielle Colette and Henry de Jouvenel were married in Paris. Colette was three-months' pregnant and the marriage was a simple one. Léon Hamel stood as her witness, and after the ceremony *people from* Le Matin *and other friends passed us on from table to table, we went from lunch to dinner, from dinner to supper until Christmas Eve, when we ended our week of activity by going to bed at seven in the morning. If this child is not the most inveterate partygoer, I give up.*[2] On December 20, the day after her wedding, Colette wrote to her former partner and friend Georges Wague and signed herself for the first time "Colette de Jouvenel." No time had been wasted, it had gone very swiftly.

⚜ THE FETTER

What did not go swiftly was the novel she was finishing. *You can't write a passionate novel while you're making love.*[1] *L'Entrave* suffers from having been written so closely to real life. After this, Colette's books were always to be set in a period long before the time in which she wrote them. Because of this, the best of her work is filtered, refined, purified, by selective memory. Here, however, we are not judging her work, but discovering her in it.

L'Entrave gives us an outline of the situation through which Colette had just passed, and in which she was to live with Sidi. The text reveals things about which Colette never spoke; it shows us that, despite the irrational and even dangerous reality of her love, she never lost her keen regard for herself. *L'Entrave* is an admirable description of how a free woman, a "vagabond," can be led so far astray that of her own free will, contentedly, she returns to the same cage from which she had managed to free herself in the past.

The text begins with the memory of the *voyage à trois* once taken with Auguste Hériot and Lily de Rême: the characters are Renée Néré, Jean and May. Under the influence of powerful carnal desire, the May-Jean pair becomes Renée-Jean. In the novel, however, May's behavior is less romantic and less dangerous than was that of the actual Panther. Renée Néré treats Jean casually—as Colette had treated Auguste, as she had dreamed of treating Henry—as an object, an instrument of pleasure. *I've heard callous young women say "For me, where love is concerned it's all or nothing." But then, a pretty nothing, well presented, is already something!* [2] An experienced woman with a past, Renée can banter: *Great transports, great sorrows—we all know what they are. Like everyone in our age of imperfect young women, we have had them.*[3] She takes pleasure in congratulating herself on what she thinks is her own impassivity: *It almost seems to me that one could remove the man sitting across from me and replace him with someone else without anything being changed.*[4] At times, lovemaking gives her the illusion that she can be self-sufficient.

Once appeased, the desire for sensual pleasure begins to fade into coldness, indifference. Aroused, it seeks only what can feed it.[5] There is no question of anything *but sensual pleasure, ever more pleasure. For that matter, we wouldn't have it any other way.*[6] And yet this "matter" gradually begins to destroy sexual compatibility, the intoxication of lovemaking. Jean is jealous of her past life, of her ex-husband, of *that shady character you married for better or for worse*, of her theatrical profession; *Jean's unconcealed contempt for my former profession reveals that he thinks about it enough to want to wipe it out.*[7] He resents being considered a sexual object. *Sometimes it seems . . . that you're using me!* Renée dislikes his being away, his society dinners. Step by step, he installs her—she installs herself—in his home and puts her into the tempting yet unbearable position of a kept woman whose idleness gives her the illusion of freedom, whose security conceals her almost Oriental dependency.

During the day, my interests are almost the same as those of Victor, the butler: "Is Monsieur going out with Madame?" "Has Monsieur returned?" "Is Monsieur going to dress?" Apart from the old friend with whom she plays interminable games of bezique when Jean is away, *if I dine in a restaurant, it's with Jean; if I go to the theater, it's with Jean.*[8] Completely dominated by the man about whom she once assured herself *it will last as long as you want it to last, and no longer,* Renée is forced to make do with the things that *content those like myself, the recreation Jean allows me by leaving me.* Pitiful female freedom, *the loveliest woman hides herself away, if only to indulge freely in her dreams.*

Freedom is only a word: *Freely . . . to be free! I say it aloud so that this lovely, faded word may regain its life, its appeal, its green reflection of a wild wing, of the forest. . . . In vain!* Travel? *I don't know how to travel. Where would I go? I'll soon find out, that is if he takes me with him.*[9]

The slightest detail, every event, is a fateful signal, like a dream one has dreamed before. A boat trip brings back *the time before my wandering life, memories of changing my home.* After their first kiss, *it seemed to me that I had just begun to perform . . . the rites of some forthcoming, inevitable ceremony.* Their first night together, *I lie awake as all women do, whether they are naive or blasée, when they begin and begin again their lives, anxiously, pressed against the side of a sleeping man.*[10]

And it comes to pass that sensual pleasure ceases to be enough. The two lovers live in silence, they communicate only when they embrace. Pleasure is silent. Once it seemed too much, now it is insufficient. *We no longer communicate save in our anxiety, since when we embrace we exchange nothing.* Renée doesn't dare to question Jean. *He was only the man who saw me naked.*[11] Each of the lovers attempts to win something from the other. *I foresaw the extent of the danger on the day I began to despise everything you were giving me . . . joyous, facile pleasure. . . . One day I began to think about what you weren't giving me. I entered the chill shadow love casts before it.* Renée lies awake watching her lover sleep, dreaming of *some miserable and pitiful death that would petrify there forever, in his impenetrable sleep, the image of my new love.*[12] It is all over. Set on the peaceful path, the trap cannot be avoided, but it can perhaps be circumvented. The man will encounter it first; history has given him a head start. *Love is this painful collision, forever renewed, with a barrier that cannot be broken down. We were like two*

*friends walking together, side by side, separated by a crystal wall
and unaware that it separated us. But love will throw us together,
and I tremble to be the first to break, I, the more fragile.*

Shared sexual harmony weighs in this unequal balance. It gives
Renée an awareness of her inferiority. The lovers go for a stroll to
the summit of a hill, where a vast landscape unrolls before them.
*You examined it in the light of history, attempting to discern all
the conquering feet. . . . And at your side I was fractious and stubborn, separate from you, distracted by a lizard that magically appeared and disappeared. . . . With the narrowed and sometimes subtle eyes of the nearsighted, a woman, I peered at the mountain. And
when you noticed me, your own attention was distracted. . . . I felt
myself far away, and yet hanging onto you, small enough to be
carried by you, heavy enough to hinder your progress. . . . You
tasted . . . the regret that makes you like a failed God, the furious
regret that you had not created me.*[13] Nearsighted, a woman—whereas
the imperial-minded man contemplates the vast extent of his conquests, she is aware only of the magic of little disappearances, the
lizard or the man. She is slowly overcome with contempt for herself,
she is ripe for servitude. As a woman, she has been born with *the
humiliation of being made to belong rather than to possess.*[14]

Jean leaves. Renée has dared tell him "I don't agree with you."
The kept woman, the woman who still held back a part of herself,
becomes an abandoned woman who lapses into neuroticism. Anything rather than his absence, anything rather than lose him. *I kneel
by the window in a posture that has already become a habit, and
I begin to suffer, routinely, as I suffered yesterday, all the yester-
days. . . . Everything I felt was so simple, in my unhappiness: he
had been beside me, he was gone, and I had no wish, no hope, save
for his return. Let him return, as my lover or not . . . let him return . . . let him return!*[15]

She is now ready to make any kind of compromise, ready to heed
the lecture in sexual morality that her friend Masseau gives her:

"*Your unhappiness, your grief, your solitude! Your dignity. To
begin with, dignity is a male shortcoming!*"

"*You, you, eternally you! You demand, you whimper, you pout,
you daydream, you disguise your eternal weakness with all of that,
your inability to possess. . . . You spend all your time setting Jean
up in opposition to yourself, he's a libertine, nothing more, but accept it! Make it your own!*"

"*But Masseau . . . what about him . . . would he let me do the same? Would he ever consider me as you say—to the extent that if he sees me in another man's arms he will cry 'Oh, how this emanation of myself can love!' "*

"That's not your affair! No business of yours at all. As though female love had anything to do with ours." [16]

The model proposed to Renée is unequivocal; it is futile to try to equalize the terms of the bargain. Jean's absence enables her to see this clearly: either submission or breakup. And she gives in, she humbles herself to get him back. And he comes back. *There is one goal for me . . . this man. To wait for him, to tremble that he might leave me, to see him escape and patiently approach him again to win him back—from now on this is my profession, my mission. Everything that I loved before I met him will then be mine again, but through him. . . . I made a vain attempt to break out, thinking that the limit of my universe was an obstacle. Many women I suppose begin by making the same mistakes as I have, before returning to their place, which is narrower than man's.* [17]

She had not lost all her lucidity; she was to nourish her resentment, the sly resentment of a slave. *I am well aware he is not perfect. If fate brings him back to me, I will still see on his face from time to time that smile like a thieving animal, the withdrawal from some painful truth, some effort. I am well aware that before he is willing to give even a bit of himself, he will be capable of demanding everything of me, excusing himself for not demanding even more!*

Colette detested *L'Entrave*, in much the same way she detested the *Claudine* novels. She struggled over the book, and when she finished it she wrote to Hamel on September 16, 1913:

I rejoice in the relief, but I vomit on it, I despise it. [18]

In *L'Etoile vesper*, she refers to the *contrived ending, the narrow corridor I tried to make my reduced characters pass through, the benevolent tone of the conclusion that nobody believes. . . . I have since attempted to rewrite the ending of* L'Entrave. *I haven't been able to do it!* [19] But obviously people were only too ready to accept this ending, so like reality, even though it did not recall for Colette her most "honorable" memories. In the end, she was too honest to ignore what she herself had written in *La Vagabonde*, before the fact, what Simone de Beauvoir has so succinctly stated with regard to a woman in love: "For women, love is a supreme attempt to overcome the dependency to which she is condemned by accepting it, but even when it is freely consented to, dependency can be lived only in fear and servility." [20]

✤ SULTANA AND MALE WHORE

And she would accept it until the end. With time, obviously, Colette considerably blackened the picture of her husband; she had deliberately accepted an inferior position, or at least she had allowed one to be forced upon her. It is not therefore surprising that she found her companion to be a clever master who used and abused all a master's prerogatives. Colette's writing gives us only a subjective notion of Henry de Jouvenel; she never claimed to have painted a portrait of him. What he represented for her, what she saw or wanted to see in him, all this describes her more than it describes him.

Her vision of him and the male characters he may have inspired can be described with two words, femininity and inertia. Whether in her fictional characters—Jean in *L'Entrave*, Farou in *La Seconde*, Herbert in *Julie de Carneilhan*, even the Blue Lieutenant in *Mitsou* or Chéri—or in allusions to Sidi in her letters, both traits recur constantly.

In the days of *Claudine* and Willy, Renaud too was often described with feminine epithets; there is a continuity in Colette's search for femininity in the man she loves that reveals a certain latent homosexuality. Auguste—"Maxime" in *La Vagabonde*—is described as completely virile; Colette was not attracted to him. In *L'Entrave*, however, she describes the *somewhat whorish physical coquetry* of Jean, and his *feminine lips*. In *Lettres de la Vagabonde*, she frequently mentions the Sultana, the male whore in Sidi. Colette finds an element of contempt in this highly carnal femininity, probably a part of what made it so erotic. *I miss dreadfully the presence of a certain contemptible person*;[1] Jean's "handsome, stubborn and wily face" betrays perfidy, impatience, emotional cowardice. Farou is "above all" a coward; Chéri is "weak"; the Blue Lieutenant is a cad; and Herbert d'Espivant is monstrously calculating and false. And to these two traits was added a domineering and easily despotic character. Like Willy, the unfaithful Sidi was a jealous husband, suspicious and easily roused to violence. This sentence of the macho Herbert d'Espivant may have been his: *You are the meadow I have ploughed, that I have mown down. But I can assure you that if others succeed me, you'll never come back to me to thrust the marks they leave on you under my nose.*[2]

And Colette makes a more direct allusion to *Him, when he spied on me from the window to see if I was deceiving him.*[3]

Masseau describes Jean in *L'Entrave* from the male point of view: *He was a fairly simple boy, born proud and brought up to be despotic because he had always seen Mama tremble before Papa, a bit humble because he had touched everything and had become attached to nothing, a little too young to be good, and yet with sufficient illusions to be revolted at the notion that a woman might occupy the largest place in a man's life.*[4]

Renée notices all the domineering, calculating traits, the *characteristics of deceit, of a kind of brutal power, of a weakness seductive enough to get him anything.*[5] And feminine, domineering, a bit cowardly as he was, he emitted a strong physical attraction that Colette found it difficult to resist, and that he used. It may have been her own weakness, her own fragile nature when confronted with the sexual attraction of a partner who made her suffer, that she is describing in this series of male characters based more or less directly on Henry de Jouvenel. Julie, still in love after three years of divorce, says flatly about Herbert d'Espivant: *Always this open credit of sensuality, this blackmail of pleasure, this pleasure-panacea, this mortal wound of pleasure—that's all he knows!*[6]

Aside from this bargained-for, traded, loaned, maybe sometimes given pleasure, Sidi was elsewhere: he was at the *Matin* offices, away at war, on official missions; he is dining out, he is in conference, negotiating, cheating on her. Colette, solidly installed in her home, her suffering, earthbound, waits for him—so clearly an airborne creature. He flies off, he escapes her, he comes back; now here, now absent, his absence is full of his presence, its weight only makes his departure more acutely felt. Until his definitive removal to other nests, he will play the role of the "determined vagabond" throughout these years, and she the one who *watches him, forever moored fast.*[7]

❧ MOTHERHOOD

In *L'Entrave*, Renée cradles a seagull in her hands and describes that mixed desire for maternity and sensuality that women feel as they grow older, *these sudden yearnings to touch, this nervous tenderness at the contact of a soft animal, I am fully aware that what is welling up is an untapped spring of love, and no one feels it as deeply as an old maid or a woman without a child.*[1] Colette de Jouvenel, called Bel-Gazou—a term meaning "fine speech" in Provençal and "pretty fawn" in Nivernais patois—was born on July 3, 1913. *My pregnancy has been nothing but an extended holiday*, her mother wrote. *You can forget the horrors of delivery, but you do not forget the long, unique holiday. I have forgotten none of it!* [2]

Conceived only a few days after Sido's death, the child was late in arriving. Colette was forty, and she noted *it is neither right nor proper to start a child by pondering over it too deeply . . . intelligent cats are usually bad mothers, sinning from an excess of zeal and distraction.* [3] During the first three months, she barely mentioned her condition, until Charles Sauerwein told her, *"Do you know what you're doing? You're having a man's pregnancy. Pregnancy ought to be more joyful than that. Put on your hat and come have some strawberry ice cream at Poirée-Blanche."* [4] During the fourth month, her friend Wague reminded her of the "Geneva business," an engagement with Wague and his wife Christiane Kerf, who was in her fifth or sixth month. In her confusion, Colette told her surprised partners . . . and then decided to go ahead with it after all. *Much moved, Georges Wague hid it all and called me a brooding owl, promising me that my child would be day-blind.* [5] Colette was given the best room, overlooking the lake:

"Now about your cravings," Wague said . . ."what have you been having for breakfast since you've become a 'fallen woman'?"

"Same as before the fall, café au lait." [6]

At 8 A.M., to spare her the "piss" the hotel served, Wague entered dressed as a chambermaid and lisping in an affected voice, followed by his wife bearing a small aluminum coffeepot emitting an odor of fresh coffee. Colette was touched and tried to thank them, but Wague, *at my thanks, assumed his haughty Basque expression, "It's not for you, it's to cut down on expenses,"* and Kerf added, *"It's not for you, it's for the child."* *That evening, during our well-rehearsed fight onstage, I felt a precautionary arm between my back and the table, helping me while appearing to hold me down.* [7]

She worked throughout her pregnancy: first in the music hall, and then on the final part of *L'Entrave*, first entitled the *Raisin volé*, the *Stolen Grape*. While still unfinished, it began to appear in installments in *La Vie Parisienne*; there was a question of which would come first, the child or the end of the novel. During her sixth and seventh months, she packed her bags and went to Limousin for the first strawberries, the early roses, the privileges and care reserved for a prospective mother. Colette refused to embroider bibs, cut out smocks or fuss over fluffy woolens. *When I tried to envision my creation, I imagined her naked, not adorned. She had to make do with a sober and practical English layette . . . bought superstitiously at the last minute.*[8] The child gave signs that it would outdistance the novel, and Colette capped her pen.

Her long holiday came to an end on a cloudless July day. *The imperious child en route to its second life mistreated my resisting but no-less impatient body. . . . When no one was looking, I unhooked the watering hose and gave the thirsty garden a good dousing.*[9]

There was the *drawn-out cry all women emit in childbirth.* Colette was given chloroform. *One last white vision, the father watching me from the doorway, and then I fell over into the black hole.*[10] As an epicurean, what surprised her was not her suffering, but the cessation of suffering. *People have no idea at all of what it is to stop suffering, or they would speak of nothing else,*[11] and then, a daughter. *Is it true, a little girl? There is a little girl . . . in this house there is an additional being.* Colette felt the anxiety of all new mothers, wondering whether she truly felt the famous "maternal instinct." The father came in with the child, *"My God, my God,"* she pleaded silently, *this is the awful moment. I feel nothing but apprehension, but fear, and I should be mad with a greedy, normal desire, with maternal joy? How can I pretend? And that's my baby girl. But no, this satisfaction that I feel at . . . having made a child worthy to live, this respectful amazement, this silliness, it's not enough, is it, it isn't maternal love?*[12]

With her fingertip, she attempted to open the damp, wrinkled and tiny hands that contracted, felt, grasped. Yes, obviously she had been expecting the emotion of this embrace, this physical pleasure, tender, amused, but . . .

No, she thought, that's still not it.

"Ah!" she cried.

"What's wrong, are you in pain?"

"No . . . Didn't you see? Didn't you see?"

"What?"

"There, look, her eyebrows. Oh, and her mouth . . . but it's you, it's you."

But no, she said to herself, that's still not it. That's only love. . . . The cry I just emitted, that was only the cry of a woman in love. . . . Ah, tiny creature with so much of him, when will I love you for yourself alone?[13]

It took time for her to determine the precise site of her love for this new person in the house, who was there without having come in from the outside, and for the austere Beauce dog to adopt it. Colette's questions were unusual questions at a time when the entire realm of motherhood was ruled by trivial prejudices. She boldly stated truths that are uncommon, even today: the maternal instinct is a creation of the male brain; the love for a child is like any other love, a feeling with its history and its individuality, it is not as "natural" as it is supposed to be. *I had to recognize that a whole body of advice, of furtive and jealous upheavals, false premonitions, even real ones, the pride of having a life I had merely created, a somewhat perfidious awareness that I had taught the other love a lesson in modesty, would finally turn me into an ordinary mother. And I did not recover my equanimity until the day intelligible speech bloomed on her ravishing lips, until awareness, mischief, even tenderness, made this commonplace toy into a little girl, and that little girl into my daughter.*[14] We can understand why a doctor would prescribe the therapy of reading Colette to his mentally disturbed patients, such a relief is it to realize, through her, that a woman who feels this mixture of sensations vis-à-vis her newborn child is not a monster; she is like all women.

Both Colette and Simone de Beauvoir describe this type of maternal behavior as "virile." Why not regard it rather as a description of a pregnancy and childbirth healthily accepted by a woman whose life is not limited to being a reproductive machine? Describing such sensations as "virile" seems unfair to Colette and to all women who have achieved success both in their pregnancies and in other activities. There is no need to glorify them with an epithet that is too much of a paradox since no man has ever managed to demonstrate what a truly "virile" pregnancy might be. Influenced by a profession that was looked on as masculine at the time—journalism, reporting, dramatic criticism—Colette was merely weighing on the scale of her own experience the fact that there was nothing incompatible between motherhood and one's work.

⚜ JOURNALIST

Journalism is a career that takes your breath away. Even when I was young, I was never able to match my slow rhythm to its tempo of "daily deadlines"! For Colette, journalism was closely bound up with her meeting and marriage with Jouvenel. She was later to admit that the profession did not suit her and that she had never liked it. After her daughter's birth, she was to remain away from the stage for nearly nine years; for five years, until the publication of *Mitsou*, she turned away from literature and devoted all her activities to *Le Matin*. Two years after she was hired, on October 30, 1913, her column *Les Contes des mille et un matins (Tales of a Thousand and One Mornings)* began to appear with the subtitle *Journal de Colette*. Six years later, she became a literary editor. Over these years, her contributions were to include far more than short stories. The war demanded men, but it demanded women as well. Colette began a career as a straight reporter. A long series of articles, interviews and portraits of political figures, reports on the first flight of the dirigible *Clement-Bayard* (June 1912), the trial of Mme Guillotin (June 1912), a balloon ascension (September 1912), the trial of the Bonnot gang (February 1913), an election-eve report and a military review (April 1913), a visit to the Salon d'Aviation (December 1913), reports from the war front (1915), the Landru trial (1912), cowboy films (1923), and a considerable amount of drama criticism.

Le Matin was a powerful and innovative newspaper; aside from its two editors-in-chief, it had a third "permanent editor." Jean Sapène was the "over-all business director," and Charles Sauerwein the news editor. They were all engaged in continual internecine bickering, and the rest of the staff frequently laid bets as to which would come out on top. Maurice Bunau-Varilla, whose name, *varilla*, means a small baton in Spanish, lived up to it by attempting to conduct everyone's activities. Colette had few dealings with him, nor with Stephane Lauzanne. Nor did she feel much sympathy with the paper's political bent at the height of its popularity. Her Sido-like skepticism toward the profession of political journalist and politician, in both of which her husband created a stir, never left her. She was also skeptical about the portion of such activities from which she was excluded. As for the atmosphere at *Le Matin: I would had to have wanted to be a part of it, and first off, I would had to have been accepted. The distance that politics forced me to maintain could be read on my face, so much so that when I was present the heated discussions cooled or went out. I was treated indulgently, with the kindness shown to village idiots.*[1] Rejected by this ultramasculine world, Colette responded with her own rejection and developed that irony women can so readily assume. Seen through informed and detached eyes, the male comedy often appears fairly insular; in the view of someone in the wings who can see their strings being twitched like so many marionettes, its characters become excited and act in often silly ways: *"Drop by the paper, my dear friend." "I certainly will,"* replies the recipient of this *invitation, none other than the head of the cabinet, the secretary of state, an ambassador from a neighboring country. Once in the build-*

ing, a mere mortal, an "old pal," subjected to "Now see here, Paul," the visitor would do his best to retain his hauteur, adjust his sealskin collar, avoid noticing anyone in the elevator, but could expect neither anonymity nor secrecy.[2]

In this *red-painted, noisy and active place,*[3] there was no lack of female company around the offices. Power, glory, money attracted a number of female parasites who would *congregate in the vast waiting rooms, detectable by their ostrich boas, their scarves to snare the passerby, their insistent perfumes of solicitation.*[4] These delicately trained vampires knew, unlike Colette, how *to distinguish between the underling in a hurry, the deputé of the day, someone from the Stock Exchange, they could pick out the "VIP," the man loaded with a wad of money and financial responsibilities.*[5] They probably also knew very well that Henry de Jouvenel, the editor-in-chief, was less impervious to their charms than anyone, and Colette mentions them with an evident and well-ripened bitterness, charged with bile, reminiscent of her earlier feelings with regard to Willy's Claudines.

Another shadow on her married life, which was a long series of "disappearances," were "male business lunches." Colette speaks of them with humor, but at the time her humor must have had to throw off a heavy cargo of bitterness at *these political, secret feeds, a freemasonry of the gullet. . . . Lunch at the Commission, weekly dinner of the "group," monthly banquet for the left-wingers in the Vivarais district. . . . In obscure temples in La Villette or Les Halles, fine wines would be drunk, arcane sauces consumed. Up the crooked stairs, Maginot's tall figure, a bottle of Richebourg under each arm, would climb. . . . Sober forty-year-olds, gay sixty-year-olds, whole hordes of "men in the public eye" made a nefarious habit of . . . gluttony. In low-ceilinged rooms they would be served by a complicitous innkeeper who would piously shut behind him the door to their "private dining room" as though to hide them. In fact, they were hiding themselves. When it comes late in a man's life, indulgence is always a bit clandestine. It enlivens, but it does not honor.*[6]

No need to add that such lunches, *a wife's nightmare,* as Colette calls them, were exclusively masculine; *I only managed to glimpse such festivities, no one desired my presence at any of them.*[7] This was what probably made them so hard for her to bear, used as she was to professional circles in which the female element was given its due, and she resisted now as she had earlier. Henry de Jouvenel's world, the world of Power, was a peripheral world much like Willy's

Parisian social circles had been; it left her with only fragmentary
memories, some pleasant, most disagreeable, none of which she was to
recall with delight.

The war impelled her further into the profession of journalism
and at the same time enabled her to escape the exclusive control of
her husband's newspaper; she had to make a living. Between 1917
and 1918, she began to write some of the earliest film criticism in the
weekly *Le Film.* Some of the articles signed "The Woman from
Nowhere" in the same magazine are probably also by her. The film
director Louis Delluc succeeded her in this position. She also wrote
articles in *L'Excelsior* and *L'Eclair.* The latter had offices in an old
building in the center of Paris; on the staff Colette found her great
friend, Annie de Pène, a *femme de lettres* like herself, and there she
met Francis Carco, looking very young in his uniform, his *eyes like
the wild animals that steal from birds' nests.* Carco was to become
one of her closest friends and companions throughout this entire
period. She began work at *L'Eclair* as a drama critic, hired by René
Wertheimer, the editor, *Jewish, literate, a family man, a kind man.*
She found it a demanding job: *The night, the war, the rain, the
snow. . . . I had asbestos soles put on my shoes, but they made them
too tight. The last subway didn't wait for me, and I lived in Auteuil.
Sometimes, around 1:30 A.M. on opening nights [Wertheimer] would
notice how tired I was, and how lonely. With casual indifference he
would suggest, "If you can wait for me another forty-five minutes,
I've got my jalopy and I'll run you home." I could wait!*[8]

After the Great War ended, everyone suddenly found that in the
newspaper business—and business in general—everything had changed.
*But life as it was prior to 14–18, gone forever and never to return,
where is it still remembered if not in my own particular fond dreams
and in collections of old lighthearted newspapers like* Gil Blas. *. . .
People stopped reading or hearing or using droll nicknames like
Félisque Faure or Nini Toutcourt, women seemed to have different
names, their breasts and buttocks had been altered, demi-mondaines no
longer lolled late in bed sipping frothy cups of hot chocolate and playing with their tiny dogs, they no longer poured half a liter of expensive
perfume into their baths.*[9] The code of male elegance changed too:
*And the vests! I can still see Jacques Liouville's vest in natural pony
skin that buttoned up the back. . . . And the neckties! Neckties in
braided rice straw with little turquoise designs, Chantilly lace shirt-
fronts on a watered-silk background, narrow sailor ties in antelope or*

hand-knit chenille.[10] After the War, journalism became more respectable and moved out of buildings *that still managed to retain the atmosphere of a provincial notary's office. There were stained-glass windows, huge American conference tables, leather armchairs, rubber flooring, dining rooms like convent refectories or penitentiaries, bars like those in ocean liners.*[11] Editorial directors were on the lookout for "personalities," and Colette was promoted to assistant editor. Journalism created the star reporter who lived dangerously and covered himself with glory. *Photographers neither slept nor ate. Roger Mathieu and I literally assaulted the train carrying Queen Marie of Romania, clinging to the bars of the royal car when it passed through Laroche in the middle of the night. God, was I afraid as the roadbed sped by beneath me! Vallier of* Le Matin *conducted his own personal investigation into the Landru affair and leaped over the wall of the notorious house in Gambais; he seemed to be able to slip through keyholes.*

"Well, Vallier," Jouvenel said, "what have you come up with?"

"Well, sir, not really very much."

He took pleasure in building suspense as he explored his pockets.

"Out with it, Vallier, out with it," Jouvenel said.

"Nothing much . . . a tooth."

And with a sudden gesture, his voice rising, he brandished a human molar with long, yellow roots.

"And a . . . ah! here it is . . the top joint of a finger."

With a coquettish grin, Vallier placed his macabre discoveries on the desk.

"Digusting! Scavenger! Necrophile! Will you get that out of here?"

The scavenger feigned insult.

"Well, you can't come back with a femur every time," he said in a wounded tone.[12]

In spite of these occasional highjinks, Colette regarded journalism as daily drudgery; she found it much more demanding than vaudeville discipline, to which she had submitted with apparent alacrity. And we should take her seriously when she states flatly that she did not like to write . . . literature, at least, which demanded more from her, was probably easier; but there were compensations: *The obsession with the late article, so many lines to be got out between midnight and 2 A.M., for years these replaced the "examination dream" in my sleeping hours. I still experience it sometimes, in alternation with the absolute necessity of singing* Les Huguenots *on the stage of the Opéra.*[13]

In this milieu—it was always her husband's milieu—she was like an invited guest. She knew the more famous journalists only through *conjugal endosmosis. Which is not a sure method of evaluation.*[14] For three years she practiced journalism in her husband's shadow; for him it served as a political platform, and in the end these years were to seem to her even less honorable than the years before. Her way of life throughout was very like that of the average middle-class "Madame Dupont." But she tried, and from time to time she was even happy. Yet still "freedom," that lovely, wingèd word, beckoned to her in the distance, toward a time when literature and her own private inclinations were to regain the upper hand.

⚜ THE SEQUESTERED MODEL

Colette was thirty-nine when she was married for the second time, forty when Bel-Gazou was born—the same age as Sido at her own birth. It was a bit late to embark on the role of traditional wife. Still, the frustration she had experienced during her eccentric first marriage and during her years on the fringes of society had also brought certain compensations. *"You will lead an upright life,"* Margot tells Renée Néré, *and for a woman an upright life is the one that leads her to her grave practically unnoticed by anyone!* [1]

Colette had sublimated her maternal model; Sido had just died. In the beginning, she played her role of "upright" wife conscientiously, with perhaps a touch of overattention to its social aspects, which did not displease her.

In marrying Jouvenel, she had risen vastly on the social ladder. She became a baroness, she had a title to maintain. Sido had looked after her children herself, and notwithstanding her several servants —common at the time—she had selected her own cuts of meat at the village butcher's. Colette had servants now, and for Bel-Gazou there was an English nanny; from 1913 to 1921, until the girl was sent away to school, Miss Draper looked after her. *All through the war a cranky foreign woman who was grumpy and ill-tempered with everyone, including herself, was shunted off to the country alone with a little girl and saw to everything, acting as gardener, cook, doctor, refusing to accept wages.*[2] Had it not been for the war, Colette would have lived the comfortable, soft existence of any active upper-class woman. Under the carved balconies of the Passy chalet, *I led a truly female life with its commonplace and curable griefs, its revolts, its laughter and cowardice. I developed a liking for decorating, for destroying. There I worked, impelled by a need for money. I spent many lazy hours.*[3] There was a legend attached to the romantic chalet: a jealous painter in love with his model had installed a street door with a wrought-iron bolt and key—*No house so faithfully counseled waiting to me.*[4] And like the beautiful, sequestered model, Colette spent hours waiting in the same room by the log fire. Married life—as it had been in the Rue Jacob in former days—was one long lesson in patience. There were to be several Henrys . . . but they were all alike in one thing. The house was more comfortable, her husband treated her with greater courtesy; for the moment, the war was at the door. Afterward he would pursue the same chimeras, power and flesh. Like her former husband, he would be home less and less often. To Carco, Colette summed up the inner pain of her marriages: "One of the best things about being in love after all is recognizing the step of a man when he climbs the stairs."[5]

At forty, it was easier to bear waiting than it had been at twenty; there were compensations and remissions. *The child's birth, the first two years of the Great War, the letters that never came, what difference did it make if I waited within the crumbling walls of the chalet —just when you think it has been overcome, the agony of waiting returns unbidden. The bar set across the window was convenient to lean on during my nocturnal vigils. And in the daytime there were other things that helped: the cat's severe immobility, the hesitant rain drops, the dog's yawns . . . and suddenly a letter would fall through the slot in the door, the dogs would jump up as though they had been called, and the whole house would cease waiting, fearing, imagining, along with me. In the cottage, covered in the summertime with flowers, with Virginia creeper hanging curtainlike in garlands, a whole world bloomed in the garden shadows. . . . Animals prospered and multiplied, cats flared their nostrils at the scent of a yellow rat, the yellow rats feared nothing but the owls. I had a flying squirrel, two grass snakes, one a viper with a pink stomach, and two green lizards.*[6] The chalet promised a future, proliferation . . . and yet one day as Colette was dashing home through a summer storm, she saw what she at first thought must be an optical illusion—one corner of the chalet had collapsed into the garden below. Passy 1913, a fragment of life. In 1917, Colette was finally forced to move to Auteuil, to the Boulevard Suchet. The disintegration of the Rue de Cortambert chalet was almost symbolic. Perhaps, like the wife it sheltered, it had lacked attention. The Great War had touched it, had quickened its natural deterioration.

❧ AUGUST 1914

In August 1914, Colette was in Rozven at her villa, across the Nez peninsula from Missy's, which she had managed to furnish and move into in the spring. As yet, the war was only a distant noise over the horizon. On June 28, the Archduke Franz-Ferdinand was assassinated in Sarajevo; on July 31, Jaurès had been assassinated in Paris.

Colette wrote a letter on August 1 to Léon Hamel mentioning the Caillaux affair and her "mad" brother-in-law Robert de Jouvenel's attack in *L'Oeuvre* against Caillaux. But she was not a woman to fill her letters with frivolous things; she gets to her serious news at once: *Hamel, brace yourself, I've been swimming, swimming on my stomach, on my back, I can turn over in the water, I swim like a top, 100 strokes at a go, and I'm having a wild time. Bel-Gazou is superb, brown as a paté-en-croûte, with muscles like her mother's and very gay.*[1] The war is only a big, black word in the headlines of the somnolent summertime newspapers. It is impossible to conceive of war in the midst of a vacation in Saint-Malo, when all one's time is spent gazing at the black mare, at the sparrow hawk as it climbs in the noontime sky and hangs motionless before its descent; a wife and contented mother, Colette ignored the war. On August 1, however, Germany, followed by France, ordered a general mobilization. On the evening of August 2, the German ultimatum was delivered to Belgium demanding right of passage for its troops. On the 3rd, Belgium rejected the ultimatum, and Germany declared war on France.

And yet the war was . . . this fish-seller demanding to be paid in hard cash, silver and bronze . . . who gazed off to sea and saw the long parade of days without bread or cider beginning to move in toward shore . . . the war was the grocer's boy on his bicycle bringing the latest rumors with the happy ringing of his bell, advice to hoard sugar, oil and gasoline . . . that was the war. In Saint-Malo where we rushed to learn the news we were met with a thunderbolt, General Mobilization.[2] As the town crier read out the proclamation, everything seemed to burst forth at once, the bells, the cries of the people, the children's tears, and the crier's drum. Out of the depths of History, the old gestures, panics, anxious disorder, visceral anxiety: *Women run from groups of other women and stop short as though struck, and then begin to run again . . . some cry suddenly and then suddenly stop as some thought crosses their mind,*

*their mouths gaping stupidly. Adolescents grow pale and stare va-
cantly, like sleepwalkers.*[3] Slowly, Colette left Saint-Malo and returned to Rozven. *Would this be the longest evening of my war,
still here and waiting to leave as the calm flatness of the sea holds the
upside-down reflections of the violent rocks?* [4]

Henry de Jouvenel was mobilized into the 23rd ground infantry
regiment. On August 12, 1914, he wrote to an old school chum from
the Collège Stanislas, Anatole de Monzie: "My dear old friend, I was
unable to see you, I'm off. I have every intention of returning. But
you never know. If by some fluke I don't come back, I beg you to
look after my family." [5] In her *Souvenirs de ma vie*, Marguerite
Moréno wrote, on the following day, a note about this August 13th:
"Colette's husband left yesterday. As soon as he donned his uniform,
he was gone far from her, from everything. This sudden transforma-
tion of a civilian into a soldier seems to change his way of thinking.
. . . Colette is being brave. All women are behaving well in this
moment."

Bel-Gazou stayed behind in Rozven and spent most of the war
either in Brittany or at Castel Novel. Colette returned to a Paris that
was being drained of men. It was the end of her honeymoon.

⚜ IN THE REAR LINES

Colette set up her wartime quarters in Paris, and the euphoric
days were over. She had to make a living. She was able to place a few
articles with *Le Matin. Our means of livelihood are limited.*[1] As the
Germans drew closer to Paris, there was talk of newspapers ceasing
publication and being replaced with bulletins issued by the War
Ministry. Women organized. Musidora, an actress who had started
out at the Ba-Ta-Clan and was to appear in the film version of *La
Vagabonde*, was living in a modern studio apartment in the Rue
Descamps. Annie de Pène, the writer and editor at *L'Eclair*, lived
at the end of the Impasse Herran in a tiny house with a covered
entryway, like a cottage. Marguerite Moréno had returned from
Argentina and was living nearby in a ground-floor apartment in a
new building in the Rue Jean de Bologne. These four neighbors
organized a kind of phalanstery: *at night when the sky was filled
with zeppelins, Musidora slept in the Rue Cortambert on a narrow
iron bed, and in the daytime she did the marketing and cooked. I
cleaned house and did the laundry. We were a good team: we would
wring out the sheets we had washed by hand by tying one end*

around an enormous copper faucet and twisting them, and Mar-
guerite Moréno, her cigarette dangling from her lips, would scatter
over our household chores the benevolent ash of rumor, true and
false, of anecdotes and predictions. Annie de Pène knew of a door-
way from which a farmer sold chickens he would toss out with a
"Catch, little lady! Four francs four sous." [2] Marguerite, who was
unparalleled at *sowing the miraculous seeds of laughter, the laughter*
of tragedy, the nervous giggling fits of wartime, insolence in the face
of approaching danger, her words as uplifting as a shot of alcohol,
kept up everyone's spirits. One night, as the cannon rumbled in the
East, *temporarily out of verbal jokes . . . Moréno picked up the*
rhythm of the shelling, with its strong and weak beats, she snapped
her fingers and tapped her heels on the floor, improvising on the spot
a parody of Spanish dancing, and with her revolving hips and rolling
eyes she gave us laughter, made us forget danger with the healthy
impertinence and temerity of a true heroine.[3]

When there was any news, it was generally bad. In September,
Sidi . . . *fighting for the past three days around Verdun, saw his*
comrade, an artillery officer, killed at his side. He jumped aside to
avoid the shrapnel and fell into a trench, injuring his foot. Alas! he's
already healed up and on his way back to the front! [4] The war was
barely two months old; there is no condition to which one adapts so
quickly. In such emergencies, women spontaneously return to long-
forgotten habits and responsibilities: *Two or three small shells this*
morning. One fell very near. . . . The other almost hit Mme de
Comminges's house, but it didn't even damage the roof.[5]

Colette was discreetly ironical about the wild upsurge of rampant,
suicidal chauvinism, the bellicose ardor that overcame the entire male
population. *Sidi, well, he's fighting; I allowed myself to write him*
that it would be nicer if he were here, that the Matin, *for God's sake,*
was still an important aspect of his duty (it was almost suppressed in
his absence, Le Matin), *and he replied with a patriotic harangue.*
Can't you just see him sitting on his horse amidst the smoke? It took
a powerful God to create soldiers like that.[6]

"My love," she wrote to Sidi, "you're not getting my letters
either. We're poor beasts. . . . I'm keeping up the morale of my
creatures here at home. But they're fairly easy to manage. Still, we
can't help having long and ridiculous arguments over the fate of our
troops and of Paris in the kitchen, and you can't work and talk
about the war at the same time." [7] "My love," Henry wrote from
Verdun on April 23, 1915, "I've begun riding, using my sword. I

yearn for cleanliness . . . there are times when living like an animal
has its advantages, since it's the only thing that makes life bearable.
. . . How happy the beasts must be these days! The endless lines of
sobbing women and mothers, the fathers who come to beg for the
bodies of their sons, and we don't have them, the letters from ref-
ugees pleading to return to their villages, even under fire, and to
whom I can grant nothing—it all makes a horrible atmosphere. My
dear love, you are still there, are you not, you still love me? Luckily
there's still that, and Bel-Gazou." [8]

Colette began working as a night-nurse at the Lycée Janson-de
Sailly on October 16: *a horrid job . . . thirteen hours on duty,
every kind of care to be provided, when morning comes everyone
is a bit haggard.* Marguerite Moréno took a similar job at a hospital
in Nice where she had taken Jean Darragon, her second husband,
who was too ill to be mobilized. "I am still at work among my leg
amputees, who are gay, and my arm amputees, who are sad," she
wrote to Colette. "In a very short time, the legless begin to draw, to
write, to make little toys and drag themselves along the floor with
their hands, joking all the while. But the armless become depressed,
it's a great humiliation for a man—perhaps the worst—not to be able
to pee without asking for help." [9]

Despite her care, Marguerite's husband died. Jouvenel remained
well. The winter was a hard one: *Sidi saw four men next to him die
from the cold.*[10]

⚜ VERDUN

There was a clandestine visitor in Verdun in December. Disguised
as a nurse, Colette made a *lovely, terrified journey* of thirteen hours
to be with her husband. Under a false name with borrowed papers
and several unexpected and possibly dangerous adventures, she
traveled on a blacked-out train from Châlons to Verdun. The shelling was continual, the darkness rent from time to time with flares.
She was impatient to get there: *Nobody slept or spoke until the
winter dawn broke, until we arrived at Verdun.*[1]

At last she was with Sidi again, in the home of a noncommissioned
officer and his wife who owned a house in Verdun and allowed her
to hide out on condition she not go outdoors or near the windows,
since a group of medical officers lived across the street. The shelling
drowned out the coke fire that sputtered and flared, and the dialogue
between her hosts and herself was *the dialogue of war, all wars*:

"*What's new?*"

"*New? Well, the butter the upholsterer's been selling is really margarine.*"

"*And? . . .*"

"*The piano seller's got a big shipment of sardines. I'm going to drop by on my way to tend to the horses.*"

"*Yes, yes, and what else?*"

"*Oh,*" the dark-haired young woman exclaimed, "*there's that it's shameful to have to pay three sous for a leek. For that matter, the subprefect is fed up, he's going to have all the rice and macaroni and potatoes brought in to the subprefecture, and then we'll see if the grocers have the nerve to . . .*"

"*Yes, yes . . . but please, what about the war?*"

"*The war?*"

I began to lose patience. "*Yes, the war! The one we can hear, that we read about, the one that's going on outside!*"

Her blue eyes crinkled with amusement, "*Oh yes, excuse me, the war. . . . Well, it's coming along, it's coming along well. Don't worry about that!*" [2]

It was always food, wherever one went, a piercing concern: how to come by a good meal, what was available to eat. Wars come and go and are all alike with their endless days of hunger interrupted by miraculous feasts that live on in the memory—a basket of scandalous truffles brought by someone on leave in the Lot region, a cream cheese from a gardener in Verdun who kept a cow in his back garden, some tiny clandestine restaurant open only at night.

War. War seen by women. Wives shut away, voluntary prisoners of love living an Oriental way of life, going out for only a few moments at night. *If we whisper about them we will not betray them. There was one who did not cross the threshold of her prison for seven months, who saw no human face save for the one she loved. They say she writes and writes and that she is the happiest of women.* [3] War enabled women to have recourse to new forms of coquetry, to add spice to their ancient village vendettas. The wife of the noncommissioned officer who had offered shelter to Colette returned home unscathed beneath a hailstorm of shrapnel:

"*How annoying,*" she cried, "*really annoying. I was forced to take shelter in the X's doorway, and we're not on speaking terms!*" [4]

Colette celebrated New Year's Eve of 1915 in the Argonne. She brought baskets of candies for the children in the devastated villages. The car moved slowly through frozen fields ploughed by artillery;

there was *a man dead beneath his cross, and another, and still another cross topped with a képi, and then soldiers, a food convoy, horses and mules.*[5] The village of Rampont had lost half its houses, but the church still stood with its broken windows; a dozen women and children were kneeling among the soldiers, and officers stood in the freezing wind. One by one, in pairs, the children emerged from the ruins. *They came timidly, silently, mischievously, to collect their toy trumpets, their cookies, their dolls. They sprang from the ruins in bunches and stood along the wall against the blackboard of the makeshift schoolroom. One ravishing child's golden hair gradually erased the chalked inscription written up behind her: "To die for one's country is the noblest of fates and the most enviable."* [6]

Despite her detachment and her sense of humor, Colette was not exempt from the militant chauvinism of this unsettled period: a German officer evacuated his requisitioned quarters in someone's home, taking with him the clock, the woman's clothing, the contents of a safe he had blown open, and the best books in the library: *What understanding can we hope for,* Colette wrote with indignation, *what bridge can be built between ourselves and a people that teaches its sons both a love for ageless books and the most practical way of blowing a safe at the same time!* [7]

She was still in Verdun in February 1915: *They say people in Germany and Austria are beginning to go hungry!* She had just experienced a bombardment, and she wrote at length to Hamel, describing the antiaircraft action against the German planes, the exploding shells, the arrival of fighter pursuit planes, another German plane. Exploding shells, bombs in the next-door garden; that round had made her insides shake and she was living in a house without electricity, lit by four candles.

⚜ COLETTE'S WAR

1915, 1916, 1917 were calmer years. For some of the time, Colette was in Italy as a reporter for *Le Matin.* The war continued, but far from the front, protected, its worst effect seemed to be Sidi's absence and the various restrictions.

In June 1915, Colette was in Rome. Henry de Jouvenel's first wife Claire Boas, the mother of his son Bertrand, had been there before her. Claire Boas had a lingering fondness for the Jouvenel name and the title of baroness, both of which had been legally taken from her in the divorce. *If you want a laugh,* Colette wrote to Léon Hamel on June 28, *I'll give you Mme Boas, who made Rome slightly more unlivable for me because of her recent visit here, during the course of which she created a good deal of disturbance using the name she is so attached to. I turn up with the same name—naturally—and everyone's first reaction is that I am some kind of imposter! It has all been straightened out now, save for the Hotel Excelsior,* her hotel, *where to put it bluntly I was refused a room. What do you say to that? It's enough to shake me out of my lethargy.*[1] She moved into the Albergo Regina in the Via Vittorio Veneto, where she had a friendly neighbor in Gabriele D'Annunzio, who lived in the apartment next door. For this Frenchwoman who had traveled so little, Rome was full of marvels. Even more than the museums, she admired the handsome men who filled the streets and the pregnant women in the poorer districts, standing opulent and massive in the sun like towers or beautiful plants heavy with fruit, around whom *sprang other wild creatures, tinier nymphs whose quantities, unlike our own miserly bourgeois women, they never think of limiting.*[2]

In July 1915, she was in Venice, where *a German Taube threatens St. George standing on his church, but eventually goes away after jettisoning three bombs in the canal. The Sunday flags float down from San Marco fanning the torrid square. And the chambermaid who brings in my tea sums up the incident in these curt, heroic terms: "It's nothing! The enemy came, we chased him off!"*[3]

Sidi joined her on leave on September 13, at Cernobbio on Lake Como. *Ah, Hamel, how lovely it all is! I've marked where our hotel is. Everything I look at is blue: Sidi, the lake, red sage flowers, morning glories, the water stairs and the ripe figs . . . I'm dizzy with it all!* He had to leave on the 22nd, and she is left with his brother— *only his brother's brother*—Robert and Robert's girl friend Zou; she misses him. On the 29th Sidi returns, and once again she is happy.

She returned to Rome in January of 1917. This time in the company of her husband, who was beginning his diplomatic and political career as the French delegate to the Allied conference. Colette strolled in the gardens of the Villa Borghese with or without Sidi— most often without, for he was extremely busy—and with her faithful dog, Gamelle. The winter was so mild that they could lunch out of doors beneath the oaks and umbrella pines. At the hotel there was wartime fare, only two choices, no butter or cheese. But Colette had orgies of white cheese between meals, she worked on *Les Heures longues,* her evocation of the war years, and awaited the arrival of her friend Musidora, who was coming to Rome on tour with *La Vagabonde*.

The letter to Hamel containing all this news is dated March 22, 1917. It was to be the last. In April this old friend, the confidant of her deepest feelings, died. As she was to do whenever death touched her deeply, Colette kept silence. When her friend Annie de Pène succumbed to Spanish influenza the following year, she had only a brief comment: *I will miss Annie de Pène a great deal, and what a stupid way to die.* She did not attend Annie's funeral, just as she had avoided the funerals of Marcel Schwob and Sido, as she was later to avoid those of Hélène Picard and Renée Hamon. At the time of Annie's death, she wrote with resentment: *She would go without lunch or dinner, or skip a meal so as not to put on weight, and the flu got her when she was defenseless, that is, with an empty stomach!* [4] When she went to visit Germaine Beaumont, Annie's daughter, who was ill, she uttered not a word of consolation, but laid a bunch of grapes on the bed and asked her, simply, "How are you feeling . . . my child?" [5]

Even such years as these pass. Apart from journalism, Colette published several books during the war: *La Paix chez les bêtes*, in 1916, is reminiscent of the *Dialogues de bêtes*, as though Colette, in a period of great human suffering, preferred to take refuge in the animal world. *Les Heures longues*, which appeared in 1917, won the admiration of Marcel Proust. *Les Enfants dans les ruines*, published the same year, and *Dans la foule* in 1918, round out her wartime productions.

Colette began her direct connection with the Seventh Art with the filming of *La Vagabonde* and her participation in *La Revue*, a film directed by Diamant-Berger. And in 1916, she had moved—an epic move, employing four wartime moving men: an old man, a fifteen-year-old apprentice, an "asthmatic pubkeeper," and Apollo.

Apollo was young, sturdy, bursting with health, and not at the front. There were grounds for suspicion on the part of a soldier's wife, intolerant of slackers. "You there, I'd like to know how it is that . . ." *His chestnut hair and heroic torso glowed with a kind of working-class mischief as he handed me his military registration booklet opened to the proper page:*

"It's all there," he said, "it's no secret. X, Denis André, twenty-eight, father of seven, exempt from military service."

In the ensuing silence, the bitter old man muttered: "Seven! Don't get too close, he may be contagious!"

"Last year," Apollo went on, "I thought I was in for it 'cause I only had five kids, and that's not enough to exempt you as a father of six. Jeezus! I said, I won't be able to stay out forever on my bronchitis, and one of these days I'll get called up; so get moving! And back to work I went, and whups! Twins! That's my own way of making weapons. And," he added, lowering his voice, "that's not to mention four more who're wandering around somewhere. . . . I only mention them . . . to brag a bit!" [6]

Colette moved out of the Passy chalet and into a small private house in the Boulevard Suchet formerly occupied by the aging actress Eva Lavallière. Since it was wartime, she left the extravagant furnishings and decorations as she found them. Both she and her predecessor found the dwelling depressing. It was uncomfortable—and did not bode well for the future. *Probably because it was unloved, the little house had shriveled up. Before me, a troubled woman eager to remain beautiful . . . in despair over her aging body, her illusions gone, childish, had languished within its walls. But I did not feel it was hostile to me. I realized how fragile it was, and I protected as best I could this dwelling that protected me so little. At the first sound of a night-time alert, from 1915 to 1918, I would open all the windows to save the glass and go back to bed. All around me, alone—my husband in the East, my child in the country—the house would reverberate like an empty barrel as the bombers flew over it.* [7] During this period, a very young girl, nearly a child—she was, in fact, thirteen—came to work for Colette during one of her visits to Castel Novel. Pauline Tissandier was a peasant girl from the Brive region with swarthy skin and slightly protruding eyes: for forty years, until Colette's death, she remained with the employer whom she loved, and who loved her.

⚜ THE WAR FOR LITTLE GIRLS

All these dark years, however, were illuminated by the "Treasure of Light" who lit up the darkest rooms, by the voice and laughter of a tiny child playing with the war as though it were only a short, mysterious word.

Bel-Gazou's war: early in the war, eighteen months old, she had evidenced her facile chauvinism by lisping her own version of the Marseillaise, *"A mon zafa de la pa-trie."*

Born twelve months before the declaration of war, Bel-Gazou experienced the confused days of mobilization, long journeys across a disordered France, more than one dramatic moment. A bull destroyed the cart in which it was being transported, like Germans destroying a church. For a few weeks in a Breton village, she reigned over a large infantry contingent. She knew all about the war! [1]

A portion of Colette's war comes to us colored and made poetic by the realism and surrealism of a two-year-old child, three, four, five, a child with no knowledge of anything but war.

At two, Bel-Gazou had a large map of Europe on the wall in her room. *Every day, she points to where her relatives are fighting: "Papa here . . . uncle there . . ." and unhesitatingly sets up a French general-staff headquarters in Sicily, at the same time providing our infantry with a highly advantageous staging area in the north of Denmark.* [2]

At four, she had her own interpretation of Red Riding Hood and the contents of the famous basket for grandmother:

"A cake? What kind of a cake?"

"Uh . . . made of puff pastry."

Her hand let go my wrist and struck her bare thigh:

"Puff pastry . . . and no one informed the mayor?"

"The mayor? Whatever for?"

"He should have been told . . . pastry is forbidden 'cause of the war."

"But . . ."

"And the mayor, he would have gone to see Red Riding Hood, and he would have said 'Sir, I'm reki . . . reki . . . rekisitioning your pastry. You can't use up flour for pastries in wartime, and you'll have to pay a thousand sous and that's it!"

"But Bel-Gazou, Red Riding Hood is a story of a long time ago. There wasn't any war then."

"No war! Aha! And why wasn't there a war?" [3]

What age was she? four, five, she spoke three languages, English, Limousin patois, and French. She shocked the inhabitants of Rozven by playing in bare legs and feet, wearing a bathing suit, spending all day on the rocks at the shore. Her mother came upon her as she was engaged in an elaborate game that consisted in writing without paper, ink or pen.

"Who are you writing to, Bel-Gazou?"

"My brother."

"Your brother? So you have a brother . . . what's his name?"

"His name is Louis Tragomar."

"And how old is he?"

"Eight."

"Where is he?"

"He's in England."
"And what does your brother do in England, Bel-Gazou?"
"He makes minitions."
I said nothing, but I was shocked. This was too much reality for a child's fantasy.
"And how would you like to have a sister, Bel-Gazou?"
"I've got one already!"
"Ah, of course. And her name?"
"La Bellaudière."
"I see! Is she older than you?"
"I think so . . . it's a long time since I've seen her."
"Why, does she live a long way from here?"
"Oh, she was taken prisoner by the Germans, poor thing."
"Imagine!"
Bel-Gazou lifts her head and looks up at me with her gaze from which astonishment and gaiety have eliminated mystery, and utters with the heedlessness of a talking bird the word she hears on all sides: *"Oh, that's war!"* [4]

⚜ THE WOMEN'S WAR

War is often no less surprising for women than for little girls; there are still things to be said about it. Aside from all the clichés concerning the sacrifices of our valiant wives, there has been no great attention paid to the ways in which women experience wars, what it means to them, what they seek in it and how they regard their male counterparts.

Colette relates her war simply, in fragments. War and love, for example. She eschews farewells on station platforms, tear-stained eyes looking for letters that will never come, aging widows with countless mouths to feed, or the sorry females who change heroes into cuckolds. Not that all these fragments of reality do not contain truth; it is just that they did not much interest Colette. In three letters —authentic or fabricated—she evoked another, less banal reality:

First, the "bachelor soldier." *"Madame, I am twenty-three years and three months old and a sergeant. I want to get married. I want to get married as soon as possible. . . . For three years, I as a veteran soldier have known, lost, rediscovered, wept over and protected some one hundred comrades of all types and ages. . . . My friends have told me enough to fill a book, but here I refer only to love stories. A hundred different love stories! Do you think, Madame, that*

*all of them are alike? You are wrong. You may want to divide them
into happy love affairs and unhappy love affairs; I tried to do this
too, mathematically, but I found it impossible because too many of
them suddenly or gradually slipped from the first category into the
second."* [1]

In the beginning, there are *"photos, passionate letters, pressed
flowers, packages of treats and expensive silk scarves."* [2] Women who
are passionately in love write every day for weeks on end, and then
every week for months on end. And one day, a postcard instead of a
blue envelope, or a mauve . . . and then nothing! Perhaps a note
breaking it off, a letter of denunciation, or silence. *"And all this time,
the married men are firm as Verdun itself. 'Here kid, have some of
this, it's pork-liver paté my little woman makes herself' or, 'Come
on, old pal, taste this chicken wing my wife sent me.' Unjustly, perhaps, I feel that my packages, the packages I get from relatives,
letters from my uncle, sweaters from my grandmother, fall short in
comparison. . . . Even the threat of death doesn't affect these fortunate men.*

" *'If I don't return,' one of them says, 'I won't mind too much. I've
got my oldest boy, who's already pretty grown up . . . the shop
will get along somehow.'*

" *'Die! Of course I don't want to! But she has such courage, I'm
sure she'll do the right thing, with me or without me!'*

*"So, Madame, in short, I've had enough! Do you understand? I
want my share. . . . Quickly, Madame, get us married! Since we
have to take care of future generations, get us married right away!"* [3]

Second letter, an unmarried woman: *"Madame, last Tuesday I read
the letter you published in your column from a young twenty-three-
year-old sergeant who wants to get married. I am replying. I am
the girl he wants. I am twenty-five years old and have forty hectares
of land in the country and a little money. . . . I'm a blonde and
I'm not bad looking, believe me. Or would he prefer a brunette? In
that case, there's my cousin, who is a bookkeeper in a bank, and her
sister is also a brunette and is assistant secretary to an important
lawyer. None of us is married. We are productive workers, we
women without sex, and we stand by and see other women getting
married all the time. Who are they? Just women, Madame, but they
are young widows, or not so young, and divorcées. . . . Why them
and not us? There's Mme G . . . who is well over forty and engaged to one of the handsomest fliers in France. And there's Mme
B . . . who had a messy divorce a year ago and is now going to*

make life pleasant for a boy in the Alpine corps who could be her son. Mme F, fifty years old and mixed up in a shady lawsuit, is about to marry a beardless young lieutenant. . . . You'll say it's all a question of dowry! Don't be misled, Madame, the officer in question is a millionaire twice over! You smile, Madame, you think I am trying to turn my private sorrow into a public affair? I won't go on . . . I'll just go on designing my old maid's costume like all unmarried girls." [4]

And third, a woman approaching middle age: *"Yes, Madame, I am one of those widows you—or rather, young marriageable girls— are reproaching for wanting to go on living. Two years ago, the war took my husband from me. Am I supposed to die too? It's too late now, I should have died at the time. . . . I am one of those harpies, those abominations who want to remarry, who do remarry, who go on telling themselves when they're over forty 'I've still got some life left in me.' In exchange for the magnificent and brave hero I had given up, I ask for merely a live man, and not even a whole one. 'Oh, you're easy to please!' your young girl will cry, 'why should you have him rather than me?' Because, I reply to her, you may be able to take such a gift, but you won't be able to keep it. . . . We know. We have been through all the sorrows of love and we know how to hold on; more than one of us want nothing but to work on a man's behalf! Of course, you have your future before you. . . . But you will fritter it away. I don't have to dream of the future to be happy in the present, I don't have to make comparisons in order to be happy. My gratitude doesn't depend on the size of the gift, and I've paid enough by now to know that life is precious enough without wanting happiness to boot."* [5]

Colette's own wisdom and the wisdom taught by wartime arrive here at this ambiguous coupling where love between an older woman and a younger man still gives rise to a certain virtuous repulsion. Subconsciously, in the sociological climate created by the war years, Colette is preparing for Chéri, she is naively giving expression to the part of herself that was beginning to identify with Léa, the embodiment of the aging mistress.

In the *Claudine* novels, Annie had spoken the words "fresh flesh" with a relish that foretells the carnal desires of the aging woman and her immodest complacency. Colette changes little: her various ages are so many molds into which she pours her eternal feelings, her guiltless and sensual love of the flesh. Her journalistic comments on this sociological wartime phenomenon are applicable to her later novels as well. *Listen, young lady! The hospital, the nursery. . . .* *When millions of men can find the strength to overcome being away from a woman, they aren't going to make do with the first woman that comes their way. My father, a Zouave, brought back only one painful memory from the battlefield, the cry, the sigh issuing from youthful mouths and gray beards alike, "Mother!" Your arms stretch out to beg, my girl, but other female arms offer a less well-thought-of but total refuge, they offer a combination of protection, love, and a devotion that is repelled by nothing, and the exhausted hero will lie easy in their embrace!* [6]

The toll taken by the war made way for Chéri, Léa's troubling charge, an ephebus torn apart by his love of a fifty-year-old woman. During the long hours of the war, Colette turned forty-five. Following the birth of Bel-Gazou and her abandonment of her profession in the theater, she began to put on weight. The imposing figure of a woman that returned to the stage during the 1920s was a far cry from the slim Colette Willy, the Vagabond. Henceforth, the former Claudine would play Léa.

⚜ WAR AND LOVE

Before *Chéri*, however, her first work of fiction since her marriage and *L'Entrave*, was to be *Mitsou*, written in 1917 and published in 1919. The novel deals with some of Colette's principal preoccupations throughout the war, and hints at the beginning deterioration of her relationship with Sidi.

She goes back to her experiences in vaudeville, now part of the past. Mitsou is a performer in that branch of Parisian show business know as the *café-concert*, the caf' conc'. Once she had been *a dressmaker, but she shuns what she knows best—poverty and the workshop—and yearns for what she is least good at: the stage.*[1] War comes. *Mitsou* is a war story. By chance, she meets the handsome Blue Lieutenant—he has no other name. They write long letters to each other. And then they meet again. By dawn, Mitsou is deeply in love with the Blue Lieutenant, and the Blue Lieutenant has grown bored with the caf' conc' singer. Mitsou, inspired by love, writes one last letter that Colette signs. Between their two situations—Mitsou and Colette —what differences . . . and what similarities.

Petite Chose, Mitsou's pal and music hall colleague—we might call her "Tiny"—is the character who personifies the common, widespread view of wartime as seen through a woman's eyes, war from the "rear" as it was then subtly called. She is not the kind to turn her back on any of the unexpected benefits offered by this prodigal era. *There hasn't been anything like it since the beginning of the world! Has there ever been a time before when the streets were full of men, all kinds of young men, handsome guys dressed up fit to kill and on the lookout for girls, drinking them in, eyeing them up and down, grinning and hungry for them? Isn't that true? And people have the nerve to say that we're only out for ourselves to get hold of their sons, their husbands, brothers and cousins! Well, Madame, is all I can say, I'm not one of your knitters or bandage-rollers. I can't send prisoners packages because I haven't got a cent! I'm just a girl who likes all she can get, and I'm not about to turn my back on some good-looking guy standing in front of me. And one who's going off tomorrow to be killed, to boot!"* [2]

The war enhanced female sexual awareness, it enabled women to make advances that they would be forced to forgo to a certain extent afterward. Female discourse changed, it became more direct, more down to earth. The term "war economy" is a common one, but "war sexuality" is seldom heard. We have mentioned food shortages, but sexual shortage leads to the same gluttonies, passionate leave time after weeks of letters, desire and frustration. In a period still full of taboos and prohibitions, when contraception was neither sure nor systematic, war enabled women to indulge their sexual desires, to discover that such desires existed and to enjoy them. The end was always imminent, and it was an end that women often considered when it was too late, when they were old.

In the face of imminent death—in a week, or month—the old prohibitions, the austere virtues, conventional coyness, hesitation, all seemed to matter very little. Everything dictated the quicker, the better. As men say, women "gave themselves," rather, they offered themselves and to themselves, pleasure, love, liaisons with young men who had the additional attraction of being heroes. He is handsome and brave; he may soon die. For once, desire and passion, ephemeral and temporary as they are, were practicable in a world in which everything was officially recognized as being ephemeral and temporary. All human aggression was turned to the war, the Great War, not the war of every day. Wartime love affairs were full of tenderness and longing. Violence was occurring elsewhere.

Petite Chose's excitement, the excitement of all women—particularly free women: divorcées, widows, older women—was also caused by the fact that free for once from an exclusive duty to one and only one man, women turned to other, broader duties that also expanded their outlook. The men were gone, and women took their places; when the men were present, women cared for them, but this ordinarily fairly unappealing task made them additionally valued during these exceptional years, and bettered their position.

Gratitude toward a careworn wife bandaging her husband's scratches and gratitude toward a wartime nurse serving all mankind are two different emotions. In peacetime, a man in his own home dreams of adventure, a substitute for war. In wartime, in his barracks or in the trenches, he dreams of women. Her hour has come. Her life is more difficult because men's work and responsibilities are added to her own traditional tasks, but at the same time all the alienation she has experienced as a woman suddenly works in her favor; she does not have to risk her life, and her importance to men and to society is qualitatively, basically, changed.

Mitsou describes the upheavals of wartime, how they alter the conventions of peace. In peacetime, the Blue Lieutenant, solidly bourgeois, recently out of school, would have paid no attention to a caf' conc' singer. His many letters to her and the length of time he is forced to wait for his night of love, both attract and arouse this young man who, in peacetime, would have quickly become blasé, whose meeting with Mitsou under ordinary circumstances would have been boring.

"*As for us, the war got us as we were coming out of school. It made men out of us, and I suppose we'll always miss not having been young men . . . boys who didn't know what it was like to be a young man during the war, trembling, excited, skeptical, resigned, wanting everything and deprived of everything, weighed down by the bitterness of feeling old but with a childish faith, unaware that these little moments 'in the rear' are ruining our brief returns to our former lives, our hometowns, our belongings, our women.*" [3] Confronted with these "mature schoolboys," these men who are too young, *like fruit out of season, ripe on one side, green on the other,* the woman's function was to redress the imbalance, fulfill his needs. It was an urgent task. And as has been noted, older women were often best prepared to perform it. Mitsou is young, but she is familiar with poverty, with hard work. She is also kept by a "man who is well off," and she regards him as something like an employer; thus she also knows what it is to be dependent, to be forced to obey an authority with which she does not agree.

Without the war, there would never have been any letters between

Mitsou and the Blue Lieutenant. Mitsou is a "wartime godmother," a pen pal. She does not send the Lieutenant the little "lifesaving packages" Petite Chose sends her boyfriends, *filled with nothing but kisses.* She is above that, even though she is only a caf' conc' singer, treated like dirt by the women who have taken "important" jobs as secretaries or telephone operators because of the war.

Are you in danger when you stand guard at night? Do you need any useless things? And the Blue Lieutenant, upstanding, serious boy that he is, replies: *No, dear Mitsou, night guard isn't too dangerous. But it is an ordeal and the burdens you have to carry—responsibility and solitude—are harder to bear at night.*[4]

The war colors every moment of the leave the Blue Lieutenant spends with Mitsou. In the restaurant, they are asked to produce their food coupons; Mitsou has an extra allotment because she works at night. *The bunch of narcissus costs twenty sous instead of ten centimes.*[5] Mitsou's constant chatter about the revue in which she is performing, entitled *Ivy on the Battlefield,* makes the Blue Lieutenant laugh. *I'm imagining the kind of people who think ivy grows on a battlefield!* [6]

The war has brought them together at the Restaurant Lavoie, Mitsou and her Blue Lieutenant, a variety performer and a product of the bourgeosie. He *looks around with the slightly fake assurance of an "experienced" twenty-three year old and with a feigned ill humor designed to warn others not to look down on Mitsou, to let them know that he is quite used to her, even blasé about her. Having directed this mute warning at two sober deputies, a pair of American Red Cross women and a quartet of tanned and boisterous superior officers, he settles down to enjoy his evening in a restaurant with Mitsou.*[7] But their surroundings, the restaurant with its hidden social pitfalls, throw a terrifyingly harsh light on the gap between their educations, their speech, their backgrounds.

"What will you have, Mitsou, Burgundy, Bordeaux, Champagne?"

"It doesn't make any difference to me—I don't know wines by places."

"I'll bet you've never seen the sea, Mitsou!"

"Of course I have, at Deauville. It was really boring. . . . I can't understand people staying outdoors all day like that. I can see going to a casino or a tea party, but standing around outdoors like they were all homeless . . ." [8]

Mitsou never takes her eyes off the Lieutenant; he observes her as she proceeds from one faux pas to another:

Mitsou, angelically: "Where are you off to? Is your stomach upset? It's on the first floor."

Robert, shocked: "Upset . . . what a thing to say, Mitsou!"

Mitsou: "Why, doesn't that ever happen to you?"

Robert, to change the subject: "The Queen of Spain is said to have no legs!"

Mitsou: "First I've heard of it! Aren't they disgusted, having a crippled queen?" [9]

Unfortunate Mitsou, unaware that a well-bred young gentleman seeks certain qualities only at specific times, and out of motives impossible to conceal from his mistress. At such times, social differences and individual shortcomings fade away; there is no more war, no more code of manners, *the struggle begins, slowly, to the sound of an ethereal moaning, to the rhythm of two bodies rocking together as though to soothe or assuage a wound.*[10] Mitsou's room is tastelessly furnished, vulgarly ostentatious, but *on the lace-hung wall, thrown against the headboard was cast for the first time a magnificent image, the shadow of the torso of a naked rider, thin-waisted, broad-shouldered, curved over his invisible mount!* [11]

When she awakens, emerging from love-satiated sleep, Mitsou feels *tired and lucid,* recalling *only the exceptional pleasure, the pleasure of having held against her a handsome body that smelled as it grew warm like scented wood when it is rubbed, a body that joined itself to hers with vegetal exactitude and precision, that way was good, this way was even better, and better as it changed. That was what made her grateful, not the acute excitement she hadn't much enjoyed.*[12]

Afterward, the Blue Lieutenant dresses and leaves, and in a letter he explains that he will not be able to keep their appointment for the following night. All of Colette's insight is bestowed on Mitsou, and between them they compose a letter that was to fascinate Marcel Proust, a letter that others have found artificial; and we must agree that the only thing about it that is really Mitsou's is the grammar:

The one good thing out of this tiresome thing that's happening to you is that now I know that you can count on me. Count on me for anything. To wait for you if you want me to, to guess if there's something you're ashamed to tell me, and you can count on me if you get the notion of saying to me right out, "it's finished between us," and I'll know how to behave so you won't have to beat around the bush.

And then there's this too, if you think I ought to get another job or learn things or change in some way or other, I can do that too,

*even if it's just to make you happy or amuse you or give you some-
thing to talk about with me. . . . In your world, a man doesn't say
to a woman "You're beneath contempt," he says "Madame, excuse
me, I'm just going out to buy cigarettes,* I'll be right back," and you
leave her for life. I'm not beneath anything, but I was really afraid
I'd never see you again, not even in a letter. . . . My love, I'll try to
be what you imagine I am. This is a big ambition, dear Blue Lieutenant, and you haven't asked me to walk alongside you for the rest
of our lives. . . . So let's start with the easiest part first, and if you're
not completely discouraged, please give me one more time your sleeping with me again, the surprise of following you so easily to where
there's pleasure, let me have the trust and friendliness of your body,
perhaps one night, touching each other, softly, they will bring me
up to you.*[13]

⚜ MARITAL PROBLEMS

There, the story breaks off, there is no way of knowing whether
Mitsou succeeds in bringing back the Blue Lieutenant; however, the
tale of Colette and Sidi went on, and reveals that Colette gradually
gave up trying to be what Sidi "imagined" her, she became aware
that she had been looking at an illusion. Colette's critics have always
been misled by the story of Mitsou and the Blue Lieutenant, perhaps
Colette herself was a bit misled. *Mitsou* has been hailed as her first
non-autobiographical novel, yet upon close examination—not too
close, since the details are deceptive—we can see that it describes
Colette's situation during this period with a fair degree of precision: a
minor variety artist meets a socially superior man with whom she falls
in love. What was Colette, after all, that she should have become the
Baroness de Jouvenel? She was a poor provincial woman, a divorcée,
a woman who had danced naked onstage. Although Mitsou's practically illiterate letter to the Blue Lieutenant after their one night
together may seem completely artificial, it still contains a vivid expression of the hopes and fears of a woman very much in love with
a man who, if he married her, would be marrying beneath his class,
a man whom she feels slipping away from her. Mitsou is not the kind

---

* The package of cigarettes is a clear reference to Henry de Jouvenel's
methods. In a conversation with the author, Bertrand de Jouvenel remarked
that his father had used this ploy in leaving his mother, Claire Boas. This is
the second instance of such behavior in Colette, the first being in *L'Entrave*,
where Jean is another character based on Colette's husband.

to "make" another career for herself, to "learn things or change in some way or other." The new baroness will manage to become an attentive wife, a model mother, a society woman. Foreign as politics and high society were to her, she was able to write in 1913 from Castel Novel: *I had the pleasure of hearing Sidi greeted as warmly as Poincaré, there were triumphal arches constructed by our mayors, lunch with the president and his wife at Brive (Mme Poincaré is charming, she wants a blue cat), cooking exhibitions, a dinner I gave for eighty-seven people, a reception at the Geographical Society. . . . And through it all, I was trying to think of a synonym for* "greedy." *No need to look, Hamel, there isn't one.*[1]

But all that was not enough to keep him. Beginning in 1917 and 1918, but mainly after the war, the couple's difficulties began to increase. Henry de Jouvenel's character began to undergo a change: he turned from journalism to politics, and this change probably had its effect on their relationship. Colette had taken up journalism partly because of her husband, but there was no question of her turning to politics, which she regarded as a foreign territory and for which she had felt a strong aversion ever since her childhood.

On July 13, 1917, Jouvenel was appointed private secretary to his friend Monzie, Undersecretary of the Merchant Navy. "I was the one," Monzie was to say, "who turned him away from journalism and lured him into Parliament."[2]

In 1918, he served as a member of the French delegation to the Disarmament Commission; in 1921 he ran in the Senatorial elections and got in on the first round of voting by 356 votes out of 707 in his Corrèze district. In 1922, as a member of his country's delegation to the League of Nations, he won approval for his disarmament proposal from the eighty-eight member nations on September 22. Henceforth, he was to occupy a more or less permanent position on the foreign affairs committee. His first important speech was made during a foreign policy debate on the Washington Arms Limitation Conference. He was a strong supporter of Briand's policy for European disarmament. In 1924, he was appointed Minister of Public Education in the Poincaré cabinet, but by then, he had already been separated from Colette for a year.

Obviously, his political functions caused him to be away with increasing frequency, and at the same time Colette was increasingly encumbered with social obligations, about which she was definitely of two minds. Bonmariage's perfidiousness toward Colette provides us with the following anecdotes, which may or may not be true:

"When he [Jouvenel] stood for the Senate in Corrèze, his opponents—the only enemy he ever had was Marcel Hutin of *L'Echo de Paris*—spread the rumor he had married a dancer. In response, Jouvenel had Colette accompany him. One hostile prefect was forced to behave in public with a rampant friendship, hat in hand.

"Once elected Senator, Jouvenel was invited to dine at the Elysée by Poincaré. He replied that he would be delighted to see the President of the Republic at any time, but that he dined every evening with Mme de Jouvenel. Poincaré hastened to invite Colette as well. Jouvenel lacked the courage of his own dignity, but he could rely on that of his wife. As long as she was married to him, she saw to it she was treated with respect and invited everywhere." [3] Here again, the author's tone clearly indicates the degree of hostility Colette must surely have encountered in the haute-bourgeoise circles to which her marriage had elevated her. It is hard to know how much it made her suffer or whether she was even truly aware of it, for she never said a word about it directly. She does, however, describe her special situation as a wife and hostess, a woman and a writer who missed nothing, and surely not the half-discreet, half-friendly contempt directed toward her. There are advantages in being an outsider looking in, and there are countless occasions on which a woman can turn such a status to good use: in a group of men engaged in "serious" affairs, once the usual compliments have been traded and the leg of lamb consumed, a woman's invisibility is practically guaranteed.

If a woman has not been bitten by the political bug before she turns forty-five, there is little chance of her falling victim to it afterward. I accepted my solitude in the midst of keen masculine conversation with good grace. . . . I would quickly carve the sizzling gigot in its earthenware dish, I would dip the foie-gras spoon into its pot of boiling water, I would slice the raspberry tarte, and the coffee cups were always warmed and the coffee hot. . . .

Occasionally, a guest would favor me with a smile, with a "Congratulations on the lamb!" or "At last, a hostess who serves really hot coffee!" and then they would return to their vehement poison. . . . And I asked nothing more. Before retiring to the little room I had set aside for myself upstairs, my dog at my heels, I would feign attention for a while, but only to be able to watch them at my leisure.[4] Colette's gaze would dwell on her inexhaustible landscape, the human face. *André Maginot's swarthy face would blush,*

*but nothing could alter the dark, Martiniquaise complexion of Henri
Lemery; some passing strong feeling would efface the usual expression on these faces with which I was familiar, the desire to please.
Forgotten and silent, I would feel vaguely guilty at spying on a spectacle not intended for my eyes. And my departure would bring these
men, caught up in their arcane affairs, back to me from what seemed
a great distance.*

*Anatole de Monzie would often take the lead in discussions. But
even when most exasperated, I felt that he maintained his self-control,
and I would quote under my breath Balzac's remark about one of
his characters who can "use fiery words without getting warm."* [5]

Francis Carco reports that one evening when Colette was feeling
bored at one of Monzie's dinner parties, she suddenly turned to her
husband and said, "It's a good thing I'm going to meet Carco later
on this evening in Montmartre. I will be able to relax with him, he
knows how to talk to women." [6]

So Colette would escape from her social duties, from candlelit
formal dinners in Anatole de Monzie's luxurious home, or in the
Boulevard Suchet, and go off to meet Francis Carco, accompanying
him on his nocturnal ramblings through another kind of Paris: low
dance halls in the Rue de Lappe frequented by Jean Lorrain and
Christian Bérard, little local nightclubs where one danced to ac-
cordion music, the Paris of Père Lunette and the era of the grand
dukes. "Bottini, the illustrator of *La Maison Philibert*, would sketch
characters that were so vividly real it was impossible to forget
them. . . . One night, in a dance hall in the Rue de Lappe that was
run by Marcel Proust's former butler, following a sudden raid by
the police and the inevitable knocks on the head from their weighted
capes, Colette stood on a table and shouted, 'That's enough—quiet
down!' " [7] They would wander down streets in the Gobelins district or the Place d'Italie, streets that still existed, where "a caf' conc'
would still be open in the neighborhood, with singers in sequined
gowns and low comedians like Dranem, performers of whimsy,
monologuists. Farther on, at the Cité Jeanne d'Arc, the hovels would
be stuffed with the treasures the ragpickers had collected from the
garbage pails. . . . Passersby would stay close to the wall and turn
to see if they were being followed. And around three in the morning, we would all end up in Les Halles, amid the noise and the bright
lights and the animation of restaurants like the Grand Comptoir and
the Baratte." [8]

Other friends, other pleasures. Colette and Henry de Jouvenel began to cross paths with growing infrequency in their house on the Boulevard Suchet.

And their daily life together must have been poisoned by other differences. For example, Colette's immoderate love of animals. For a while she kept a tiger cat at the Boulevard Suchet, a baby panther named Ba-Tou, who would sleep peacefully at Virginia the chambermaid's feet while she was mending. Was Henry de Jouvenel the kind of man to have been truly gratified at seeing his home transformed into a zoo? *"When I enter a room in which you are alone with your animals,"* my husband used to say, *"I always have the feeling I'm intruding. One day, you'll disappear into the jungle."* [9] And Ba-Tou had to be dispatched to the Jardin des Plantes.

Their differences were further increased by financial problems. It would seem that Colette Willy's familiar round of creditors and bailiffs was not completely absent from her second marriage. "I dash about, I struggle," she said to Carco, "against the most embarrassing and threatening thing of all, being broke!" Bonmariage called it a wedding of "hard-up and poverty. Being broke means the usual shortage of cash on the part of people who live a bohemian life. Being hard up is the condition of people who earn a million a year and spend a million five in the same amount of time. Colette was broke, but Jouvenel was hard up." [10]

A letter of Colette dated early in September of 1917 provides a discreet echo of such subtle distinctions. She refers to *the very common crisis of being broke.* In the same letter, she mentions the manuscript of *Mitsou* that had been lost in the subway. It would seem that she had returned to literature because she was in need of money. And the deterioration of her relationship with Sidi must also have played its part. As has been noted earlier, her only overt allusion to a somewhat shaky financial relationship is contained in *Julie de Carneilhan.* This novel, written in 1941—and therefore years after Jouvenel's death—describes the atmosphere of their married life. Earlier, before their marriage, Herbert and Julie experience a "crisis of being broke," which Julie manages to overcome by selling a diamond necklace. Herbert gives her an I.O.U., which she still retains. Then Herbert marries again, a beautiful and wealthy woman named Marianne. Like everyone who has "real" money, Marianne is not overly generous, particularly toward her spendthrift husband, and Herbert is in dire straits. Relying on the dignity of his present wife and the remnants of his former wife's love for him, Herbert sets up a plot to extract money from Marianne by making her think it is really intended for Julie. He asks his former wife for the I.O.U. and persuades his new wife to repay his debt to her . . . and then he borrows money from Julie a second time. Julie is poor but proud; she allows him to get away with it out of love. Marianne is rich and proud, and she too goes along out of love. Herbert sends his wife to Julie bearing the money, ostensibly to thank her. Marianne believes she is repaying the million francs, but Herbert has only slipped 100,000 francs into the envelope, a ten percent tip and no word of thanks.

This plot, with all its complex psychological and financial components, may have been invented by Colette from start to finish; as things stand now, there is no way of knowing any more than this. But it should be considered. Whatever the real basis for the story, at least it reveals fairly clearly that after her experiences with Willy and Henry de Jouvenel, Colette had come to see her economic relationships with men as fairly unusual. In her books, the man Colette loves is usually a kept man of some sort; venal women are rare. Even Léa, a "professional beauty," keeps Chéri as her gigolo, even though he himself is rich.

It is very hard to establish whether all this is merely a transposition of a more general pattern in her life, of Colette's feeling that she is "giving" more than her partner, or whether she actually experienced—in whole or in part—this sort of financial transaction with her second husband. It is a fact that after his divorce from Colette, Henry de Jouvenel was to marry a very rich woman named Dreyfus, who may have inspired the character of Marianne in *Julie de Carneilhan*. The novel is built on a triangle: two women versus a man who is their moral inferior. Julie's sigh says a great deal about Colette's own feelings: *Herbert, ah, Herbert; my loves, my best days, my deepest grief. Herbert!* How can anyone distinguish between the discourse of love and the discourse of fiction?

⚜ ON JEALOUSY IN LOVE

For a man who is a public figure, the period he enters upon first emerging from his early obscurity is a very difficult one, Colette wrote many years later, drawing up a balance sheet, *for it is at that point that he experiences the illusion of being universally admired. He tends to indulge in the ingenuous satisfaction of the yearnings he experienced when a poor student and until he was past forty. If he hesitates, his country clamors that "he needs it." He wanted every-*

thing, like many people who are born poor. He wanted this decora-
tion, this land, this white cattle in those green fields, this million,
just one more. . . . And this post . . . this beautiful woman, all I
have to do is reach out for it.[1] Colette was obviously thinking of
Henry de Jouvenel, at least in part, when she wrote these lines. Politics helped him realize his desire never to be poor again; his desire for
women long predated his success. And his hunger for them was never
appeased; so many women flock to a public figure! Natalie Clifford
Barney has the following comment on Colette's relationship with
her second husband: "Colette, an inveterate gambler, may not have
realized that the game in which she was engaged would be over the
head of her gallant, who ended up gallantly offering to marry her.
I felt misgivings when Colette married Henry de Jouvenel and set
up housekeeping, lovingly and bravely, in a real house with a fine
husband, a baby, a nursemaid, servants, etc. In spite of their many
common tastes, *eating and lovemaking among them,* and despite their
common interest in their work at *Le Matin,* I had no reason to think
that this union, apparently so happy, would last. . . . For that matter, how could this tall, dark man in his prime, both intelligent and
vain, who was so attractive to women—and so attracted to them—
be stopped short and tied down to only one woman, even if that
one woman were Colette, Colette who offered him not only total
love, but also her original mind, a whole new world?

"In her office at *Le Matin* I chanced to witness one of the first
disturbances in her marriage, to which Colette had totally abandoned
herself in spite of her instinctively wary nature, in the first full bloom
of her happiness.

"On that particular evening, having completed her newspaper
tasks, Colette was sitting at her desk and we were chatting together
when Henry came in, apparently in the best of humor, gave me a
friendly greeting, and then turned offhandedly to Colette:

" 'You needn't wait dinner for me this evening.'

"Colette was taken aback. 'Will you be home early?'

"At this question, Jouvenel, who was standing behind Colette's
chair, stared straight at me—he didn't seem at all put out at having a
witness to this first occasion—and said:

" 'No, I'm afraid I'll be late. And above all, don't wait up for me!'

"The blow had been struck, and Jouvenel enjoyed showing how
much he meant to her; in the face of Colette's bewildered silence he
went on relishing the suffering of this person who was superior to
him in every way, above all when it came to love. What could have

been more natural than that Jouvenel, during this trial period of his fidelity, should have grown bored with having his voracious sexual needs frustrated, with his restricted female diet, with the limits put on his male vanity?" [2] He was not to remain bored for long. And again, Colette experienced those things she had tried so hard to avoid after her first marriage: *jealousy, demeaning espionage, ritual ferocity. . . . I had occasion to plumb the depths of jealousy, to inhabit those depths and dream of them for a long time. It is a place where one can manage to live, however, and if I once in my writing compared it to Hades, as everyone does, I trust that word will be put down to my lyric bent. Rather, it is a kind of gymnastic purgatory where all the senses are able to work out, one by one, as in every gymnasium. Of course, I mean jealousy based on some motivation, some valid cause, not monomania. One's hearing is sharpened, the eye becomes virtuosic, the step quick and silent, the sense of smell more acute. . . . All the rest is a series of events that are either won or lost—won most usually.*

What did I say? I told him that He met Her every day at the same tea shop, I was sure of it! The rest is all competition, beauty contests, good health, stubbornness . . . even salaciousness . . . the rest is all hope! [3]

In her meditation on jealousy, which marked the years of her marriage to Jouvenel as did other things, Colette denies that *their disease keeps jealous people from living, working, even behaving like proper people. Even when jealousy erupts with one of its favorite symptoms, the urge to kill. The female faculty of foresight, of being able to imagine what may or will happen, is one men are not very familiar with. A woman is well aware of the crime she may one day commit. . . . But what criminal woman in love has not been disappointed by her very crime? It was better when I was planning it. Is it always like this, dark and somber with blood on the rug? And that look of mysterious discontent, of disapproving sleep on that face, is that really death?* [4] Crime is a fool's game in which human beings united in a common, universal urge to kill are divided into two categories: those who kill, and those who do not. *Like everyone else, I have hoped for worse than death for one woman, two, three women. . . . Here I am speaking of that sympathetic brand of black magic that can't really seriously hurt anyone, not even the one working the spell, if used against healthy people. You are satisfied at achieving a vague disquiet, a languor, the little shocks caused by a finger laid on the shoulder. But such messages are sent by love as well as hatred.*

I cannot guarantee they are completely innocuous.[5] (In a short story entitled *La Lune de pluie* Colette shows that such practices were not without danger.)

For that matter, Henry was fickle and he even managed to make other women jealous of his wife. Colette too ran risks, was the object of threats in the *season of fairly vivid jealousy* when she allowed herself to indulge in these particular processes of elimination. *One rival fearful for her own happiness was thinking as intently on me as I about her. However, I made the mistake of allowing my writing to distract me and take up my time, and I abandoned my daily, secret threats. In short, I left off doing my curses for three or four months, whereas Mme X devoted all her many leisure hours to hers. And the results were equally one-sided. First, I fell into an excavation on the Place du Trocadéro and then I caught bronchitis. And then, on the subway, I lost the last half of a manuscript I was taking to the publisher, and I had not made a copy. A taxi driver stole a 100-franc note from me when I asked for change and left me standing at night in the rain without a cent. A mysterious epidemic carried off three of my angora kittens.*[6] A letter from Colette to Georges Wague enables us to date the period of Mme X, and her maledictions in early September 1917; *I've had to get busy the past three or four weeks and work my way out of a crisis—of the usual being broke. (We all know what that's like, I'm sure!) And on the way out of said crisis, I lost in the subway a manuscript I was delivering [Mitsou] and I didn't have a single line of draft for it. So of course, that wasn't very pleasant, and then that same evening Sidi found me in bed shivering with a hot-water bottle and it was around eighty-five degrees outdoors!*[7]

This "woke" Colette from her inattention and sent her back to keeping up her side in the *exchange of mental missiles with Mme X to bring an end to the series of misfortunes.* It was just enough of a full-time occupation to keep women from being bored. But jealousy is also a passion that becomes dull and loses its point. . . . *I was not the only one to regret it, because we fought without any deep feeling of antipathy. Time has a way of recompensing honorable adversaries. As soon as she ceased being mine, my adversary charmed me with a few anecdotes amusing solely to the two of us:*

"One day I went all the way to Rambouillet to kill you." The rest of her story was a farce involving a missed train, an automobile breakdown, a gold chain purse that split open and vomited out an indiscreet revolver onto the Rambouillet sidewalks, unexpected en-

*counters and a friend who read Mme X's murderous purpose in her
brown eyes and dissuaded her from it with affectionate tact. . . .*

*"My dear," she cried, "just think of all the pitfalls fate erected
between us in Rambouillet! Can you deny that they were put there
by providence?"*

"Of course not. But don't forget the important one."

"Which one is that?"

"I wasn't in Rambouillet. I haven't been near it all year!"

"You weren't there?"

"Not in Rambouillet."

"That's the last straw!" [8]

As for Henry de Jouvenel, he was the stakes in the game, not its
referee. With this blonde woman, with that lovely brunette *whose
hair was like mine*, threats were exchanged directly, like reflections
in a mirror, *an incessant emanation that began to endanger the lover
himself. . . . "What are you thinking about?"* he would ask them.
They were thinking about me. "Where are you," he would ask me,
*"on the moon?" I was with the person being agitated by my invisible
presence. We overlooked nothing, neither they nor I.*

Jealousy has many side effects. Concisely, Colette lists them all.
Alongside the urge to kill is the willingness to step aside in favor of
a rival; she judges this severely:

*I committed only one real fault, I did it again, and I was punished
for it. It was only justice. They say you should never give a knife
or a scissors as a present. I would add, nor a man. First, because no
man—even though he swear it on our heads or on the Holy Book—
is ours to give. He may seem to go along, he may appear to take pleasure in it, but his nature will never let him forgive us. And since he
rarely forgives the fortunate recipient, you discover once again that
your renunciation has spoiled everything.*[9] The gratuitous giving of
the man one loves to one's rival recurs several times in Colette's books,
and on each occasion she condemns it. In *L'Etoile vesper*, in the days
when she was settling old accounts, she wrote: *Misia even gave the
husband she loved to a rival. Not an unusual attempt. Many of us
have tried it, taking advantage of a momentary—nearly fatal—unhappiness at a moment when the rival is at the height of her innocence,
her beauty, her irrationality, begging us to release him to her. This is
more than enough to persuade us to make what people call "a beautiful gesture of reconciliation," for which we don't get a shred of
pity or a word of thanks.*[10]

Colette condemns compromise in general, although she herself practiced it. A pox on forgiveness and conjugal weakness! *The greatest imbecility is the one literature calls "the eternal triangle." Its shocking variations, its gymnastic, "human pyramid" implications quickly bring an end to hesitant polygamies. What woman, however upset and stupid, can really believe that one and one will add up to three? Some detached observer once noted that in a trio of lovers, there was always one who was being deceived, and probably two. I like to think that the one most often deceived is the patriarchal male, the clandestine Mormon, and he deserves it, being no better than a commonplace provocateur, a "small time pacha."* [11]

These triangles so pleasant for the "patriarchal male" can turn into a special new relationship in which the two favorites form a league against the "pacha"—one of her nicknames for Henry—*and such leagues are less rare than one might imagine. However, having exited from a narrow tunnel, having eschewed the heavenly paths of Llangollen, their union will by preference be a secret one.* [12]

It is quite clear that Colette had at least one of such relationships in which two women join together *despite a man and in profound and growing indifference to that man.* Such a relationship can easily remain platonic, and probably was in this case. Germaine Patat, who owned her own dressmaking shop, was Henry de Jouvenel's official mistress in around 1922, and Colette's friend. Colette wrote from Rozven on July 12, 1922: *Sidi, Zou-Robert and Germaine arrive tomorrow.* Zou was Robert de Jouvenel's companion. On November 1, 1923, Colette mentions a lunch with the prefect of Tulle, which she attended together with Germaine. The best comment on this friendship, which continued even after Jouvenel had left both of them, is contained in Colette's novel *La Seconde.* The story analyzes with great lucidity the manner in which Fanny, the wife of the popular playwright known as "Grand Farou," joins with her husband's secretary Jane in a kind of complicitous friendship: *Each recognized in the other a skilled worker from the French middle classes, painstaking workers who ignored their own difficulties and the toil of their forebears. Among the proud and scrupulous lower middle class, girls are still taught that their beds must be made before they leave for school, their bicycles polished, their cotton gloves washed in the sink.* [13] Fanny gradually comes to rely absolutely on Jane's attentive and tender companionship; when she finally discovers that Jane is her husband's mistress, things have gone too far. *If I am supposed to hate everyone who has addressed Farou with 'tu,' I'd be shaking hands with nobody but men.* [14]

Faced with the frankness of the women's rivalry, the craven Farou withdraws as Willy had done in the past, as Henry was in the process of doing, and takes a position "above it all." "*A man in that situation? There's not one out of a hundred that can come out of it with any advantage, not to mention honor!*" [15] Jane says. The only thing he fears is gossip. There must be no scandal. "*I am fully confident that nothing concerning the three of us,*" Farou says, "*will provide fodder for public opinion. Not even office gossip! I'm absolutely confident!*" [16]

But Fanny has had enough of jealousy. *She looked back to the earlier days of her love when she had wept out of jealousy in front of Farou, silent, detached, and withdrawn to one of those summits from which a man antagonistically watches his most precious possession, his superfluous burden, storm and descend into the void.*[17] But even Farou's highly effective strategy for pleasure, not without its dangers, is able to distract her from the knowledge that feeds her jealousy, "One is so alone with Farou." And Jane is so comforting in her affection, *Fanny, you are such a better woman than Farou is a man. Much, much better.*[18] Here we have an echo of Natalie Barney's estimation of the Jouvenels, and probably of other people's as well. Fanny reflects on Jane's potential expulsion: *At the end of a week, he'll have found somebody else. . . . But I won't be able to replace her. He is destined to seek out his favorite, Eastern kind of pleasure. He will retain his innocence, his solitude, his profession. But with whom will I be able to form a couple again? Two people are not too much to be alone with Farou . . . against Farou.*[19]

Leaving Jane and Fanny to pursue their own brand of consensual polygamy, Colette eventually broke up her own vicious triangle, as she had in Willy's time. She remained friends with Germaine Patat. And after her, there were others. One of the women who appeared later on seems to have been Marthe Bibesco. Colette makes a mysterious reference to her in one of her letters to Marguerite Moréno: *Sidi, who made me start early because he wanted to get there before we did hasn't even shown up yet. However, his letter informs me that he left Paris right after we did. . . . Love, amour . . . a good anagram for amour: Rouma. All you have to add is "nia" and you come up with a woman built like a horse and who foals two-volume novels. Poor Sidi has no luck at all! I expect him at any moment, from one hour to the next, from one day to the next, one week to the next.*[20] According to Robert de Jouvenel, this last liaison of his father was approved of by his grandmother, Mamita, who was pleased that her son was finally having an affair with someone of his own rank . . . Marthe Bibesco was a princess!

Fickle and violently jealous as he was, however, Henry de Jouvenel did not get rid of Colette without her managing to take revenge, according to Natalie Clifford Barney. And vengeance inspired by love, unconscious or calculated, ambivalent and so close to hatred, often leads to a new love. And how refined vengeance can become when the old love and the new love share a resemblance based as much on biology and heredity as on fantasy.

In the meantime, during the years after the war Henry de Jouvenel pursued his love affairs and Colette turned to works about love; the subconscious is not limited by space and time, it can examine the prehistoric past or peer into the future. *Everything you write about happens*, Colette wrote to Bertrand de Jouvenel, and elsewhere she noted: *how judiciously one of my husbands remonstrated with me, "Can't you write a book that isn't about love, adultery, a mixture of semi-incest and separations! Isn't there more in life?" If his age had not urged him to philander—for he was indeed handsome and charming—to rush off to lovers' trysts, he might perhaps have taught me the place love ought to play in a novel and outside of one. But he left . . . and I dedicated, incorrigibly, another chapter to love, to the loss of love, a chapter blinded by love.*[21]

Following *Chéri*, a product of the war, came *La Fin de Chéri*, a product and an evocation of the postwar period. The loss of everything familiar, the need to invent the new and the unknown, these have always been painful processes for individuals as well as for societies. However, the "psychological crisis" of the postwar period was primarily a male crisis; women had not been affected by the pre-1914 myths to the same extent as men; they were the victims or beneficiaries of such myths, not responsible for them. They emerged from the war with their status improved; they had taken advantage of men's absence to assume new responsibilities, to acquire some measure of independence. Colette's writing throughout this period expresses this kind of female postwar victory.

⚜ THE SOLDIERS RETURN

Postwar; the aftermath. Everything that had existed "before" was dead and buried in the shell holes. Everyday life, buried by the war beneath more pressing concerns, seemed hard to disinter . . . perhaps because it had been forgotten, perhaps she had grown older without realizing it. *La Fin de Chéri*, an austere novel, so different from *Chéri* although theoretically a continuation of that story, managed to recall the atmosphere of the immediate postwar period, albeit written later. Even though older, Chéri resembles Jouvenel, if only because of his generation; he is more like a father than a son. Like Henry de Jouvenel, he is conscious of belonging to an old aristocracy of feudal barons.

The prewar idleness and way of love have disappeared, as have their wartime counterparts, military sloth and illicit affairs. Everyone now *seemed to be a victim of St. Vitus's dance. The work, the bustle, duty, women serving their country. . . . My eye! and everyone money mad. . . . They're so businesslike, these women, that they make you disgusted with business.*[1]

A leftover from the vanished Belle Epoque, a stranger in his own home, cut off from the *demi-mondaines* in their carriages in the Bois de Boulogne and separated forever from Léa, their symbol, who is now an old woman gone to flesh, Chéri is overcome with what the next postwar generation was to call "nausea," with an awareness of the absurd: *I've come to the conclusion that everyone is a bastard. . . . No, I don't believe we're living through great times, at the dawn of something, some kind of rebirth. . . . What about the supply scandals in the army, blankets, noodles, Legions of Honor? You make jokes about sessions in the Chambre des deputés and about the Lenoir son's accident. Mme Caillaux fascinates you, and the Thermes de Passy. . . .*

"*Don't forget Landru.*"

"*Landru doesn't count, that's from before the war. Landru is old hat. But the rest . . . well, as I said, everyone's a bastard.*"[2]

The postwar Chéri is contemporary with the first Dadaist manifestos, with the wave of youthful postwar suicides—Jacques Vaché, Arthur Cravan, Jacques Rigaux—with the first crop of surrealists in revolt against the high-flown sentiments of the era: "*You're suffering from the sickness of the times,*" Léa scolds Chéri. "*You're just like all your friends, you're looking for some kind of paradise you think you earned in the war, aren't you? Your victory, your youth, your beautiful women. . . . They owe you everything—they promised everything, and it was only right they should . . . and what do you find? A dull and ordinary life! So you wax nostalgic, you get lazy, you're disappointed, neurotic.*"[3]

Chéri embodies the "fatigue" of Henry de Jouvenel and other men Colette knew in this period, the war hero's disenchantment with a society that was rebuilding in a fever of consumption and money-making, a society in which women were playing a far more active role than before. Colette gives Léa an indulgent attitude toward the parvenu, both financial and sexual parvenus: *The other evening, I was dining in one of those restaurants that still manage to see to the protection of our stomachs and uphold the good reputation of our cuisine. . . . The door opened and a nouveau-riche couple came in. . . . The woman removed her gloves, threw back her sables and dazzled the other wealthy patrons with the glitter of 200-thousand francs worth of diamonds, two in her ears, two on her fingers, no more.*

"What're ya gonna have?" she asked her husband.

He hesitated, rubbing his stomach.

"I dunno. Nuthin' temps me. I've got a kinda pain."

"What about some stew? At least the broth here still smells like it had some meat in it. For me, I'll have . . . just a minute, Delphin, don't be in such a hurry. I'll have some hors d'oeuvres, and go heavy on the potato salad! And legga lamb, okay, but let me take a look at it first, you can't trust anybody. And willya change the table-cloth . . . I want it changed, I don't eat off mended linen."

My friend murmured under her breath, "I can't say that sitting next to such people gives me much of an appetite."

"But whyever not? At least they know how to eat. Did you see her inspect that leg of lamb and test the cheese with her fingertip? Let them be," Colette concludes, as impertinent and down-to-earth as Léa, *"what's wrong with her and her scads of money shocking the stuck-up, sterile, wealthy French Old Guard? It loathes everything, it's behind the times where every art form is concerned, it sticks with out-of-date talent through laziness and false modesty and an utter lack of imagination."*[4]

But in part of her mind she sympathized with Chéri's nostalgia: surrounded by Léa's old photographs, her old portraits of herself, he eagerly listens as the old woman (*"La Copine"*) speaks to him, as if the present had ceased to exist. *Together, they regained contact with an era that had become superfluous, bypassing all the untimely dead, and the "Copine" extended toward Chéri a footbridge of names, the names of invulnerable old men, of old women still prepared to do battle or frozen in their final avatar never to change.*[5] Although he is a child of the prewar world, Chéri was a postwar creation; a youthful idler drained of vitality by his mistress and by his wife, he becomes a thing, an object. *Edmée overlooked the fact*

*that the female's appetite to possess everything tends to emasculate
all her most vibrant conquests, that it can reduce a magnificent and
inferior male to the status of a mere courtesan.*[6] Since the war had
destroyed so many men, the women who had taken over their functions while it was being waged were now all the more unwilling to
relinquish them.

⚜ A RISING TIDE OF WOMEN

The feminist movement had made great strides during the war.
Having become indispensable factors in the economic functioning of
society, women now raised their voices in demands that were pacifist, pro-birth control, suffragist. The trial of Hélène Brion in 1918
was a good illustration of the links between the feminist and pacifist
movements: a socialist and teacher, she was brought to trial for "de-
featism." Many women rallied to her cause, among them Séverine
and Marguerite Durand. In 1916 *La Voix des femmes*, a feminist and
pacifist newspaper, was founded by Louise Bodin.

Paradoxically, opposition to the government's policy of encourag-
ing large families was strengthened by the huge fatality rate during
the war: "The creation of life is already a terrible dilemma," a woman
wrote in December 1917 to *La France féminine*, "but to create it for
the sake of possible future holocaust is even more terrible!" Many
women revolted against the "blood tax" that was being demanded
of them. Women were being asked to respond to ever-increasing demands, and the suffragist movement grew in strength. "As a childbearing machine, a laboring machine, a tax-paying machine, all of
which ensure the State of immense returns, the woman now being
called into duty also has the right to participate in guiding the affairs
of State," Marie de la Hire wrote, and she drew up a program providing for the election of a female deputy from each département.
Political discontent was increased by labor unrest. Overworked, exploited and exhausted, women organized widespread industrial strikes,
and in 1927, even though the number of women employed in industry had sunk to the prewar level, they were admitted to union
membership on an unrestricted basis.

Even though they fell far short of demands being made, some laws
were passed giving widows and divorcées child custody rights.
Minimum salaries for home labor were established. The number of
secondary schools for girls increased, although until 1914 their curriculum was still different from that in boys' schools. Many basic

rights were extended to single women—unmarried, widowed or divorced—only because of their position as heads of family. Barrès enraged feminists by putting forward a bill aimed at limiting the right
to vote to war widows, an attempt to replace the soldiers who had
been eliminated at the polling places. As the men returned from the
front, they were reinstated and given preference over women; new
laws were passed to protect working women (maternity leave, the
right to work sitting down, no night shifts), and these had been
greeted with disfavor by employers. Yet a great many more women
now found it necessary to work for a living. Competition was keen,
and women were offered less important jobs and lower salaries.[1]

But at least women had gained from their wartime experience an
awareness of their identity and a desire for independence; they had
learned to get away from home and earn their living, they had
traveled, they had been forced to make decisions, to raise their children on their own, to live alone. Less idle and submissive than before
the war, women were now prepared to face their responsibilities
and demand their rights rather than return to their former "privileged" positions. It was scarcely surprising that the returning men
found themselves strangers in their own homes in the face of this
new and growing female awareness. And this sensation was in addition to the traumas of war from which many if not all of them were
suffering. Upon encountering the new life being led by his mother
and his wife, Chéri feels dispossessed. This inner crisis of the male
conscience was part of the overall "crisis of the European conscience," making it difficult for men who had escaped the bloodbath
to adapt, at least for several years. But of course, many women managed to forget the war and to regress to their former status.

For her part Colette began to be increasingly aware of her own
need to become something more than merely Jouvenel's wife, a position
for which she appears to have begun preparing as early as 1913. Having
been forced to support herself since 1914, she began a gradual return
to literature in 1917, and up until her separation in 1923 she bravely
continued with her work as a journalist and as a literary editor.
Despite the fact she was now a baroness, she returned to the stage
in 1922. She found a nucleus of new friends who were not necessarily also her husband's, and gradually she began to move toward the time when she would give him up, her lover, her protector,
the guarantor of her social status and her name; she began to prepare to return to being what she was: simply Colette. None of this,
of course, was accomplished without pain, without deep inner tur-

moil. As always, Colette found herself at a crossroads of two kinds of history, History with a capital letter, and her own. She could attempt to ignore the former, but she was unable to help being affected by it. Like many other women, the postwar years found her attempting to solve many feminine contradictions, and it was during these few years, from 1918 to 1923, that she began to confront them head on.

✢ AT ROZVEN

1918–Mid-June: *I've been experiencing difficult days and nights,* Colette wrote. *Sidi has been in the thick of the fight. He's been reported either dead or a prisoner. He has fought like a tiger, and like a fine, brave man.*[1] At end of October: *Dear old friend, I'm on vacation in the country with Sidi and my daughter, but all good things come to a speedy end.*[2]

The war was over. It was a tremendous turning point in her life and in the lives of those around her. Before the war, she had still been a young woman starting a new life, a new profession, new social circles, a child. The war had turned her into a middle-aged woman, a woman again betrayed and entangled in lies and the atmosphere lies create. She had thought her life settled forever, but little by little, she began to realize that she would have to reevaluate her choices. In 1917, she had begun work on a novel. The manuscript of *Mitsou*, completely rewritten, was published in 1919. In 1918, she had been appointed literary editor of *Le Matin;* her secretary, Claude Chauvière, was to write a book about her recalling this period when Colette was tilting with editorial windmills: "Some unknown censor returned some of her articles and stories to her editorial office with marginal questions indicating passages to be altered. For example, the phrase 'pregnant woman' was queried. One wonders what term they might have suggested as a replacement. In *Le Matin*, she published *Le Blé en herbe, La Femme cachée*, etc. She told me:

" 'Sapène was the one who taught me the difficult and salutary gymnastic feat of writing reviews of plays and performances in twenty lines. A minimum amount of words for the maximum effect.'

"Her office was full of pencils, photographs, caricatures; she had a desk on a dingy and dusty rug. There were wicker chairs and a telephone. On the other side of the window, a bit of chimney. . . . His Majesty Arthème Fayard, handsome, elegant and a light eater, always told with astonishment how he had found Colette sitting down to a fine cheese and a good bottle of wine. She could digest anything—including news of revolutions, murders, great changes in the world —nothing disturbed her appetite." [3]

In the beginning, she had been deluged with manuscripts from young friends to whom she tried to lend a hand. Bertrand de Jouvenel recalls reading manuscripts for her and that, as a young, demanding adolescent, he was far more severe than she. Later on, she took to handing these out to various readers and read only the best herself.

Above all, however, this period was a time for friendship, for happy group vacations at Rozven. *I can never recall this season of my life without the golden memory, the echo of soft laughter that lifted my heart, the laughter and the wispy hair of Germaine Beaumont*—the daughter of her friend Annie de Pène, her secretary at *Le Matin* before the advent of Hélène Picard. *To this great writer, so like a blond child, I owe many precious hours and unforgettable vacation days in Brittany. I can still see her on some precipitous coast-guard path, bent down and stretching out her hand to pick up, as if it were a flower, a large, slate-colored grass snake that pecked at her nose like a gander. . . . In the foam of Brittany's midsummer seas, we spent many Septembers together, writing, collecting crayfish and mulberries, making simple nightdresses for ourselves in flowered cretonne bought at the dry-goods shop in Saint-Coulomb. Germaine Beaumont wrote letters in verse "because," as she said, "it's easier." As we sewed, we would chat. . . . She is my fondest memory from my days with the big newspapers.*[4] Germaine Beaumont wrote: "I can testify to her regular working hours, to the order that prevailed in her office, to the care with which she read the stories she had to choose from for her column *A Thousand and One Mornings*. And in addition to this editorial work, she performed the demanding task of a dramatic critic." [5]

Germaine Beaumont's best memories were also of vacations at Rozven, where Henry de Jouvenel seldom put in an appearance, busy elsewhere with his political and amorous duties. They were a large and happy group of friends: Léopold Marchand and his wife Mitz; the Francis Carcos; Germaine Beaumont; Hélène Picard, Colette's secretary and herself a writer. Léopold Marchand was a "huge fun-loving man, eighteen years younger than Colette, whom Colette called 'tu,' whereas he always addressed her as 'Madame,'" with a respectful 'vous.'" He was an important figure on the Parisian theatrical scene, and helped Colette turn *Chéri, La Vagabonde* and

La Seconde into plays; he remained her faithful friend. His wife, "Miche," was a Polish Jew whose entire family was to be wiped out in the next war. In despair, she committed suicide during the Occupation. Colette had met him around 1919 at *Le Matin*, and he had submitted stories to her. It was in this period that he began to replace her former companion, Léon Hamel, the "Silent One" in the *Correspondance de la Vagabonde*, and he joined her for many happy holidays at Rozven. There would be long walks, swimming, collective sewing sessions, feasts and reading aloud from serials that made them shriek with laughter; everyone had a passion for party games. One, invented by Léopold Marchand, was a variation of the surrealists' famous "blind" group drawings and consisted in supplying an adjective picked at random to fill up the blanks in an otherwise innocuous story.

" 'Listen, everyone,' Léo would begin. 'I'm going to start: We were walking through a bloodless and caramelized rain . . .'

" 'Léo, you're making that up,' Colette would say.

" 'No, Madame, no—I never allow myself to make things up.'

" 'Take his paper away from him,' Colette ordered me.

"I was honor-bound to say that Léo had not been making it up.

" 'Fine,' Colette would say. 'Go on.'

" 'When we chanced upon a waggish manse where the drunken serving girl served us gothic berries with a glass of camphorated water. . . .'

"Another game consisted in making up backgrounds for characters Léo had drawn, and this too reached absurd heights. Francis Carco would sing to us, his repertoire ranging from folksongs to the Bat' d' Af, by way of Le Chat Noir." [6]

Another of Colette's secretaries at *Le Matin*, Hélène Picard "blew into our Ile de France like a southern storm." She was the widow of a subprefect and had "flooded her husband's subprefecture with poetry." Had it not been for Colette, Hélène would have lived a life of poverty and solitude. "Colette found an apartment for her, installed her in it, and looked after her with apparent amusement, with constant and effective solicitude . . . she saw to it that this elfin creature had enough for herself and her charming side lines." [7]

It would appear that Hélène Picard was in love with Francis Carco, a love unreciprocated but abetted by the women. Carco relates that upon arriving one summer in Rozven by train, "Colette welcomed us and laid concupiscent eyes on Hélène . . . indeed, unable to resist, our hostess surreptitiously took up a long pair of scissors, sneaked up behind Hélène and snipped off her hair. As it fell around her feet, she cried out in her childish, plaintive voice:

" 'Oh, Colette, my Colette!'

" 'It suits you much better that way,' Colette said." [8]

In 1920, the year *Chéri* was published by Fayard, "we would empty the windows of the Saint-Malo antique dealers of the glass paperweights and globes that she collected. *Chéri* was bringing in unexpected royalties. I remember Bel-Gazou riding a white horse and . . . calling from the hallway in a strange and, she hoped, disguised voice: 'The postman's here to collect . . . give what you can, it's for the yearly calendar.' " [9] And Bel-Gazou would run off to spend her money on "treats at the grocers or the nearby pastry shop." She was seven years old. During the happy summer vacations in Rozven or Castel Novel, she was inseparable from two boys with the same last name as herself, her half-brothers Bertrand and Renaud de Jouvenel.

⚜ BEL-GAZOU

Toward the end of her life, Colette began to spend a great deal of time sorting through old photographs. She collected them in cardboard folders, with inscriptions: "Animals and Friends," "Places and Music Hall," "Children and Houses." We pause at the latter. *The children, my own and the children of two other women, are together as I wanted them to be in their childhood. There they are among the houses that they and I both stopped in, and when one of them now entertains himself with the photograph drawer, his attention is at once drawn to the basic element, the decor:*

"*Ah, there's the little building they tore down to make the garage. . . . A strange notion, rather than putting the garage behind the barn.*"

"*Why didn't you say something at the time?*"

He shrugs. "What good would it have done?" He, the eldest, was an old-fashioned, stubborn child, weighed down by that courteous antagonism that reduces the father-son relationship to a minimum:

"*And here are the hazel trees. . . . Some of them were red ones!*"

"*Filberts.*"

"*Filberts, all right . . . Purist!*" . . .

There is a candid photograph of these three offspring of various maternal beds. They are not very attractive looking, but the photo-

*graph has caught them being almost theatrically themselves, the elder
doing his bad imitation of Musset with dirty blond unkempt hair, his
gaze open, charming, irresponsible and affected. The second, thirteen,
shut in, thinking only of himself, a brutal little poet who would
rather have died than admit he was unhappy and sensitive, rather
than share an iota of his lyrical outpourings.*

*And with them is my daughter in all the glory of her seven years,
flourishing and impenetrable!* [1]

This was in 1920. Bel-Gazou was seven, Renaud—the son of Isabelle
de Comminges, the Panther—thirteen, and Bertrand, the son of Claire
Boas, sixteen. *The boys were not very close when they were growing
up. One of them called me "My dear Mother," and the other called
me "Madame." Perhaps he was the one who liked me best. Since
these photographs were randomly taken on the coast of Brittany, we
scarcely ever saw them again, half-naked, scratched by the porous
rocks and the sea salt, we scarcely ever saw them again all three together.* [2]

When Colette remembered the carefree vacation days from 1920
on, the time when the two boys, one sixteen to twenty and the other
twelve to eighteen, included in their mysterious adolescent adventures the Bel-Gazou of six to ten, she must have recalled another
happy band some forty years further back in time when the boys
were called Achille and Léo, the little girl Minet-Chéri. There is
sometimes an almost palpable link between Gabrielle and Colette.
The château in Castel Novel or the house in Rozven might be Saint-
Sauveur, Sido might replace Colette, and Gabrielle Bel-Gazou. The
mysterious "Watcher" who moved about in the night-time attic and
prevented the over-excited children from falling asleep could just as
easily have been a part of life in Claudine's Puisaye an entire generation earlier.

*Sunday—the children look strange this morning. I saw them look
the same way once before when they were planning to put on a performance of their play* The Ghost of the Commander *in the attic.
. . . But that's an old story. Bertrand is eighteen now, and as is
fitting for his age he has plans to reform the European financial system; Renaud, who is past fourteen, thinks of nothing but assembling
and dismantling engines; and Bel-Gazou's questions to me this year
are of a depressing banality. "When we get to Paris can I wear long
stockings?"* [3] After standing watch, with much fright and various
conflicting explanations, Colette and the two boys eventually solved
the mystery of the Watcher: *"He," white and gigantic,* was an *imag-*

inary creature bigger than a hunting dog; he walked a certain number of steps across the attic floor, muttered a brief magic spell, and vanished through the window into the night.

Thursday—the youngest boy is sitting at his desk composing a lengthy narration of a trip. Title: "Hunting with the Grand Duke in Southern Africa."

The elder has "forgotten" the beginning of a poem on my desk: The pulse of the night, the weighty vision/Of shadow in the light, the gray apparition. . . . Everything is back to normal! [4]

La Maison de Claudine was written at a time when the group of children around her must have led Colette's thoughts back to the days of her own childhood, and it evidences a certain confusion between the generations. Bel-Gazou was growing up. She was no longer the lively and secretive child who had called the cows home in her heavy Limousin accent. At first, Colette had adored her little girl because of her strong resemblance to her father. Her letters refer to it constantly: *My daughter is a radiant little heifer who is like Sidi feature for feature;* [5] *aside from being a magnificent child, she looks so much like him that I am amazed . . . she has six teeth;* [6] *my daughter is magnificent, like a smaller Sidi. Her resemblance to Sidi is remarkable.* [7]

During the war, Colette had seen little of her daughter living with her English nanny in the country. In October 1918, she wrote, *My daughter is a love.* [8] In April 1920, *my daughter is like a progressive peasant girl,* [9] *my daughter, bursting out of her skin, is going off to school;* [10] in 1921, *my daughter is herding in the cows,* [11] *she says she is going to marry and have seven children, the man of her dreams is a farmer.* [12] On April 28, 1921, *My daughter is like an Eros, elegant, toothless and robust;* [13] but on August 17, *she is a love, I had to give her a good slap the other day*; in September 1921, *She's an awful bossy Sidi.* [14]

Something seemed to go wrong in 1922, at the same time that things began to go wrong with Henry de Jouvenel. On July 12, Colette wrote from Rozven: *My daughter is insufferably independent!* [15] and on May 12, 1922, to Marguerite Moréno, from Paris, she announced the purchase of *school things*. In September 1922, *My daughter reigns over the Château de Launay, orders the meals. . . . Ah! la-la, she's asking for a few good slaps.* [16] From Rozven on July 16, *she's a wild thing and is going to be brought under control when school starts.* [17] August 12, she mentions her *abominable independence* [18] and her *insolent expression,* and in July she is *a monster who'll be sent off to school soon, and that's that!* [19]

Beginning on the first of October 1922, Bel-Gazou—who hence-forth will no longer be "Bel-Gazou," but rather "my daughter," or "Colette"—was sent off to boarding school in Saint-Germain-en-Laye. In 1923, her parents were separated. She was to remain in boarding school for practically the whole of her school years, and she found it difficult to bear. From now on, she saw her mother only for part of the summer. She attended schools in Saint-Germain and later in Versailles. In 1925, she was sent to England and spent the month of September at Saint-Jean-de-Braye in the Loiret, with Germaine Patat.

We may wonder at Colette's reasons for forcing her daughter to undergo the trial of boarding school at nine years of age, when she herself had been kept so tenderly and so warmly by Sido's side throughout her own childhood. Natalie Clifford Barney discreetly remarks on "the growing resemblance between the daughter and the detested husband [that] may have been a trial to Colette's maternal feelings." [20] We know that in the beginning this resemblance played a large part in her feelings of mother love, but she turned against her daughter all her resentment toward the father she was herself turning away from, and she was "evenhanded in her resentment." [21]

Colette indirectly attempted to justify her actions in *Aventures quotidiennes*, maintaining that *the boarding school principle is obviously monstrous, but recourse to it is probably henceforth inevitable.* The corruption of boarding school is less damaging than that of a home in which only a *thin cord* holds mother and father together, and where a child is exposed to *a precocious education of the bitterest sort.* Less damaging are *study-hall whispering, papers or books sneaked from desk to desk,* certainly less damaging than a *family quarrel, conversations full of hidden meanings,* the sound of *insults, servile pleading or slammed doors.*[22] The atmosphere at home must obviously have been unbearable, and Colette had valid motives for removing her daughter from it. Yet she never found a suitable occasion to take her back, and despite her strong affection for her daughter and her daughter's tender admiration for her, their relationship was far different from the special one she herself had had with Sido. An extract from a letter written when Colette was at the house in the Boulevard Suchet—around 1926—reveals the tenor of their relationship over the years; her preaching is softened with tenderness, but her over-all tone is one of faultfinding:

"My dear, you've been kept in. Why didn't you tell me, since you've known you had this black mark hanging over your head for two weeks? In the hopes of seeing you, I had put off a short but necessary trip to Rozven. . . . It's not a very serious thing, except that being kept in, along with your other black marks, reveals a state of mind, your state of mind. You've been impertinent to your teachers and your fellow students. . . . I could have so easily fallen into this sin of self-complacency myself, brought up as I was in a village very like Varetz and surrounded by peasant children who were slow to learn. But a kind of scruple kept me from feeling superior, from thinking I was some kind of *rara avis*. And this scruple has enabled me to make a name for myself in literature. . . . I kiss you, my dearest, with all my heart. But stop wasting your time! Being kept in, black marks, reprimands, pouting, bad humor, all that's just a waste of time. Life is so short. . . . With all my heart, your mother and your friend." [23]

It must be noted that in 1926 Colette had other loves on her mind. Yet it seems she was always to have something else on her mind. From Minet-Chéri to Bel-Gazou, the generations have changed; they are not alike. Colette was not the unique mother Sido had been.

Comparisons of letters from Sido to Colette with those from Colette to Bel-Gazou make this very clear. And yet, she cherished her emotional relationship with her daughter in her "royal chambers," in her most secret and innermost heart. *For if I see no objection to putting, in print, into the hands of the public certain altered fragments of my emotional life, I may be permitted to tie tight and secret into the same sack everything having to do with a preference for animals and for—also a question of taste—the child I brought into the world.*[24]

Colette can be seen attempting to solve this further contradiction by her not always successful efforts to correct her own imperfections, to become a Sido for Bel-Gazou. She, in the end, was well aware of it when she wrote as epigraph to *La Naissance du jour: In reading me, do you imagine I'm painting my portrait? Patience! It is only my model.*

⚜ THE KID

"She was my father's wife, and I always regarded her work as a part-time job. I called her 'Aunt Colette,' and she usually called me 'The Kid,'" wrote Renaud, the younger son, the Panther's son, stressing the almost conspiratorial bond between them. And Colette:

One of my most vivid memories is of a child who had been neglected in every respect, so much so that my inability to remedy the situation seemed almost criminal.[1] Renaud attended the public school of the Immaculate Conception in Pau, and seems to have been equally neglected by both his busy and fickle father, with his "durable and remarkably unfair wrath," and his mother, who was wildly jealous of Colette and engaged in an *emotional competition in which she [Colette] did not compete.*[2] Colette was fond of the abandoned and tyrannized boy and took him on vacations with her. *I can only come to Rozven for September*, Colette wrote him in 1923. *I'm afraid of creating trouble for you if I ask you there. However, if you can get permission for a few days of sand and sun, my house is yours, my child.*

Renaud remembers the house on the Boulevard Suchet, where in the somber ground-floor salon was a piano upon which she played and a picture she had painted, for she painted and made tapestries. "I seem to recall having seen and heard meowing in that salon the tiger cat someone once gave her, to my father's displeasure. There was also an unexpected squirrel that leaped onto my father's shoulder as he was leaving the bathroom, giving him a terrible fright despite the fact he had just returned from the battle of Verdun, and there was even a snake that would writhe about on the table during meals and that obviously didn't remain long in the house."[3]

His most vivid recollections of Colette are at the family château, Castel Novel, "an enchanting retreat the Princesse Bibesco called the 'leafy château' and Aragon 'the pink château in Corrèze,' both epithets deserved since it was built of pink stone and offered a high rear wall the color of old, blackish ivy. There, Aunt Colette's room was on the second floor, a huge room with the biggest bed in the world, made especially for her and covered in pink toile de Jouy, my father making do with a smaller room hung with fabric that had greenish figures of monkeys illustrating the fables of La Fontaine."[4]

Even more vivid were Renaud's memories of his childhood spent with Bel-Gazou, leagued with her against the demanding race of parents, of whom "Aunt Colette was one, whereas Bel-Gazou and I were the kind of children who were always doing something forbidden, or at least questionable. One evening, in the midst of a meal," Renaud relates, "Bel-Gazou was bitten by a wasp. Aunt Colette gave her a good scolding for having excited the notoriously docile creature with her frightened gestures." As for his father, whose favorite he says he was, Renaud retained a certain feeling of admiration: "She

called my father Pacha or Sidi or both, he was quite another sort of
person. Aristocratic—perhaps a bit tetched on the subject of nobility
—and a sincerely democratic radical socialist of the old school, so far
as I know he never abandoned either his hauteur or his bourgeois
prejudices, for it is possible to be both bourgeois and aristocratic. In
his way, he was very like Déroulède in that he was unable to countenance any criticism of France, even in jest, and had a high conception of his duties as a statesman, as his country's ambassador in
fact and in life, both in and outside the Senate; he was respected
enough to be given what amounted to a state funeral, he hated in-
trigue, trickery or deals, and was shocked at political cowardice of
any kind, to the point where he flew into one of his most violent
rages when Daladier resigned in the aftermath of the 1935 riots; he
carried honesty so far that he would refuse to speak to intriguers and
arrivistes, and his name was always being put forward for cabinet
posts, although he was too independent to be appointed a minister as
frequently as some others." [5] Renaud's flattering portrait of his father
obviously bears little resemblance to the one we find in Colette's
books and letters, and her erstwhile stepson came to treat her with
fairly severe contempt: "He was so different in quality that I am
unable to understand what attracted him—setting aside the aesthetic
tastes of the period—to this literary debutante—everyone was well
aware, much more so than anyone is today, that she had been one
of those half-naked dancing girls whose naughty photographs are
still preserved in certain albums. And his choice is all the more surprising in that he always expressed his fear that I would fall for some
'actress,' in the days I frequented the Pitoëffs. He must have had a
taste for the plebian." [6] "I still have," Renaud de Jouvenel adds,
"love letters from Colette to Henry de Jouvenel indicative of a love
that extended to humility." And he also accuses Colette of "exaggeration": "I have noted this in her published letters in which she
mentions me; I can scarcely recognize myself in the character she
describes. This is because she was overly fanciful and saw people
through a magnifying glass, one that both deformed and idealized
them." [7]

His ungracious attitude toward his stepmother can perhaps be explained by his deep sense of solidarity with Bel-Gazou; he felt that
her mother had practically abandoned her. Perhaps it can be explained by other events that will occur later, or perhaps there are
motives of which we are unaware. He obviously reacted against the
"plebian ex-dancer," as did other members of his family and his social

class. His mother, Isabelle de Comminges, "was quick to remind you of her genealogy and that the Comminges had three centuries' priority over the Jouvenels. From the vantage point of those three centuries, she looked down upon the rest of the world, treated the Bourbons as usurpers, and vilified anyone who lacked class." [8] But whatever his motives, he is totally unjustified if we are to go by Colette's letters to him, which extend from 1920 to 1952 and are full of tender affection. Published correspondence indicates that their relationship was never broken off. In July 1924, after the death of Robert de Jouvenel, the following passage expresses the crisis through which Colette passed at the time of her second divorce:

Such a great deal of work! Yes, a great deal! How would I get along otherwise? This is hardly a time for rest. Kid, I have been going through a hard time and it's not over yet. But I have no intention of mixing you up in bitter things that are too grown-up for you. Just think of me, sometimes, with affection; it would be exactly as if you were a believer and were praying for me.[9]

⚜ CHÉRI

And then, there was Bertrand. He did not enter Colette's life prior to 1920, and before him came *Chéri*, which appeared in installments in *La Vie Parisienne* from January 3 to June 5.

Chéri had sprung up along with a character named Clouk in eight stories published in her column, *A Thousand and One Mornings*, between 1911 and 1912. According to Colette, Chéri's first embodiment was Clouk, a short, red-haired fellow with a polyp, and that suddenly Clouk *grew pale and lost consciousness and faded away to nothing, to awake handsome in the arms of Léa, who named him Chéri*. In fact, Clouk and Chéri were both born at approximately the same time and combined to give birth to Fred Peloux, nicknamed Chéri, the young, twenty-five-year-old lover of Léa, a fiftyish *demi-mondaine*.

The plot of *Chéri*, the ending of Léa and Chéri's relationship when Charlotte Peloux arranges a marriage between her son and Edmée, the wealthy young heiress of another *demi-mondaine*, could have been based on several similar stories Colette witnessed in the real world. The society of aging former *demi-mondaines* offered a wealth of material about similar liaisons between youthful gigolos and fading cocottes. One of the models for Léa was Suzanne Derval, and Colette's earlier acquaintance with Liane de Pougy, Emilienne d'Alençon and La Belle Otéro also helped her create the character. For the second time in her career as a writer, Colette produced an archetype: Claudine had been "touched up" for her by Willy, but Chéri was completely her own; the character immediately became immensely popular. The dearth of men after the war also played a part in making the novel successful beyond all expectations. Like *Claudine*, it was an enormous *succès de scandale*, in addition to which it achieved the more "classic" type of success by embodying its period. Men were scandalized: *Men were very hard on it, particularly men who were no longer young. Those most affected by the curse of age showered me with blame.* . . . *"What can have come over you," one of them said to me, "to make you put such a rare—not to say unusual—type as your Chéri into a story? And this world of . . . this world of whores . . . of . . ."*

Instead of flaring up like a chestnut in the fire, I kept my mouth shut. I realized that a lover devastated by a great and unique love affair must needs be regarded by all virtuous male incompetents as a "pale gigolo," a "faggot."[1] Later, we will briefly examine the severe criticism, sometimes almost a delirium of hatred, leveled against *Chéri* and against its background of the *demi-mondaine* world, that world of well-fed and lovely women attempting, over the aroma of creamy hot chocolate between their lace sheets, to forget the irrevocable loss of a last lover. Colette was accused of having picked her characters out of the mud, of having them engage in immoral liaisons. Had the same story been set in the "real" world of the Boulevard Saint-Germain rather than in the *demi-monde* of the cocottes, it would have been unanimously proclaimed a masterpiece. We need only remember Benjamin Constant's *Adolphe*. What character is more banal in our literature than the young man who parts from an aging mistress in order to live his own life and ends up marrying an innocent young girl!

Aside from the fact that Colette had chosen an "improper" social milieu for her novel, the masculine public was further enraged by the very element that entranced the female public: Chéri was still deeply in love with Léa, and later, in *La Fin de Chéri*, his love would kill him; Constant's Adolphe, at least, acts like a man. Disgusted with his aging Eléonore, he struggles against the pity that prevents him from breaking with her; she manages to solve her lover's dilemma by her opportune death. But the fact that the handsome, voluptuous Chéri should be so much in love with Léa that he would sacrifice his youth to her was greeted with approval solely by women. *At the time of Chéri's*

*success, only the women supported me, I can be proud of that. I am
referring to the phalanxes of Léas. They had very private ways of
greeting me, of applauding me, of showing their friendship, putting
their approval into a handshake, a glance. The most beautiful of these
women, and the closest to the utter ruin of her beauty, cried word-
lessly to me, "Ah, yes . . ." Another, faded like a rose crushed beneath
the weight of a happiness soon to end, took a moment when we were
alone together to tell me everything in three small words, "Ah, the
bastard!"* [2]

André Gide was one man who wrote her an enthusiastic letter:
"Madame, one word of praise I am sure you scarcely expected to
receive is mine. . . . And for my part, I am equally surprised to find
myself writing to you, surprised at the great pleasure I received from
reading you. I devoured *Chéri* at a gulp. What a wonderful subject
you have taken up! And with what intelligence, mastery and understanding of the least-admitted secrets of the flesh." *

Then there is the personal part, the mystery. Chéri, of course, has
some of Henry de Jouvenel's traits, a kind of coquetry, a kind of
"feminine" cruelty. And Léa resembles Colette in her age—give or
take a few years—and in her penchant for renunciation for the sake
of freedom, in the abstention Colette prized so highly. And there is yet
another element that arises out of the relationship between Colette's
writing and her subconscious, and this is the part played by premoni-
tion. Colette was a seeress, a sorceress, a magician, a Sibyl who strewed
the leaves of her books to the winds of gossip like so many arcane
oracles. She herself was often surprised by this, and in *La Naissance
du jour* she wrote, *I made up Léa with foreboding;* almost perplexed,
she told Bertrand de Jouvenel: *Everything one writes comes to pass.*

---

* In the *Journal des débats*, October 13, 1920, Jean de Pierrefeu wrote an
especially severe criticism, concluding with: "Her art depicts strange, vulgar
and boring milieus . . . it is time for her to find new characters. She has too
much genius . . . to persist in slumming." Colette replied serenely: "But what
has come over you, my dear Pierrefeu, and all the rest of you who are trying
to reform me? Is dealing with poor creatures—and Léa, and Chéri even more
than she, are poor creatures—such a vile thing? I cannot see it that way, I'm
afraid. It seems to me that I've never written anything as moral as *Chéri*."
(Quoted in *Catalogue de l'exposition Colette*, Bibliothèque Nationale, Paris,
1973.)

Jean Cocteau wrote: "Chéri is a fairy tale, the tale of a white cat and a
tiger cat: the kind of cross between an alley cat and a wild beast that the
English in the Indies call a *golden cat*. [In English in original] You are the
only one who can turn our mud into soap bubbles. Everything is made irides-
cent by your touch. I love you. Jean." (Ibid.)

❧ Bertrand de Jouvenel

And so it happened that on a spring evening in 1920, a very young man named Jouvenel—he was sixteen and a half—entered Colette's salon in the Boulevard Suchet. He was, in fact, her stepson. He had been kept away from her by his mother, Claire Boas, and had not yet met this woman she considered her principal rival—nor did Colette know him, although she had been married to his father for approximately seven years.

During these seven years, Henry de Jouvenel's relations with his first wife had gone from bad to worse. Claire Boas had soon made it very clear that although she may have relinquished her husband, she had no intention of giving up the grand and aristocratic title that had gone along with him. All the rancor of their separation and divorce centered around this name. The first Baroness de Jouvenel used it not only in private life but also in public, where her political activities were eventually to impinge on those of her former husband. During the war, her salon on the Boulevard Saint-Germain, absent her husband, became a political center, and along with her Slavic nationalist friends she was active in preparations for the Peace Conference. Henry's political career was getting off the ground in these same years, and a certain embarrassing confusion ensued. We will recall that upon Colette's arrival in Rome in 1915 she found she had been preceded at her hotel by another Baroness de Jouvenel and was treated as an "adventuress." Added to this, there were the first wife's more direct personal insults; jealous of her rival, she forbade her son to visit the apartment of "that woman," and even Henry saw him only on rare occasions. He was slow to anger, but once the war was over, he was forced to take legal steps to prevent his wife from continuing to usurp a name which was no longer hers. Whereupon Claire Boas became greatly concerned—willing to use her son to achieve her aims, she sent him to call on her rival.

The spring of 1919—more likely the spring of 1920; Bertrand was sixteen and a half. The literary reference of course can be found in Raymond Radiguet's *Le Diable au corps*, whose hero is a schoolboy like Bertrand, although somewhat older. Bertrand has been living in Versailles in the home of an old maid; he is stubborn, poetic, studious, perhaps a bit hot-headed like many adolescents of his age and generation. Wary of girls, he dislikes dancing and prefers to devour the books in his father's library and to dream of future fame as a biologist or an historian.

Bertrand was tall and awkward, his eyes a metallic blue, and he probably had some of his father's charm; so he appeared with a pounding heart, a bouquet of flowers under his arm, on a certain landing on a certain stairway in a building on the Boulevard Suchet.

He was shown into the salon, a room crammed with objects and overlooking a small garden; he recalls that he was so paralyzed with shyness that he went to stand in the darkest corner of the room. Suddenly, the door to an inner room was flung open and a woman moved to the windows, looked around, saw no one, and murmured to herself, "But where has the child got to?" She turned and saw him, and he had the impression that she melted into him.

So the meeting between the young man and his father's wife took place. The boy was disturbed, seduced by a combination of imposing strength and gentleness—part coquetry and part maternity—that emanated from this forty-seven-year-old woman. Her eyes seemed to promise him a refuge against the world and himself. The young know what allegiance means.

The ice had been broken. Their first meeting led to a freer relationship. There were luncheons on Sunday in the Boulevard Suchet, at which Colette, Henry and his brother Robert honed the boy's critical turn of mind; there were vacations in Brittany in Colette's house.

In the spring of 1920, Colette wrote to Marguerite Moréno: *She* [Claire Boas] *has entrusted her son to me, he is charming*. Henry, Colette and Bertrand had come away together, but the demands of Jouvenel's life—either public or private—had called him back to Paris. Stepmother and stepson remained behind, perhaps in the company of Colette's friends the Carcos, Germaine Beaumont, Hélène Picard.

And Bertrand attended Colette's school, the school of life: "think of a garden in Brittany, by the sea. It is early morning and she has been awakened by the melancholy two-note whistling of those birds we call *courlis*. . . . She sits in delightful loneliness on the damp and salty grass and her hand enjoys the roughness of the herbs. The sound of the waves fills her mind, she looks now at them, now at the flowers, which are moving faintly upward as the weight of the dew dissolves. The earthly paradise is here: it is not lost for her; others merely fail to see it, indeed shut themselves out from it. . . . She is completely unconscious of political events, wholly devoid of any ambition; indeed, she is incapable of any planning or scheming in any realm, even to gain or retain any human affection." [1] The entire story of Bertrand and Colette is contained in these vibrant and discreet lines he published in English upon her death.

She taught him to admire along with her the indescribable splendors of creation, and gave him a book "aptly entitled *Le Paradis Terrestre*" with "admirable photographs of the 'desert de Retz.' " She taught him to watch the "rapidly changing color of the sky, the increasing roar of the incoming sea," the polish of a pebble picked off the beach, to watch the "prompt dartings of a shrimp which feels that the tide will liberate it from its narrow pool." She was never so happy as when she was allowed to communicate to another her marvel at small miracles, "like the flashing of scales in a fisherman's net."

And she was happy then, with this passionate adolescent avid for life at her side; she generously dispensed the fruits of the earth she knew so well how to taste, to teach others to enjoy. In a single summer, Claire Boas found her son transformed, she detected her rival's hand and protested that she had changed him, corrupted him; she made threats, issued prohibitions. Bertrand seldom if ever saw Colette during the school year. In the summer of 1921, however, despite the pressure put upon him, the adolescent boy returned to Rozven. He and his stepmother went together by train and were alone for a while, but Colette had been forewarned and she treated him with a cool indifference that wounded him. Shy, with the presumption of the very young, he wanted to be her companion once again. And was she not responsible for this creature she had tamed? Neglected by her husband, Colette was lonely; Bertrand was at a rebellious age. They came together again, and the bond formed between them was of a kind to leave its imprint. His legal mother was alarmed and issued threats; his father became irritated in his turn and attempted to separate them by sending his son abroad. Family relations deteriorated to the point where, following a violent argument between husband and wife on the subject of Bertrand, Henry de Jouvenel slammed out of his domicile on the Boulevard Suchet, leaving his son in residence behind him. There was scandal. Bonmariage, always ready to defame Colette whenever the opportunity arose, faithfully reports the gossip: "The drama of the divorce would be too delicate a subject to mention had Colette herself not written a somewhat overly detailed account of it in *Chéri*. Léa is Colette, Chéri is Hyppolyte.

"Racine shows a Phèdre tormented by her guilty love, but it is not incestuous. . . . And nothing happens, absolutely nothing. The Boulevard Suchet was something else again."

The scandal was based on misapprehension: Colette had written *Chéri* before meeting Bertrand. But scandal cares little for historical facts; it feeds on gross deformations of such facts. Once the sound and fury had died away, there was nothing but a once-young man's voice, remembering: "Few of us—'they have ears and hear not'—hearken to this song of all things created: Colette has done nothing else in her eighty years of earthly pilgrimage. No author has been more persistently misunderstood; she has been represented as an evil counselor of purely carnal pleasures—it is true enough that, in her most vital days, she eagerly picked the fruits of the earth, without discriminating those which were forbidden—but this is only the lesser part of her story.

"Love has two faces, *agape* and *eros*, a deep understanding and appreciation of the lovable and a petulant willfulness to seize it. It is not easy to divorce them: Colette was immensely rich in the former and therein lies her greatness; for the latter, she suffered ample retribution." [2]

⚜ THE CUCKOO'S EGG

Other contemporaries—aside from Bonmariage, of course, who fell upon the affair as the choicest of tidbits for gossip—expressed themselves with great circumspection. Natalie Clifford Barney wrote that "Colette, stubborn and willful as she was, did not look upon it in that way, and her vengeance was swift; Henry de Jouvenel, whose *amour propre* was far more damaged than his affections, took refuge at his mother's while awaiting finalization of their divorce." [1] To Francis Carco, Colette reported Sidi's behavior: "Every evening, after one of the quarrels he was such an expert at, he would dash out of the room and shut himself in the bathroom, where I could hear him heaving heartrending sighs late into the night. Naturally, I didn't believe him for a minute, but it still touched me to witness his unhappiness. Finally my curiosity got the better of me and I went to see what was going on. He was stretched out flat on the tiles. Only the sight of his clothing carefully arranged on a hanger saved me from rushing to his assistance—and falling into his trap. Can you beat that!" [2] The atmosphere in the Boulevard Suchet had obviously become sufficiently impossible for Bel-Gazou to be sent away and to explain the difficulties Colette was experiencing.

From 1920 to 1924, Colette's letters make frequent mention of Bertrand. According to the latter, some 300 letters from Colette to him have been lost, and these clearly would have told us more about her relationship with the boy than the few notes that we have. In her letters to others, she always mentions him with a mixture of maternal tenderness and amused irony: [3] *Bertrand de Jouvenel is here too, his mother entrusted him to me for the sake of his health and his unhappiness* [4] (this is during that second summer in Brittany to which Bertrand de Jouvenel makes reference); on September 22, to Marguerite Moréno, written from Castel Novel: *Bertrand follows me around like a puppy.*[5] 1922, Colette calls Bertrand a weak and fragile adolescent, he is her *leopard*, her *big whippet of a boy.*[6] *Bertrand is like a little lovebird with serene little kisses,*[7] he is a good *big little boy, this morning in the ninety-degree heat he was sucking sugar candy into a point with all the solemnity suitable to his seventeen years.*[8] *Here, nothing new, except for a child who was turned over to me all worn out by the excessive altitude, tennis, dancing, too many costume balls— in short everything forced on him by his nefarious mother.*[9] We gather that Bertrand's family made attempts to lure him away from Colette by providing a multitude of distractions. *He doesn't look well at all, and yet I assure you that he's been very well behaved. They're going to stick him away in the snow this winter—without his blessèd mother.*[10] *Bertrand has the flu . . . it's a bad time for him, since today he's twenty and flu doesn't make you feel any younger.*[11] Henry de Jouvenel had left the family domicile sometime in December 1923. Shortly thereafter, Colette wrote to her friend Christiane Mendelys, on January 6, 1924: *I've been alone here for a month. He left without a word while I was off on a lecture tour. I'm getting a divorce!* [12] A few days later, still in January, she went skiing in Switzerland with Bertrand *looking like a mountain asparagus*; he *is fine as long as I nag him,* and *whenever we go out together he takes wonderful care of me, since he's a marvelous skier.*[13] In April, Bertrand went to Prague for a few months; *he was right to go, first because it's the beginning of his career, and on the way, in Strasbourg and Nuremberg, he experienced his first triumphs; there were receptions and applause. He already holds forth before an audience with that strange aplomb his parliamentary genes have given him. . . . He was right to take his time and profit from this trip that was meant to be a forced exile. Thank God, I've not been a bad counselor to this child.*[14]

In 1924, Colette mentions Bertrand's first steps in his brilliant career with the skeptical humor she reserved for the "serious" activities of people close to her. *Bertrand is in Paris for a week, the imbecile! He is organizing some kind of democratic youth group or some other fantasy.*

He should be back on the 15th, I believe. I am angry with him for interrupting and compromising my work. In thirteen days, he gained two kilos. How discouraging such creatures are! [15]

At the end of August, Bertrand went to Geneva to preside over the congress of the Fédération Internationale de la Jeunesse Etudiante, covering himself with glory. *America has just invited him to make a triumphal tour at immense fees, and Clauzel wanted to keep him there (Geneva) as a First Secretary at the League of Nations . . . it's like the brilliant and precocious ripeness of an apple with a worm at the core. It'll be good for him to be off to the peaks after that. I have the impression that all this rash behavior, which I am alone in fighting against, will end up very badly.* [16]

Colette was greatly upset; during this same period, she refers to Bertrand's friends as *little Satans, low-class politicos, a pack of yapping puppies. Just to tell you that my wilful child is still working himself up to a breakdown. To hell with this vain concern, this beating of our wings over a bird from a cuckoo's nest.* [17] The cuckoo's egg is piling success on top of success in Geneva; a newspaper goes so far as to print that his father *is truly fortunate to be able to have the advantage of his son's counsel.* [18]

In a letter to Léo Marchand dated January 21, 1925, Colette wrote: *I'm very put out with you because of the rude way you left Paris. If you keep it up, you'll soon be as impolite as Bertrand.* [19]

It was the end. She makes no further mention of Bertrand de Jouvenel until August 1946, when she tells Marguerite Moréno that one of his sons has died. *He has another one, three months old, not the same wife. How the "sultan's children" have managed to follow in his disorderly footsteps!* [20]

And the chapter closed. Onto this adolescent boy, so like Sidi in some respects, Colette was to project a part of her love for his father; later, her feelings would be tinged with her resentment toward that father and, on a deeper level, with her nostalgic tenderness for all frail adolescents, for romantic youths, both in real life and in her fictional Chéri.

What interest can there be in finding out that somewhere there is a very old young man, white-haired and bent, who managed to avoid the suicide I forced on Chéri? Colette replied to a blushing young journalist in 1945, in response to the question whether Chéri had truly existed. *Young man, I could have told you "Yes, I knew Chéri, like temptations, there were many of him." Every woman has her own troubles, and the comparisons she can make with other troubles.* [21]

Chéri, of course, is not Bertrand. But following Bertrand, another young, high-spirited man in love began to appear in Colette's work, sometimes in the foreground, sometimes in the background of the main narrative. He is always a dark figure, devastated to some degree by his love for an older woman who is always more or less his father's lover: in *Le Blé en herbe*, Phil is the timid pupil of a strong-willed Dame Blanche. According to Colette, the genesis of the novel was an old idea for a one-act play she had once attempted to write for the Comédie Française. *The curtain rises, the stage is dark, two invisible characters are talking about love with a great deal of perception and experience. The dialogue ends, the lights come up, and the astonished audience discovers that the speakers are fifteen and sixteen years of age, respectively. I wanted to demonstrate that passionate love knows no age, that it always speaks the same language. . . . In the story I simply added a few landscape descriptions of the Cancale region I loved so much.* According to Bertrand de Jouvenel, Colette was also basing her work on a crush he had had on a girl his own age years before, while on vacation a long way from Brittany, an affair he had told Colette about.

Tony d'Espivant commits suicide because of Julie de Carneilhan, his father's first wife. "Farou the younger" pines for Jane, the elder Farou's mistress. Jean Farou, perhaps, is the closest to real life; women do not take him seriously and he broods on his hatred and contempt for his father, the weak, fickle older man, and on his schoolboy crush for one of his father's women:

"*Jean will meet us at the Vaudeville," Fanny said.*
"*Where is he having dinner?"*
"*He has a committee meeting."*
"*A committee—he has a committee?"*
"*He's seventeen years old."* [22]

Although *Chéri* preceded Bertrand, *La Fin de Chéri* was contemporary with him. *In Chéri and La Fin de Chéri*, Colette explained, *I merely wanted to say that when a woman of a certain age has an affair with a very young man, she is in less danger than he of being permanently marked by the experience afterward. No matter what he does, in all his subsequent liaisons he will be unable to keep from remembering his old mistress.*[23]

This personal echo, which gradually fades into the sounds of the world, is further refined by Colette in *La Naissance du jour. After the first love, married life turns into a bureaucracy*, she writes, *in which all we are entertained or amused by is the balancing act that*

*at a certain point impels an older man toward a young girl, Chéri
toward Léa. . . . The perversity of gratifying an adolescent lover
doesn't actually ravage a woman. On the contrary, giving becomes
a kind of neurosis, an egotistical frenzy, "Here's a new tie for you,
a cup of warm milk, a living part of myself, a package of cigarettes,
conversation, a trip, a kiss, advice, the protection of my arms, an
idea! Take them! And if you don't want me to burst with everything
I have to give you, I advise you not to refuse. I cannot give you less.
Learn to live with this!"* [24] *And such neurotic generosity is shared
when the adolescent also has a mother still young enough to be a
rival to his older mistress. The "rivalry in giving" . . . poisons both
female hearts and leads to . . . a battle of vixens in which maternal
fury is equally savage and indiscreet. You sons too well loved . . .
you cannot go from one mother to another without betrayal, try as
you will.* [25]

Years earlier, while writing *L'Entrave*, Colette had discovered that
to ask was to give; that giving was taking. It is not our job to discern
whether—in her life as in her work—this adolescent was one who
did not get what he so continually demanded. There are many readings of *La Fin de Chéri*. Enough to note the emergence of the
androgynous adolescent boy at this stage in her life: perhaps for Colette it indicated a recurrence of her search for feminine elements
in the object of her love. The maternal relationship is reversed now,
however; she has become the mother.

⚜ THE END OF THE NAMELESS YEARS

Between 1920 and 1923, Colette was mentally preparing for her
separation from Henry de Jouvenel. As it had with Willy earlier,
the door to her cage opened wider, and she began to live increasingly
for herself. In 1920, she was named a Chevalier of the Légion
d'Honneur; in 1921, *Chéri* was turned into a play by Léopold
Marchand, and on February 28, 1922, she returned to the stage for
the first time in seven years to appear in the role of Léa for the play's
hundredth performance. In 1923, *La Vagabonde* was in turn presented on the stage. In November–December 1923, just prior to her
separation from Jouvenel, she went on a lecture tour, during which
she sedulously refrained—understandably—from commenting on the
married couple and married life.

Her last years with Jouvenel, however, were marked by two even
more important events: in 1921, at Bertrand's urgings—he was eager

to see her turn away from the sophisticated milieu of *Chéri*—she published *La Maison de Claudine*, her first delving into her past, her first *recherche du temps perdu*. In 1923, signing herself for the first time simply as "Colette," she published *Le Blé en herbe*: twenty-three years had passed since *Claudine à l'école*, she was just fifty years of age.

And behold, legally, in literature and in life, I'm down to nothing but one name, my own. Has it really taken, to reach this point, to return to it, thirty years of my life? I may even end up believing it was worth the price! [1]

So we come to the end of the story of a woman without a name who struggled for fifty years to obtain . . . one single name, a woman's name. Need we note that it was nevertheless her father's family name? The tale of female identity is an ambivalent one. It should be too facile to date Colette's true independence from this moment. But is anyone ever free? Until her death, there would always be fetters to hinder and restrict her freedom.

Henceforth, however, her status, her life, was to be an individual one. There would be no cage from which she would have to escape in order to write, to act, and nothing to impede her doing either. Man had finally been shorn of his magical and commanding force; he no longer either barred doors or opened them. For Colette, the days of compromise and sharing were over. She entered on a period in which the *Bel Aujourd'hui*, the lovely present, fleeting and evanescent, mingled with that brilliant Yesterday still preserved in the azure springs of the past. For her, it was time to start on the path home.

Colette in 1917

Henry de Jouvenel

Henry de Jouvenel with his and Colette's daughter in London around 1925

Colette in 1929

Colette in 1937

Bertrand de Jouvenel

Maurice Goudeket

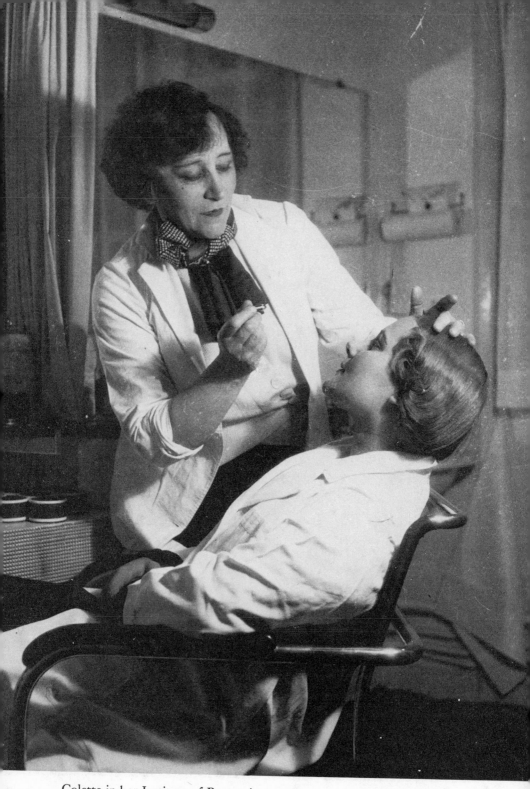

Colette in her Institute of Beauty in 1932

Colette in the garden of the Palais-Royal (1938)

A portrait of Marguerite Moréno

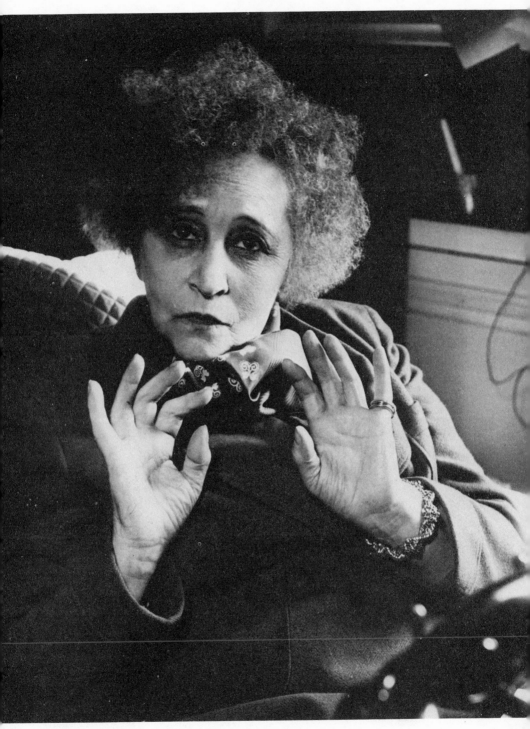

Colette in 1948

Colette with members of the Académie Goncourt, December 1949

A drawing of Colette made by Jean Cocteau in the kitchen with flour and charcoal

Colette on her balcony (1941)

Colette and Cocteau (1944)

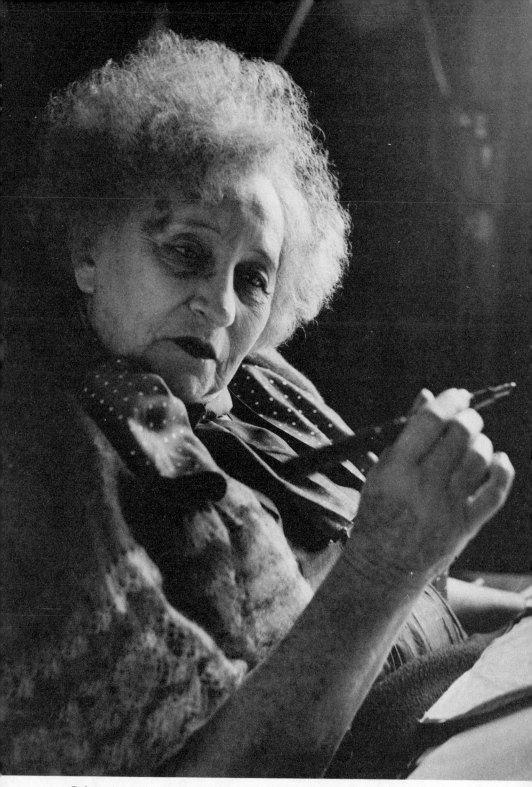

Colette in 1954, the year of her death

V
COLETTE
The Path Back

"Doesn't it bore you," I asked her one day when we were out walking, "to return by the same way?"

"It's not the same way, because we're going backwards."

MAURICE GOUDEKET, *Près de Colette*

Have I now reached the point at which one cannot begin again? Everything is so like the early years of my life, and little by little I can recognize—by the way my country property has become smaller, my cats and old bitch dog have grown old, by my wonder and my serenity that wafts toward me from far away—I recognize the path back.

COLETTE, *La Naissance du jour*

By dint of repetition, by doggedly proceeding with one's past strapped to one's back, one ends up by advancing, even if only in a circle; the path leads back to the beginning, the same but different. There is no sure way to gauge the effect of time on the human entity: I can scrutinize the many photographs that span Colette's life—as she herself must have done so often—but the passage of time is imperceptible. Each photograph is like the one before and yet different in some indefinable way. In the twilight, day fading into night, we cannot see clearly how we have got from the wise blond child with her long braids to this old woman with the deep lines engraved around her vivid eyes; and the same holds true for literature. From Claudine to Renée, from Renée to Léa—from Renaud to Jean, from Jean to Chéri—the woman grows older, her companion younger. The same, and yet other.

During 1922, 1923, 1924, the years when her second marriage was falling apart and becoming only a remembered disaster, while the last vestiges of her youth she had managed to salvage were slowly fading, a change began to occur in Colette. She began to turn inward, and in her writing she set out to restore entire sections of her past, a restoration begun in Saint-Sauveur in Claudine's house and continued on, fragment by fragment, until it began to touch upon and mingle with the present, momentarily, only to escape from her again. Gigi, her last imaginary daughter, her ultimate twin, produced when she was seventy-one, lives in the same period—literary and historical—as the first Claudine, the period of cocottes and their training. In closing the circle, Colette spent the last thirty years of her life working on a project she began before she had turned forty, *when you set out across the undulating barrier, if you have not left behind you bit by bit your curly hair, your teeth one by one, your members one by one worn out, if the dust of eternity has not closed your eyes to the wondrous light before your final hour, if you have kept hold until the end of the friendly hand guiding you—lie down smiling, sleep well the sleep of the chosen.*[1]

1924. Times were hard. Henry had left the conjugal roof in December 1923. Bertrand was in the house in the Boulevard Suchet until 1925. Colette faced many problems, the main one financial. It was difficult for her to continue on at *Le Matin* after her separation. *I am very tired*, she wrote, *after a week of uncertainty, will I stay on at* Le Matin *or move over to the* Journal; *I think the* Journal *will take me so long as—disontologically—I keep on vacillating and living on my savings for three months between the two papers. Vacillating, fine; living on my savings, it won't work.* Before moving to *Le Journal*, she wrote weekly columns in *Le Figaro* and later *Le Quotidien*, as well as for *L'Eclair*. She left *Le Matin* as of February 16, 1924 and began a period of frantic activity. A January letter to Hélène Picard sets the tone of her days: *My dear little Hélène, I'm working away from 8:30 to 1 A.M. . . . on an eleven-page synopsis of a complete five-act play I turned over to Léo at lunch today with two hours of exhausting palaver. At three, I had an appointment with Mouthon, the editor of* Le Journal. *He is starting up a weekly and offers me a job. Two more hours of palaver and figures. . . . At five at Armand Colin on the Left Bank. . . . Six-thirty, at the Maison de Blanc I tried on a wool suit with pants for the snow, at seven I took the next* Journal de Colette, *which was written last night between ten-thirty and one, to* Le Matin.[2] She went off to ski with Bertrand, but further troubles awaited her upon her return. She failed to obtain the literary editorship on *Le Quotidien*, which would have ensured her a certain material security; journalism didn't pay enough; Jouvenel was no longer there to add his weight as a public figure and husband. She returned to her earlier loves, literature and theater. In 1924, she published a short story with the evocative title *La Femme Cachée* ("The Hidden Woman"), and included it in a collection of articles entitled *Aventures quotidiennes* that came out in the middle of the year; she began work on *La Fin de Chéri*, published in 1925.

At the end of 1924, the Casino de Monte Carlo theater conceived the notion of performing *Chéri* with a cast consisting of authors rather than actors; she appeared as Léa along with Tristan Bernard, Jacques Deval and Léopold Marchand. The following year, 1925, she agreed to appear in the play during February and March, this time with a professional cast that included her friend Marguerite Moréno in the role of Charlotte Peloux. In Marseilles in December Pierre Fresnay appeared as Chéri with the same cast. She acted in the play throughout 1925 in Paris and on tour in various spas, Royat, Toulouse, Foix, Cauterets, La Bourboule, Saint-Jean-de-Luz, Deauville, and she appeared in *La Vagabonde* in Monte Carlo.

As in her earlier vaudeville days, the critics were sharply divided over her talents as an actress. *La Revue de Paris*, on which Colette was to begin her long career as a drama critic in 1929, was full of praise, Albert Flament comparing her to a "Renoir with delicious arms." *Fantasio*, however, was more severe: "Colette is making a mistake. She writes remarkable books, and no actress can replace her in that domain. Let her pursue that course, and let the actresses do the acting." And *Le Mercure de France* and André Rouveyre: "Mme Colette shouldn't be misled! The audience is there out of curiosity about the writer."

Colette went on imperturbably, but not for much longer. In 1926, when she was fifty-three, she gave up her escapes onto the stage, her lifelong attempts to avoid her demanding and exclusive profession as a writer. Her final appearance in the public eye after her farewell to the stage was to be her attempt to start an *institut de beauté* in 1930. For this last project, however, she needed someone who was in some way a businessman, and in 1925, she met him.

⚜ AN ENCOUNTER

Natalie Clifford Barney's remark about Colette continued to apply as she grew older. How difficult it was to be alone! Bertrand vanished from her life in the beginning of 1925. But in April she had already met the man who was to become her traveling companion, Maurice Goudeket. We have the details of their meeting from him. When he saw Colette for the first time, he was around thirty-five years old, sixteen years younger than she. His father Dutch and his mother French, Maurice was a son of the Jewish middle class. Born in Paris in 1889, he had left France at the age of three for Amsterdam because of his father's business—he was a dealer in diamonds. The family returned to Paris permanently in 1900, and from then on his life was much like that of any other middle-class Parisian boy. Well-educated, he had had literary aspirations as an adolescent and had led the kind of life typical of his background. He tells us that he had never experienced any great passion before meeting Colette; in 1925, he was a dealer in pearls, having abandoned his intellectual aspirations at his father's behest. He notes that like other adolescents of his generation, he had read Colette at fifteen or sixteen, and "with the overweening pride and chimerical wit of that age, I informed my parents, 'I'm going to marry that woman, since only she will be able to understand me.' " [1] We are not absolutely obliged to believe this. "It was at the home of some society people where I dined fairly frequently. I had met Marguerite Moréno there earlier. One evening, with no forewarning, I entered the salon and there was Colette, who had come with her great friend Moréno. She was wearing a print dress and lying on her stomach on the sofa. With her upraised head and tousled hair, her bare arms and her beautiful plump wrists, she looked to me like a huge cat stretching itself." [2]

Goudeket felt that Colette was extremely self-absorbed, and his first reaction was wary. "I talked banalities to her, and she replied with a naturalness I mistook for artificiality." When the conversation became general, Colette did not join in. The evening dragged on. She was not enjoying herself, and neither was he. A month later, he saw her briefly in the wings at the Renaissance, where she was appearing as Léa. At Easter, Goudeket decided to spend a few days on vacation in Cap d'Ail at a hotel where mutual friends who knew Marguerite Moréno—the Bloch-Levallois—were also staying. He drove down to the coast with Marguerite in his chauffered car. A few days later, Colette announced her arrival; she intended to drive down with Pierre Moréno, Marguerite's nephew, companion and "Little Slave," as Colette called him, in the new Renault Henry de Jouvenel had given her.

And she arrived. No one saw her during the daytime. She went out to work. In the evening, the party turned to playing *Taminti*—Maurice played only too well. Someone remarked, "Oh, with Maurice, it's difficult, he's as calm as . . . as . . . ."

"Colette threw me a look over her cards and completed the comparison: 'Like a covered flame,' she said, to my astonishment." [3]

Chance threw them together on the return trip. Goudeket had received a message requiring his presence in Paris and planned to return by train, while Pierre Moréno was to run in the car on the return trip and Colette would take Goudeket's car with the chauffeur. Owing to luck—or a series of mishaps—things turned out otherwise. Goudeket was unable to find a seat on the train and was "forced" to return in his own car with its passenger. As a gesture of thanks, Colette invited him to lunch at the house on the Boulevard Suchet where she was, by now, living alone. They said little to each other since the butler was present, "the vestige of a baronetcy that suits me like a feather on my behind," Colette said. [4]

She signed her latest book for him, *Aventures quotidiennes*, and wrote a phrase perhaps more penetrating than it appeared: "To

Maurice Goudeket, distinguished adventurer." He took the pre-
caution of leaving the book behind, and she sent it to him with a
note: "For having forgotten this book, you deserve to be shorn of
one of the epithets. Which are you more fond of, 'adventurer,' or
'distinguished'?"

Goudeket proved worthy of both. "A gift of roses accompanying
my apologies," he notes, "enabled me to pursue things." [5]

They continued chatting together, evening after evening and late
into the night, endlessly. "Sometimes I would ask rude questions,
but she never attempted to evade them . . . never. Save for literature, we talked about everything. One night . . . I had not brought
my car and she walked out to the taxi with me. Already inside, I
murmured a few tender words to her, but she ignored them. Instead,
she turned to the driver and, pointing at me, she spoke with her
customary familiarity and bluntness: 'Take it away . . . and don't
damage it.' " [6]

From Colette's point of view, although the affair seemed so familiar, how different was its form, its sensitivity! She does not tell
us what happened, she "tells herself," partly in her *Lettres à Marguerite Moréno*, who was—if the expression is not too debauched—
Colette's "best friend." In their egalitarian and uncompetitive correspondence, we can enjoy the highest type of female relationship,
without boasting or braggadocio, void of any desire to save face, full
of jokes and mutual understanding. What one of them does not say,
the other understands to perfection and expresses her concern . . .
her justifiable concern.

It is May 1925, the "probationary" period following the trip to
Cap d'Ail, the Arabian nights. The principal characters are Maurice
Goudeket, Andrée Bloch-Levallois—Colette nicknamed her "the
Chihuahua" after the wild mountain dog—who was evidently much
attracted to Goudeket, the Chihuahua's husband Bernard Bloch-
Levallois—sometimes also a Chihuahua by metonymy, Colette herself
and Marguerite Moréno, the friend and go-between in this miniature
world within Paris, who was out of town staying at a house she
owned in Touzac, in the Lot.

From Colette, Paris, May 7, 1925: *I didn't see your friends yesterday or today, but a little while ago the gracious Chihuahua telephoned and tenderly wailed about the misadventures of your journey.
Two days ago, she and Bernard came with Goudeket to take me to
the theater, and afterward we had a cold supper in Goudeket's chilly
but attractive apartment. Last night, I had a long conversation with*

this boy, I think it would be very good for him to let himself go a little. My dear soul, how I'd like to talk to you.[7]

May 11, 1925: *I have long chats with our friend Goudeket, preferably at night. And your friends make me booze. . . . Such is my life. And quite agreeable, I must confess.*[8]

May 13, 1925: *Of course I'm behaving! I haven't seen the Chihuahua save over the telephone since Sunday. She's caught a bladder attack, she should have thrown it back. . . . Last night, we—Goudeket and I—had another of those conversations that begin at ten to midnight and end at four twenty-five in the morning. Yes. Do you believe? I'm rather beginning to like riposting with a certain finesse and perceiving that my companion takes it all in through his antennae! Are you happy—orgies of Vittel water, oranges and grapefruit and cigarettes. Yes, of course you are. Me too. It would do no good to say more at the moment.* You, you don't hear with your antennae but with your heart when I talk, your heart is all ears.[9] (emphasis added)

May 18: *I'm waiting for my nightly story teller . . . shhh! he's having lunch here, don't say anything about it.*[10]

A letter at the end of May 1925 recalls one Colette had written some fourteen years earlier to Léon Hamel recounting her tragic-comic adventures with the Panther. Now the Panther has been succeeded by a Chihuahua; the dog is wild but well behaved in comparison to the big cat. And Colette is also tamer. *A week of drama is over; this unhappy woman, somehow* sensing *what was going on, turned into a harpy and came out with her unbridled passion for this boy. She has pursued him, she has pursued me, everywhere—on the telephone, at everyone's house, at all hours of the day and* night, *she has interrogated my maid, my secretary, my friends the Marchands. Fortunately, I decided to tell all . . . it was all very simple.*

"My God, where were you, at such and such and such a time?"

"Oh . . . out."

"But your friends told me . . ."

"My friends are hardly inquisitors."

"But I want you to be happy and . . ."

"Don't worry, I'm seeing to it. And because you are really a charming creature, stay charming, stop thinking that friendship and investigation are one and the same."

Not a name had been pronounced. She said:

"Very well, I'll go. But promise me that if you are happy, I'll know it!"

No sooner had I achieved my happiness, than I left the scene of my felicity and dashed to the telegraph office.

The boy is exquisite. I would prefer to leave it at that.[11]

Anything she may add later is redundant. She mentions masculine grace, a *dark, dark, dark boy.* The Chihuahua, having been told all by the dark boy, calms down and a reign of trust ensues. Colette is in limbo. *Ah! la-la and la-la again and so on. She's a fine one, your friend. Here she is up to her neck in a real mess, up to her lips, further than that! Oh, the devilishness of quiet people. That means Maurice the Kid. Do you want to know what Maurice the Kid is like? He's a bastard and a this and a that, and even a nice guy, with a skin like satin. That's as far as I've got. My dear soul, I kiss you over and over. And best wishes to the Little Slave.*[12]

Then Marguerite suddenly roused herself. She had known her Colette for years, this wife-mistress whose companions were always "little slaves." She replied by return mail:

"This is a fine kettle of fish! Now you've done it!

"You've really fallen into the soup this time!

"Can't you ever live in peace, unhappy woman!

"You no sooner get a slave than, poof! you turn him into a master!

"Ah, you may well say la-la, and la-la again!

"Will you 'get hold of yourself' once and for all—perhaps an unfortunate phrase to write to you, or to him. . . . When I desperately tried to get you to come here, I knew what I was doing. . . . When I'm not there, you cut loose. . . . However, I forgive you. And it makes me happy to see you like this, people don't have wonderful adventures, and perhaps even 'better' than a wonderful adventure, everytime they turn around. That 'better' is all up to you." [13]

However, despite her friend's fears, Colette did not turn her slave into a master, and he did not become a slave—she was incapable of that. This time, she managed to turn him into a companion.

⚜ WOMEN AMONG WOMEN

At forty—is this the age when women, setting aside their traditional rivalry over men, can finally develop lasting ties with other women?

Marguerite Moréno and Colette were friends for fifty years; they had met in the 1900s when Colette was living in the Rue Jacob and

Marguerite was married to Marcel Schwob. Their friendship grew over the years, as did their correspondence—especially during the war, and afterward. "I don't believe Colette confided as much," Goudeket wrote, "to any other friend. Her other woman friends that I knew—because of age differences, authority, and because it was Colette's nature—were all somewhat tutelary where she was concerned." [1]

Colette persuaded Moréno, a tragic actress who felt she was only suited to verse drama—and she was admirable—to turn to comic roles. At the age most actresses begin to think of retirement, Marguerite Moréno embarked on a second career that was to be even more brilliant than the first, as a comedienne. Her greatest role was as the Madwoman of Chaillot. Despite her daily, sometimes twice daily, performances at the Athénée, she always found time to visit Colette.

"And you don't even look tired!" I said admiringly.

"Macolette, you can be sure that if I don't look tired it's because I'm not tired. What I'm doing isn't very hard. The Madwoman is a very long and eccentric part with no secrets about it. . . . Do you know what I think? Who can I tell if not you? It's my opinion that anybody could play the role. Only . . . nobody knows that. On second thought, it's probably best that aside from the two of us, nobody finds out." [2] Marguerite, Colette's equal in personality and talent, was a true "pal," with that word's connotations of esteem and complicity. But Colette's friendships with other women, women who flocked to her and with whom she exchanged a vast correspondence, all had that touch of "tutelage"—to borrow Maurice Goudeket's term—we might call "maternal." The basic pattern was based on the bond between protector and protégée. Of course, Colette chose her protégées according to her tastes, her liking for people who agreed with her own personal ethics. In return, she received their unswerving canine veneration; a situation that became increasingly familiar when she reached middle age.

Hélène Picard, a poetess in love with Francis Carco, had been her secretary at *Le Matin* after Germaine Beaumont and before Claude Chauvière; she always addressed Colette with the formal *"vous,"* whereas Colette called her *"tu,"* and looked after her faithfully, particularly in later years when she fell victim to a bone disease.

"She lived in Vaugirard in a room at the top of the building that she had furnished with seraphic images, opalines and blue parakeets, a tiny ethereal universe." [3] Since she was unable to move, Colette came to visit her. Her letters to Hélène extend from 1920 to 1945.

Nearly the same age as Colette, she aroused all her maternal instincts; she worries about Hélène's health, her diet, what she eats. She sends her packages of candy, beauty products, things for the parakeets, blue writing paper, flowers. Hélène became her literary protégée; Colette helped in getting her the Prix de la Renaissance Politique Littéraire for *Le Mauvais Garçon* in 1928 and wrote countless letters to newspaper editors on her behalf. For Colette, poetry always came before prose, and she admired her friend's proficiency in the art she valued so highly. "You possess the resounding line and the violet brilliance." On occasion, Colette would confide certain details of her private life to Hélène, but generally, aside from many sincere expressions of affection, that was infrequent. She sympathized with Hélène's physical suffering and the restraint with which she accepted it.

Hélène is perhaps typical of the feminine type that aroused Colette's tender solicitude although unlike her in every way: Colette seemed to see Hélène as a kind of fallen angel, an ethereal "bohemian," both vulnerable and wild, passionate, but modest to the point of coldness. She also had the ability to be alone that Colette lacked. She called her "Hélène of the Heights," "Celestial Hélène"; her life was "luminous," but at the same time she spoke openly about the most basic facts and needs of her daily life. Colette, as she grew older—like Sido—developed the same penchant for vulnerable, weak creatures, particularly when they were attempting to be stoic and stubborn. We may be surprised at the contrast between this mystical and vegetarian "bohemian," with her exaltations, and the somewhat carnivorous Colette we have come to know. However, Colette's friendships with women apparently very different from herself— from Renée Vivien in the distant past to Hélène, Claude Chauvière and Renée Hamon—fulfilled some deep and inner predilection. It was not a question of intellectual liaisons, such as male writers often enjoy. Colette's correspondence has nothing in common with the correspondence of Gide or Flaubert; there are no grand ideas, aesthetics, politics or philosophy discussed in her letters, and even a paucity of allusions to literature. It is the correspondence of an ordinary woman firmly anchored in solid, everyday things, giving her "news," news of herself, of the people around her, of her animals, her disappointments and her joys, and demanding the same of her correspondent. Her choice of correspondents—her choice of friends —reveals the same tendencies as her writing and is based on the same ethic.

Such too was the relationship she cultivated with Renée Hamon, a young woman from Brittany in love with the sea and adventure who had gone round the world on her bicycle—not to mention visits to many distant lands afterward. Renée was the "Little Pirate," and Colette wrote many letters to her, attracted by her independence, her sense of adventure, her readiness to make the trips Colette dreamed of. Renée had all the qualities Colette prized in her female friends: she was not afraid to make daring decisions, she did enterprising and even shocking things with considerable physical courage. And she too was unhappy; she had had a difficult childhood, she had lost a child, her love life was stormy. A secretive woman, she placed the same value on friendship as Colette and devoted herself to the older woman in a way that was sure to win her affection. She became gravely ill with cancer, converted to Catholicism and suffered enormously until she died.

To Colette, she was a younger sister, a daughter, an intimate young friend: she called her the "Little Pirate," "My Wingèd Messenger," "My Poor Escapee," "The Dry-Docked Pirate," and told her "I am your lifebuoy, your plump lifebuoy."

Renée Hamon was "a tiny, blond and shapely woman, although her head was a bit large, she carried it high and proudly." [4] Colette describes her in movement, running *her narrow hands through her hair, ruffling it, closing her eyes, pursing her lips . . . crinkling her narrow eyes, humming and chortling.*[5] Renée Hamon was *a little bit of a woman who took the notion a few months ago to go off to have a look at the other side of the earth! Alone, her luggage as light as her pocketbook, she went . . . fearing neither God nor the devil nor man, nor murderous weather nor crossing the Pacific in a sailboat . . . nor cooking on some Tahitian ship and washing down the bridge.*[6] She returned from her travels with a book entitled *Aux Iles de Lumière* that appeared with a preface by Colette, a study of Gauguin, and fragments of a journal consisting almost entirely of lengthy praises of Colette. As for Colette, she showered her with literary advice, she made her privy to her inner life, her past, she talked to her about Polaire, homosexuality, monogamy. Her letters to Renée Hamon are like friendly chats, tender conversations in which the elder gives advice, asks questions, and listens: *I received your letter, my Little Pirate, and both the photographs. The one showing you collapsed on your luggage on some distant sandy shore gave me a start, and a kind of envy. . . . You look so alone and small there on the sand, beneath the feathery palms.* In creating her

"*Toutounier*," the nestlike bed on which the sisters cling to each other to gain warmth and forget their misfortunes in love, their worries over money, Colette worked from a palette impregnated with the colors of Renée, the adventurous sister.

As Renée succumbed to her disease and began to weaken, Colette's concern increased, as did her activities on her behalf. She sped up publication of Renée's *Amants de l'aventure*, published in 1943 and dedicated to her. *Should I tell you your book is like you? Yes, I will, at the risk of making you vain. It has taste, color, the inimitable ring of the truth.* Early in 1943, Renée too was baptized and received her First Communion, and Colette accepted and approved her conversion: *They* [the nuns] *make good company, the murmur of prayers is a nice, soft sound.*[7] She had gone to light a candle for her in Notre Dame des Victoires in 1942, as she was to do for Pierre Moréno in 1944. It would be wrong to think of Colette as having been herself affected in any religious way, of having turned to the church; she merely accepted the ritual, a purely individual ritual, and it is also a sign of her anxiety, one of the names of love. Her religious tolerance was so ingrained that she had no need to be aggressive; she was not anticlerical but merely skeptical, with a mixture of poetic incredulity and a liking for the occult. In the final days of Renée's illness, beneath Colette's anxiety and concern we can sense the stirrings of revolt: *I find that such suffering is really too great for such a tiny body* (June 27, 1943); *it is hateful to feel powerless* (July 8, 1943); *the poor human body, so humble and so touching. I am filled with rage, revolt, impatience when I think of you. . . . I too am praying in my fashion* (July 27, 1943).[8] Her friendship with Renée Hamon was *bathed in a poetry appropriate to it.* Every winter, Renée had sent Colette daphnes, laurel flowers from Brittany, and she brought back for her from her voyages collections of seashells; according to the season, there had been Brittany *galettes*, candies, Vannes chocolates, chestnuts, oysters, and precious food packages during the war.

There were other woman friends. Claude Chauvière was another "tutelary" friend; she wrote a book about her memories of her protector, another long hymn of praise. The inequality of their relationship leaps from every page, and the book sins from an excess of wonder, an almost servile willingness to excuse rebuffs or ill-temper. True, as Natalie Clifford Barney remarked to Jean Chalon, Colette was very open to flattery. And she was equally sensitive to homage from a chosen protégée whom she also loved for herself. And what tenderness and solicitude she offered in exchange!

Claude Chauvière also became a convert, and Colette agreed to act as her godmother.

There were other friendships with "fellow writers" like Lucie Delarue-Mardrus, a woman of her own age and generation. Anna de Noailles discovered in Colette's garden plants whose sonorous names she eagerly and fatuously used in her own poems. She was a woman as affected as Colette was simple, brilliant in polite conversation where Colette offered her no competition—fortunately, since it was extremely difficult to get in a word when the poetess was holding forth.

First in her affections, however, appear to have been Marguerite, Hélène and Renée—and in her correspondence. She was to write a long passage about Hélène in *L'Etoile vesper*, and of Marguerite in *Le Fanal bleu*, her last works.

"Once she gave her friendship," Goudeket wrote, "it was never withdrawn, but she was unable to be other than clear-sighted when it came to her friends' failings. . . . One day, I felt duty bound to tell her of something one of her friends had done behind her back. 'Do you think I didn't know?' she replied. And she added, 'Poor thing!' She overlooked much, she knew nothing superficially." [9] She even knew this truth, which she uttered with a sigh: *Our friends have a difficult time liking our friends.*

Can a daughter be called a friend? Colette would have probably answered in the negative; with her rigorous female sensibility, she knew that after a certain age *succeeding generations are not meant to live together*.[10] And yet most of her friends were younger than she, and they became progressively younger as time went on.

When she refers to the adult Bel-Gazou in her letters, she pays little attention to the "tutelary" link between them. She either expresses admiration for her daughter, a beautiful girl who drives her own car at high speeds, has *breasts like a young negress and swims like a shark, dancing the fox-trot with her friends*, or she complains, without animosity, that the girl never writes or comes to see her. In other words, she was more curious than anything else; owing to some trait she never admitted or recognized, Colette's daughter escaped her. Her letters tell us that Colette de Jouvenel, after years of boarding school, passed a stenographer's course and went on to get her baccalauréat degree. In the summers she often visited her mother at La Treille Muscate. In January 1933, she refused to accompany her father when he was appointed Ambassador to Rome.

It was none of my business, but it was also important to see that Jouvenel didn't purely and simply go off and leave the child without any means of support.[11] In the summer of that same year, Colette de Jouvenel worked as an assistant on the film *Lac aux dames*, for which her mother had written the dialogue. Her half-brother Renaud, with whom she was always very close, had married Arlette Dreyfus, the daughter of Henry de Jouvenel's third wife, and Colette saw the couple from time to time. On August 11, 1933, her daughter married, and two months later, on October 8, Colette announced: *She's getting a divorce. For an unimpeachable motive: physical disgust. That's something nobody can argue with, right?*[12] Following her divorce, Colette de Jouvenel spent a great deal of time at Curemont, her estate in the Corrèze, making occasional trips to Paris to see her mother. *Where is my daughter?* Colette asked toward the end of her life, and supplied her own calm reply: *where she wants to be, which is a nice fate at her age. She will come when she wants to see me, with her dark chestnut eyes and her mouth—as one used to say—like a little bowl of strawberries. She will turn up unexpectedly, and I will give her a few traditional words of advice, "Have you got on a sweater under your jacket? Your skirt is too short. Watch out for the traffic . . ." She laughs. We both laugh.*[13] Bel-Gazou was already thirty years old.* Time was running out.

⚜ THE SEDENTARY VAGABOND

Until the war, Colette and Maurice led quiet, active lives together; of the two great cares with which her life had always been fraught—unhappy love affairs and financial straits—the former had vanished for good. But money remained a problem; Colette undertook a variety of activities, journalism, travel, changing apartments, film, starting an *institut de beauté*, and literature—she published many books between 1923 and 1939, among them some of her most important.

To start with, she moved; she had to get rid of a residence that reminded her of past unhappiness. *Devoid of its master, the house on the Boulevard Suchet had lost its soul. Yet it was a nice house. . . . No, we were the nice things about it. With us gone, separated, once the great tidal wave of love had vanished on the horizon, it was like one of those seaside villas: at high tide, they are charming, but low tide*

---

* Colette wrote loving dedications to her daughter. In her copy of *La Seconde*: "To the first . . . in my heart." (quoted by Claude Chauvière, *Colette*, Firmin-Oidot, Paris, 1931).

uncovers the slimy beach stinking of rotten mussels.[1] So she rented out the aristocratic hôtel on the Boulevard Suchet, last remains of her ephemeral baronetcy.

Now where would she go? Apartments were in short supply in the 1920s; *by a stroke of luck—more scary than unexpected—my perplexity was confronted with a rainbow, the curve of an entresol window looking onto the garden of the Palais-Royal.* The address was 9, Rue de Beaujolais, a fateful address, at least for Colette and her descendants, at *a modest rent, a ceiling I could touch with my hand—just seven feet high—a long, fifteen-yard area I could set up according to my taste. . . . "Be careful not to jump for joy,"* a waggish friend advised, *"or you'll crack your skull."*

"I'll jump for joy when Quinsson, who owns the theater next door, lets me have the apartment upstairs," I replied.[2]

In the gracious adjoining garden, the cat and the bulldog were to enjoy a deserved peace after years of social pretense. Colette had come down again in the world in her entresol apartment—in danger, it would appear, of collapsing into a ground-floor apartment: *"My floor is buckling," I informed Monsieur Ventre. "No, Madame, not buckling. Sinking!" "Where to?" "Ah, Madame, to wherever God wills!"* [3]

What did it matter—Goudeket had his apartment in the Avenue du Président Wilson. For Colette, the apartment was less admirable than the *domain surrounding it.* In the neighborhood were *Les Halles, full of produce . . . streets lined with restaurants, nearby theaters, the Tuilleries gardens, the quais, the islands in the Seine—impossible to enumerate all the things that lit up my life. On moonlit nights, the Carrousel was all silvery, the gardens blue and black, the joined cats drunk with the magic of it all.*[4]

The cavern in which she set up housekeeping may once have been the vantage point for Regency *demoiselles de plaisir,* the "Beavers," who were called "Half-Beavers" because of their half-moon windows; for Colette, the sunlight was too feeble. The first winter she came down with bronchitis, and again the following year, and so on—once again she began to talk of moving.

In the interim, she also changed what she called her "natal sky." Brittany recalled a past she was eager to forget; in their first summer together, Goudeket had taken her to Provence, and she made a sudden decision to sell Rozven and buy a modest four-room house, lacking modern conveniences, in the neighborhood of Saint-Tropez. There was a small, wisteria-covered terrace, a garden, a pine wood, fig trees, and a bottomless well. Colette was enraptured. *You only have to cross the vineyard and a coastal path and a little deserted beach to reach the sea.*[5] The property was called Tamaris-les-Pins, *a good name for a railway station,* Colette remarked, and she renamed it La Treille Muscate on the spot.[6] *Is this to be my last house? I pace it out, I listen to it during the brief, inner night that seems to fall around us just after midday. The cicadas and the new wattling protecting the terrace creak together. Some unknown insect is crushing bits of cinder between its elytra . . . and the west wind blowing watchfully around my walls leaves the flat, dense sea hard and calm, a rigid blue that softens as the day draws to a close.*[7]

Her domain seemed to be shrinking, returning to a more manageable size; in her social life too, Colette went back to being what she was: a writer with a middle-class background painstakingly making her living with her pen. *Many stages have been attained and passed. The faraway, ephemeral château gives way to my little house. Properties strewn across France have little by little narrowed down to this, in response to a wish I never dared express in the past . . . once again, there are devoted and competent servants. The maid digs in the garden with delight, the cook does the laundry.*[8] The granite towers of Castel Novel faded along with her memories of the Great War.

Whatever she may have thought, however, she had not yet found her final home. By 1931, she had grown tired of her cave in the Palais-Royal and begun looking for some *high-up airy, light* apartment; she found what she wanted on the top floor of the Claridge Hotel. *Two small, adjoining rooms under the roof, two twin balconies on the edge of the rain gutter, red geraniums and strawberry plants in pots, most of my furniture, and all my books on the wall.*[9] Living in a hotel was convenient; food was sent up from downstairs ready to eat, and the pipes were warm.

The aftermath of the Depression of 1929 had affected the pearl trade. Bankrupt, Goudeket was forced to give up the chauffeured car that had helped seduce Colette and turn to the subway; he also gave up his apartment and took the room next to Colette's. They lived there from 1931 to 1936. Colette made contact with the world in the elevator: Englishwomen in Liberty silks and pink chiffon, Hindu princes, Moroccan pachas, candidates in the Miss Universe contest. One day on the way up to her room she shared the elevator with a man who bowed courteously. *"Madame doesn't recognize Monsieur Alexandre?" the elevator boy asked me. Shortly afterward, the famous financier was no longer "Monsieur Alexandre," he was Stavisky, scandal, fruitless escape, botched suicide far away in the corner of his room.*[10] To all outward appearances, in his smart hat that *didn't suit him,* Stavisky seemed to Colette to be only another character in the drama of hotel life, most of whom remain anonymous: the man who was murdered, the madman, the lovers united in double suicide, mere figures, evanescent phantoms *without substance, hotel ghosts.*[11] Friends moved in, liked living there, got bored and moved out again. She stayed at the Claridge until the hotel went bankrupt, even though the service declined, the furnace grew cold. In 1936, followed by Goudeket, she alit on the uneven numbered side of the Champs Elysées in an *eighth-floor apartment all bonbons and hairpins,* in the Marignan building.

⚜ A CAREER IN ANOTHER KIND OF BEAUTY

In the meantime, Europe was hit by the Great Depression and financial hard times had arrived. His business destroyed by the Depression, Maurice Goudeket, crestfallen, *put his tail between his legs and attempted to pick up the pieces.*[1] 1931 was a particularly difficult year; Maurice was *cleaned out*[2] and desperate. They lit on something they could do together. The plan was to set up an *institut de beauté,* apparently an old dream of Colette's, and early in 1932 she wrote: *Maurice is scraping away, scraping away, and we are living close to the bone, and yet we are opening a business.*[3] It is hard to tell who made the decision. Goudeket blames Colette for the fiasco; according to him, she was impelled toward this new interest out of a desire to escape the strain of writing she was finding increasingly difficult to endure and of a longing to renew contact with other people, people she didn't know, average people. It would be a "human profession, one that would allow you to come and go, to handle things, to work with real substances."[4]

Colette herself relates that the idea had been suggested to her some years earlier by André Maginot, of the famous Line: *Even at the time, I had in mind the notion to make up some perfumes and beauty products. My commercial zeal met with no encouragement. For myself and my female friends I boiled up some quince paste and its mucilaginous seed coverings, I beat up cold cream and pressed out cucumber juice. . . . Why not? The Duchess Sforza, née Antoko-leski, had set me an example by opening an old-fashioned apothecary shop.*[5]

Colette, with her basic, down-to-earth tastes, fantasized pounding and kneading, willful dreams, the dreams of a woman aware of her own body, a woman long familiar with home methods of turning everyday substances to use. She "adored working with the human face. She would alter her friends' hairdos, brandishing the scissors. Not even the casual visitor was spared." [6] In addition, she had a deep and long-standing passion for makeup left over from her music hall days, a passion she indulged until her death. And indeed, makeup is an indispensable adjunct of the "hidden woman." In the symbolism and conventional signs of Colette's world, it filled a role analogous to that of Style in literature, footlights in the theater. The main purpose was to dazzle. For Colette, there was an additional ethical purpose: just as the dignity of a sufferer entails silence and dissimulation, so makeup was the dignity of the woman growing old, deformed. In her youth, Colette had danced naked, but she had never shed her powder puff. When old and bedridden, she surprised all her visitors with her coquetry—her powder, rouge, the kohl for her eyes, were never out of reach; in the morning, she refused to be seen without makeup, even by Goudeket. It was a matter of courtesy. Thus she enthusiastically fell in with the idea of launching a "laboratory" for beauty with her companion. Goudeket insists he tried to dissuade her, that he even considered refusing to take part, and that he only gave in to spare her any later regrets. "I knew that she could console herself if she failed, but not if she had failed to try." A bit complacently, he adds, "It was not to be the only occasion on which I was forced to allow her to navigate in dangerous waters, always ready to take over the wheel should shipwreck seem imminent, rather than fetter her." [7]

In June 1932, therefore, Colette temporarily laid down her pen and opened a boutique in the Rue de Miromesnil. Following Maginot's suggestion, she wrote "My name is Colette and I sell perfumes." The details of her business fascinated her; she visited the laboratory where her products were made up, choosing, tasting, sniffing, happy among the test tubes and retorts. In love with the magical, alchemical aspects of the whole operation, she oversaw everything—flasks, packaging, prospectuses and instructions for use. She drew her own caricature for the lids of the powder boxes. In the September issue of *Vogue* she published an advertisement she had written, explaining her new career and recalling past history:

"The public may well be surprised . . . that I have turned from writing novels to manufacturing products for increasing, creating and preserving beauty. I too am amused when I look back over my own past and recall the time when everyone was astonished that a

lazy and obedient wife had become a writer. . . . And I had scarcely
earned a bit of fame as an author than I turned to the stage, 'went
on the boards,' as one said in those days. I did a little mime, a little
dancing, a little acrobatics, and I was harshly criticized—'How can
you, who . . . who . . . are an established writer . . . how can
you display yourself on the boards where . . .' "

And indeed, this new undertaking earned her some disapproval.
At fifty-nine, comfortably ensconced as a *femme de lettres*, having
finally gained respect, an officer of the Légion d'Honneur since 1928,
she suddenly turned into a businesswoman, a beautician. "So now,
in my later years, I am upsetting the whole thing, manufacturing and
selling 'beauty products' at an age when others are settling their
affairs, I am daring to start anew! I'm a lost cause." And can we
imagine André Gide or Paul Valéry turning to hairdressing or becoming high-class masseurs at sixty! Even André Malraux, the great
adventurer of French literature, made do with becoming a cabinet
minister at forty-five and settling down.

But Colette was unwilling to settle down. She knew that if she
had an audience, it was not the same as the audience for Proust; it
was drawn from the people. "People I don't know stop me in the
street with 'Madame, is it really true that you're opening an institute
. . . a store, near the Rue Beauveau?' I get letters—some signed, some
anonymous—full of approval, disapproval, asking questions, demonstrating to me the import of the decision I've taken without really
being aware of its gravity. . . . A teacher in a distant village writes,
'Madame, you've no right to . . .' whereas fifty-year-old women
beg 'Save me! Create potions, perform miracles, save me from my
wrinkles!' " The sorceress in Colette responded and revealed a part—
but only a part—of her secrets, the secrets that Sido had imparted to
her: "In those distant days I already knew how to melt ointments in
a playing card held over a candle without burning it. I had learned to
prepare rose vinegar to treat chapped hands almost as well as my
mother. . . . Later, I was taught the mysteries of quince water . . .
the art of beating up cold cream white as snow, smooth and smelling
of pure wax and rosewater, I've been using it for over thirty years
. . . but on the subject of a special pomade of mutton grease, I will
remain silent, nor will I reveal a word about twenty other magical
potions."

For, deep down, she felt there was really not all that much difference between her new profession and writing; she had never thought
of the latter as sacrosanct. "I find the women beautiful as they emerge

from beneath my writer's fingers, and I enjoy touching living flesh, heightening its colors, concealing its defects with my disinterested fingers, inspired by a kind of benevolent, maternal feeling." She felt that at last she was working with living things. Colette's naive advertisements reveal a creative drive, despite her attempts to hide behind the publicity for her business. Her thoughts on aging women, her willingness to believe in her own witchcraft, in legends about the fountain of youth, are all contained in them. "And I know so well what ought to be spread upon a distracted female face, so full of hope in its decline; I have long contemplated this endless landscape of the human face and I know it intimately. . . . I see women standing at the door to my establishment, I look at them, I have to restrain myself from telling them 'Go out and give pleasure, go out and love, go out and suffer and wound, go out and play!' "

In her spotless shop, she was the fairy godmother in a white smock, in her laboratory, surrounded by her equipment. She also had a branch in Saint-Tropez.

But the witchcraft failed to work; perhaps it was because of Colette's somewhat special concept of youth and beauty. "Imagine my surprise," Natalie Clifford Barney wrote, "while walking one evening on a quai in Saint-Tropez, to come upon Bel-Gazou, barely recognizable beneath the cheap-pink and bruise-blue makeup slathered over her lovely high cheekbones and youthful eyelids. The makeup made her look like a loose woman rather than the somewhat wild child she was. I learned that this attempt at beautification had been made by Colette's maternal hands. . . . In an attempt to support the enterprise, the famous aging beauty Cécile Sorel agreed to submit to a treatment, but Colette changed her mind from one eye to the other, resulting in an asymmetry that doubled the great actress's age and discouraged further volunteers." [8] Of course, it was a bad time to launch a business—in the middle of the Depression—and there was considerable competition from American and British firms. The institute's *succès d'estime* was owed far more to Colette's popularity as a writer than to her aptitude as a makeup artist. And her new profession brought her face to face with the thing she was trying to get away from: writing. Clients always ended up by asking for what they had really come for: her signature in a book. Her demonstrations of her wares in the provinces often ended up as literary lectures, tiring on two counts. She became aware that her personal appearances were essential to the business and would continue to be for a long time to come, and that profits were not high enough to enable her to take a complete rest from writing. As it had in the music hall and journalism, literature managed to find her out, no matter where she went to escape from it. And so she went back to it.

⚜ Près de Maurice

Goudeket had been forced to turn to less high-flown activities. In 1933 he sold washing machines and *a charming utensil for unclogging drains and toilets, a masterpiece of good taste and ingeniousness, which I have chosen to call "the ferret."* [1]

In December, he turned to journalism and wrote a novel that was never published. On April 3, 1935, after ten years of life together, they were married.

By the way, we're married, Maurice and I. . . . The ceremony took seventeen minutes from start to finish, with a wedding party consisting of two witnesses. What other way was there? in over ten years, we've just never had a morning free to make things legal. [2] Goudeket's masculine version: "It was at the time Colette and I were asked—on different levels—to report on the maiden voyage of the *Normandie*. Would we be able to live together openly in puritan America? 'What if we got married?' I said jokingly, 'then there won't be any problem.' Colette looked at me, and it was only then that I realized how much this cementing of our relationship meant to her." [3] In any case, even if—as Goudeket suggests—she had not been expecting a proposal of marriage, she was to recall the ceremony: * *It wasn't cold that morning, just a soft snow! It hung from the yellow catkins of the hazel trees and fell so densely that I asked my old companion and new husband to stop the car so that I could hear the snow whispering as it fell on the dead leaves. And the luncheon menu was appropriate to this wintry spring. There was succulent ham cooked in a pot-au-feu with pink fat and crackling and a bouillon redolent with celery, nutmeg, horseradish. . . . And can there be a wedding without champagne? Yes, if instead of champagne you have one of those secret wonders that constitute the*

---

* Goudeket relates that in order to avoid publicity he had sought a dispensation from publishing the banns. He was told that his desire for discretion was an invalid motive, but that he could plead fear of scandal and should declare that since the whole neighborhood thought they had been married for years, it would create a scandal if their public marriage revealed they hadn't been married all along.

glory of French inns, in this case a nameless vintage that was dark and golden as a Spanish reliquary and stood up to the pork and the cheeses.[4]

Finally freed from the fetters reality attaches to desire, Colette had chosen her husband of her own free will. She was to be Colette, never Colette Goudeket, either in private or as author. Was this finally the fulfillment of her dream at thirty, the dream of a free and equal love? Maurice Goudeket makes only direct appearances in Colette's writing; her correspondence gives us an official image filtered through her conscious mind. It is the image of a companion, literally, of a person with whom one shares food, games, vacations, friends. Over the years, the "Devil," "the dark, dark boy," became the "great guy," the calm and equal comrade, a quiet man born "under the sign of propriety." A bit of a dilettante, easygoing, he communicated his own serenity to his feline companion. Goudeket was not to inspire a work of fiction, as Jouvenel had earlier. Only unhappy love affairs make good stories.

It must be said that he did not alter her pessimism with regard to men and love affairs. From *Le Pur et l'Impur* (1932) to *Julie de Carneilhan* (1941), her distrust remained unaltered. Having managed to become a man's friend, Colette did not change her views with regard to her age-old adversary. Does this mean that her unhappy past experiences had had a more profound effect on her than this last and happy encounter, or is it rather that she was now resigned to her knowledge and merely altered her desires, bringing them into line with reality? She was still obsessed with a fear of solitude; more than anything else, Colette did not want to grow old alone.

Together, they boarded the *Normandie* and celebrated in their cabin with Léopold Marchand, Claude Farrère, and other friends. As a going-away present, Colette gave herself a hamper of food and spent the five days' crossing in boredom, while the Minister of Commerce who was on board representing the government spent the trip buttonholing other passengers to inquire anxiously "Have you by any chance heard whether I'm still in power?"

Besieged by reporters at the pier and questioned about her sandals and her bare feet, she gave a reply that bemused the readers of the next day's newspapers: "Because it makes walking easier." In New York, Goudeket and Colette did what ordinary tourists do; they visited the Empire State Building, spent hours in Woolworth's, and finally encountered a cat. "At last, someone who can speak French,"

Colette exclaimed. This one famous anecdote appears to have summed up their visit to the capital of the American Empire. Colette was not then an exportable commodity.

Earlier, they had traveled throughout Europe, to Spain and Tangiers, and had sailed the North Sea on Henri de Rothschild's yacht, the *Eros*; on this voyage, fittingly enough, Colette concocted a book on "those pleasures lightly referred to as physical," *Le Pur et l'Impur*. There were visits to zoos in Antwerp and to the Sarrasini Circus in Berlin. The Berlin city fathers refused a permit for its eighteen superb white elephants to parade across the city to salute Colette in front of her hotel; Sarrasini himself had promised her this treat, and had planned to appear dressed as a maharajah in white silk. Two years later, having been ordered to purge his circus of Jews and other "half-breeds," Sarrasini fled Nazi Germany. The elephants perished in a fire on the dock in Antwerp, Sarrasini of despair in South America.

Of all foreign countries, Colette was most inspired by North Africa. The Glaoui invited her to Morocco in 1926, and she returned on lecture tours. She contemplated the full moon over Fez, saw the snow glittering atop the Atlas Mountains, the sands and the blue and green enameled terraces under the muezzins' descant; she saw pink almond trees and date palms, pomegranates, Moorish cafés, and stuffed herself on *pale cakes bathed in succulent oil with green olives, chicken smothered in fresh fava beans with their puckered skins, lamb stuffed with fennel, lamb with cumin, zucchini, lamb prepared with twenty spices.*[5]

In 1938 they returned to Fez as reporters for *Paris-Soir* to cover a notorious trial. Oum el Hassen, a Moroccan prostitute well known to the French army for "her wild race's affection for the French race," had hidden French officers in her home during the uprisings in 1912 and 1925. In short, she had sold herself in two ways, with a whorehouse for French officers outside the walls of Meknès. Some of her clients had gone so far as to request the Légion d'Honneur for this great friend of France. Then came disappearances, discoveries of boiled human flesh, of cut-up bodies and walled-up girls, and an investigation was demanded: in her old age, Oum el Hassen had turned her drugged fantasies into criminal acts.

Almost with condescension, Colette reported, *she deigned to identify a dismembered corpse as that of one of her girls. . . . She did not deny that during the search of her house a feeble sound of a scratching fingernail had emanated from behind a wall. Broken down, the*

wall vomited out its secret: four female children and a boy of around
fifteen. . . . Out of fourteen prostitutes, four were dead, three had
disappeared, seven were crippled for life, all within the space of
less than a year.[6] Oum el Hassen was sentenced to fifteen years' hard
labor. Yet she had been a great friend to France. For once, French
and Moroccans found themselves agreed on one point: the victims
were, *after all, only women.* It is perhaps difficult to go along with
Colette completely when she comments: *What words or pictures*
can we use to bring Oum el Hassen to understand what we mean by
cruelty; accused of murder and brutality as she is, how can she com-
municate to us her conviction that she is innocent? What we call
cruelty has been the ordinary, bloody, happy commonplace of her
life since childhood. . . . Where could she have learned that there
are limits to the punishment that can be meted out to women, to
creatures, that is, who as such have no value at all? [7]

⚜ ONE OF THE GREAT ONES

After Oum el Hassen's trial, Colette never went back to North
Africa. Ever since her music hall days, traveling had merely recalled
to her the old vagabond life. Travel led to imaginings, but other
people went away, not she. So long a voyager, Colette settled
down to being her true self, a sedentary creature.

Claude Chauvière, so close to Colette's life at a certain period, has
drawn a vivid sketch of her daily routine: " 'I'm hungry,' Colette
would exclaim, just as shortly before she had exclaimed 'I'm thirsty!'
Overflowing with life and activity, she always glowed with physical
pleasure . . . passive, idle, a bit of a glutton, she bit into apples and
disemboweled chocolate éclairs.

" 'Pauline, I'm so hungry I'm going to be sick!'

"Then she would tend the fire, setting the logs, adding charcoal,
poking at it and shoveling the ashes, working the bellows . . . she
was fond of buying things, less fond perhaps of paying for them.
'I loathe money, and it's because I dislike it so much that I like to
imprison as much of it as I can in my drawer.'

"She was like a nomad in her confused fear that if she settled down
she would fall apart; there were no clocks or calendars in the house.

"The cat stalks solemnly among the carafes and the compote dishes.

"Colette fondles her precious stones, carves the leg of lamb, adjusts
the radiator. 'Maurice, dip your lettuce in your sauce, it's better that
way. Have some of my marc, I made eighteen liters this year. . . .'

"Women with names like Moune, the Countess, Nathalie, Miche, call on the telephone, and with its help Colette talks to Ferenczi and Flammarion, she goes from Luc-Albert Moreau to Léon-Paul Fargue, from *Candide* to *Vogue*. . . .

"Now she wants to go to the cinema. Now she has an appointment with her dressmaker for a fitting, one with Gaston to have her hair done, and then she has to buy mangos at H., coffee at C. And she hasn't powdered her face yet. She bounds into the bathroom, there are noises of faucets and crystal. She fills the apartment with steam and rearranges the flowers. And she has mislaid a file folder, the one for the living. There are three: one for the dead, one for publishers, and the one she cannot find. Drawers and bookcases are opened and shut. Panic. The telephone continues to connect and disconnect people, people come and go as though there were a revolving door." [1]

Between 1933 and 1938, Colette was drama critic on *Le Journal* and *L'Eclair*, *La Revue de Paris* and *Le Petit Parisien*. Her best pieces were collected in the volume entitled *La Jumelle noire* in her complete works. She undertook innumerable activities; she would take on anything, from publicity for a new brand of tobacco to "the text of an enchanting new edition of antique flower paintings by Redouté." [2] She wrote dialogues for films, for *Lac aux Dames*, directed by Marc Allégret in 1933, for *Divine* of Max Ophuls in 1934, and for the French version of *Mädchen in Uniform*. *La Vagabonde* was brought to the screen in 1930 by Solange Bussy, starring Marcelle Chantal.

At the same time, her official honors turned her into one of the best-known women of her time. In 1923, she was interviewed about her possible candidacy for the Académie Française, an institution on principle closed to women. Candidacy entailed paying a certain number of official and formal "calls." Colette replied:

Never, understand never, do I pay calls, even on my best friends. Why should I pay calls on a bunch of old men who've never been introduced to me? Monsieur, you can say that I have no desire to become part of a group that insists on women being the first to pay calls on men.[3]

She was appointed a commander of the Légion d'Honneur in 1935 and was named to fill Anna de Noaille's seat in the Belgian Royal Academy of French Language and Literature.

Honors, however, did not turn Colette into a "public figure."

From the year of their meeting up until the war, she and Goudeket spent each summer in La Treille Muscate. The house underwent yearly improvements; it became increasingly comfortable but decreasingly private as Saint-Tropez grew in popularity. In the earlier years, Colette lived the quiet life of an ordinary woman on vacation, rising early, working in the garden in the morning, swimming and devouring "Provençal repasts of green melons, anchoiade, stuffed racasse, rice with fava beans, bouillabaisse and aioli." [4] She made new friends with people like Kessel and the painters living in Saint-Tropez, Dunoyer de Segonzac, who illustrated the text of La Treille Muscate, Luc-Albert Moreau, the illustrator of La Naissance du jour, and his companion Hélène Jourdan-Morhange; she got to know André Villebeuf, part-owner of "Le Maquis" on its neighboring hill, the critic Gignoux, Thérèse Dorny, Segonzac's wife to be, Nora Auric. In Paris they also saw Luc-Albert Moreau and Hélène, who owned a house near Montfort in Mesnuls. Every Sunday, Goudeket and Colette would go out for lunch bearing the one cheese out of a hundred from a shop in the Place de la Madeleine and chops from a butcher who respected Colette as a fellow expert. Once a year there would be truffles—"Bank account permitting. For Colette always said 'If I can't have an abundance of truffles, I'll do without.' She would eat them as if they were potatoes." [5]

Just before the war, they moved for the final time. From both their Parisian apartment and their house in Provence. Before the impending upheaval, there was a final change of scene, but Colette was used to moving with little warning. In 1938, she returned to the Rue de Beaujolais through a series of astonishing strokes of luck, beginning with an interview in which she confided to a tenacious reporter: "To begin with, I've only moved fourteen times, and every time it was because I was forced to do so. For example, ten years ago when I was living in the Palais-Royal, I moved heaven and earth to get the apartment on the first floor of my building; if I had been successful, I would never have budged."

The interview was printed in Paris-Midi and on the following day, Colette received this letter:

"Madame, I read in Paris-Midi that you are still desirous of renting the first-floor apartment, 9, Rue de Beaujolais. I am the occupant of said apartment, and I am prepared to turn it over to you." [6]

So she returned to the Palais-Royal, to its habits and customs, with the joy of a prodigal daughter. The village was unchanged: the gentleman who cultivated miniature cactuses in his window was still there, as was the man who strolled in the garden in straw sandals. There was Renée, a streetwalker from the Cher district, who asked Colette for one of her books, "the saddest one," and who shared her territory with an authentic countess of seventy-one who bathed early each morning at the public faucet on the sidewalk. Colette observed the amenities she valued so highly and returned to being a citizen of a garden she was never again to leave. As for La Treille Muscate, owing to the growing fame of both Colette and the Côte d'Azur, it had become uninhabitable. Campers invaded the garden, along with autograph-seekers and the curious. It was purchased by the actor Charles Vanel, who sold it shortly afterward. Her increasing distaste for owning property abated temporarily when she spied a wisteria vine growing on a little house with a large garden in Méré, outside Montfort-l'Amaury. This was in 1939. Between the two wars, Colette's literary activity had been unceasing—it was a pity so few people read her well. "Colette does not enjoy the place due her in literature," Benoîte Groult was to write, "and the same holds true for all female writers." [7]

❧ So few people read her . . . well

Literature is a poor provider . . . for women, a well-known fact. But Colette was demanding, she wanted to be paid what she was worth. When Arthème Fayard was attempting to get her to sign with him, he told her, via René Bizet: " 'Your prices are my prices.' The figure she asked took him aback, but he paid it. . . . At *Les Nouvelles Littéraires* there were protests: 'André Gide only asks a quarter of that for an article!'

" 'That's André Gide's fault!' Colette replied." [1] It was her opinion that everyone's interest would be served if the well-known names raised their prices. Albeit looked down on by intellectual or moralizing critics, her books sold well. On several occasions, however, scandal stopped serial publication. Curiously, as she progressed from a young woman through middle age and became old, her life became less scandalous, her work more so.

Le Blé en herbe began publication as a serial in *Le Matin*; halfway through the book, the editor halted publication—his readers were protesting against the daring notion that a fifteen-year-old boy might be taught the pleasures of the flesh by an older woman, and that he would take advantage of her lessons to initiate his fifteen-year-old girl friend, all told with a naturalness and sobriety of expression, by a woman. This was something the average reader in 1922, the era of Freud and Breton, was not about to countenance.

La Seconde also appeared as a serial, in *Les Annales*. Pierre Brisson, the editor, requested changes, a few slight alterations—but upon receiving the first issue, Colette found the following puzzling sentence: *"Jane deleted her son with a delete.* 'I told you,' said Colette to the dismayed Pierre Brisson, 'that the deletions would show!' " [2]

Ces Plaisirs, later retitled *Le Pur et l'Impur*, dealing frankly with sexuality in general and homosexuality in particular, suffered the same fate as *Le Blé en herbe*. Publication began in the weekly *Gringoire* in 1932, and the editor stopped publication after the second issue. He wrote Colette a letter in more or less the following terms: " 'Dear friend, this time you've gone too far. I'm getting protests from every side. I am thus forced . . .' " [3] The scandal that had surrounded her life and that would henceforth be confined to her books was to hang over her until her death. "Criticism" with regard to Colette is highly instructive in this regard, demonstrating as it does that talent does not overcome scandal but rather feeds it, particularly if the talent is a woman's talent.

She has been particularly ill read. First, because scholars and intellectuals have systematically kept her apart from so-called serious literature. And secondly, because her work has the reputation of being unfit for certain readers. She has been relegated to a kind of Index owing to three historic ambiguities involving temperament and status: she was a "non-intellectual" writer in a century of cerebral literature with philosophical tendencies; she had a questionable social, moral and religious status in a period that was still extremely puritanical; she was a freedom-seeking woman in an age of male dominance. These ambiguities have worked to discourage—up until the end of the 1960s—all impartial attempts at serious criticism of her work.

The "intellectual" critical faction was led by Julien Benda; he began by deploring the fact that Colette did not know Latin,* and maintained that she was incapable of depicting "the purer instincts," or "the female soul in all its changing facets." Guilty in his opinion of what he calls 'Belphégorism," Colette, in his view, described only

* We recall that the female secondary school curriculum set up by Camille Sée in 1880 did not include the classical humanities. In any event, Colette's only diploma was her elementary school certificate.

"the baser emotional states." Unfortunately, her work reflects only "life, and not life as seen through the operation of the intelligence." [4] The reader of Colette is in a most unfortunate position, forced to resign himself to the fact that intellectual content is absent in her work, and further deprived of any spiritual satisfaction because "Colette's art is based solely on the senses." [5] In fact, a continual theme in all these accusations treats with the matter of the senses. There is no emotion or cerebration in her work; her mind is a *tabula rasa*: "The world she creates," writes Claude Boncompain, "is a world without a soul . . . or one peopled with base characters unduly preoccupied with the flesh . . . although her brush may evoke on occasion the great Venetian painters, she lacks the somber light of a Goya, any glimmer of thought as in Rembrandt." [6]

The fatal word is out: the flesh! And if only she were tragic . . . but no, she isn't even unhappy. According to Marcel Thiébaut she contaminates the entire uplifting concept of love: "Twenty generations of humanity have found in love the pretext for lyricism, they have identified it with ecstasy or religion. For Colette, it is merely desire, an excuse for sensual gratification or intoxication." [7] Gonzague Truc echoes his words and deplores her limited and atheistic novels, remarking that Colette "devoted herself to pleasure in mere things, the last recourse of all who are unable to attain knowledge of the Author of all things." [8] In his proselytizing frenzy, however, Mauriac forgives the sinner, "this pagan and carnal creature who leads us irresistibly to God"! [9] At least he gave her credit for not attempting to convert others to her evil ways. But Abbé Bethléem thought otherwise; in his *Novels Approved and Proscribed*, he fulminates against "the effects of her highly scandalous literature," and exclaims: "Beware of approaching too near the sewer in which she disports herself, for fear of being spattered with its filth." [10] Other critics joined in accusing Colette of crimes against humanity; she makes it vile, bestial. André Billy stated: "If, on the scale of intellectual values, metaphysical thought occupies the highest degree, Colette's art must be relegated to the lowest, since it is made up entirely of animal instinct!" [11] Jean de Pierrefeu went so far as to maintain that Colette's writing dealt with the "night of the brain, the end of all culture, and entails the definitive impoverishment of the human being, debased to a bestial level." Colette's heroines occupy some "primeval forest where they cavort, pursued by a male." [12] And many others stigmatized her offenses against morality. Even André Gide expressed dismay that Colette was "somewhat contaminated by a facetious, sophisticated and repellent society," one he had himself frequented, fortunately protected from it—thank God!—by a vestige of puritanism.

In addition to immorality and lack of spiritual values, Colette was also accused of the common failing of female writers: Trahard calls attention to her inability to achieve "form" in her work. "It is rare indeed that she manages to construct a novel in a solid manner. George Sand was little better at construction, nor any other woman. There is no example of a woman who is a great architect, since reasoned, geometrical—painstaking and unified—construction is incompatible with spontaneous *élan*. . . . Colette's art is therefore an art of mere execution." In addition, "Colette is not creative, since true creators are able to rise above their own personalities . . . she forgets herself so rarely in her work that her male characters are always less well formed than her female characters." [13] And of course men are so rarely treated elsewhere in literature that Trahard's distress at Colette's failure is totally justified! But even Henriette Charasson, a woman, has deplored "the powerlessness to overcome their own nature so characteristic of female authors." [14] Paul Souday expresses indignation that any writer should base his literature on himself: "Madame Colette never evidences scientific perspective or olympian serenity; she nearly always produces only personal literature." [15]

From this brief and far from exhaustive survey, drawn at random from the period 1920 to 1960, it is easy to see the extent to which criticism of Colette has been bogged down in the morass of common prejudices with regard to women. Attacked by the puritanical right wing, but equally disdained by the surrealists, existentialists and practitioners of the *nouveau roman*, she nevertheless retained a faithful public, especially women, a public of readers who were "non-intellectual" and unaffected by the vagaries of literary fashion. And as usual, the generation following her own proved even more narrowminded. Her contemporaries Valéry, Proust and even Montherlant had viewed her accomplishment with considerable clarity, even if they were not particularly loquacious about it, and Jean Cocteau admired her and paid her homage.

Women courageous enough to deal frankly with sexual problems, the problems of their own sexuality, have always been accused of immorality. Even Simone de Beauvoir was condemned for writing pornography following the publication of *La Deuxième Sexe*. Yet Colette totally ignored disapproval and insults; she was untouched by reprobation. "You don't say," was her simple reply. Insults, defamation, injustice and perfidy rolled off her back without affecting her.

She neither pretended to the role of celebrated author, nor did she defend herself. She merely went her way.

In the social sense of the phrase, she was never a *femme de lettres*, but she could and did converse with Valéry on the technical secrets of their craft; like two high-class artisans, they would compare notes on tricks of the trade, alchemical formulae.

"On the other hand, André Gide and she, although curious about each other, found themselves with nothing to say when they were finally brought together, and Gide admitted it." [16]

As an interview subject, she was the journalists' despair when it came to eliciting definitive pronouncements on literature. Léo Paillet asked her what profession she would choose if she were given her life to live over again; "Grocer," she replied. Where literary matters were concerned, her view was that of a tired laborer: "One writes, but the only good thing is living!" [17]

⚜ THE RETURN TO HER PAST

Her inner journey gradually began to have less and less connection with the outward activities and rhythms of her daily life. On the threshold of old age, she began to separate herself from the present. The era of *L'Entrave*, of literature drawn directly from life, dealing with nearly contemporary events in the world, was over. Her close friends, those who had known her in the past, must have had difficulty recognizing their Colette in the author of *Ces Plaisirs* or *La Naissance du jour*. After turning fifty, after her second divorce and the unpleasantness it entailed, her books changed. They began to turn slowly back to the past, to a journey back in time, away from the present, in a kind of renunciation. The processes are associated, for it is in her search for lost time that Colette returns to the subject of Sido and her special place in her life; and from Sido, she takes her example, she derives her need to "renounce." She gains a different perspective on freedom and fetters, one that leads her to action and dispossession. Colette's old age began at this point: the past began to take over, her mental landscape narrowed down without her gaze losing any of its acuity.

At the end of this path there will be a paralyzed old woman whose eyes have ceased to dwell on anything that cannot be seen from her own window, an old woman about whom Jean Cocteau remarked, "she was inexhaustible about anything concerning the Claudine period,

and appeared not to recognize our own, or even to attach any importance to it." [1]

La Fin de Chéri was written after the separation from Henry de
Jouvenel and it is full of resentment. Chéri commits suicide because
Léa has grown too old and cannot love him. When she kills off one
of her male characters, Colette is always committing a premeditated
crime. In her sacrifice of a handsome young man to a woman's old
age, there is a ferocity that reflects a basic female fantasy.

Willy once ironically noted the unlikelihood, the unbelievability,
of the twenty-five-year-old Werther's suicide for the sake of his sixty-
year-old Charlotte, and from his own male point of view, he was
not entirely wrong. However, when read in conjunction with *Chéri*,
La Fin de Chéri tells another story. In the first novel, the young man
leaves Léa, his "Nounoune," and gets married. A few months later,
he is drawn back to her and sees the signs of age, the stigmata, that
will separate them forever. Léa renounces him and sends him away.

The war intervenes. Bertrand comes and goes. Colette then writes a
sequel: *La Fin de Chéri* opens with Chéri's final visit to Léa; she is
now an old woman, dead to him. The book is about mourning. Unable
to overcome his grief, the young man goes to her home and
seeks to recapture his beloved by examining portraits and photographs of Léa as a young woman; surrounded by her image, he commits suicide while she is away attending *her mother's funeral*. Replacing Chéri with Minet-Chéri, the text becomes a tale of the death of
childhood, of Sido's death. Chéri kills himself because the Nounoune
he loved has been taken from him; similarly, Minet-Chéri, the infant
Gabrielle, is dead with Sido. Such a reading, only one of many possible readings, casts light on a subconscious process; there are other
texts from the same period that reveal this return to Sido more overtly.

La Fin de Chéri was written in 1923, but was not published until
1926. *La Maison de Claudine* dates from 1922, *La Naissance du jour*,
1928, *Sido*, 1930.* All of these books evoke Colette's childhood and the
central character in her own life, Sido. From this point, and up until
Gigi, text after text will recount in reverse the story of Colette's
life. "Between Colette's childhood and *La Maison de Claudine*, followed by *Sido*, there was approximately the same length of time as
between her young womanhood and *Mes Apprentissages*," Goudeket

---

* Certain sections of *Sido* and *La Maison de Claudine* were written as separate
pieces before appearing in book form.

notes.[2] Five years after Willy's death, the latter volume describes Colette's initiation into literature and love during the Belle Epoque. *Le Pur et l'Impur* describes Lesbos and her years with Missy; *Gribiche* is set in the music halls. In *La Seconde* (1929) and *Julie de Carneilhan* (1941), Colette returns to the period of her second marriage with Jouvenel. The circle is closed with *Le Képi*, and particularly with *Gigi*, her last published fiction. *Gigi* is based on an actual event of the 1920s, but is set in 1900, her days with the cocottes and her engagement to Willy being brought forward slightly to that time.* Like *Julie de Carneilhan*, it was written in the midst of the war, at a time when Colette was filled with anxiety over Goudeket; both books are a fresh and untarnished description of a bygone era.

This lapse of time between events lived and events written clearly shows that a part of Colette was already becoming detached from the life around her and journeying back in time without thought for chronology. Other texts—*La Chatte* and *Duo*, concerning jealousy, or *Le Toutounier*, which describes a relationship between two women, a "sisterhood"—are also part of a subconscious return to the maternal symbol. All the female characters, or the very young men who are their equivalents—Alain in *La Chatte*, for example—forgo sexuality in death or escape and return to their origins, to the source. This origin is represented by various metaphors, usually feminine—a cat, the Château de Carneilhan, the "Other" who is both rival and mother, the womblike bed of the sisters in *Le Toutounier*. For Colette, growing old meant taking refuge in femininity, returning to and assuming the maternal form. The text that most clearly evidences this is *La Naissance du jour*.

❧ "THE SUPREME CHIC OF KNOWING WHEN TO STOP"

La Naissance du jour is an accounting, a program for "knowing when to stop." It is a sketch of the meaning Colette at fifty would seek to realize in her old age. It is a dialogue with Sido's ghost. *Here, when I no longer thought to follow her save on the other side of life,*

* "It is based on the marriage of Yola Enriquez, a young student at the Conservatoire, to Henri Letellier, owner and editor of *Le Journal*. The girl's aunt was the owner of a hotel in Saint-Raphael where Colette had stayed in 1926 and had encountered the main characters in the story, then recently married. Sixteen years later, in an attempt to distract herself from the war, she used these facts as the basis for a romantic novel." (Quoted in *Catalogue de l'exposition Colette*, Bibliothèque Nationale, Paris 1973.)

here below is there still some garden path where I can retrace my own footprints? Is there still a maternal phantom in an old-fashioned blue satinette dress at the edge of the well, filling her watering cans? This cool spray, this sweet enticement, this provincial spirit, in short this innocence, is this the enchanting appeal of one's declining years? How simple it all is! [1]

At the "break of day," Colette evokes the maternal ghost in her house, La Treille Muscate. Sido embodies the call of the springs, associated with spray, liquid. It was in these years that Colette was enchanted to discover that she had the power to find water, to "divine." She wrote to Goudeket: "I'm a diviner, a diviner beyond divination! I'm puffed up with pride, a foolish fond pride." [2]

Like Sido, she would go *straight to the secretly glittering water hidden from the light, the sleeping stream, hearts unable to expand. She would hear the liquid sob, the long subterranean chiming, the sigh.* [3]

The book is full of this regained possession of the springs: *Do you imagine as you read me that I am portraying myself? Be patient, this is merely my model.* [4]

At the beginning of the book, Colette seeks absolution from her model. She lays her venial sins at her feet. Her mother will recognize them as like her own, the forbidden fruits she had attempted to grasp from life by moving her old armoire at seventy-eight, by chopping wood in the courtyard. Yet Colette's were sins of the flesh. She has just met Goudeket. Like her mother, she too rises *at dawn, before anyone else is up, standing on the threshold crossed by a nocturnal visitor, half-naked in a fluttering robe, my arms trembling with passion and shielding—oh! I should hide myself for shame—the thin shadow of a man.* [5]

And Sido's benevolent regard takes in the invisible correspondences that shatter and fragment men's souls: *"Stand back and let me see," my beloved ghost would say. . . . "Ah! you are embracing my pink cactus that has outlived me. How it's grown and changed! . . . Stay there, and may you both find rest, you and he, the man who survives, whom you embrace, for I see that he is really my pink cactus that has finally decided to bloom."* [6]

Sido sees the man her daughter loves almost ironically, as a pink cactus. There is no difference between *helping an exhausted horse along with hand and shoulder,* in *wrapping a muddy dog in a fold of your skirt,* in *sheltering some child . . . who is none of ours,* or in *enfolding in impartial arms a stammering lover on the brink of more dangerous abysses.*[7] There is only one love, one virtue: "never give pain."

The flesh, the demands of the senses, are sinful only when one is no longer physically worthy. *I am counting on a future that is measured in hours.*[8] And at the same time, she asks Goudeket: *Will you still be my friend when spring comes?* From spring to spring, how quickly the blossoms seem to fall!

Growing old is recognizing that as they decline, face and body must forgo what has occupied them: *one of the great banalities of life—love is beginning to withdraw from mine.* The veteran of the battles of love lays down her arms, not without a sense of wonder: *It is the first time . . . I must now live and even die without either my life or death being dependent on someone I love, it's extraordinary.*[9]

Her friends, friends who aways gave her the supreme proof of their affection by *showing a spontaneous aversion to the man I loved,* will doubtless be pleased.[10] Hadn't the best moments in these friendships been the ones when she had returned to them as a wounded lover still *hot from the battle, licking my wounds, analyzing my tactical mistakes, with such pleasure in partiality, accusing my enemy of crimes and defending him unreasonably, and secretly clutching his letters, his pictures, "He was so charming . . . I should have . . . I shouldn't have . . ." And then reason would take the upper hand . . . such is the pattern of suffering, like clumsiness in love, like the duty to contaminate, innocently, any life lived by two people together.*[11]

Suffer, yes, I knew how to suffer, she reflects, *but how childish it was!* As Sido had exclaimed concerning love, great, unreasonable, devastating love: *"How trivial!"* [12]

And how undignified. *Love is not an honorable emotion.*[13] Sido, who was all wise, knew nothing of the impure regions in which Colette had wandered, she knew nothing of La Boétie's bizarre paradox, "voluntary servitude." *She who tamed animals, cared for children, tended growing things, she was spared the discovery that some animals seek death, that some children beg to be defiled, that some closed flowers demand to be forced open and crushed underfoot.*[14]

The pangs of jealousy, the torture of possession and the frustrated desire to possess—all began to fade. *My mother knew, she who had only learned by "getting burned," as she said, she knew that one possesses by renouncing, and only by renouncing.*[15]

Possession was an illusion, the possession of men, animals, objects, houses . . . time goes by and fades into timelessness. One is no longer the mistress of one's body. It is time to renounce. For Colette, there had always been only one kind of love, physical love. And love must be renounced. All plants, animals, men, germinate and flower in the same way. *There is only one animal.* Animals must be renounced. In order to return to the beginning, possessions must be laid aside.

But renunciation is not some kind of mystical asceticism, there are also compensations: when the soiled sheets are thrown off, one arises into joy, into the dawn. The renunciation of one sort of relationship with man enables one to gain a better hold on him, *Man, my friend, let us rest here together! I have always enjoyed your company. And now you look at me so gently. From the confused mass of cast-off femininity, you see emerge . . . a drowning woman. . . . Behold, your sister, your companion, your equal, a woman who has escaped age to become a woman. Like you, in your image, her neck has grown thick, her body as its grace gradually fades is strong, she has an authority that tells you you can no longer make her despair, or only purely and without passion. Let us stay together, there is no longer any reason for you to leave me forever.*[16]

As for the difference in age, *I never think of age difference . . . no more than I do the opinion of imbeciles . . . what difference can fifteen years make to us? We are certainly less preoccupied with it than some mature man who continues to fall in love with innocent young girls. . . . We only think of it to the extent that we protect ourselves with coquetry, we seek health, adornment, affectionate tricks, and these are the lot of young women too.*[17]

In *La Naissance du jour,* Colette rejects Vial, whereas in real life she was accepting Goudeket. The latter was much surprised. The answer is to be found in the text itself, as Colette evokes the days when she was creating the character of Léa, the days with Henry de Jouvenel, *while I was describing this lonely woman, I would show my life, page by page, to a man, asking him, "Have I lied well?" And I would laugh, my forehead seeking his shoulder, just below his ear where I could nibble it, for I could not escape the belief that I had lied. . . .*

"You're there, aren't you? You're there?" But what I held was already only a fallacious solidity. Why did he stay? I inspired confidence in him. He knew that I could be left alone with matches, gas, firearms.[18]

Sido was gone, but Maurice was there. There would be no reason for him to "leave forever" a woman who was gradually ceasing to be what one calls a woman—that bizarre contraption for which there is no male equivalent—a woman who was turning into a person, a companion. The well-earned victory of a woman who has grown old. Such renunciation, so much lost time, to become at last a human being! Colette both renounced Goudeket and kept him by her. He himself mentions that "she was the one who, preventing me, was later to decide that we as a couple would transmute love into friendship." [19] In her inner life, the "hidden woman" followed Sido's plans. She did it in stages; it was difficult, since *the greater difficulty lies not in giving, but in not giving everything.* Here too, Sido had gone before her, clearing the way. She had played chess with the wool merchant, and *when I become too inept and disgraceful, I'll give up doing that too, like everything else, out of decency.*[20] The lines at the end of her final letter in the book slant down. *She was so brave, but she is still afraid, dreading being dependent, dependence of any kind.*[21] One must have patience, know how to wait, to relinquish in one's turn. *Only to wait, waiting is a lesson taught in a good school, where they also teach elegant good manners and the supreme elegance of knowing how to give way.*[22]

Not possessing money is only one stage in letting go. There were others; she considered giving up meat, *but not this year, I'm too hungry, but some day I will be a vegetarian!*

"Why?"

"It would take too long to explain. When one aspect of cannibalism fades, the rest vanish in turn, on their own, like fleas off a dead hedgehog.[23]

She relinquished her animals. Her life with Goudeket included two animals, both females: Souci the bulldog bitch, and Chatte, the cat. They died within three months of each other, the cat first, then the dog. After thirteen years of life with them, "Colette expressed her grief with her habitual restraint. She simply kept silent for a few days." [24] Many years later she sighed, *when I give up hymning the final cat, I will have become mute about everything.*[25] Nor was the dog replaced. Colette no longer walked easily, and she was unable to give her animals enough exercise.

She relinquished objects, tiny objects, glass balls, gold chains, silk scarves, picture books, things that had been with her for years and of which she was truly fond. *I should have given it away*, she would tell herself, *someone took pleasure in it, real pleasure. . . . Ah! no; no, I don't want to, I want to keep it.*[26] She argued with herself, blaming her *magpie, squirrel, dormouse instincts . . . the reflexes of a miser, a shrinking of the aptitude for possessions, a diminishing of the thing possessed. . . . Shall I give it away? Give it away, profit from the moment I still cherish the thing I want to give.*[27] Yet it was so hard! . . . she would rest her hand upon the colored bead, the bibelot, the braided gold. But once she begins to give, she cannot stop: *I began to understand that my ruthlessness was only to give the lie to growing old. If I give up the toys of old age, relax my fingers, once I empty the box, the drawer, I discover I no longer really desire anything.*[28] She had carefully saved a dress belonging to her mother; now it was used to cover the manuscript of *Sido, the blue dress is still dressing Sido.*[29] She acceded to the scissors, to turning the dress into a book cover.

She burned her love letters. *Born in the flames, most of them perished in the flames.*[30] She abandoned the novel and turned to shorter forms out of preference, *Bella Vista, Chambre d'Hôtel, Gigi,* fictions more intricately worked, stripped down, finely wrought. After *Gigi,* she felt she no longer had the strength to create and sustain a character, and she wrote no more fiction. Her final books, *Le Fanal bleu, L'Etoile vesper,* stroll in the past, like essays, in *the lovely past in the sun's rays, gray with mist, childish, transparent, blooming with modest joys, scarred with such cherished griefs.*[31]

All her long road toward freedom ended in this natural old age, in acceptance of the fact that every acquired object had found its place. These are the only conditions under which the path back can be followed. Death, after all, is the voyage on which we need take nothing. And on Colette's path, there were already many dead before her.

⚜ THE DEAD

Inside, I reproach them for dying; I call them careless, thoughtless. How dare they do that to me![1]

We doubt she reproached Willy, who died on January 12, 1931, followed by Henry de Jouvenel in October of 1935.

I'm sure his wife must be extremely unhappy, she wrote, ambiguously.[2] Polaire died alone in the hospital on October 11, 1939, shunned by her dog who disliked sick people. Her brother, Léo Colette, *an old sylph, his wings matted by the rain,*[3] went from her in March 1940 depriving her of the things *he alone held, our ancient possessions, our secret rhymes, the topography of our natal village.*[4] Renée Hamon died in Brittany at the end of October 1943. Colette wrote to the companion of her final years, *I know the poor child had to die, that it was necessary, desirable, that there was no other way out. But now that it's over, I am—we—are revolted.*[5] Missy committed *a kind of hara-kiri* in 1944. A year later, Colette lost her friend Hélène Picard. She did not attend the funeral, but sent violets, and *what a joy for me that my legs kept me from seeing the sight that would have destroyed her vivid image.*[6]

I had never imagined Marguerite would leave me. And Colette could not forgive her. She died on July 14, 1948: *We didn't deserve that!* While she was alive, they had often been unable to see each other, but there had been the telephone, letters. When she died, the newspapers were full of her pictures, images of her.

Now I have everything but her.[7]

Growing old means watching others die. And now, for the young as for the old, millions died and never returned.

⚜ THE OCCUPATION

Colette's writing does not deal at any length with the period between the wars. She had already begun her return to the past. She says nothing of the Bolshevik revolution, the rise of fascism, the Front Populaire, the Spanish Civil War, Munich . . . nothing. There is mention of Hitler in a letter, one or two reports of trials, Stavisky . . . She had turned her back on History, but it was to catch up with her: the Nazi occupation centered in on her and her Jewish husband.

August 1939 began very like August 1914, deceptively so. She was on vacation in Dieppe with Goudeket and the Léopold Marchands. Swimming, relaxation, euphoria. They put off their return to Paris until late in the season. At the first alert, everyone went down into the cellar, but the concièrge had left the key to the street door behind in his loge. After that, Colette refused to take shelter even during the heaviest bombardments in 1944. She stored up provisions, filled the coal bin, organized forays into the countryside, spoke on shortwave radio.

June 11, 1940. Paris nervously prepared for the exodus. Cars were loaded, bags packed, papers were burned in the ministries. Colette, Pauline and Goudeket set out from the house in Méré for the Corrèze and found France *falling over itself*. Colette de Jouvenel had offered them shelter at her property of Curemont; there was a knoll where two medieval châteaux were crumbling to bits, and a dwelling had been set up along the outer wall. They lived by the radio, like everyone else, and Colette wrote her *Journal à rebours*; it was her way of ignoring what was happening. But the times were not propitious for adventurings into the past. After three weeks, the couple set out to return to Paris by way of Lyons; it was early August.

"When we arrived at the border control for the Occupied Zone, a German found nothing suspicious about me," Goudeket relates. "But for Colette it was another matter. 'You, Jew!' he said. . . . He examined Pauline. She had jet-black hair, large yellowish eyes, a swarthy complexion. 'You, certainly Jew!' the German insisted." [1] Suddenly, Goudeket intervened. " 'You're making a mistake,' I told the German in his own language, 'I'm the only one here of Jewish birth.' " After consultation with a disgusted young officer, the car, "loaded with the refuse of humanity," was turned back.[2]

They returned to Lyons. Provided with a letter of recommendation from the Swedish consulate, their second border crossing was made with "courtesy and clicking heels." Colette had disregarded her companions' pleas and had slipped a tiny loaded revolver into the finger of her glove; replying to the Germans, she "casually waved this empty glove with its . . . rigid loaded finger . . . in their faces." [3]

On December 12, 1941, at 7:20 A.M., the door of the apartment in the Rue de Beaujolais resounded to the blows of a fist. A German officer wearing a helmet and *Feldgendarmerie* insignia around his neck had arrived to arrest Goudeket. Colette got up, she helped him pack his suitcase. "The Feldwebel was waiting. The other exit from the apartment was guarded by an ordinary soldier, a fanatical redhead, far more aggressive than his superior.

"She went with me to the top of the stairs. We looked at each other. We were both smiling, we exchanged a hasty kiss.

" 'Don't worry,' I said, 'It will be all right.'

" 'Off you go,' she said to me, giving me a friendly tap on the shoulder." [4]

Over a thousand people were arrested that day. It was the first big round up of "prominent French Jews." They were taken to the manège at the École Militaire. Among them, René Blum—brother of Léon—Jean-Jacques Bernard, Arnyvelde, and other of Goudeket's acquaintances. In the evening, he slept at the Compiègne detention camp, unaware that he had risked being deported directly to Germany: the French railway had been unable to provide for both their transport and the trains for Wehrmacht soldiers on Christmas leave, and the latter were given precedence.

Colette never recovered from the shock of this early-morning invasion of her home. Every time the bell rang, she would start in fear, her mouth would tremble, the corner of her eye would twitch. It was too late, at sixty-eight years of age, to forget *the sound of foreign voices, the noise of nailed boots, and the ringing of the bell . . . and then the softer sound of the footsteps of the man descending the stairs, his little suitcase in his hand. . . . When they went away, that man and the two hundred others they had picked up, they joined the anonymous dead. Frozen and silent as the dead. There were no voices, there was no writing, nothing was left to show they were alive.*[5]

Yet she managed to control herself; she frantically set about making up packages out of nothing to send to him . . . and above all to arrange for his freedom. At first, there were dark and sinister days of waiting in the Palais-Royal . . . *shouts, appeals, one night when the thorough and bureaucratic enemy systematically rounded up all the neighborhood Jewish children, their mothers, separating Jewish husbands from their wives and locking them away in vans, women and children in others vans. . . . How could I compare my own nightmarish loss with separations such as those?* [6]

One day a piece of lined paper no larger than a subway ticket arrived, covered with a new, unaccustomed, cramped handwriting. It was a list, a litany, asking for butter, preserves, sugar and above all bread, *bread, for God's sake bread*, and the word *lard* in huge letters. There was worse to come: *After January 1, 1942, the thermometer began to drop. Eight, twelve below zero centigrade, fourteen below on the plains of Compiègne. But the word "deportation" began to appear more and more often in the newspapers, on people's lips . . .* and many women learned with shock that *what we had thought was the worst that could happen was about to become worse still.*[7]

She had connections. She went to see anyone who could help, Germans, collaborators, men in the resistance. Would Sacha Guitry intercede? Others? Her daughter, a member of the resistance in the Corrèze? One writer, a former prisoner who had been released after agreeing to collaborate, suggested a way out:

" 'I've found a solution for your husband. I can get him a permanent job from "these persons" in the Compiègne camp. He will be well treated and fed.'

"Colette made a face.

" 'You've no other choice, my dear friend; otherwise it means death.'

"She shuddered.

" 'If there's no other way,' she finally said, 'I'll have to put up with it. Will it be hard work?'

" 'Not at all, he won't have to do a thing.'

" 'Well, that's not so bad,' she replied.

" 'He will only have to furnish—oh, just once in a while—a few bits of information about his fellow prisoners. You see, it's a job as a trustee.'

" 'I refuse,' Colette said, completely calm.

" 'I didn't quite understand, my dear friend. Perhaps you've not understood me. The other alternative is death. You understand, death!'

" 'Well, then I choose death!'

" 'I hope you are going to consult your husband!'

" '*We* choose death,' Colette repeated, still without raising her voice." [8]

He was released. He arrived at the second-floor apartment in the Rue de Beaujolais and undressed completely on the landing *to leave behind with his clothing the larger part of the souvenirs he had brought crawling back from Compiègne.* We know how emaciated the deportees were, *his cheeks and forehead were greenish white, the rims of his eyes orange, his lips gray.* [9]

Colette wasted few words in describing the war: *I love nothing the war years brought . . . dry-eyed, I longed like everybody else to return to the days before the war, days we had all thought so dull before we found out what kind of days were to follow. Among other worldly things, I longed for freedom to enjoy my sorrow! Oh, what crying jags I will indulge in when things are all right again! That's what one says.* [10]

Goudeket spent the rest of the war in hiding, first in the Free Zone and later in Paris, where at night he slept in the attic of the building, under the eaves. The war went on, through the invasion of Italy, the gradual withdrawal of German troops from Russia, the Allied landing, the bombings in the spring of 1944. Like all villages, the Palais-Royal offered its own passive resistance, produced its own martyrs and traitors. Renée from the Cher still plied her ambulatory trade. Winter and summer, Colette would watch her as she leaned against the grille, striking up occasional conversations with her. In 1942, she disappeared; in 1943, a woman Colette did not recognize at first greeted her in the street.

"*Is that you, Madame Renée?*"

"*Well,*" she replied, "*it is and it isn't.*" *She shifted her weight onto one leg.*

"*I've been in Munich. And other places.* They *picked me up. . . .*"

"*Yes, in Munich . . . first in a restaurant where* They *made me wait table. And* They *forced me to pick up red-hot plates just off the stove, metal pots, with nothing to hold them with. Look at my fingers now, like claws. I can barely sew, me who used to do fine needlework. . . . And then I was sent to prison. . . . You can't imagine what it's like there.* They *shut up an eighteen-year-old girl without any light. . . . I'm getting out, it stinks of Kraut around here!*" [11]

One of the Palais-Royal shopkeepers had a passion for blue parakeets. Tons of food seemed to come into and go out of his shop. The entire neighborhood disapproved; it was taking a fairly high moral stand during this difficult period. The bookseller offered Goudeket a hideaway, a cushion and a lamp concealed behind his Gustave Dorés. In case of an alert, he only had to slip out of the apartment by a rope ladder and hide in the shop below, which was left unlocked. A poetically inclined German strolled in the gardens, a *lover of art and beauty*, and angered the inhabitants of the Palais-Royal. He had three loves, tropical birds, romantic novels and objets d'art. *In fact, where romantic fiction was concerned, he purchased things like* Eperon and the Whips, Flagellations, *the* Empress of Polished Leather, *and other edifying volumes*.[12] He dropped in to visit the antique dealer with annoying frequency. "*The chandelier? I've just sold it, sir, just this minute. See, they're taking off the price tag . . . the little chair? Oh, sir, it's not authentic, it's only a poor copy, any connoisseur would notice in a second. . . . I'm sorry, sir, that opaline lamp is not for sale, someone left it to be repaired.*" [13]

Colette waited patiently. In *De ma fenêtre* she writes with simplicity traditional words of advice, good sense, how to keep from feeling hungry and cold, how to "hold out." She was in no condition to go underground; she was an old woman, terrified for her companion, overcome by the horrors in the newspapers and the rumors flying about. They were troubled times. Reports were contradictory, there were clandestine radios, whispered denials. Paris was beginning to fill up with *men in hiding, with invisible allies, with enemies who never slept. . . . Names whispered the evening before would suddenly be denied, Leclerc, Koenig. . . .*

Toward the end, the great leaders had no names, they became one glorious They.

"They *are in* Antony! *. . .* They *are outside Châtillon. . . . no,* They're *still fighting. . . .* They *are repairing the road so the tanks can get through. . . .* They *are coming. . . .* They *are here!"* [14]

And then, the Liberation. *Men, women wept and laughed, they cheered and waved their arms, kissing strangers, taking each other by the arm they marched blindly forward, singing, dancing, bearing torches.*[15]

⚜ THE LIBERATION

Liberated—and old. Colette turned seventy-two in 1945. Now she looked like her last pictures, the huge mop of white crinkled hair and the beautiful face with its vivid eyes set in their wrinkles. In 1931, she had fallen into a ditch and broken her leg while on vacation at La Treille Muscate. The injury to her heel spread to her hip, probably creating a lesion. A few years later, the joint became arthritic.

The trauma of Goudeket's arrest and her anxieties under the Occupation had weakened her. She had begun to suffer acutely in 1943; it was the prelude to years of physical pain. She gradually became immobile, renouncing mobility as she had renounced so much else; she used a cane, then two canes, then a wheelchair for out of doors and another for moving about inside the apartment. At last she was confined to her bed, which she transformed into a dwelling. Goudeket cared for her, filtered out visitors.

Publicly, her life was brilliant; she was given countless honors. She succeeded Sacha Guitry in the Académie Goncourt in 1945 and became its president in 1949; she was named a Grand Officer of the Légion d'Honneur. Her final books created no scandals—on the contrary—the days of censorship were in the past. In 1948, her complete works were published; *Chéri* was performed at the Théâtre de la Madeleine, and she rehearsed the actors from her couch. *La Seconde* was revived in 1951 with André Luguet, Hélène Perdrière and Maria Casarès, and the actors came to perform scenes for Colette in the Palais-Royal. *Claudine à l'école* was made into a film, but her greatest success was with *Gigi* starring Danièle Delorme, *Julie de Carneilhan* with Edwige Feuillère, and the screen adaptation of *Chéri*. In 1951, Anita Loos adapted *Gigi* for the American stage; Yannick Bellon made a film of Colette at home in the Rue de Beaujolais. In Monte Carlo, Colette discovered a young Anglo-Saxon ingénue and exclaimed, "Here is our Gigi for America, you needn't look any further." The young actress was named Audrey Hepburn; her performance made *Gigi* into an international triumph for them both.

Was Colette aware of how popular she was? On her eightieth birthday, there were unusual celebrations, her photograph was in every newspaper. When she appeared in the lobby of the Hôtel de Paris in Monte Carlo ensconced in her wheelchair, many stood up and applauded. "Oh Maurice," she said, "see, they remember me from last year." [1]

Her last books reveal the further shrinkage of her field of vision, "although the star (*L'Etoile vesper*) still shone down on the world, the lamp (*Le Fanal bleu*) shed its light only on the objects within its shaded range." [2] The blue lamp of this title is the lamp Colette made for herself using a rolled sheet of her favorite blue paper as a shade. Her world shrank from the landscape she could see outside her window to the interior of her room. She had always been nearsighted, or so people had told her. What she saw, she saw clearly. More than anything else, she still wanted surprise, *Surprise me, make an effort to surprise me, I cannot do without these last glimmers.*

She was curious about physical pain. She tested her powers of endurance, her aptitude for *honorable suffering, for conversing with the presence of pain.*[3] She wanted to remain alert and refused tranquilizers, sleeping pills. There were moments of weakness, of revolt, *That's it, I've had enough! I want my leg back! Everyone seems to think it's natural I should be in such a state, so old, so many honors. . . . But there is all this pain, these restrictions! I've had enough! A miracle, a miracle, My God, it's high time!* [4] At the same time, she took pains not to disturb those around her. She did not complain. If she had to suffer, she would make pain a *vivid call to life,* a rising and falling rhythm independent of herself, she would give it her attention. At her age, after all, Sido had still trotted around moving furniture. She would outdo Sido. The woman who had been a dancer had to forgo walking; the woman who had valued physical well-being above all things, the pleasure of being in full possession of her health, her strength, was forced to resign herself to a slow decline.

Around her, the Palais-Royal was like another Saint-Sauveur. Jean Cocteau was living in the same apartment in which "Barras had invented Bonaparte." [5] Madame Colette, as she was now called, this woman who had fought so hard to win her own name, became the "president of the Palais-Royal," whose residents "taking the few steps that led into the Rue de Richelieu, would say 'I'm going up to Paris.'" [6] The center of this village was the Grand Véfour restaurant at the corner of the Rue Montpensier, Cocteau's street, and the Rue de Beaujolais, Colette's. Whenever she expressed a desire to eat there, "two robust kitchen helpers would bring up a kind of sedan chair" on a signal from the owner, Raymond Olivier, and carry her down to the restaurant, where he would shower her with attention.

One day, when the entresol of the building caught fire, Olivier dashed upstairs before the smoke became impenetrable. Colette was difficult to transport. "But since you're here, there's no reason not to have some coffee," she calmly said, seeing her exit blocked by the flames. The firemen arrived with a ladder in the nick of time. The Palais-Royal harbored a band of friends and neighbors, Christian Bérard, Emmanuel Berl, Mireille, Pierre and Hélène Lazareff, Hervé and Gérard Mille, Jean Cocteau and Jean Marais—the "Jeannot" of *Le Fanal bleu*, with his "purity," "his sonorous, savage voice," and their dog Moulouk, *who watched for him when he was gone and reverted to being a puppy when he looked at it.*[7]

Colette continued to write on her lap desk, a gift from the Princesse de Polignac, telling about her friends and their visits to her, about the everyday events in the Palais Royal, stories of children— How can one ever stop writing?—in spite of her "lack of vocation," a claim she made often, despite her dislike of discipline, the perfection she had always imposed on her work.

I believed that the task of writing was like any other task, once you laid down your tools you joyfully cried "The End!" And you clap your hands, and from them pour grains of sand you believed to be precious. . . . And it is then, in the letters written by those grains of sand, that you read the words "To be continued." [8]

In the grains of sand, she could read back her fate as a writer who had been "invented," fabricated by a merchant. And now she saw this habit of writing coming to an end. Lying on her couch, she watched the fire, her last "living creature," leaping and immaterial, and she created a tapestry as she wrote, *Guided by the same hand, pen and needle, the habit of work and the wise desire to bring it to an end, to form friendship, to separate and come together again. My slow messengers, go out to the countryside. . . . I can see the edge of the road from here.*[9]

All around her were her round objects; on the mantelpiece were her spheres of Chinese crystal, the symbols of her imaginary course. She returned to where she had begun, to the crystalline springs, she began to look like Sido. Her memory grew away from the present, it kept intact the footsteps of the past. Two months before her death, she came upon a photograph taken in her school in Saint-Sauveur, showing her among some thirteen little girls from eight to twelve, and she could name them all, one after the other, without hesitation.

She gradually fell silent, she went out on two occasions in the car, holding out her hands in a gesture of marvel. "She became interested in fewer things, but in those few she was no less interested." [10] Pauline cared for her devotedly, carrying her to her bath, lifting her out, waiting on her throughout the day, arising three times every night and keeping watch outside her door. She died peacefully, surrounded by her own. On July 20, 1954, her daughter, Pauline and Goudeket stood vigil. On the previous evening, she had had a lucid hour, "her hands fluttered around her like wings. . . . Her arm described an arc embracing all she had ever showed me:

" 'Look,' she said to me, 'Look, Maurice!' " [11]

"The next day, she woke and spoke in silent syllables, intelligible only to herself." [12] On the evening of August 3, Colette slept. Pauline and Maurice Goudeket were watching. "It was very hot, the sky was overcast and the Palais-Royal was deserted. Colette's breathing became harsher and we looked at each other, Pauline and I. It lasted some fifteen minutes. We sat without moving. Suddenly there was silence, and Colette's head slowly drooped to one side, in an infinitely graceful movement." [13]

Her "instinctive fondness" for the curve, the sphere, had brought her full circle, and the circle closed. Perhaps, at the very end of her journey back, she had found the unfettered radiance of her mother's body.

Epilogue

Colette was the first woman to be honored with a State funeral. A catafalque covered with the French flag was set in the *cour d'honneur* of the Palais-Royal. Philippe Hériat reported the ceremony and noted the particular homage paid by the women of Paris. Hundreds of people, most of them women, passed before the coffin. "Among the many floral tributes was a wreath from those in the music hall and the circus, beside a wreath of red roses whose ribbon in the Belgian national colors bore the name 'Elizabeth' . . . the violet dahlias from *Les Lettres françaises* were propped against the aristocratic flowers from *Le Figaro*."

The Catholic church refused to sanction a religious funeral for a woman who had acted on the stage, who had been twice divorced.* Many Catholics protested. The British writer, Graham Greene, addressed a letter of protest to Cardinal Feltin, the Archbishop of Paris. Maurice Goudeket, later a convert to Catholicism, regretted not being able to put a cross on her tombstone.

This was Colette's last scandal; her work and her life were still faintly redolent of hellfire. None of this would have concerned her, just as the scandals of her life had bored her. Where religion was concerned, she was nearer to a kind of paganism vaguely tinged with Catholicism than to any set orthodoxy. Death did not interest her either, she had said so. And funerals even less so. She never went to them.

She would have smiled at the anecdote told by her friend Jean Cocteau: "Dialogue between Pauline and Madeleine [Cocteau's old servant] on the day of Colette's funeral:

"Pauline (from beneath her black veil): 'Ah, it's you, Madame Madeleine.'

"Madeleine: 'Yes, Madame Pauline, I've come to weep for Monsieur Jean.' "[1]

In a *Tale of a Thousand and One Mornings* she once wrote about the Montmartre cemetery, Colette had criticized burial and praised

---

* The refusal of the Church's authorization was based rather on her personal status vis-à-vis the Church than on any considerations of her work as a writer.

cremation, Fire, ready to spring up and destroy, purify, joyfully dispersing our remains.

In her *Journal intermittent*, she had written: *I tell myself that the material remains of a person are a poor thing, and that the dead have nothing more to do with the living . . . A memory, an image, the unforgettable sound of a voice, a poignant handwriting . . . only there does a person return, in the hours of tender remembrance and despair.*

She is buried in Père Lachaise, where a simple marker of stone bears the inscription: Here Lies Colette 1873–1954.

Chronology

<table>
<tr><td>1829
September</td><td>Birth of Jules-Joseph Colette, Colette's father, at Toulon, Mourillon.</td></tr>
<tr><td>1835
August</td><td>Birth of Adèle-Eugénie Sidonie Landoy, Colette's mother, in Paris, Boulevard Bonne-Nouvelle.</td></tr>
<tr><td>1857
January 15</td><td>Marriage of Sidonie Landoy and Jules Robineau-Duclos, landowner in Puisaye, in Brussels.</td></tr>
<tr><td>1858</td><td>Birth of Léon Hamel.</td></tr>
<tr><td>1859</td><td>Birth of Henry Gauthier-Villars, "Willy."</td></tr>
<tr><td>1860
August</td><td>Birth of Héloise Emilie Juliette Robineau-Duclos, the "sister with the long hair."
Captain Colette arrives in Saint-Sauveur.</td></tr>
<tr><td>1863
January</td><td>Birth of Edmé-Jules-Achille, half brother of Colette; birth of Missy.</td></tr>
<tr><td>1865
January</td><td>Death of Jules Robineau-Duclos, Sido's first husband.</td></tr>
<tr><td>December 20</td><td>Marriage of Sidonie Landoy and Captain Jules Colette (set up housekeeping, Rue de l'Hospice).</td></tr>
<tr><td>1868</td><td>Birth of Léopold Colette, "Léo," Collette's brother.</td></tr>
<tr><td>1873
January 28</td><td>Birth of Sidonie-Gabrielle Colette in Saint-Sauveur en Puisaye (Yonne).</td></tr>
<tr><td>1876</td><td>Birth of Henry de Jouvenel.</td></tr>
<tr><td>1880
(seven years
of age)</td><td>Captain Colette retires.</td></tr>
<tr><td>1884
(eleven years
of age)</td><td>Visit of Colette to Paris, Rue Saint-Roch.</td></tr>
<tr><td>1885
(twelve years
of age)</td><td>Marriage of Juliette Robineau-Duclos and Dr. Roché.</td></tr>
</table>

1889

(sixteen years of age) July 1, 2	Birth of Maurice Goudeket, in Paris VIIIe. Sidonie-Gabrielle Colette awarded her *brevet élémentaire* in Auxerre; end of schooling. Visit of Colette to Paris.
September	Birth of Jacques Gauthier-Villars; Colette begins reading the *Lettres de l'Ouvreuse*.

1890

(seventeen years of age)	Public auction of Colette's birthplace. Family moves to Châtillon-sur-Loing (today, Châtillon-Coligny) to the home of Achille.

1891

(eighteen years of age)	Willy is thirty-two. Death of Jacques's mother; Sido reconciled with Juliette.

1892

(nineteen years of age)	Jacques cared for in Châtillon. Visit of Colette to Paris, at the home of Mme Cholleton.

1893

(twenty years of age) May 15	Marriage to Henry Gauthier-Villars, "Willy." Honeymoon in the Jura.
June 28	Couple moves to the Rue Jacob. Colette is introduced into various literary and musical salons. She meets Anatole France, Proust, Marcel Schwob, Catulle Mendès, Marguerite Moréno, Pierre Louÿs, Jean Lorrain, Lucie Delarue-Mardrus, Gérard d'Houville, Paul Valéry, Fargue, Rachilde and Vallette, Ravel, Debussy, d'Indy, Fauré, Reynaldo Hahn.

1894

(twenty-one years of age)	The Kinceler episode. Ecole Polytechnique ball. After a serious illness, Colette goes to convalesce in Belle-Isle-en-Mer with Willy and Paul Masson. *Claudine à l'école* begun (between May and November).

1895

(twenty-two years of age) July	Willy and Colette make a trip to Saint-Sauveur, where they stay at the school.
September	Willy and Colette attend the Bayreuth Festival.
October	First draft of *Claudine à l'école* begun.

1896

(twenty-three years of age)	Visit to Uriage (the Arriège of *Claudine s'en va*). Bayreuth Festival (*Ring*).

| January | Draft of *Claudine à l'école* finished and relegated to a drawer by Willy. |

1898
(twenty-five years of age)

Marriage of Achille.
Willy rediscovers *Claudine à l'école*.

1899
(twenty-six years of age)

Willy seeks publisher for *Claudine à l'école*.
Bayreuth Festival (*Ring, Parsifal, Meistersinger*).

1900
(twenty-seven years of age)

Publication of *Claudine à l'école* under Willy's signature.
L'Aiglon, by Rostand; *Lord Jim*, by Conrad; Freud's *Science of Dreams*; *Le Rire*, by Bergson.
Colette makes short trip to London.

1901
(twenty-eight years of age)

Claudine à Paris.
Bayreuth Festival (*Flying Dutchman, Parsifal*); Georgie accompanies Willys to Bayreuth; the couple moves to 93, rue de Courcelles (XVIIe), and later to 177 bis.

1902
(twenty-nine years of age)

Claudine en ménage, signed by Willy.
Purchase of Les Monts-Boucons (Casamène, in *La Retraite sentimentale*).

January 22

Claudine à Paris, by Willy, Lugné-Poe and Charles Vayre, presented at the Théâtre des Bouffes Parisiens, with Polaire in the title role.
Henry de Jouvenel appointed editor-in-chief of *Le Matin* along with Stéphane Lauzanne. He is twenty-six.

1903
(thirty years of age)

Claudine s'en va published, signed Willy.
Willy prosecuted for *La Maîtresse de Jean*.
Claudine au concert column in "collaboration" with Willy.

October 31

Birth of Bertrand de Jouvenel.

1904
(thirty-one years of age)

Minne (Willy).
Dialogues des bêtes published, signed Colette Willy. She retains this signature until 1923.
Sale of Les Monts-Boucons.

1905
(thirty-two years of age)

Les Egarements de Minne, signed by Willy.

May 1	Legal separation (*séparation de biens*) filed. *Sept dialogues de bêtes*, with preface by Francis Jammes, signed Colette Willy.
September 17	Death of Jules-Joseph Colette. First mime lessons with Georges Wague.

1906

(thirty-three years of age)	Colette moves to 44, Rue de Villejust. Also lives at the Rue Georges-Ville, near the Etoile. Colette writes *La Retraite sentimentale*.
February 6	Première of mimodrame *Le Désir, l'Amour et la Chimère* at the Théâtre des Mathurins, based on a scenario by Francis de Croisset.
March	Theatrical debut of Willy in *Aux Innocents les mains pleines* at the Théâtre Royal.
October 1	Première of *La Romanichelle* at the Olympia with Colette Willy and Paul Frank.
November	Interlocutory divorce decreed.
November 28	Première of *Pan* with Colette Willy as Paniska, Théâtre Marigny.

1907

(thirty-four years of age)	*La Retraite sentimentale* published by Colette Willy.
January 3	Moulin Rouge scandal with *Rêve d'Egypte*.
February 13	Final divorce action declared.
March 13–16	*Rêve d'Egypte* performed in Nice.
April 27	Colette submits her first serial (*Les Vrilles de la vigne*) to *La Vie Parisienne*.
November 2	Première of mimodrame *La Chair*, with Colette Willy, Georges Wague and Marcel Valée (Christiane Kerf takes over the role in May 1908) at the Apollo. Summer in Crotoy at the mouth of the Somme with Missy at the Villa Belle-Plage.

1908

(thirty-five years of age)	*Les Vrilles de la vigne*, by Colette Willy.
March 10	First lecture at the Centre Fémina.
August 28	Colette performs in the play *Son premier voyage*, by Xanrof and Gunrin, in Geneva.
November 18–29	Performs Claudine, created by Polaire, for fifteen performances of the play in Brussels at the Alcazar (Missy in Brussels).
End of September	Moves to the Rue Saint-Sénoch.
December 10–17	Season at La Scala in Lyons with *Claudine à Paris*.

1909
(thirty-six years of age)   L'*Ingénue libertine*, by Colette Willy.

January–February   Performs in *En camarades*, written by herself, at the Théâtres des Arts and the Comédie Royale (with her dog).

February 14–17   *La Chair* in Brussels.

April–June   Tour in the south of France with *La Chair* and *Claudine à Paris* at the Gaité-Rochechouart.

                      La Chair performed in New York at the Manhattan Opera House.

                      Willy sells the rights to the *Claudine* novels to various publishers.

1910
(thirty-seven years of age)

February   *La Chair*, Brussels.

February–March   *La Chair* in Grenoble and Nice.

May 21–October 1   *La Vagabonde* appears in serial form in *La Vie Parisienne*.

June 21   Final divorce decree pronounced.

September 21–29   *La Chair*, Dijon.

November 14   Première of *Claudine*, three-act operetta by Willy, Henri Cain, Edouard Adenis and Henri Moreau, at the Moulin Rouge.

December 2   Colette begins publishing in *Le Matin*, where she meets Henry de Jouvenel (with *La Poison*, the first short story in the *Music Hall* series).

                      La Vagabonde obtains three votes for the Prix Goncourt.

                      Colette travels with Auguste Hériot (Naples and Nice).

1911
(thirty-eight years of age)   *La Vagabonde* published by Ollendorf.

                      Purchase of the house at Rozven.

April 15–27   *La Chair* at the Gaité-Montparnasse.

June 23–July 2   Series of performances of *La Chair* in Geneva and Lausanne.

July 31   Letter concerning the "Panther."

August   Première of mimodrame *Bat' d' Af'*.

                      Reprise of *La Chair* at L'Etoile-Palace.

                      Première of mimodrame, *L'Oiseau de nuit*, at the Gaité-Rochechouart (title suggested by Colette).

August 25   Moves to Hôtel Meurice.

October	Moves to Rue Cortambert.
	Colette hired by *Le Matin* to provide a column per week.
1912	
(thirty-nine years of age)	Colette appears at the Ba-Ta-Clan in *La Chatte amoureuse*, part of the revue *Ça grise*.
June 13	Colette goes up in the dirigible *Clement-Bayard*.
June 16–17	Reports on the Grand Prix de l'Aviation et l'Aero-Club de France in Angers for *Le Matin*.
September 26	Sido dies.
December 19	Colette marries Henry de Jouvenel.
1913	
(forty years of age)	*L'Entrave*, *l'Envers du music-hall*, *Prrou, Poucette et quelques autres*, published by Colette Willy. Colette uses this signature until 1923.
January	Report on the election of President Raymond Poincaré at Versailles.
July 3	Birth of Colette de Jouvenel, "Bel-Gazou," in Paris.
October 30	"Journal de Colette" added as byline to her column *Contes des mille et un matins*.
December 31	Death of Achille Robineau in Paris.
1914	
(forty-one years of age)	
August 2	Henry de Jouvenel mobilized in 23rd Infantry Regiment.
	Colette night-nurse at Lycée Janson-de-Sailly and leaves for Verdun in December, spending New Year's Day in the Argonne.
	Meets Francis Carco at *L'Éclair*, where Annie de Pène is editor.
1915	
(forty-two years of age)	Trip to Rome and Venice.
	Contributes to *Le Film* (edited by Diamant-Berger).
1916	
(forty-three years of age)	*La Paix chez les bêtes*.
	Assists Georges Wague in obtaining a class in pantomime at the Conservatoire.
	The film, *La Vagabonde*, is made in Italy, with Musidora.

1917	
(forty-four years of age)	Colette moves to 62, Boulevard Suchet, Auteuil. *Les Heures longues, Les Enfants dans les ruines* published. Jouvenel begins his political career, appointed French delegate to the Allied Commission in Rome, where Colette accompanies him.
1918	
(forty-five years of age)	*Dans la Foule.* Death of Annie de Pène. Jouvenel member of the French delegation to the Geneva Disarmament Commission.
1919	
(forty-six years of age)	*Mitsou, ou, Comment l'esprit vient aux filles,* published (followed by *En Camarades*). Colette named literary editor at *Le Matin*. Meets Léopold Marchand.
1920	
(forty-seven years of age)	
January 3–June 5	*Chéri* appears in serial form in *La Vie Parisienne* and is published in book form. *La Chambre éclairée.*
Spring	Bertrand de Jouvenel (aged sixteen) pays a call on his stepmother.
September 25	Colette named chevalier of the Légion d'Honneur.
Summer	Vacation in Rozven with Bertrand de Jouvenel.
1921	
(forty-eight years of age)	*Chéri* made into a play by Colette and Léopold Marchand.
December 13	Première of *Chéri* at the Théâtre Michel. Henry de Jouvenel elected senator from Corrèze.
1922	
(forty-nine years of age)	*La Maison de Claudine, Le voyage égoiste.* The family home in Saint-Sauveur purchased by M. Ducharne.
September 22	Henry de Jouvenel appointed French delegate to the League of Nations.
February 28	For the 100th performance of *Chéri*, Colette appears in the role of Léa.
April	Trip to Algeria. *Le Blé en herbe* is published in serial form in *Le Matin*; written at Rozven.

1923

(fifty years of age)	*Le Blé en herbe, Rêverie de nouvel an,* published with signature Colette.
February	Première at Théâtre de la Renaissance of *La Vagabonde,* adapted by Colette and Léopold Marchand.
March	Colette takes *Chéri* on tour.
November–December	Colette gives a series of lectures in the south of France.
December	Separation of Colette and Henry de Jouvenel.

1924

(fifty-one years of age)	
January	Skiing with Bertrand de Jouvenel.
	La Femme cachée, Aventures quotidiennes.
February	Colette ends her collaboration with *Le Matin.* She begins appearing regularly in *Le Figaro, Le Quotidien, L'Eclair,* etc.
March 29–June 1	Henry de Jouvenel appointed Minister for Public Education in the Poincaré cabinet.
December	Performs in *Chéri* in Monte Carlo and Marseilles.

1925

(fifty-two years of age)	
February–March	*Chéri* presented with Colette, Marguerite Moréno at the Théâtre-Daunou and the Théâtre de la Renaissance (support of Henri de Rothschild).
March 21	Première of *L'Enfant et les sortilèges,* libretto by Colette, music by Maurice Ravel, in Monte Carlo.
April	Colette meets Maurice Goudeket.
June	Colette spends her first vacation in Beauvallon in Provence.
August	Colette performs in *Chéri* in various casinos and spas.
October	*Chéri* in Brussels.
December	*Chéri* in Marseilles with Colette, Marguerite Moréno and Pierre Fresnay.
	Henry de Jouvenel appointed High Commissioner in Syria.

1926

(fifty-three years of age)	*La Fin de Chéri.*
February 1	*L'Enfant et les sortilèges* presented at the Opéra-Comique.

February	Colette invited to Morocco by the Glaoui. Purchases La Treille Muscate in Saint-Tropez. Colette moves in for the summer.
End of December	Performs *La Vagabonde* in Monte Carlo with Paul Poiret.

1927
(fifty-four years of age) Colette moves to 9, Rue de Beaujolais (entresol apartment) where she is to live until February 1930.

1928
(fifty-five years of age) *La Naissance du jour*; *Renée Vivien*.
November 5 Colette named officer of the Légion d'Honneur.

1929
(fifty-six years of age) *La Seconde*; *Sido ou les Points cardinaux. Regarde*.
March Trip to Spain and Tangiers.
June Visit to the Antwerp zoo.
September Begins work as a drama critic on *La Revue de Paris*.

Henry de Jouvenel reelected senator from the Corrèze.

Death of "Mamita," mother of Henry de Jouvenel.

1930
(fifty-seven years of age) *Sido, Histoires pour Bel-Gazou*.
February Trip to Berlin. Visit to the Sarrasini Circus.

La Vagabonde made into a film by Solange Bussy, with Marcelle Chantal as Renée Néré.
July Cruise with Henri de Rothschild in the *Eros* through the North Sea.

1931
(fifty-eight years of age) *Supplément à Don Juan*.
Colette moves to the Claridge hotel on the Champs Elysées.
January 12 Death of Willy.
February 24–March 7 Lecture tour in Austria and Romania.
April 5–23 Lectures in North Africa.
September 5 Breaks her leg.
December 4 *Ces plaisirs* appears in serial form in *Gringoire* until January 2, 1932.

1932
(fifty-nine years of age) *Paradis terrestres, La Treille Muscate, Prisons et paradis, Ces Plaisirs*.

June 1	Colette opens a beauty institute at 6, Rue de Miromesnil, Paris (with the support of the Pacha of Marrakesh and the Princesse de Polignac).
Summer	Lectures and demonstrations to promote her line of beauty products.

1933
(sixty years
of age)

La Chatte.
Colette writes dialogue for Marc Allégret's film
Lac aux dames.

June–July

October 8 — Colette begins weekly drama criticism in *Le Journal.*

1934
(sixty-one years
of age)

Duo, La Jumelle noir, volume one.

September — Writes dialogue for Max Ophuls's film *Divine.*

1935
(sixty-two years
of age)

First Cahier de Colette.
Second Cahier de Colette.
Third Cahier de Colette.
La Jumelle noir, second volume.

April 3 — Colette marries Maurice Goudeket.

June — Voyage to New York, maiden voyage of the *Normandie.*

October — Death of Henry de Jouvenel (following a visit to the Salon d'Automne).

1936
(sixty-three years
of age)

Fourth Cahier de Colette.
Mes apprentissages; Chats.

February 26 — Colette promoted to commander, Légion d'Honneur.

March — Moves to the Marignan building.

April 4 — Acceptance speech at the Académie royale de langue et littérature de Belgique, where Colette succeeds to the chair of Anna de Noailles.

1937
(sixty-four years
of age)

Claudine à l'école made into a film by Serge de Polignac.
Bella Vista; Splendeur des papillons; Claudine et Les Contes de fées.
La Jumelle noire, volume three.

1938
(sixty-five years
of age)

Paris. La Jumelle noire, fourth volume.
Trip to Fez for *Paris-Soir* (trial of Oum el Hassen).
Sale of La Treille Muscate.

Colette moves to 9, Rue de Beaujolais, first floor, where she will live until her death.

October 10   *Duo* adapted by Paul Géraldy and performed at the Théâtre Saint-Georges in Paris.

Maurice Goudeket turns to journalism (*Paris-Soir*, *Match*, *Marie-Claire*).

1939
(sixty-six years
  of age)   *Le Toutounier.*

October 11   Death of Polaire.

August   Vacation in Dieppe with Léopold Marchand.
Purchase of Méré (Villa le Parc in Montfort l'Amaury).
Colette begins to suffer from arthritis.

1940
(sixty-seven years
  of age)   *Chambre d'hôtel.*
Colette makes a series of broadcasts to America.

March 7   Death of Léo Colette, her younger brother.

June 12   Colette goes to Curemont en Corrèze to her daughter (the exodus from Paris).

September 11   She returns to Paris.

1941
(sixty-eight years
  of age)   *Journal à rebours*; *Julie de Carneilhan.*

December 12   Maurice Goudeket arrested by the Germans.

1942
(sixty-nine years
  of age)   *De ma fenêtre.*

February 6   Maurice Goudeket freed.

1943
(seventy years
  of age)   *Le Képi*; *De la patte à l'aile*; *Flore et Pomone*; *Nudité.*
Colette begins suffering acutely from arthritis of the hip. Has increasing difficulty moving about.

1944
(seventy-one years
  of age)   *Gigi.*
Trois . . . Six . . . Neuf.
Broderie ancienne.
Missy commits suicide at eighty-one years of age.

1945
(seventy-two years
  of age)   *Belles Saisons.*

| May 2 | Colette is unanimously elected to fill the post of Sacha Guitry on the Académie Goncourt (the first female member). |
| | She names Maurice Goudeket as her heir in her will. |

1946
(seventy-three years
of age)   *L'Etoile vesper; Flore.*

March–April   Trip to Geneva, where Colette undergoes treatment for arthritis.

July   Treatment at Uriage.

1947
(seventy-four years
of age)   Second cure in Geneva. Colette resigns herself to being immobile.

1948
(seventy-five years
of age)   *Pour un herbier.*
                                 Oeuvres complètes begin to be published.

July 14   Death of Marguerite Moréno.
                                 Gigi made into a film by Jacqueline Audry and Pierre Laroche.

1949
(seventy-six years
of age)   *Le Fanal bleu.*
                                 Colette collects her newspaper articles into *Trait pour trait*, *Journal intermittent*, *La Fleur de l'âge*, *En pays connu.*

October   Elected president of the Académie Goncourt, succeeding Lucien Descaves.
                                 Chéri, reworked by Colette, is performed at the Théâtre de la Madeleine, directed by Jean Wall.
                                 Julie de Carneilhan brought to the screen with Edwige Feuillère.

1950
(seventy-seven years
of age)   First trip to Monte Carlo at the Hôtel de Paris, where she returns each year.
                                 Chéri made into a film.

1951
(seventy-eight years
of age)   Première on Broadway of *Gigi*, adapted by Anita Loos, starring Audrey Hepburn.
                                 La Seconde made into a film with Maria Casarès, Hélène Perdrière and André Luguet.
                                 Film by Yannick Bellon on Colette.

1953
(eighty years
of age)   *Paradis terrestre*, with photos by Izis.

January	Colette receives Grande Médaille de la Ville de Paris.
April 13	Première of *Ciel de lit* (The Fourposter), by Jan de Hartog, adapted by Colette, at the Théâtre de la Michodière.
April 20	Colette is made a grand officier of the Légion d'Honneur, installed by André Marie, Ministre de l'Education Nationale.
May 2–9	Douglas Dillon, Ambassador of the United States, presents her with the citation of the National Institute of Arts and Letters of America, in the presence of the Prince of Monaco, Roland Dorgelès, Prof. Mondor and Maitre Maurice Garçon.

1954
(eighty-one years of age)

January 9	Première of Claude Autant-Lara's film of *Le Blé en herbe*.
February 22	Première of *Gigi* at the Théâtre des Arts, directed by Jean Meyer, with Evelyne Kerr.
August 3	Death of Colette.
August 7	Secular state funeral. Colette is buried in the Père Lachaise cemetery. Letter of protest from Graham Greene.

Notes

Foreword
1. Elena Gianini Belotti, *Du côté des petites filles*, Des femmes, 1973

I Gabrielle—The Child's Way

The Cradle
1. *Le Fanal bleu*, Flammarion, Paris, 1976
2. Ibid.
3. *La Maison de Claudine*
4. *Sido*
5. *La Maison de Claudine*
6. Research by M. Amblard, quoted by M. Raaphorst-Rousseau, *Colette, sa vie, son oeuvre*, Nizet, Paris 1964

Sido, Beneficent Goddess
1. *La Maison de Claudine*
2. Les Etudes ardennaises, quoted by M. Raaphorst-Rousseau, op. cit.
3. Ibid.
4. *L'Etoile vesper*
5. *La Maison de Claudine*
6. Raaphorst-Rousseau, op. cit.
7. Les Etudes ardennaises, April, 1957
8. *Sido*
9. *La Maison de Claudine*
10. *Lettres de Sido à Colette*, Le Figaro Littéraire, January 24, 1953
11. *En pays connu*
12. *La Maison de Claudine*
13. Ibid.
14. Ibid.
15. Raaphorst-Rousseau, op. cit.
16. *Le Figaro Littéraire*, November 1, 1956
17. *Aventures quotidiennes*

Captain Jules Colette, the One-Legged Zouave
1. *Le Pur et l'impur*
2. *Les heures longues*
3. Ibid.
4. *Sido*
5. Ibid.
6. Ibid.
7. *Journal à rebours*
8. Research by M. Amblard, quoted by M. Raaphorst-Rousseau, op. cit.
9. *La Maison de Claudine*
10. Annie Leclerc, *Parole de femme, Grasset*, Paris 1974

Celebrating Deeds and Days

1 *L'etoile vesper*
2 Ibid.
3 *Journal à rebours*
4 Ibid.
5 Ibid.
6 Ibid.
7 Ibid.
8 Ibid.
9 Annie Leclerc, op. cit.
10 *Les Vrilles de la vigne*
11 Ibid.
12 *En pays connu*
13 Ibid.
14 *Les Vrilles de la vigne*
15 *Paysages et portraits*

The Primal Source

1 *Sido*
2 *Journal à rebours*
3 *Sido*
4 *Claudine en ménage*
5 *Sido*
6 *Paysages et portraits*

Female Lore

1 *Journal à rebours*
2 Ibid.
3 *Sido*
4 Ibid.
5 Ibid.
6 *La Maison de Claudine*
7 Ibid.
8 Ibid.
9 *Sido*

The Wild Brothers

1 *Claudine à l'école*
2 *Journal à rebours*
3 *Sido*
4 Ibid.
5 *La Maison de Claudine*
6 *Journal à rebours*
7 *Sido*

My Long-Haired Sister

1 *Sido*
2 Ibid.
3 Ibid.
4 Ibid.

5 Ibid.
6 Ibid.
7 Ibid.
8 Raaphorst-Rousseau, op. cit.
9 *La Maison de Claudine*
10 Ibid.
11 Ibid.
12 Ibid.
13 Annie Leclerc, op. cit.

"The Pure and the Impure"
1 *La Maison de Claudine*
2 Ibid.
3 Ibid.
4 Ibid.
5 Ibid.
6 Ibid.
7 Ibid.
8 Ibid.
9 Ibid.
10 Ibid.
11 Ibid.
12 Ibid.
13 Ibid.
14 Ibid.
15 Ibid.
16 Ibid.
17 Ibid.
18 Ibid.
19 Ibid.
20 Annie Leclerc, op. cit.
21 *La Maison de Claudine*
22 Ibid.
23 Ibid.
24 Annie Leclerc, op. cit.
25 *La Maison de Claudine*
26 Ibid.
27 Ibid.
28 *Claudine à Paris*

Sido, Practicing Pagan
1 *La Maison de Claudine*
2 *Sido*
3 Ibid.
4 Ibid.
5 Ibid.
6 Ibid.
7 *Les Vrilles de la vigne*
8 *Sido*
9 Ibid.

The Provinces

1 Margaret Crosland, *Colette, A Provincial in Paris*, Peter Owen, London, 1953
2 *Journal à rebours*
3 *Sido*
4 Ibid.
5 Ibid.
6 Ibid.
7 Ibid.
8 Ibid.
9 *La Maison de Claudine*
10 Ibid.

Public School and Social Decline

1 *Claudine à l'école*
2 *Aventures quotidiennes*
3 Prost, *Histoire de l'enseignement en France*, Armand Colin, 1968
4 Jean Larnac, *Colette, sa vie, son oeuvre*, Krâ, Paris 1927
5 *Editions des femmes*, Paris 1973
6 *Claudine à l'école*
7 Ibid.
8 Ibid.

School Days

1 *Claudine à l'école*
2 Ibid.
3 Ibid.
4 *Claudine à Paris*
5 *Journal à rebours*
6 Ibid.

Girl Friends

1 *Paysages et portraits*
2 Ibid.
3 Ibid.
4 *La Maison de Claudine*
5 Ibid.
6 Ibid.

Saint-Sauveur: The Other Side of School Life

1 *La Maison de Claudine*
2 Léon Dubreuil, *Le brevet de Colette, Le Cerf-volant*, no. 2, July 18, 1957
3 *Claudine à l'école*
4 Ibid.
5 André Gaucher, "Son Excellence, le Dr. Merlou," foreword, Société nouvelle d'éditions parisiennes, 1906
6 Lettres d'institutrices rurales d'autrefois. Association des amis du musée pédagogique (inquiry undertaken by Francisque Sarcey in

1897 following the publication of Léon Frapié's controversial book, *L'institutrice de province*)

The Daughters of the Poor in the Nineteenth Century

1 *Claudine à Paris*
2 Michèle Blin, "Une pédagogie pour jeunes filles pauvres de *Claudine à l'école* à *Mes apprentissages*," *Revue Romantisme*, 13–14, 1976
3 Lucille Sauvan, *A Training Course for Primary School Teachers*, Pitois-Levrault et Cie, Paris
4 *Claudine à l'école*
5 *Les femmes et le travail du Moyen Age à nos jours*, various authors, Editions de la Courtille, Paris 1975
6 Julie Daubie, Librairie de Guillaumin et Cie., Paris 1860
7 Evelyne Sullerot: *Histoire et Sociologie du travail féminin*, Edition Gauthier, Paris 1968
8 *Journal à rebours*
9 Daubie, op. cit.

II   WILLY—Days of Contempt

A Mixture of Satyr and Prince Charming

1 Natalie Clifford Barney, *Souvenirs indiscrets*, Flammarion, 1960
2 *Mes apprentissages*
3 *La Vagabonde*
4 *Mes apprentissages*

Henry Gauthier-Villars, Father/Husband

1 Quoted in *Catalogue de l'exposition Colette*, Bibliothèque Nationale, Paris 1973
2 Sylvain Bonmariage, *Willy, Colette et moi*, Editions Frémanger, Paris 1954
3 Paul d'Hollander, *Colette à l'heure de Willy*, thèse dactylographiée, 1976 (in preparation, Presses de l'Université de Montréal et Editions Klincksieck)
4 Willy, *Commentaires et indiscrétions sur les "Claudine,"* Pro Amicis, Paris 1962

Curious Engagement

1 *Lettres inédites de Sido à Colette*, Raaphorst-Rousseau, Rice University Studies, 1973
2 Ibid.
3 Ibid.
4 Ibid.
5 *Noces*
6 d'Hollander, op. cit.
7 Pierre Champion, *Marcel Schwob et son temps*, Grasset, Paris 1927
8 *Willy et Meg Villars*, Société d'éditions et de publications, Paris 1911

The Wedding

1 *Noces*

2 Ibid.
3 Ibid.
4 Simone de Beauvoir, *Le deuxième sexe*, Gallimard, Paris 1951
5 *Noces*
6 Ibid.
7 Ibid.
8 Simone de Beauvoir, op. cit.
9 Ibid.
10 *Noces*

Ingénue and Libertine
1 Marie-Jeanne Viel, *Un mariage pas comme les autres*, Paris-Presse l'Intransigeant, March 1957
2 *Claudine à Paris*
3 *Mes apprentissages*
4 Ibid.
5 *Trois . . . Six . . . Neuf*
6 *Mes apprentissages*
7 Ibid.
8 Claude Boncompain, *Colette*, Confluences, Lyons, 1945
9 *La Vagabonde*
10 *Mes apprentissages*

Baptism
1 *La Vagabonde*
2 *Mes apprentissages*
3 Ibid.
4 Ibid.
5 Ibid.
6 Ibid.
7 Ibid.
8 Ibid.

Marcel Schwob, Sacha Guitry, and Others
1 Champion, op. cit.
2 *Mes apprentissages*
3 Yvonne Lanco, *Colette à Belle-Isle-en-Mer*, March 1955
4 *Mes apprentissages*
5 Ibid.
6 Ibid.
7 *Lettres à ses pairs*
8 *Mes apprentissages*

A One-Man Band in the Belle Epoque
1 *Lettres à ses pairs*
2 A. Ketchum, *Colette ou la naissance du jour: étude d'un malentendu*, Minard, Paris 1968, and Charles Ledré, *Histoire de la presse*, Fayard, Paris 1945
3 *Henri de Madaillan*, quoted by Bonmariage, op. cit.

Rue Jacob: La Vie de Bohème

1 Claude Chauvière, *Colette*, Firmin-Didot, Paris 1931
2 *Mes apprentissages*
3 Ibid.
4 Ibid.

"De la musique avant toute chose . . ."

1 La Hire, *Ménage d'artistes*, Bibliothèque Indépendante d'Editions, Paris 1905; "Colette Willy," *Revue illustrée*
2 La Hire, op. cit.
3 *Revue illustrée*, cf. supra.

A Provincial Girl in Salon Society

1 *En pays connu*
2 *La Vagabonde*
3 *La Jumelle noire*
4 Léo Paillet, *Dans la ménagerie littéraire*, Baudinière, Paris 1925

The Slave Trade—One Character in Search of Authors

1 *Mes apprentissages*
2 Ibid.
3 Ibid.
4 Ibid.
5 Marcel Thiébault, "De Claudine à Colette," *Revue de Paris*, August 1957
6 *Mes apprentissages*
7 *Le Képi*
8 *Mes apprentissages*
9 H. Martineau, "Jean-Paul Toulet, collaborateur de Willy," *Mercure de France*, October 1956
10 Ibid.
11 Ibid.
12 *Mes apprentissages*
13 d'Hollander, op. cit.

White Slavery: The Claudine Novels

1 d'Hollander, op. cit.
2 Jeanne Roge, *La Grive*, "Les sources de Colette"
3 *Mes apprentissages*
4 Ibid.
5 Ibid.
6 H. Lefebvre, "Une heure avec . . . Colette," Interview, *Nouvelles Littéraires*, March 27, 1926
7 d'Hollander, op. cit.
8 *Mes apprentissages*
9 Ibid.
10 Willy, *Commentaires et indiscrétions sur les "Claudine,"* op. cit.
11 Unpublished letter from Colette to Rachilde; quoted in *Catalogue de l'exposition Colette*, op. cit.

12 Ibid.
13 d'Hollander, op. cit.
14 *Mes apprentissages*

The Belle Epoque and Its Creatures
1 Jean Cocteau, *Colette*, Grasset, Paris 1955
2 Ibid.
3 Ibid.
4 Ibid.
5 Ibid.
6 Natalie Clifford Barney, op. cit.
7 Ibid.
8 Bonmariage, op. cit.
9 *Aden Arabie*
10 *Mes apprentissages*
11 Paillet, op. cit.
12 *Mes apprentissages*
13 Ibid.
14 André Billy, *L'époque 1900*, Editions Jules Taillandier, Paris 1956
15 Ibid.
16 *Mes apprentissages*
17 Ibid.
18 Ibid.
19 Ibid.
20 Ibid.

Claudine and the "Affair"
1 Bonmariage, op. cit.
2 Willy, *Souvenirs littéraires et autres*, Montaigne, Paris 1925
3 *En pays connu*
4 Ibid.
5 George Painter, *Marcel Proust, a Biography*, Chatto & Windus, London 1961
6 Willy, *Commentaires et indiscrétions sur les "Claudine,"* op. cit.
7 *Claudine à Paris*
8 Willy, cf. supra.

Some Women
1 Jean Larnac, *Histoire de la littérature féminine en France*, Krâ, Paris 1929
2 Sylvia Weil-Sayre and Mary Collins, *L'Histoire du féminisme en France*, and Maïté Albistur and Daniel Armogathe, *Des femmes*, 1977, *L'Histoire du féminisme français.*
3 Carpentier, *Divorce et séparation du corps*, Larose, 1829
4 Article 217, Code Civil, Loi de 1804
5 Carpentier, op. cit.
6 Ibid.
7 Article 217, Code Civil, Loi de 1804

The Scandalous Claudines

1 Sacha Guitry, quoted in La Hire, op. cit.
2 M. Boulestin, *Petite Revue du Midi*, 1903
3 Willy, *Commentaires et indiscrétions sur les "Claudine,"* op. cit.
4 Ibid.
5 Ibid.
6 *Lettres à ses pairs*, Colette to J. Muhlfeld, early 1902
7 d'Hollander, op. cit.
8 Paul d'Hollander has undertaken a comparison between this edition of *Claudine amoureuse* and the manuscript of *Claudine en ménage* retained by Paul Barlet. According to him, Willy can be given credit for 380 changes in punctuation, 176 substitutions, corrections, additions, suppressions of notes and 50 changes in sentences. Later, Colette removed many of the considerable changes made by her collaborator from the collected edition, among them a conversation concerning writers and certain passages dealing with the character of Maugis.

Polaire

1 Jean Cocteau, *Colette*, op. cit.
2 *Mes apprentissages*
3 Ibid.
4 Ibid.
5 Ibid.
6 Ibid.
7 Ibid.

Maugis the King

1 *Mes apprentissages*
2 Ibid.
3 La Hire, op. cit.
4 *Mes apprentissages*
5 Raaphorst-Rousseau, op. cit.
6 E. Charles, "Le Cas Willy," *Revue Bleue*, 1905
7 Ibid.

The Vicious Triangle

1 Bonmariage, op. cit.
2 *L'Etoile vesper*
3 *Lettres de Sido*, Le Figaro Littéraire, January 24, 1953
4 d'Hollander, op. cit.
5 Bonmariage, op. cit.
6 *Mes apprentissages*
7 Ibid.

Voluntary Servitude

1 *Claudine en ménage*
2 *Mes apprentissages*
3 Ibid.

The Isosceles Triangle

1 *La Vagabonde*
2 Claude Chauvière, op. cit.
3 *Mes apprentissages*
4 *Le Pur et l'Impur*
5 Bonmariage, op. cit.
6 *Claudine en ménage*
7 Willy, *Commentaires*, op. cit.
8 d'Hollander, op. cit.
9 Willy, *Commentaires*, op. cit.

A La Suivante!

1 *Dialogues des bêtes*
2 *Mes apprentissages*
3 *Trois . . . Six . . . Neuf*
4 Ibid.
5 *Mes apprentissages*
6 *La Vagabonde*

The Stubborn China Repairer

1 Natalie Clifford Barney, op. cit.
2 *Mes apprentissages*

The Claudine Epic: From the Cage to the Door

1 *Claudine à Paris*
2 Ibid.
3 *Claudine en ménage*
4 *Claudine s'en va*

The Chrysalis

1 *Trois . . . Six . . . Neuf*
2 Ibid.
3 *Mes apprentissages*
4 Ibid.
5 Ibid.
6 d'Hollander, op. cit.
7 *Mes apprentissages*
8 Ibid.
9 Ibid.
10 Ibid.
11 Ibid.

Getting Out: The Poetry of Expulsion

1 *Mes apprentissages*
2 Ibid.
3 Ibid.
4 Ibid.
5 Ibid.
6 Ibid.
7 Ibid.

8 Ibid.
9 d'Hollander, op. cit.
10 *Mes apprentissages*
11 Ibid.
12 Ibid.
13 Ibid.
14 Ibid.

III COLETTE WILLY—COLETTEVILI—Free and Enslaved

The Escape
1 Bonmariage, op. cit.
2 *La Vagabonde*
3 *Trois . . . Six . . . Neuf*
4 Ibid.
5 *Gribiche* (Bella Vista)
6 *Trois . . . Six . . . Neuf*
7 *Mes apprentissages*
8 Ibid.

The Moulin-Rouge Scandal
1 Fernand Hauser, *Le Journal*, November 17, 1906
2 *Lettres de la vagabonde*, footnote to letter to Christiane Mendelys, November 25, 1906
3 d'Hollander, op. cit.
4 Jean Larnac, op. cit.

Divorce
1 Letter contained in the catalogue of the bookseller Bernard Collet
2 d'Hollander, op. cit., quoted from "Willy et Colette, un couple célèbre de la Belle Epoque," *Oeuvres libres*, October 1959
3 *La Vagabonde*
4 *Mes apprentissages*
5 *Lettres de la vagabonde*
6 d'Hollander, op. cit.
7 Willy, *Commentaires*, op. cit.
8 Ibid.
9 Bonmariage, op. cit.
10 *Lettres de la vagabonde*
11 *La Vagabonde*
12 *Lettres à ses pairs*
13 *La Vagabonde*

The Farcical Baroness
1 H. Martineau, op. cit.
2 Ibid.
3 Ibid.
4 Willy, *Lélie, fumeuse d'opium*, Albin Michel, Paris 1911
5 Ibid.
6 *Lettres de la vagabonde*

A Rough Life

1 *La Vagabonde*
2 Bonmariage, op. cit.
3 *La Vagabonde*
4 *Dialogues des bêtes*
5 *La Vagabonde*
6 Ibid.
7 Preface to *Lettres de la vagabonde*, Claude Pichois and Roberte Fortin
8 Ibid.
9 *Lettres de Sido, Le Figaro Littéraire*, January 24, 1954
10 Ibid., letter dated February 16, 1908
11 Ibid.
12 Letter from Sido dated March 1, 1909, private collection, quoted in *Catalogue de l'exposition Colette*, op. cit.

Another Step Down in the World

1 *Lettres à ses pairs*
2 Quoted in *Catalogue de l'exposition Colette*, op. cit.
3 *Les Vrilles de la vigne*
4 Ibid.
5 Ibid.
6 Ibid.
7 Ibid.
8 *La Vagabonde*
9 Ibid.
10 Ibid.
11 Ibid.
12 Ibid.
13 Ibid.
14 Ibid.

The Female Cavalier

1 *Mes apprentissages*
2 *Le Pur et l'Impur*
3 Bonmariage, op. cit.
4 Ibid.
5 Ibid.
6 Ibid.
7 Ibid.
8 *Le Pur et l'Impur*

In Lesbos

1 Jean Chalon, *Portrait d'une séductrice*, Stock, Paris 1976
2 Ibid.
3 *Le Pur et l'Impur*
4 Ibid.
5 Ibid.
6 Ibid.

The Amazons

1 *Le Pur et l'Impur*
2 Chalon, op. cit.
3 George Painter, op. cit.
4 Ibid.
5 Chalon, op. cit.
6 Natalie Clifford Barney, op. cit.
7 Lucie Delarue-Mardrus, quoted in Painter, op. cit.
8 *Le Pur et l'Impur*
9 Ibid.
10 Ibid.

Gomorrah as Seen from Sodom

1 Painter, op. cit.
2 *Le Pur et l'Impur*
3 Painter, op. cit.
4 *La Vagabonde*
5 S. de Beauvoir, *Le Deuxième Sexe*, vol. 2, op. cit.
6 H. Harris, *L' approfondissement de la sensualité dans l'oeuvre de Colette*, Nizet, Paris 1976
7 *Le Pur et l'Impur*
8 Ibid.

The Ladies of Llangollen

1 *Le Pur et l'Impur*
2 Ibid.
3 Ibid.
4 Ibid.
5 Ibid.

Missy, the Good Fairy

1 *Le Pur et l'Impur*
2 *Les Vrilles de la vigne*
3 *Lettres de la vagabonde*
4 Chalon, op. cit.
5 S. de Beauvoir, op. cit.
6 *La Vagabonde*
7 *Les Vrilles de la vigne*
8 Ibid.
9 Remy de Gourmont, *IIIe Lettre à l'Amazone*, Mercure de France, Paris 1913

Mirages of Male-Female?

1 *Le Pur et l'Impur*
2 Ibid.
3 Ibid.
4 Ibid.
5 S. de Beauvoir, op. cit.
6 *Le Pur et l'Impur*

Notes

Ibid.
Ibid.
Ibid.
10 Françoise d'Eaubonne, Buchet Chastel, 1962

The End of the Boulevard
1 André Billy, *L'Epoque contemporaine*, Jules Taillandier, Paris 1956
2 Ibid.
3 *Lettres à Marguerite Moréno*
4 Billy, op. cit.
5 Ibid.
6 Ibid.
7 *Paysages et portraits*

Opium Dens—The Lament of the Nightingale
1 *Le Pur et l'Impur*
2 Ibid.
3 Ibid.
4 Bonmariage, op. cit.
5 Billy, op. cit.

From the Lapin Agile to the Semiramis Bar
1 Billy, op. cit.
2 Bonmariage, op. cit.
3 *Lettres de la vagabonde*
4 *Paysages et portraits*
5 Ibid.
6 *La Vagabonde*

Hide and Seek with the Audience
1 *Gribiche (Bella Vista)*
2 *La Vagabonde*
3 S. de Beauvoir, op. cit.
4 Yannick Resh, *Corps féminin, corps textuel*, Klincksieck, 1973
5 Ibid.
6 *La Vagabonde*

"Let Out a Breast!"
1 *Les Vrilles de la vigne*
2 *L'Entrave*
3 *Mercure de France*, June 1, 1926
4 *Mercure de France*, December 1, 1913

Traveling Companions, Enfants du Paradis
1 F. Lefebvre, *Une heure avec . . .* fourth series
2 *La Vagabonde*
3 Ibid.
4 Ibid.
5 Ibid.
6 *L'Envers du music-hall*
7 *La Vagabonde*

8 Ibid.
9 Ibid.
10 Ibid.
11 Ibid.
12 Ibid.
13 Ibid.
14 Ibid.
15 *L'Envers du music-hall*
16 Ibid.
17 Ibid.
18 Ibid.

The caf' conc'—Total Exploitation
1 *Gribiche*
2 *L'Envers du music-hall*

Miseries
1 *L'Envers du music-hall*
2 Ibid.
3 Ibid.
4 Ibid.
5 Ibid.
6 Ibid.
7 *Gribiche*
8 Ibid.
9 Ibid.
10 Ibid.
11 *L'Envers du music-hall*
12 Ibid.
13 Ibid.

The Variety Girls: Factory and Laundry
1 *Gribiche*
2 *L'Envers du music-hall*
3 Ibid.
4 Ibid.
5 Ibid.
6 Ibid.
7 Ibid.
8 Ibid.
9 Ibid.
10 *La Vagabonde*

Strike
1 *La Vagabonde*
2 *L'Envers du music-hall*
3 Ibid.

Carnal Sirens
1 *La Vagabonde*
2 S. de Beauvoir, op. cit.

3 *La Vagabonde*
4 Ibid.
5 Ibid.
6 Ibid.
7 Ibid.
8 Ibid.
9 *Les Vrilles de la vigne*
10 Ibid.
11 *La Vagabonde*
12 Ibid.
13 Ibid.
14 Ibid.

Willfully Free
1 *La Vagabonde*
2 *La Naissance du jour*
3 *La Vagabonde*
4 Ibid.
5 Ibid.
6 Ibid.
7 Ibid.
8 Ibid.
9 Ibid.
10 Ibid.

The Springs of Writing
1 *La Vagabonde*
2 Ibid.
3 Ibid.
4 Ibid.

IV COLETTE de JOUVENEL—Sharing at Noon

The Trap
1 *La Vagabonde*

The Baron
1 *Troix . . . Six . . . Neuf*
2 *Lettres de la vagabonde*
3 Ibid.
4 Ibid.
5 *Dictionnaire des parlementaires français*, biographical notes on ministers, députés and sénateurs from 1889 to 1940, vol. 6, P.U.F., 1970
6 *L'Entrave*

The Cat and the Panther
1 *Lettres de la vagabonde*, Claude Pichois's note to letter from Colette to L. Hamel
2 Ibid.
3 Letter to Renaud de Jouvenel, Autumn 1937, *Revue de Paris*, December 1966

4 *Lettres à ses pairs*
5 *Lettres de la vagabonde*

Sidi: Early Skirmishes
1   *Trois . . . Six . . . Neuf*
2   *L'Etoile vesper*
3   *Lettres de la vagabonde*, letter to Christiane Mendelys, August 29, 1911
4   Ibid., letter to Léon Hamel, end of April 1912
5   Ibid., letter to Hamel, June 10
6   Ibid., July 10, 1912
7   Ibid., July 20, 1912
8   Ibid.
9   Ibid., August 6, 1912
10 *Julie de Carneilhan*
11 Ibid.
12 *L'Entrave*
13 *Lettres de la vagabonde*, to Léon Hamel
14 Ibid.

Sido's Death
1   *Lettres inédites de Sido à Colette*, op. cit.
2   Ibid.
3   *La Naissance du jour*
4   Ibid.
5   Ibid.
6   Ibid.
7   *La Maison de Claudine*
8   Ibid.
9   *Lettres inédites de Sido à Colette*, op. cit.
10 *Lettres de la vagabonde*

A Real Baroness
1   *Lettres de la vagabonde*
2   Ibid.

The Fetter
1   *Lettres au petit corsaire*, 1939
2   *L'Entrave*
3   Ibid.
4   Ibid.
5   Ibid.
6   Ibid.
7   Ibid.
8   Ibid.
9   Ibid.
10 Ibid.
11 Ibid.
12 Ibid.
13 Ibid.
14 Ibid.

15   Ibid.
16   Ibid.
17   Ibid.
18   *Lettres de la vagabonde*
19   *L'Etoile vesper*
20   S. de Beauvoir, op. cit.

Sultana and the Male Whore
1   *Lettres de la vagabonde*
2   *Julie de Carneilhan*
3   *La Naissance du jour*
4   *L'Entrave*
5   Ibid.
6   *Julie de Carneilhan*
7   *L'Entrave*

Motherhood
1   *L'Entrave*
2   *L'Etoile Vesper*
3   Ibid.
4   Ibid.
5   Ibid.
6   Ibid.
7   Ibid.
8   Ibid.
9   Ibid.
10   Claude Chauvière, op. cit.
11   *Paysages et Portraits*
12   Ibid.
13   Ibid.
14   *L'Etoile vesper*

Journalist
1   *L'Etoile Vesper*
2   Ibid.
3   Ibid.
4   Ibid.
5   Ibid.
6   Ibid.
7   Ibid.
8   Ibid.
9   Ibid.
10   Ibid.
11   Ibid.
12   Ibid.
13   Ibid.
14   Ibid.

The Sequestered Model
1   *La Vagabonde*

2 *Paysages et Portraits*
3 *Trois . . . Six . . . Neuf*
4 Ibid.
5 Francis Carco, *Colette mon ami*, Rive Gauche, Paris 1965
6 *Trois . . . Six . . . Neuf*

August 1914
1 *Lettres de la vagabonde*
2 *Les Heures longues*
3 Ibid.
4 Ibid.
5 Extract from a letter belonging to Maître Louis Guitard and Mme Ginette Guitard-Auviste, quoted in *Catalogue de l'exposition Colette*, op. cit.

In the Rear Lines
1 *Lettres de la vagabonde*, letter to Christiane Kerf
2 *Le Fanal bleu*
3 Ibid.
4 *Lettres de la vagabonde*, letter to Léon Hamel, September 17, 1914
5 Ibid.
6 Ibid.
7 Letter belonging to Mme Colette de Jouvenel, quoted in *Catalogue*, op. cit.
8 Letter from H. de Jouvenel belonging to Maître Guitard and Mme Guitard-Auviste, quoted in *Catalogue*, op. cit.
9 *Le Fanal bleu*
10 *Lettres de la Vagabonde*

Verdun
1 *Les Heures longues*
2 Ibid.
3 Ibid.
4 Ibid.
5 Ibid.
6 Ibid.
7 Ibid.

Colette's War
1 *Lettres de la vagabonde*
2 *Les Heures longues*
3 Ibid.
4 *Lettres de la vagabonde*, letter to Georges Wague
5 Ibid., quoted by Claude Pichois
6 *Les Heures longues*
7 *Trois . . . Six . . . Neuf*

The War for Little Girls
1 *Les Heures longues*
2 Ibid.

3 Ibid.
4 *La Chambre éclairée*

The Women's War

1 *La Chambre éclairée*
2 Ibid.
3 Ibid.
4 Ibid.
5 Ibid.
6 Ibid.

War and Love

1 *Mitsou*
2 Ibid.
3 Ibid.
4 Ibid.
5 Ibid.
6 Ibid.
7 Ibid.
8 Ibid.
9 Ibid.
10 Ibid.
11 Ibid.
12 Ibid.
13 Ibid.

Marital Problems

1 *Lettres de la vagabonde*
2 *Dictionnaire des parlementaires français,* op. cit.
3 Bonmariage, op. cit.
4 *Trait pour trait*
5 Ibid.
6 Carco, op. cit.
7 Ibid.
8 Ibid.
9 *La Naissance du jour*
10 Bonmariage, op. cit.

On Jealousy in Love

1 *L'Etoile Vesper*
2 Natalie Clifford Barney, op. cit.
3 *Le Pur et l'Impur*
4 Ibid.
5 Ibid.
6 Ibid.
7 *Lettres de la vagabonde*
8 *Le Pur et l'Impur*
9 Ibid.
10 *L'Etoile Vesper*
11 *Le Pur et l'Impur*

12 Ibid.
13 *La Seconde*
14 Ibid.
15 Ibid.
16 Ibid.
17 Ibid.
18 Ibid.
19 Ibid.
20 *Lettres à Marguerite Moréno*
21 *La Naissance du jour*

The Soldiers Return
1 *La Fin de Chéri*
2 Ibid.
3 Ibid.
4 *La Chambre éclairée*
5 *La Fin de Chéri*
6 Ibid.

A Rising Tide of Women
1 These data are taken from Mary Collins and Sylvie Weil-Sayne, *Les Femmes en France*, Charles Scribner's Sons, New York 1974

At Rozven
1 *Lettres de la vagabonde*, Colette to Georges Wague
2 Ibid.
3 Chauvière, op. cit.
4 *L'Etoile Vesper*
5 Germaine Beaumont, André Parinaud, *Colette par elle-même*, Le Seuil, Paris 1951
6 Ibid.
7 Ibid.
8 Francis Carco, op. cit.
9 Ibid.

Bel-Gazou
1 *L'Etoile Vesper*
2 Ibid.
3 *La Maison de Claudine*
4 Ibid.
5 Letter to Marguerite Moréno, spring 1914
6 *Lettres de la vagabonde*, May 6, 1914
7 Ibid., November 1913
8 Ibid., October 1918
9 Ibid., April 1920
10 Letter to Marguerite Moréno, 1920
11 *Lettres de la vagabonde*, April 28, 1921
12 Ibid., May 1921
13 *Lettres à Marguerite Moréno*, April 28, 1921
14 Ibid., August-September 1921

15 *Lettres de la vagabonde*
16 *Lettres à Marguerite Moréno*
17 Ibid.
18 *Lettres de la vagabonde*
19 Ibid.
20 Natalie Clifford Barney, op. cit.
21 Chauvière, op. cit.
22 *Aventures quotidiennes*
23 Chauvière, op. cit.
24 *La Naissance du jour*

The Kid
1 Letter to Renaud de Jouvenel, autumn 1937, op. cit.
2 Ibid.
3 Ibid.
4 Ibid.
5 Ibid.
6 Ibid.
7 Ibid.
8 Ibid.
9 Ibid.

Chéri
1 *L'Etoile Vesper*
2 Ibid.

Bertrand de Jouvenel
1 Bertrand de Jouvenel, "Colette," *Time and Tide*, August 14, 1954
2 Ibid.

The Cuckoo's Egg
1 Natalie Clifford Barney, op. cit.
2 Carco, op. cit.
3 *Lettres à Hélène Picard, Marguerite Moréno*, and *Lettres de la vagabonde*
4 *Lettres à Marguerite Moréno*
5 Ibid.
6 Ibid.
7 Ibid.
8 *Lettres de la vagabonde*
9 *Lettres à Marguerite Moréno*
10 Ibid.
11 *Lettres de la vagabonde* (letter to Léo)
12 Ibid.
13 Ibid.
14 Ibid.
15 *Lettres à Marguerite Moréno*, letter dated August 12
16 Letter to Léo, August 24, 1924
17 *Lettres de la vagabonde*, end of August, 1924
18 Ibid.

19 Ibid.
20 *Lettres à Marguerite Moréno*
21 *L'Etoile Vesper*
22 *La Seconde*
23 Interview in *Nouvelles Littéraires*, quoted by Jean Larnac, op. cit.
24 *La Naissance du jour*
25 Ibid.

The End of the Nameless Years
1 *La Naissance du jour*

V COLETTE—The Path Back

The Roaring Twenties, Hard Times
1 *Les Vrilles de la vigne*
2 *Lettres à Hélène Picard*, January 12, 1924

An Encounter
1 Maurice Goudeket, *Près de Colette*, Flammarion, Paris 1956
2 Ibid.
3 Ibid.
4 Maurice Goudeket, *La Douceur de vieillir*, Flammarion, Paris 1966
5 Ibid.
6 Goudeket, *Près de Colette*, op. cit.
7 *Lettres à Marguerite Moréno*
8 Ibid.
9 Ibid.
10 Ibid.
11 Ibid.
12 Ibid.
13 Ibid.

Women among Women
1 Goudeket, *Près de Colette*, op. cit.
2 *Le Fanal bleu*
3 Goudeket, *Près de Colette*, op. cit.
4 Ibid.
5 *Lettres au petit corsaire*
6 Quoted in Goudeket, *Près de Colette*, op. cit., text of a radio broadcast
7 *Lettres au petit corsaire*
8 Ibid.
9 Goudeket, *Près de Colette*, op. cit.
10 Ibid.
11 *Lettres à Hélène Picard*
12 Ibid.
13 *L'Etoile Vesper*

The Sedentary Vagabond
1 *Trois . . . Six . . . Neuf*
2 Ibid.
3 Ibid.

4   Ibid.
5   Goudeket, *Près de Colette*, op. cit.
6   Ibid.
7   *La Naissance du jour*
8   Ibid.
9   *Trois . . . Six . . . Neuf*
10   Ibid.
11   Ibid.

A Career in Another Kind of Beauty
1   *Lettres à Marguerite Moréno*, August 26, 1931
2   *Lettres de la vagabonde*, September 1931
3   Ibid., early 1932
4   Goudeket, *Près de Colette*, op. cit.
5   *L'Etoile Vesper*
6   Goudeket, *Près de Colette*, op. cit.
7   Ibid.
8   Natalie Clifford Barney, op. cit.

Près de Maurice
1   *Lettres à Hélène Picard*
2   Ibid.
3   Goudeket, *La Douceur de vieillir*, op. cit.
4   *L'Etoile Vesper*
5   *Journal à rebours*
6   Ibid.
7   Ibid.

One of the Great Ones
1   Chauvière, op. cit.
2   Raaphorst-Rousseau, op. cit.
3   *Le Fanal bleu*
4   Goudeket, *Près de Colette*, op. cit.
5   Ibid.
6   Ibid.
7   Benoîte Groult, *Ainsi soit-elle*, Grasset, Paris 1975

So Few People Read Her Well
1   Chauvière, op. cit.
2   Goudeket, *Près de Colette*, op. cit.
3   Ibid.
4   Julien Benda, *Belphégor*, Paris 1924
5   Lalou, *Histoire de la littérature française contemporaine*
6   *Confluences*, op. cit.
7   Marcel Thiébaut, *Revue de Paris*, August 1957
8   Gonzague Truc, *Madame Colette*, 1941, Corrêa
9   François Mauriac, "Chéri et La Fin de Chéri," *Revue hebdomadaire*, 1927
10   January 15, 1938
11   *Fraternités littéraires*, 1932

12 *Journal des débats*, October 1920
13 *L'Art de Colette*, Jean Renard, 1941
14 *Vingt-cinq ans de littérature française*, 1926
15 *Les Livres du temps*, 1932
16 Goudeket, *Près de Colette*, op. cit.
17 Chauvière, op. cit.

The Return to Her Past
1 Jean Cocteau, op. cit.
2 Goudeket, *Près de Colette*, op. cit.

Leaving Off, "The Supreme Chic of Knowing When to Stop"
1 *La Naissance du jour*
2 Goudeket, *La Douceur de vieillir*, op. cit.
3 *La Naissance du jour*
4 Ibid.
5 Ibid.
6 Ibid.
7 Ibid.
8 Ibid.
9 Ibid.
10 Ibid.
11 Ibid.
12 Ibid.
13 Ibid.
14 Ibid.
15 Ibid.
16 Ibid.
17 Ibid.
18 Ibid.
19 Goudeket, *Près de Colette*, op. cit.
20 *La Naissance du jour*
21 Ibid.
22 Ibid.
23 Ibid.
24 Goudeket, *Près de Colette*, op. cit.
25 *La Naissance du jour*
26 *Le Fanal bleu*
27 Ibid.
28 Ibid.
29 Ibid.
30 Ibid.
31 Ibid.

The Dead
1 *Le Fanal Bleu*
2 *Lettres à Hélène Picard*
3 *Lettres à Marguerite Moréno*
4 Ibid.
5 *Lettres au petit corsaire*

6 *Lettres de la vagabonde*
7 *Le Fanal bleu*

The Occupation
1 M. Goudeket, *Près de Colette*, op. cit.
2 Ibid.
3 Ibid.
4 Ibid.
5 *L'Etoile Vesper*
6 Ibid.
7 Ibid.
8 Goudeket, *Près de Colette*, op. cit.
9 *L'Etoile Vesper*
10 Ibid.
11 Ibid.
12 Ibid.
13 Ibid.
14 Ibid.
15 Ibid.

The Liberation
1 Goudeket, *Près de Colette*, op. cit.
2 Ibid.
3 *L'Etoile Vesper*
4 Ibid.
5 Cocteau, op. cit.
6 Ibid.
7 *Le Fanal bleu*
8 Ibid.
9 *L'Etoile Vesper*
10 Goudeket, *Près de Colette*, op. cit.
11 Ibid.
12 Ibid.
13 Ibid.

Epilogue
1 Cocteau, op. cit.

Bibliography

Many of Colette's books are difficult to obtain or are out of print in French; some have never been translated into English. The following chronological listing gives the publisher, place and date of the first edition of each work included in the bibliography prepared for the *Oeuvres complètes de Colette* published by Le Fleuron, Flammarion, Paris, 1948–1950, 15 volumes.

The French title entry is followed by the most recent American edition of the work in English translation where such exists; if no American edition has been published, the English edition is listed. Some of these titles are also out of print. The history of Colette in English translation is lengthy and fairly confusing, beginning in London in 1912 and doubtless continuing as these words are being written. A detailed examination of the history of Colette's work in English translation can be found in Eleanor Reid Gibbard's "A Chronology of Colette in Translation," published in volume 23 of *Philological Papers*, January 1977, to which the present bibliography is indebted.

In the present biography, all translations from French works, including those of Colette, are by Richard Miller.

❧ WORKS BY COLETTE

Claudine à l'ecole, Paris, Ollendorff, 1900. (*The Complete Claudine, Claudine at School*, New York, Farrar, Straus and Giroux [Noonday], 1976, trans. Antonia White.)

Claudine à Paris, Paris, Ollendorff, 1901. (*Claudine in Paris*, ibid.)

Claudine en ménage, Paris, Ollendorff, 1902. (*Claudine Married*, ibid.)

Claudine s'en va, Paris, Ollendorff, 1903. (*Claudine and Annie*, ibid.)

Minne, Paris, Ollendorff, 1903.

Les Egarements de Minne, Paris, Ollendorff, 1905.

Dialogues de bêtes, Paris, Mercure de France, 1904. (*Barks and Purrs*, London, D. Fitzgerald, 1913, trans. Marie Kelly.)

Sept dialogues de bêtes, préface by Francis Jammes, Paris, Mercure de France, 1905. (ibid.)

La Retraite sentimentale, Paris, Mercure de France, 1907. (*The Retreat from Love*, New York, Bobbs-Merrill, 1974, trans. Margaret Crosland.)

Les Vrilles de la vigne, Paris, Editions de la Vie parisienne, 1908.

L'Ingénue libertine, Paris, Ollendorff, 1909. (*The Gentle Libertine*, New York, Grosset & Dunlap, 1941, trans. Rosemary Carr Benet, 1931.)

La Vagabonde, Paris, Ollendorff, 1911. (*The Vagabond*, New York, Farrar, Straus & Giroux [Noonday], 1976, trans. Enid McLeod, 1954.)

L'Envers du music-hall, Paris, Flammarion, 1913. (*Mitsou and Music-Hall Sidelights*, New York, Farrar, Straus & Giroux [Noonday], 1967, trans. Anne-Marie Callimachi, 1957.)

L'Entrave, Paris, Libraire des Lettres, 1913. (*The Shackle*, New York, Farrar, Straus & Giroux [Noonday], 1976, trans. White, 1963.)

Prrou, Poucette et quelques autres, Paris, Libraire des Lettres, 1913.

La Paix chez les bêtes, Paris, Arthème Fayard, 1916 (new edition of preceding work). (*Creatures Great and Small; Creature Conversations; Other Crea-*

tures; Creature Comfort, New York, Farrar, Straus & Cudahy, 1957, trans. McLeod, 1951.)

Les Heures longues, 1914–1917, Paris, Arthème Fayard, 1917.

Les Enfants dans les ruines, Paris, Editions de la Maison du Livre, 1917.

Dans la foule, Paris, Georges Crès et Cie, 1918.

Mitsou ou Comment l'esprit vient aux filles, Paris, Arthème Fayard, 1918. (*Mitsou and Music-Hall Sidelights, supra*, trans. Raymond Postgate, 1957.)

La Chambre éclairée, Paris, Edouard Joseph, 1920.

Chéri, Paris, Arthème Fayard, 1920. (*Cheri* and *The Last of Cheri*, New York, Farrar, Straus & Giroux [Noonday], 1976, trans. Roger Senhouse, 1951.)

La Maison de Claudine, Paris, J. Ferenczi et fils, 1922. (*My Mother's House* and *Sido*, New York, Farrar, Straus & Giroux, 1975, trans. Una Vincenzo Troubridge and McLeod, 1953.)

Le Voyage égoïste, Paris, Editions d'Art Ed. Pelletan, 1922. (Selections in *Journey for Myself: Selfish Memories*, New York, Bobbs-Merrill, 1972, trans. David LeVay.)

Le Blé en herbe, Paris, Flammarion, 1923. (*The Ripening Seed*, New York, Farrar, Straus & Giroux [Noonday], 1975, trans. Senhouse, 1955.)

Rêverie du nouvel an, Paris, Stock, 1923.

La Femme cachée, Paris, Flammarion, 1924. (Selections in *The Other Woman*, New York, N.A.L. [Signet], 1975, trans. Crosland, 1971.)

Aventures quotidiennes, Paris, Flammarion, 1924. (Selections in *Journey for Myself: Selfish Memories, supra*.)

Quatre saisons, Paris, Philippe Ortiz, 1925.

L'Enfant et les Sortilèges. Musique de Maurice Ravel, Paris, Durand et Cie, 1925. (*The Boy and the Magic*, New York, Putnam, 1965, trans. Christopher Fry.)

La Fin de Chéri, Paris, Flammarion, 1926. (*Cheri* and *The Last of Cheri, supra*.)

La Naissance du jour, Paris, Flammarion, 1928. (*Break of Day*, New York, Farrar, Straus & Giroux [Noonday], 1975, trans. McLeod, 1961.)

Renée Vivien, Abbéville, F. Paillart, 1928.

La Seconde, Paris, Ferenczi et fils, 1929. (*The Other One*, Greenwood Reprints, 1972, Elizabeth Tait and Senhouse, 1960.)

Sido, Paris, Editions Krâ, 1929. (*My Mother's House* and *Sido, supra*, trans. McLeod, 1953.)

Histoires pour Bel-Gazou, Paris, Stock, 1930.

Douze dialogues des bêtes, Paris, Mercure de France, 1930. (*Creatures Great and Small*, etc., *supra*.)

Paradises terrestres, Lausanne, Gonin et Cie, 1932.

La Treille muscate, Paris, Aimé Jourde, 1932.

Prisons et Paradise, Paris, Ferenczi et fils, 1932. (Selections in *Places*, New York, Bobbs-Merrill, 1971, trans. LeVay and Crosland.)

Ces Plaisirs, Paris, Ferenczi et fils, 1932 (title changed to *Le Pur et l'Impur* in 1941). (*The Pure and the Impure*, New York, Farrar, Straus & Giroux [Noonday], 1975, trans. Herma Briffault, 1967.)

La Chatte, Paris, Bernard Grasset, 1933. (*The Cat*, New York, Popular Library, 1974, trans. White, 1953.)

Duo, Paris, Ferenczi et fils, 1934. (*Duo* and *The Toutounier*, New York, Bobbs-Merrill, 1975, trans. Crosland.)

La Jumelle noire, Paris, Ferenczi et fils, 1934–1938.

Discours de réception à l'Académie royale de Belgique, Paris, Bernard Grasset, 1936.

Mes apprentissages, Paris, Ferenczi et fils, 1936. (*My Apprenticeships*, New

York, Farrar, Straus & Giroux [Noonday], 1978, trans. Helen Beauclerk.)
Chats, Paris, Jacques Nam, 1936.
Splendeur des papillons, Paris, Plon, 1937.
Bella-Vista, Paris, Ferenczi et fils, 1937. (*The Tender Shoot and Other Stories*, New York, Farrar, Straus & Giroux [Noonday], 1975, White, 1958.)
Le Toutounier, Paris, Ferenczi et fils, 1939. (*Duo* and *The Toutounier, supra.*)
Chambre d'hôtel, Paris, Arthème Fayard, 1940. (*Gigi, Julie de Carneilhan* and *Chance Acquaintances*, New York, Farrar, Straus & Giroux [Noonday], 1976, trans. Patrick Leigh Fermor, 1952.)
Mes cahiers, Paris, Aux Armes de France, 1941.
Journal à rebours, Paris, Arthème Fayard, 1941. (*Looking Backwards*, Bloomington, Indiana University Press, 1975, trans. David LeVay.)
Julie de Carneilhan, Paris, Arthème Fayard, 1941. (*Gigi, Julie de Carneilhan* and *Chance Acquaintances, supra.*)
De ma fenêtre, Paris, Aux Armes de France, 1942. (Selections in *Looking Backwards, supra.*)
De la patte à l'aile, Paris, Corrêa, 1943.
Flore et Pomone, Paris, Editions de la Galerie Charpentier, 1943.
Nudités, Bruxelles, Editions de la Mappemonde, 1943.
Le Képi, Paris, Arthème Fayard, 1943. (*The Tender Shoot and Other Stories, supra.*)
Broderie ancienne, Monaco, Editions du Rocher, 1944.
Gigi et autres nouvelles, Lausanne, La Guilde du Livre, 1944 (*Gigi, Julie de Carneilhan* and *Chance Acquaintances, supra.*, trans. Senhouse, 1952. Selections in *The Tender Shoot and Other Stories, supra.*)
Trois . . . Six . . . Neuf . . ., Paris, Corrêa, 1944. (Selections in *Places, supra.*)
Belles saisons, Paris, Editions de la Galerie Charpentier, 1945
Une Amitié inattendue. Correspondance de Colette et de Francis Jammes. Introduction et notes de Robert Mallet, Editions Emile-Paul frères, 1945.
L'Etoile Vesper, Genève, Editions du Milieu du Monde, 1946. (*The Evening Star: Recollections*, New York, Bobbs-Merrill, 1974, trans. LeVay.)
Pour un herbier, Lausanne, Mermod, 1948. (*For a Flower Album*, David McKay, 1959, trans. Senhouse.)
Trait pour trait, Paris, Editions Le Fleuron, 1949.
Journal intermittent, Paris, Editions Le Fleuron, 1949. (Selections in *Places, supra.*)
Le Fanal bleu, Paris, Ferenczi et fils, 1949. (*The Blue Lantern*, New York, Farrar, Straus & Giroux, 1975, trans. Senhouse, 1963.)
La Fleur de l'âge, Paris, Editions Le Fleuron, 1949.
En pays connu, Paris, Editions Manuel Bruker, 1949. (Selections in *Places, supra.*)
Chats de Colette, Paris, Albin Michel, 1949.

Theater

Chéri. Comédie en quartre actes, par Colette et Léopold Marchand, Paris, Librairie théâtrale, 1922 (adapted by Anita Loos, New York, David McKay, 1959.)
Le Ciel de lit (*The Fourposter*), comédie de Jan de Hartog. Adaptation française de Colette, Paris, France-Illustration, 1953.
Gigi, Adapté pour la scène par Colette et Anita Loos, Paris, *France-Illustration*, supplément théâtral et littéraire, 1954. (Acting edition published in London, 1956.)

Posthumous works

Paysages et Portraits, Paris, Flammarion, 1958. (Selections in *Places, supra,* and *The Other Woman, supra.*)
Lettres à Hélène Picard, Paris, Flammarion, 1958.
Lettres à Marguerite Moréno, Paris, Flammarion, 1959.
Lettres de la vagabonde, Paris, Flammarion, 1961.
Lettres au petit corsaire, Preface de Maurice Goudeket, Paris, Flammarion, 1963.
Contes de mille et un matins, Paris, Flammarion, 1970. (*The Thousand and One Mornings*, New York, Bobbs-Merrill, 1973, trans. Crosland and LeVay.)
Lettres à ses pairs, Paris, Flammarion, 1972.

Complete works

For the definitive edition of her complete works, Colette suppressed several texts, considerably reworked others and wrote prefaces. Certain hitherto unpublished works were included in this edition. The final volume included a bibliography of all of Colette's writings as of June 1950. The entire edition is now out of print. A luxury edition in 16 illustrated volumes was published in Paris by the Club de l'Honnête Homme, 1973, including some posthumous pieces.

I. *Claudine à l'école, Claudine à Paris.*
II. *Claudine en ménage, Claudine s'en va, La Retraite sentimentale.*
III. *L'Ingénue libertine, Les Vrilles de la vigne, Douze dialogues des bêtes, Autres bêtes.*
IV. *La Vagabonde, L'Entrave, Dans la foule.*
V. *L'Envers du music-hall, Mitsou, La Paix chez les bêtes, Les Heures longues, La Chambre éclairée.*
VI. *Chéri, La Fin de Chéri, Le Voyage égoïste, Aventures quotidiennes.*
VII. *La Maison de Claudine, Sido, Noces, Le Blé en herbe, La Femme cachée.*
VIII. *La Naissance du jour, La Seconde, Prisons et paradis, Nudité.*
IX. *Le Pur et l'Impur, La Chatte, Duo, Le Toutounier, Belles Saisons.*
X. *La Jumelle noire.*
XI. *Mes apprentissages, Bella-Vista, Chambre d'hôtel, Julie de Carneilhan.*
XII. *Journal à rebours, Le Képi, De ma fenêtre, Trois . . . Six . . . Neuf . . .*
XIII. *Gigi, L'Etoile Vesper, Mes cahiers, Discours de réception.*
XIV. *Le Fanal bleu, Pour un herbier, Trait pour trait, Journal intermittent, La Fleur de l'âge, En pays connu, A portée de la main.*
XV. *Théâtre: Chéri, La Vagabonde, En camarades, La Décapitée, L'Enfant et les Sortilèges, Mélanges, Bibliographie.* Paris, Flammarion, Le Fleuron, 1948–1950.

Theatrical works based on novels

Claudine, operetta in three acts. Music by Rodolphe Berger, Paris, Heugel (1910).
Chéri, comedy in four acts by Colette and Léopold Marchand, Paris, Librairie théâtrale, 1922.
La Vagabonde, comedy in four acts by Colette and Léopold Marchand, Paris, *La Petite Illustration*, Theatre, April 14, 1923.
Duo, play in three acts based on the novel by Colette, by Paul Géraldy, Paris, *La Petite Illustration*, February 11, 1923.

Gigi, stage adaptation by Colette and Anita Loos, Paris, *France-Illustration*, supplément théâtral, 1954.

Of the many books written about Colette and her work, the following are of particular interest:

Boncompain, Claude, *Colette*, Lyons, Lyon Confluences, 1945.

Bonmariage, Sylvain, *Willy, Colette et moi*, Paris, Editions Fremanger, 1954, 316 pp.

Carco, Francis, *Colette, mon amie*, Paris, Editions Rive-Gauche, 1965, 125 pp.

Chauvière, Claude, *Colette*, Paris, Firmin-Didot, 1931, 302 pp.

Cocteau, Jean, *Discours de réception à l'Académie Royale de langue et de littérature française de Belgique*, Paris, Grasset, 1955, 117 pp.

Crosland, Margaret, *Madame Colette, A Provincial in Paris*, London, Peter Owen, 1953, 222 pp. (in English).

Davies, Margaret, *Colette*, London, Oliver and Boyd, 1961, 120 pp. (in English).

Goudeket, Maurice, *La Douceur de vieillir*, Paris, Flammarion, 1965, 226 pp.

————, *Près de Colette*, Paris, Flammarion, 1965, 263 pp.

Hollander, Paul d', *Colette à l'heure de Willy*, Presse de l'Université de Montréal; *Claudine en ménage*, édition critique, Montréal, Klincksieck, 1975.

Larnac, Jean, *Colette: sa vie, son oeuvre*, Paris, Krâ, 1927, 233 pp.

Mitchell, Yvonne, *Colette: A Taste for Life*, New York, Harcourt, Brace Jovanovich, Inc., 1975, 224 pp. (in English).

Raaphorst-Rousseau, Madeleine, *Colette, sa vie, son art*, Paris, Nizet, 1964, 318 pp.

Willy, *Indiscretions et Commentaires sur les "Claudine,"* Avant-propos de Pierre Varenné et Alfred Diard, Paris, Pro Amicis, 1962, 37 pp.

Catalogue of Colette Exhibition, Bibliothèque Nationale, 1973.

Phelps, Robert, *Earthly Paradise, An Autobiography Drawn from Her Lifetime of Writing*, New York, Farrar, Straus & Giroux [Noonday], 1975. (Selections from her *Oeuvres completes*, 15 vols., translated, some for the first time, by Briffault, Derek Coltman, McLeod, Beauclerk, Troubridge, White and Senhouse.)

Index